CRIMINAL LAW: MODEL PENAL CODE

by

MARKUS D. DUBBER
Professor of Law and Director of the Buffalo Criminal Law
Center at the State University of New York, Buffalo

TURNING POINT SERIES®

New York, New York
FOUNDATION PRESS
2002

Foundation Press, a division of West Group, has created this publication to provide you with accurate and authoritative information concerning the subject matter covered. However, this publication was not necessarily prepared by persons licensed to practice law in a particular jurisdiction. Foundation Press is not engaged in rendering legal or other professional advice, and this publication is not a substitute for the advice of an attorney. If you require legal or other expert advice, you should seek the services of a competent attorney or other professional.

Turning Point Series is a registered trademark used herein under license.

COPYRIGHT © 2002 By FOUNDATION PRESS
                         395 Hudson Street
                         New York, NY 10014
                         Phone Toll Free 1–877–888–1330
                         Fax (212) 367–6799
                         fdpress.com

All rights reserved
Printed in the United States of America

ISBN 1–58778–178–6

TURNING POINT SERIES

CIVIL PROCEDURE

Civil Procedure: Class Actions by Linda S. Mullenix, University of Texas (Available 2003)

Civil Procedure: Economics of Civil Procedure by Robert G. Bone, Boston University (Available October 2002)

Civil Procedure: Preclusion in Civil Actions by David L. Shapiro, Harvard University (2001)

Civil Procedure: Jury Process by Nancy S. Marder, Illinois Institute of Technology (Available 2003)

Civil Procedure: Territorial Jurisdiction and Venue by Kevin M. Clermont, Cornell (1999)

CONSTITUTIONAL LAW

Constitutional Law: Equal Protection by Louis M. Seidman, Georgetown University (Available December 2002)

Constitutional Law: Religion Clause by Daniel O. Conkle, Indiana University, Bloomington (Available 2003)

CRIMINAL LAW

Criminal Law: Model Penal Code by Markus D. Dubber, State University of New York, Buffalo (2002)

Criminal Law: Habeas Corpus by Larry W. Yackle, Boston University (Available 2003)

INTERNATIONAL LAW

International Law: United States Foreign Relations Law by Phillip R. Trimble, UCLA (2002)

LEGISLATION

Legislation: Statutory Interpretation: Twenty Questions by Kent R. Greenawalt, Columbia University (1999)

PROPERTY

Property: Takings by David Dana, Northwestern University and Thomas Merrill, Northwestern University (2002)

CORPORATE/SECURITIES

Securities Law: Insider Trading by Stephen Bainbridge, UCLA (1999)

TORTS

Torts: Proximate Cause by Joseph A. Page, Georgetown University (Available December 2002)

To
Herbert Wechsler
(1909–2000)

*

Acknowledgments

I am happy to acknowledge those who helped me write this book, in one way or another, at one point or another. They include Guyora Binder, Rosanna Cavallaro, Lutz Eidam, Sara Faherty, Shubha Ghosh, Stuart Green, Tom Green, Kent Greenawalt, Tatjana Hörnle, Cornelius Nestler, Paul Robinson, Rob Steinfeld, Lou Swartz, Bob Weisberg, and Leo Zaibert. My criminal law students in Ann Arbor (fall 2001) and in Buffalo (spring 2002) patiently endured a series of drafts and gave me useful comments.

*

About the Author

Markus D. Dubber is Professor of Law and Director of the Buffalo Criminal Law Center at the State University of New York, Buffalo.

*

TABLE OF CONTENTS

ACKNOWLEDGEMENTS	VII
ABOUT THE AUTHOR	IX

Introduction 1
§ 1 A Key to the Model Penal Code and to American Criminal Law 1
§ 2 Origins: The ALI, Legal Process, and Treatmentism 7
    § 2.1 Criminal Propensities 12
    § 2.2 The Model Penal and Correctional Code 14
    § 2.3 The Structure Of The Model Penal Code 17
§ 3 The Model Penal Code in a Nutshell: Section 1.02 23
    § 3.1 The Prerequisites of Criminal Liability: Definitions of Crimes and of Criminals 26
    § 3.2 The Analysis of Criminal Liability: Three Levels of Inquiry 28

Chapter 1 "Conduct That Inflicts or Threatens Substantial Harm to Individual or Public Interests" —Level One 32
§ 4 "Conduct . . ." 33
    § 4.1 Actus Reus 33
        (A) Act 33
        (B) Voluntariness 34

TABLE OF CONTENTS

§ 4	"Conduct . . ."—Continued	
	(C) Omission	35
	(D) Possession	40
§ 4.2	Mens Rea and Offense Elements	42
	(A) Element Types	43
	(B) Rules of Interpretation	52
	(C) The Modes of Culpability	60
	(D) Matching Conduct to Offense	80
§ 4.3	Intoxication and Mistake	82
	(A) Intoxication	84
	(B) Mistake	90
§ 4.4	Liability for Another's Conduct	105
	(A) Instruments	107
	(B) Complicity	110
	(C) Corporations	125
§ 5	". . . That Inflicts or Threatens . . ."	127
§ 5.1	Causation	128
§ 5.2	Inchoate Offenses	141
	(A) Attempt	144
	(B) Conspiracy	162
	(C) Solicitation	173
	(D) Renunciation	177
§ 6	". . . Substantial Harm to Individual or Public Interests"	179
§ 6.1	Substantial Harm	180
§ 6.2	Individual or Public Interests	183
Chapter 2	**"Unjustifiably"—Level Two**	186
§ 7	Defenses in General	186
§ 8	Necessity	194
§ 9	Defense of Persons (Self and Others) and of Property	202
§ 9.1	Self–Defense	203

TABLE OF CONTENTS

§ 9 Defense of Persons (Self and Others) and of Property—Continued
    (A) Use of Force Upon or Toward Another Person 204
    (B) Belief 205
    (C) Necessity 206
    (D) Unlawfulness 208
    (E) Immediacy and Protection 215
    (F) Self- and Other-Defense 217
    § 9.2 Defense of Property 218
    § 9.3 Deadly Force 223
§ 10 Law Enforcement 231
§ 11 Consent 238

Chapter 3 "Inexcusably"—Level Three .. 247
§ 12 Excuses in the Model Penal Code 247
§ 13 Duress 251
§ 14 Entrapment 259
§ 15 Ignorance of Law 262
§ 16 Provocation and Diminished Capacity 265
§ 17 Insanity and Infancy 271

Conclusion 282
§ 18 Analysis of Criminal Liability 284

APPENDIX MODEL PENAL CODE 287

TABLE OF CASES 459
TABLE OF MODEL PENAL CODE SECTIONS AND STATUTES 463
INDEX 469

Criminal Law: Model Penal Code

Introduction

This book is an introduction to the Model Penal Code. It doesn't cover everything that's in the Code. Instead it illustrates how the Model Penal Code fits together, both as a code of criminal law and as the most systematic account of American criminal law we have.

§ 1 A Key to the Model Penal Code and to American Criminal Law

To understand the structure of the Code is to understand the Code. And to understand the Code goes a long way toward understanding American criminal law. The key to the Model Penal Code therefore turns out also to be the key to American criminal law.

Oddly enough, the Model Penal Code, although hailed as "the principal text in criminal law teaching"[1] and "the point of departure for criminal law scholarship,"[2] still awaits an introduction, four dec-

1. Sanford H. Kadish, The Model Penal Code's Historical Antecedents, 19 Rutgers L.J. 521, 521 (1988).

2. Id. To get an overview of scholarly perspectives on various aspects of the Code, the symposia on the Code are a good place to start. See Symposium on the Model Penal Code, 63 Colum. L. Rev. 589 (1963); The 25th Anniversary of the Model Penal Code,

ades after its completion in 1962. So far the Code has been left to speak for itself, with mixed results. The Code is remarkably precise, but it is not easy reading. (More than once the Code drafters traded comprehensibility for comprehensiveness.) It didn't help matters that the Code found itself dissected into snippets of various shapes and sizes sprinkled in among the assortment of materials that make up a traditional criminal law casebook.

I still remember when I first encountered the Model Code in my first-year criminal law class. After wading through a series of more or less entertaining cases from a spattering of jurisdictions and a smattering of decades, which didn't even pretend to add up to a coherent body of doctrine, we ran smack into the Code's mens rea provisions.[3] Suddenly there were detailed and complex definitions of concepts like "purpose" and "recklessness," carefully crafted to fit into some general scheme of things that we could only guess at. Suddenly words mattered; words even retained their meaning from one rule to the next! Everything was connected to everything else, and everything seemed to be pro-

19 Rutgers L.J. 519 (1988); The Model Penal Code Revisited, 4 Buff. Crim. L. Rev. 1 (2000).

3. § 2.02. Unless otherwise indicated, all citations are to the Official Draft of the Model Penal Code, Model Penal Code (Official Draft and Explanatory Notes: Complete Text of Model Penal Code as Adopted at the 1962 Annual Meeting of The American Law Institute at Washington, D.C., May 24, 1962) (American Law Institute 1985), and to the American Law Institute's official commentaries on the Code, Model Penal Code and Commentaries (Official Draft and Revised Comments 1980–85) [hereinafter Commentaries].

vided for, somewhere, somehow. It was only a matter of time before the complete artifice of criminal law would emerge before us, with its principles, rules, and exceptions interwoven in a rational and systematic way.

Alas, that time never came. The mirage of coherence vanished almost as soon as it had appeared. Before we knew it, we were back reading opinions from throughout space and time, which often enough seemed to have only one thing in common: they all appeared in one and the same, our, casebook.

Very quickly the Model Code turned from a beacon of hope into a source of annoyance. Rather than making sense of the mess, it added to it. Now we were responsible not only for the law of fifty-two jurisdictions (including federal criminal law and the District of Columbia), but fifty-three.[4]

What originally had appeared as the Model Code's strength now simply complicated things unnecessarily. Not only did the "MPC rules" on this or that add to the existing pile of "common law" rules; their meticulous detail seemed to stem less from a drive to systematize but from a less benign urge to inflict gratuitous pain on overworked law students.

And why did we have to bother with this fantasy jurisdiction anyway? What was the point of torturing us with the intricate rules of a piece of model

4. Fifty-four if you count the cadre of English cases, old and new, that continue to appear in American criminal law casebooks.

legislation that, unlike the Uniform Commercial Code we encountered in contracts, hadn't been adopted in toto by a single jurisdiction?

Never mind what the Model Penal Code said; why should it matter what it said?

This book provides answers to both questions, or rather the tools for answering them. In fact, it's based on the assumption that the answer to both questions is the same: the Model Code's nature as a systematic code of criminal law. Once one grasps the Code's system, the answers to particular questions of doctrine fall into place. At the same time, to grasp the Code's system is to appreciate its enormous usefulness for anyone trying to get a handle on the often chaotic rules of American criminal law, from students to teachers to lawyers to judges to legislators.

This book thus aims to make good on the Model Penal Code's promise of coherence, something teachers usually don't have the time to do in a course already overflowing with rules from here and there and on this and that. As a systematic backdrop, a conceptual backbone, the Model Code can fulfill its potential as a tool for teaching and learning American criminal law. You won't find the entirety of American criminal law in the Code, nor anywhere else for that matter—there's just too much of it. There are so-called "common law" rules which tend to differ from jurisdiction to jurisdiction, from law school to law school, and even from criminal law class to criminal law class. In this chaos, the

Code can provide a safe haven for the bewildered student of criminal law.

If there is such a thing as a common denominator in contemporary American criminal law, it's the Model Penal Code. And that's how this book treats the Code, rather than as yet another source of alternative rules on whatever topics a criminal law course can accommodate.

Criminal law casebooks devote considerable space to the Model Penal Code, mostly by inserting Code sections, and sections of sections, between their primary sources: appellate court opinions. This book supplements these casebooks by stringing the excerpts together and placing them into the context of the Code as a whole. That way the connections between otherwise disjointed excerpts will become clearer, something that in turn will help students make better sense of the excerpts themselves.

The criminal law—and most criminal law exams—come down to a single, basic, question: who is liable for what? The Model Penal Code provides a key to the answer. That key lies in the Code's structure. That's why to understand the Model Penal Code is also to understand criminal law. Even though the particular answers along the way may differ from jurisdiction to jurisdiction, the general path of analysis is the same. (If it weren't, there would be no point in teaching "criminal law," as opposed to Indiana criminal law, federal criminal law, and so on.) And there's no better tool for understanding the analysis of criminal liability than the Model Penal Code.

An important reason why the Model Code is the key to American criminal law in fact, and not only in theory, is that so much of American criminal law derives from it, one way or another. Most obvious is the Code's influence in the forty or so jurisdictions that recodified their criminal law on its basis, including New York, Texas, Illinois, Pennsylvania, and New Jersey.[5] Even though none of these revisions adopted the Code as a whole, all of them were influenced by it to a greater or lesser extent. To get a sense of the Model Code in action, as well as to explore principled alternatives to Code approaches to particular issues, we will follow the American Law Institute's official commentaries on the Code and pay particular attention to the New York Penal Law.[6]

The Code continues to influence the criminal law in "non-MPC" jurisdictions as well. These include two important jurisdictions where the national recodification effort triggered by the Code failed miserably, California and federal criminal law.[7] As evi-

5. Richard Singer, The 25th Anniversary of the Model Penal Code: Foreword, 19 Rutgers L.J. 519, 519 (1988).

6. See, e.g., Commentaries § 3.02, at 18; Commentaries § 3.06, at 97. For added perspective, we will take occasional glances at tort law, especially the ALI's Second Restatement, which was drafted at about the same time as the Model Penal Code, and at German criminal law, the most influential system of criminal law in the civil law tradition. Cf. Commentaries § 3.02, at 11; Commentaries § 210.3, at 65.

7. The authoritative history of the federal effort is Ronald L. Gainer, Federal Criminal Code Reform: Past and Future, 2 Buff.

dence of its nationwide impact, the Code has been cited in over 2,000 opinions from every American jurisdiction. Courts in non-MPC jurisdictions frequently draw on the Code's analysis to elucidate unsettled issues, such as the mental state requirements of particular offenses, even if they end up rejecting the particular solution proposed by the Code drafters. By last count, the Code has been cited in over 100 California and over 500 federal opinions, including more than 100 Supreme Court opinions. Where does a federal appellate court turn when faced with an ambiguous criminal statute? To the Model Penal Code.[8] The Supreme Court? To the Model Penal Code.[9] And a California court? Ditto.[10]

No criminal lawyer today can afford not to know the basics of the Model Penal Code. And to lay out these basics is the aim of this book.

§ 2 Origins: The ALI, Legal Process, and Treatmentism

To get a handle on the Model Penal Code, it helps to know something about where it came from and

Crim. L. Rev. 45, 92–139 (1998). On the failure of the California reform, see Philip Hager, Fired Scholars Defend Penal Code Revisions, L.A. Times, Sept. 22, 1969, at 3; 22 Stan. L. Rev. 160, 162 (1969) (letter of Herbert L. Packer) (both cited in Sanford H. Kadish, Fifty Years of Criminal Law: An Opinionated Review, 87 Cal. L. Rev. 943, 949 (1999)).

8. See, e.g., United States v. M.W., 890 F.2d 239 (10th Cir.1989) (arson (18 U.S.C. § 81)).

9. See, e.g., United States v. United States Gypsum Co., 438 U.S. 422, 443–44 (1978) (Sherman Act).

10. People v. Carr, 97 Cal.Rptr.2d 143 (Cal.App.2000) (reckless burning of any structure, forest land or property) (citing In re Steven S., 31 Cal.Rptr.2d 644 (Cal.App.1994)).

who drafted it.[11] Although it was drafted between 1952 and 1962, the origins of the Code lie in the 1930s. That's when the American Law Institute decided to tackle criminal law and criminal procedure. An organization of distinguished jurists, founded in 1923 "to promote the clarification and simplification of the law and its better adaptation to social needs, to secure the better administration of justice, and to encourage and carry on scholarly and scientific legal work," the ALI took a look at American criminal law and procedure at the time and was so appalled by what it saw that it decided that, unlike in other areas like torts or contracts, more than a mere "restatement" of the law was called for. What was needed was a fresh start in the form of *model codes*. The Model Code of Criminal Procedure was completed in 1930. The Model Penal Code was next, but its drafting was postponed until after World War II.[12]

After the war, Herbert Wechsler, a Columbia law professor, was put in charge of the Model Penal Code project. Wechsler had laid out the plans for a comprehensive reform of American criminal law in a monumental 1937 article, entitled modestly and somewhat misleadingly "A Rationale for the Law of

11. See generally Markus Dirk Dubber, Penal Panopticon: The Idea of a Modern Model Penal Code, 4 Buff. Crim. L. Rev. 53 (2000); see also Sanford H. Kadish, The Model Penal Code's Historical Antecedents, 19 Rutgers L.J. 521 (1988).

12. A Model Code of Pre–Arraignment Procedure followed in 1975.

Homicide."[13] Wechsler consolidated these ideas into a program for the Model Penal Code, which began as two memoranda to the American Law Institute and ended up as a Harvard Law Review article.[14]

These two articles contain the blueprint for the Model Penal Code. They are required reading for anyone who wants to penetrate the depths of the Model Code and its underlying approach to the criminal law.

For everyone else, here's a quick summary. Wechsler was a leading proponent of what came to be known as the Legal Process school—a moniker derived from the phenomenally influential and, until recently, remarkably unpublished, casebook of the same name by Henry Hart and Albert Sacks.[15] Its Legal Process pedigree accounts for several features of the Model Code.

First, the Code is a model piece of *legislation*. Its goal was to transfer the power to make criminal law from the common-law making judiciary to the statute-law making legislature. "No conduct constitutes an offense unless it is a crime or violation under this Code or another statute of this State."[16] Common law crimes were no more.

13. Jerome Michael & Herbert Wechsler, A Rationale of the Law of Homicide (Parts I & II), 37 Colum. L. Rev. 701, 1261 (1937).

14. Herbert Wechsler, The Challenge of a Model Penal Code, 65 Harv. L. Rev. 1097 (1952).

15. Henry M. Hart & Albert M. Sacks, The Legal Process: Basic Problems in the Making and Application of Law (William N. Eskridge, Jr. & Phillip P. Frickey eds., 1994).

16. § 1.05(1).

Second, the Code is *comprehensive*. In its effort to guide the courts' discretion in applying the rules generated by the legislature, the Code left little to chance. Given too much wiggling room, ingenious judges might try to circumvent the prohibition of common law crimes. That's why the Code reads— and looks—as much like a criminal law textbook as it does like a code.[17] It was meant to teach criminal law to criminal justice professionals.

Third, the Code is a *code*. It attempted to construct a rational system of criminal law, rather than a compendium of existing rules. This system served certain "purposes," which the drafters, in an unusual step, made explicit.[18] Those purposes were then implemented in the "principles," "provisions," and "definitions" that make up the bulk of the Code.[19]

Fourth, the Code is *pragmatic*. Legal Process was a way of making policy first and a theory of law second. Now there's no point to a policy that's not implemented. And implemented the Code was, more or less completely, in the majority of American jurisdictions.

For our purposes, the latter two characteristics are most significant because they turned the Code

17. This feature of the Code distinguishes it from other influential modern criminal codes, and makes it a much better teaching vehicle. The German Penal Code, for instance, doesn't define actus reus, mens rea, causation, or consent.

18. § 1.02.

19. See, e.g., art. 2 ("general principles of liability"); pt. I ("general provisions"); pt. II ("definition of specific crimes").

into the key to American criminal law. Its "principled pragmatism"[20] ensured that the Code was more than an elaborate theoretical construct, but a model system of criminal law that could have an impact on the actual law in our statute books and courtrooms.

Wechsler was not only committed to the Legal Process way of doing things. He also subscribed to another orthodoxy of his time: treatmentism. Growing out of the beginnings of the new science of criminology at the turn of the twentieth century, treatmentism called for the replacement of punishment with treatment. According to treatmentism, crime was a disorder that required diagnosis and treatment. Penal treatment was prescribed based on a penological diagnosis that roughly distinguished between two types of offender: those who could be cured and those who couldn't. The former were subjected to rehabilitative, the latter to incapacitative, treatment.

In the treatmentist model, criminal law was not a matter of meting out just punishments, but a matter of administering indicated treatments. A rational system of criminal law, or rather of criminal administration, was a system that prescribed and then administered the proper treatment based on a correct diagnosis. This was precisely the sort of policy challenge that the Legal Process school was designed to meet. And meet it the Model Penal Code did.

20. Herbert L. Packer, The Model Penal Code and Beyond, 63 Colum. L. Rev. 594, 594 (1963).

§ 2.1 Criminal Propensities

That the Model Code wholeheartedly endorsed the then-orthodoxy of treatmentism is not of merely theoretical interest. The Code as a whole doesn't make sense unless one keeps the centrality of treatmentism in mind. Moreover, when confronted with a particularly ornery Code provision, it helps to remind oneself that all the drafters were doing was to "describe the character deficiencies of those subjected to [the criminal law] in accord with the propensities that they ... manifest."[21] In the end, it often enough comes down to this diagnosis of propensities, and of the propensity to commit crimes in particular. The concept of criminal dangerousness might come in handy, for instance, when a particular case (or exam question) requires drawing the line between preparation and attempt, or between purpose and knowledge, or to assess the availability of defenses like claim of right (in larceny), renunciation, or self-defense. So one might reason, for instance, that "Mr. X is guilty of attempted burglary because his preparatory actions had been so extensive as to suggest a strong propensity to commit crimes, and the crime of burglary in particular." Or, perhaps, that "a finding of purposeful behavior in this case would be inappropriate since the defendant did not possess that high degree of criminal disposition, that exceptional criminal energy, which

21. Commentaries §§ 220.1 to 230.5, at 157 n.99.

distinguishes purposeful from merely knowing conduct."[22]

Depending on a particular teacher's approach to the Model Code, considerations of this kind can be made more or less explicit. (The Code drafters themselves were not always as open about their reliance on dangerousness diagnoses as in the passage quoted above, often preferring instead to speak in vaguer terms of "individual culpability" and the like.) Even if they remain implicit, these considerations help bring some analytic clarity into tricky questions of doctrine.

Penal treatment supplements the Code's primary goal, the prevention of crime. The Code pursues its preventive goal in two steps. First, it tries to deter crime.[23] Second, if that attempt fails, it *treats* those it couldn't deter, that is, it "subject[s] to public control persons whose conduct indicates that they are disposed to commit crimes."[24] The attempt at deterrence of course fails untold times every day. And so it turns out, in fact, that treatment, despite its officially supplementary status, appears as the tail that wags deterrence's dog.

Once diagnosed as disposed to commit crimes under the Code's first half, offenders are sent on for treatment according to the elaborate set of correctional guidelines laid out in the Code's second, and much neglected, correctional half: parts III and IV.

22. For a discussion of the notion of "criminal energy" in German criminal law, see Tatjana Hörnle, Distribution of Punishment: The Role of a Victim's Perspective, 3 Buff. Crim. L. Rev. 175, 198–200 (1999).

23. § 1.02(1)(a); § 1.02, at 3 (explanatory note).

24. § 1.02(1)(b).

The Code's first half gets all the attention in criminal law classes, and rightly so, since it's there that we find the stuff of substantive criminal law, including general principles of liability (part I) and specific offenses (part II). But the first half is merely a setup for the second. The first half (the "Penal Code" proper) provides the tools for diagnosing the criminal disposition, which is then treated according to the second half (the "Correctional Code"). Put both halves together and you have the "Penal and Correctional Code" that the Model Penal Code set out to be.[25]

§ 2.2 The Model Penal and Correctional Code

Again, the Model Penal Code is only the first half of a comprehensive code of criminal and prison law that also includes a Model Correctional Code. To ignore this fact is to ignore the treatmentist orientation of the Model Penal Code and therefore to run the risk of misreading not only its general approach, but also its specific provisions. Every section in the Model Penal Code should be read with an eye toward its role in the general treatment scheme envisioned by the Code drafters.

Let's take a brief look at the overall structure of the Model Penal and Correctional Code to place our subject, the Model *Penal* Code, in the proper context. In this way, we can better appreciate the full scope of the drafter's treatmentist ambition, and the Penal Code's place within it.

The Penal Code makes up the first two parts of the Model Penal and Correctional Code, the Correc-

25. § 1.01(1).

tional Code the latter two. Part I, the general part, is devoted to "General Provisions." Offense definitions appear in part II, the special part, entitled "Definition of Specific Offenses":

Part I. General Provisions
Part II. Definition of Specific Offenses

Like the Penal Code, the Correctional Code consists of two parts:

Part III. Treatment and Correction
Part IV. Organization of Correction

Part III lays out the principles of penal enforcement, i.e., of "treatment and correction." It specifies how the general treatment parameters set by a court-imposed sentence were to be applied in practice, and revised if necessary.[26] So every type of sentence laid out in the Penal Code—probation, fine, imprisonment, and parole—finds its enforcement analogue in the Correctional Code:[27]

26. Every felony prison sentence was provisional. During the first year of correctional treatment, the "Commissioner of Correction" could petition the court to resentence the offender, if he was "satisfied that the sentence of the Court may have been based upon a misapprehension as to the history, character or physical or mental condition of the offender." § 7.08.

27. In arts. 6 & 7. Well, almost every type of sentence. For obvious reasons, capital punishment—famously placed in noncommittal brackets by the Code drafters—has no analogue in the realm of "treatment and correction." Cf. § 210.6. The Code's death penalty provisions significantly shaped the Supreme Court's attempt to construct a constitutional system of capital punishment. See Markus Dirk Dubber, Penal Panopticon: The Idea of a Modern Model Penal Code, 4 Buff. Crim. L. Rev. 53, 71 (2000).

Art. 301 Suspension of Sentence; Probation
Art. 302 Fines
Art. 303 Short–Term Imprisonment
Art. 304 Long–Term Imprisonment
Art. 305 Parole

To get a sense of the detail with which the Code regulated the application of penal treatment, consider the range of topics covered in article 303, on "short-term imprisonment." (The treatment focus also comes through loud and clear, once again.)

§ 303.1 State and Local Institutions for Short–Term Imprisonment; Review for Adequacy; Joint Use of Institutions; Approval of Plan of New Institutions

§ 303.2 Records of Prisoners; Classification; Transfer

§ 303.3 Segregation of Prisoners; Segregation and Transfer of Prisoners with Physical or Mental Diseases or Defects

§ 303.4 Medical Care; Food and Clothing

§ 303.5 Program of Rehabilitation

§ 303.6 Discipline and Control

§ 303.7 Employment and Labor of Prisoners

§ 303.8 Reduction of Term for Good Behavior

§ 303.9 Privilege of Leaving Institution for Work and Other Purposes; Conditions; Application of Earnings

§ 303.10 Release from Institution

The final part of the Correctional Code, "Organization of Correction," set up the administrative bureaucracy necessary to implement the detailed provisions of part III. These institutions once again mirrored the various types of treatment available:

Art. 401 Department of Correction
Art. 402 Board of Parole
Art. 403 Administration of Institutions
Art. 404 Division of Parole
Art. 405 Division of Probation

§ 2.3 The Structure Of The Model Penal Code

It's important to understand the Model Penal Code's place in the overall structure of the Model Penal and Correctional Code. Even more important for our purposes, however, is to understand the Model Penal Code's structure taken by itself.

In a sense, the Model Penal Code's structure *is* the Model Penal Code. The Code wears its conceptual coherence on its sleeve. So comprehensive and integrated is the Code's conceptual structure that its table of contents could easily serve as the outline for a criminal law exam. Try doing that with codes untouched by the Model Code, like the federal criminal code, or the California penal code.

The Model Code drafters imposed structure on chaos wherever they turned. For example, the Code systematized the special part of criminal law by categorizing offenses by the interests and institutions they are designed to protect, such as the state, the person, property, or the family. Before the Code, the preferred method of organization in American criminal codes was the alphabet. In 1948, four years before the Model Code project began in earnest, Congress decided to revise the vast body of federal criminal statutes that had accumulated over a century and a half. That revision, "for which the spadework was done by the hired hands of three commercial law-book publishers, on delegation from a congressional committee desirous of escaping the responsibility of hiring and supervising its own staff,"[28] consisted of placing the existing statutes in alphabetical order. The federal criminal code, Title 18, has retained this ordering to this day, more or less.[29] Efforts to recodify federal criminal law on the basis of the Model Penal Code failed in the early 1980s.[30]

28. Henry M. Hart, Jr., The Aims of the Criminal Law, 23 Law & Contemp. Probs. 401, 432 n.70 (1958).

29. *Less* because, in its continuous generation of federal crimes, Congress on occasion has found even the alphabet too demanding a structural device. So, for instance, the chapter on "child support" (18 U.S.C. ch. 11A) precedes that on "chemical weapons" (ch. 11B), and "importation of explosive materials" comes after "explosives" but before "extortion," (chs. 39–41). The struggle to alphabetize was not limited to American criminal law. Cf. S.F.C. Milsom, Historical Foundations of the Common Law 417 (2d ed. 1981) (remarking that English "criminal law had by the eighteenth century attained an incoherence which seemed to defy even the modest order of the alphabet"); R. Burn, Justice of the Peace and Parish Officer (1st ed. 1755) (headings include, in order, "Game; Gaming; Gaol and gaoler; Gunpowder; Habeas corpus; Hackney coaches and chairs") (cited in Milsom, supra).

30. See Ronald L. Gainer, Federal Criminal Code Reform: Past and Future, 2 Buff. Crim. L. Rev. 45 (1998).

The Code's greatest structural contribution, however, came not in the special part, but in the general part of criminal law. Before the Model Penal Code, American criminal codes had no general parts to speak of. Central concepts like actus reus or mens rea remained undefined. Defenses were treated in the context of particular offenses, chief among them homicide and larceny, rather than as general principles of criminal liability that applied to any and all offenses. The federal criminal code, to return to our example, is still without a general part worth its name. Title 18 contains no general provision on jurisdiction, voluntariness, actus reus, mens rea, causation, mistake, entrapment, duress, infancy, justification, self-defense, or inchoate offenses.

Most importantly, for our purposes, the Code's structure bears within it a roadmap for the analysis of criminal liability in every case that an American lawyer, judge, or law student might come across.

Once again, the Model Penal Code consists of two parts, the general and the special part:

Part I. General Provisions
Part II. Definition of Specific Offenses

The general part includes general principles that apply across the board to all offenses defined in the special part. These principles are divided into five articles:[31]

Art. 1 Preliminary
Art. 2 General Principles of Liability

[31] We'll ignore the last two articles (6 & 7), which are dedicated to the law of sentencing.

20 INTRODUCTION

Art. 3 General Principles of Justification
Art. 4 Responsibility
Art. 5 Inchoate Crimes

Article 1 deals with a number of issues at the boundary between criminal law and criminal procedure, including jurisdiction and venue,[32] the statute of limitations,[33] double jeopardy,[34] and proof requirements.[35] Most relevant for our purposes, it spells out the purposes of the Code,[36] establishes the principle of legality (in the sense that the legislature holds the monopoly in criminal lawmaking)[37] and defines certain key concepts.[38]

Article 2 is the heart of the Code's general part. Here we find provisions on the core principles of criminal liability, including:

§ 2.01 actus reus
§ 2.02 mens rea (and § 2.05)
§ 2.03 causation
§ 2.04 mistake (§ 2.04(1))
§ 2.06 complicity

In addition, the drafters began addressing possible defenses to criminal liability, such as:

§ 2.04 ignorance (§ 2.04(3))
§ 2.08 intoxication

32. § 1.03.
33. § 1.06.
34. §§ 1.07–.11.
35. § 1.12.
36. § 1.02.
37. § 1.05.
38. §§ 1.04 & 1.13.

- § 2.09 duress
- § 2.10 military orders
- § 2.11 de minimis
- § 2.12 entrapment

The treatment of defenses begins in earnest in article 3, dedicated to "general principles of justification." The justification defenses covered include:

- § 3.02 necessity
- § 3.03 public duty
- § 3.04 self-defense
- § 3.05 defense of another
- § 3.06 defense of property
- § 3.07 law enforcement
- § 3.08 special responsibility

Article 4 concludes the Code's consideration of defenses, completing the list of excuse defenses begun in article 2 with excuses based on the actor's nonresponsibility due to incapacity:

- § 4.01 insanity
- § 4.10 immaturity

Finally, article 5 deals with inchoate crimes. It's a code within a code, specifying the general principles of inchoate liability, including possible defenses, and defining both inchoate crimes and quasi-inchoate—possession-related—crimes at the same time:

- § 5.01 attempt
- § 5.02 solicitation
- § 5.03 conspiracy
- § 5.06 possession of dangerous instruments (and § 5.07)

By defining specific offenses, rather than setting out general principles of liability, the article on inchoate crimes already stands with one foot in the special part.[39] That part, the second half of the Penal Code, is devoted exclusively to the definition of offenses. It's here that we find the stuff of criminal law, the crimes that make the criminal law what it is. These are divided into the following categories of criminally protected interests:

Offenses against the existence or stability of the state[40]
Offenses involving danger to the person
Offenses against property
Offenses against the family
Offenses against public administration
Offenses against public order and decency
Miscellaneous offenses:[41]

  Narcotics
  Alcoholic beverages
  Gambling
  Offenses against tax and trade laws

It would be interesting to take a closer look at the drafters' choice of interests worthy of penal protection, and at their assignment of particular offenses to particular interests. Why, for instance, should the criminal law be enlisted to protect "the family"

39. In fact, several criminal codes revised on the basis of the Model Code place the definition of inchoate offenses not at the end of the general part, but at the beginning of the special part. See, e.g., N.Y. Penal Law arts. 110–115.

40. Model Penal Code 123 (Proposed Official Draft 1962).

41. Id. at 241.

as a social institution, assuming there is any way of determining what that institution consists of today? And what is abortion doing among offenses against the family, if it is to be retained in a criminal code at all?[42] New York, for example, didn't follow the Model Code's lead and instead codified abortion under "offenses against the person."[43]

But, for our purposes, an overview of the protected interests is good enough. As already mentioned, this book follows the practice of most introductory courses in American criminal law in focusing on the criminal law's general part, i.e., on part I of the Model Code. Still, specific offenses—most notably homicide in its various permutations—will inevitably be considered when it comes to illustrating the workings of the general principles in particular cases. Even the choice of offense categories will come up, if only briefly, when we home in on each of the Model Code's prerequisites for criminal liability, as outlined in its purposes section, § 1.02. (One of them is interference with the "individual or public interests" enumerated in the special part.)

§ 3 The Model Penal Code in a Nutshell: Section 1.02

If the Model Penal Code is the key to American criminal law, then section 1.02 is the key to the key.

42. § 230.3.

43. N.Y. Penal Law §§ 125.40–.60; but see id. § 125.05(1) (defining "person" as "a human being who has been born and is alive").

Section 1.02 is the Model Penal Code in a nutshell. It compresses the Code's elaborate analytic structure into a single statement of the prerequisites of criminal liability. And that's precisely what one would expect from a self-consciously systematic statement of criminal law, a *code*: Section 1.02 lays out the "purposes" that the remainder of the Model Penal Code works out in detail, applying them to particular issues in the analysis of criminal liability.

If it gets any attention at all, section 1.02 tends to be treated as a compendium of so-called theories of punishment, retribution, deterrence, incapacitation, and rehabilitation. And it is indeed a good exercise to try to match up the various purposes listed in section 1.02 with different rationales of punishment.[44] Here's one way of matchmaking, necessarily truncated in the absence of a prolonged discussion of the various theories of punishment, and yet specific enough—I think—to suggest the futility of the exercise:

(1) The general purposes of the provisions governing the definition of offenses are:

(a) to forbid [→retribution?] and prevent [→deterrence] conduct that unjustifiably

---

44. Note that § 1.02 actually contains two lists of "general purposes," one covering "the provisions governing the definition of offenses" (presumably pts. I & II of the Code, the "Penal Code," though the general part (pt. I) doesn't define offenses, except perhaps for art. 5, on inchoate crimes), the other applying to "the provisions governing the sentencing and treatment of offenders" (pts. III & IV, the "Correctional Code," though presumably arts. 6 & 7 of the Penal Code, on "authorized disposition of offenders" and "authority of court in sentencing," as well).

and inexcusably inflicts or threatens [→incapacitation?] substantial harm to individual or public interests;

(b) to subject to public control persons whose conduct indicates that they are disposed to commit crimes [→incapacitation];

(c) to safeguard conduct that is without fault from condemnation as criminal [→retribution (as limiting principle)];

(d) to give fair [→retribution] warning [→deterrence] of the nature of the conduct declared to constitute an offense;

(e) to differentiate on reasonable grounds between serious and minor offenses [→retribution, deterrence, incapacitation, or rehabilitation, depending on what "reasonable grounds," "serious," and "minor" mean].

(2) The general purposes of the provisions governing the sentencing and treatment of offenders are:

(a) to prevent the commission of offenses [→deterrence];

(b) to promote the correction and rehabilitation of offenders [→rehabilitation];

(c) to safeguard offenders against excessive, disproportionate or arbitrary punishment [→retribution, deterrence, incapacitation, or rehabilitation, depending on what "excessive," "disproportionate," and "arbitrary" mean[45]]

(d) to give fair [→retribution] warning [→deterrence] of the nature of the sentences that may be imposed on conviction of an offense;

(e) to differentiate among offenders with a view to a just [→retribution?] individualization in their treatment [→rehabilitation, incapacitation];

(f) to define, coordinate and harmonize the powers, duties and functions of the courts and of administrative officers and agencies responsible for dealing with offenders [→rehabilitation, incapacitation];

(g) to advance the use of generally accepted scientific methods and knowledge in the sentencing and treatment of offenders [→rehabilitation, incapacitation];

(h) to integrate responsibility for the administration of the correctional system in a State Department of Correction [→rehabilitation, incapacitation].

§ 3.1 The Prerequisites of Criminal Liability: Definitions of Crimes and of Criminals

But section 1.02 does so much more than locate the Code within the matrix of punishment theories. It tells us not only what sort of conduct is criminal,

45. For an elaborate deterrence-based account of proportionality, see Jeremy Bentham, An Introduction to the Principles of Morals and Legislation ch. xiv (1781).

but also what sort of person is to be punished (or rather treated) for having engaged in it. Right at the outset, it defines both the crime and the criminal, or the offense and the offender.

This is a crime:

conduct that
unjustifiably and inexcusably
inflicts or threatens
substantial harm to
individual or public interests.[46]

And this is a criminal:

a "person[] whose conduct indicates that [he is] disposed to commit crimes."[47]

The rest of the Code merely puts meat on these general definitions, and on the definition of crime in particular. Likewise, the bulk of this book unfolds the doctrinal rules packed into section 1.02's definition of the prerequisites of criminal liability.

At the outset, however, it's important to be clear on the relation between the definitions of crimes and criminals contained in section 1.02. As we will see, the Code is committed to the idea that no one should be punished unless and until he has committed a crime, no matter how disposed to committing crimes he may be. The concept of crime, in this sense, is prior to that of a criminal: one must commit a crime before one can be labeled a criminal. At the same time, it's not as though the two

46. § 1.02(1)(a).
47. § 1.02(1)(b).

questions are entirely unrelated. As we saw earlier, the entire Code is designed to diagnose criminal dangerousness. Rules about whether a crime has been committed, therefore, will try to weed out those who lack that predisposition and even to differentiate between different levels of that predisposition. And that's why our exploration of the Code's definition of crimes will also have to keep in mind its definition of criminals.

The criminal law—and the Model Penal Code—is concerned first and foremost with general rules governing the question whether a crime has been committed. These general rules provide an analytic framework of criminal liability that is applied to particular cases, in order to determine whether a particular person is criminally liable for a particular crime, i.e., whether he is guilty. That analytic framework is what this book, and the Model Penal Code, is all about.

§ 3.2 The Analysis of Criminal Liability: Three Levels of Inquiry

The Model Code defines a crime as "conduct that unjustifiably and inexcusably inflicts or threatens substantial harm to individual or public interests." Criminal liability thus has these three components:

1. conduct
2. without justification and
3. without excuse

To count as a crime, "conduct" must, however, meet several additional criteria, namely it must:

a. inflict or threaten
b. substantial harm to individual or public interests

And if we put the two together, we get the Model Penal Code's complete scheme of criminal liability:

A person is criminally liable if he engages in

1. conduct that
   a. inflicts or threatens
   b. substantial harm to individual or public interests
2. without justification and
3. without excuse.

The Model Penal Code, and therefore this book, does no more than elaborate on this basic structure of criminal liability.

You might have come across other schemes of criminal liability, such as the one said to underlie the "common law." It's difficult to crystallize a single liability scheme from hundreds of years of Anglo–American common law. Still, it seems clear enough that a crime in the common law sense consists of two "offense" elements:

1. actus reus (the guilty act) and mens rea (the guilty mind).

Actus reus and mens rea are necessary, but not sufficient, prerequisites of criminal liability under the common law. Owing to the hopelessly confused common law concept of mens rea, which after centuries of judicial expansion and contraction came to encompass everything and nothing, it's difficult to say what else is needed for criminal liability exactly. It's safe to say, however, that courts from early on recognized that criminal liability required both a criminal "offense" (consisting of actus reus and mens rea) and the absence of "defenses." Particularly in the law of homicide, which has always managed to attract the lion's share of doctrinal attention, courts generally divided these defenses into two types, justifications and excuses.[48] Criminal liability thus attached to an offense committed:

2. without justification and
3. without excuse.

The analytic schemes of the Model Penal Code and the common law are more or less interchangeable, depending on how one views the connection between conduct and mens rea. The Model Code defines conduct as encompassing both: conduct is "an action or omission and its accompanying state of mind."[49] Replacing "actus reus and mens rea" with "conduct," the common law scheme of criminal liability therefore looks like this:

1. conduct
2. without justification and
3. without excuse

48. 4 William Blackstone, Commentaries on the Laws of England 178–88 (1769) (justifiable and excusable homicide). It's not an accident that Wechsler first sketched his plan for a fundamental revision of American criminal law in an article ostensibly dedicated to the "law of homicide." See Jerome Michael & Herbert Wechsler, A Rationale of the Law of Homicide (Parts I & II), 37 Colum. L. Rev. 701, 1261 (1937).

49. § 1.13(5).

The "common law" and the Model Penal Code thus do not differ in their general analysis of criminal liability.[50] That's why the Model Penal Code serves as the analytic backbone of American criminal law, common law or not. Where the two differ, on occasion, is at the level of particular rules. But this we'll see in greater detail as we work our way through the three levels of the Model Code's analysis of criminal liability, next.

50. There are also obvious similarities to the dominant analytic scheme in the civil law tradition, first developed in German criminal law. See, e.g., Wolfgang Naucke, An Insider's Perspective on the Significance of the German Criminal Theory's General System for Analyzing Criminal Acts, 1 BYU L. Rev. 305 (1984); George P. Fletcher, Rethinking Criminal Law 575–79 (1978).

CHAPTER 1

"CONDUCT THAT INFLICTS OR THREATENS SUBSTANTIAL HARM TO INDIVIDUAL OR PUBLIC INTERESTS" —LEVEL ONE

The Model Penal Code's inquiry into criminal liability begins with the question whether the defendant (procedurally speaking) has engaged in conduct. Thoughts aren't punished, no matter how evil. And neither are certain movements that don't qualify as conduct. Once it's clear that some sort of conduct has occurred, we need to see if that conduct qualifies as *criminal* conduct. Conduct is criminal if and only if it matches the definition of an offense in each of its elements. These elements include, according to the Model Penal Code, conduct, attendant circumstances, and result, plus the states of mind associated with each.

Assuming the match between offense definition and conduct can be made, we move on to the next step in our inquiry into criminal liability, the question whether the facially criminal conduct was justified (chapter 2). If it wasn't justified, we then see if it can be excused nonetheless (chapter 3). And only if it can't be excused either, do we declare the defendant guilty of the crime, i.e., criminally liable.

§ 4 "Conduct ..."

Before we can match conduct to crime, we first must decide if conduct of any kind has occurred. The requirement that criminal liability can be imposed only on the basis of conduct is often called the "actus reus" principle. Only an actus can blossom into an actus reus, an "evil act," even if the actor happens to be as reus as they come.

§ 4.1 Actus Reus

The Model Penal Code is emphatic about its adherence to the act requirement. Its very first "general principle of liability" proclaims that "[a] person is not guilty of an offense unless his liability is based on conduct that includes a voluntary act or the omission to perform an act of which he is physically capable."[1]

(A) Act

So to qualify as conduct, behavior must be an act and it must be voluntary. The Code defines the former, but not the latter, at least not directly. An act, according to the Code, is "a bodily movement whether voluntary or involuntary."[2] So just lying

1. § 2.01(1).

2. § 1.13(2). If you think it makes no sense to speak of an *involuntary* act, you're in good company. See, e.g., Oliver Wendell Holmes, The Common Law 45–46 (Mark DeWolfe Howe ed., 1961) (1881) ("A spasm is not an act. The contraction of the muscles must be willed."); Restatement (Second) of Torts § 2. Note, however, that the distinction between act and voluntariness within a few years of the Code's publication had attained something like constitutional significance. Robinson v. Califor-

around, or just thinking evil thoughts, will not a crime make. Or so it seems.

Thinking evil thoughts is never enough, but lying around doing nothing may be. That's because conduct also includes "the omission to perform an act of which [one] is physically capable." Doing nothing therefore constitutes conduct, somewhat surprisingly, if it's interpreted as not doing something one could have done. And, as we'll see shortly, not doing something may even be *punished* if one not only could, but *should*, have done it.

(B) Voluntariness

The more important aspect of the act requirement is its second component, voluntariness. Here the best the Code could do was provide an indirect definition, by listing acts that don't qualify as voluntary (though for each of these one might wonder whether they should count as "acts" in the first place):

(a) a reflex or convulsion;

(b) a bodily movement during unconsciousness or sleep;

(c) conduct during hypnosis or resulting from hypnotic suggestion.[3]

The Code comes closest to an affirmative definition of a voluntary act when it includes among involuntary acts:

nia, 370 U.S. 660 (1962) (constitutionalizing act requirement); Powell v. Texas, 392 U.S. 514 (1968) (refusing to constitutionalize voluntariness requirement).

3. § 2.01(2).

(d) a bodily movement that otherwise is not a product of the effort or the determination of the actor, either conscious or habitual.[4]

This is the first, but it will not be the last, multiple negative we'll come across in our exploration of the Model Penal Code. If an *involuntary* act is "a bodily movement that otherwise is not a product of the effort or the determination of the actor, either conscious or habitual," we may be permitted to infer that a *voluntary* act is "a bodily movement that [is] a product of the effort or the determination of the actor, either conscious or habitual."[5]

(C) Omission

But the absence of bodily movement, now labeled an "omission," also can give rise to criminal liability, the act requirement notwithstanding. Not just any omission will do, only an omission that violates an explicit obligation to act. These obligations can come in two forms:

(a) the omission is expressly made sufficient by the law defining the offense; or

(b) a duty to perform the omitted act is otherwise imposed by law.[6]

Here the Code is drawing a useful distinction between direct and indirect omission liability, one that the common law obscures. Direct omission

4. Id.

5. Cf. Restatement (Second) of Torts § 2 ("act" defined as "external manifestation of the actor's will").

6. § 2.01(3).

liability, covered under (a), is imposed for violations of statutes that explicitly criminalize failures to do this or that. For example, the Model Code provides that one way of "committing" the crime of theft of deception is by "fail[ing] to correct a false impression which the deceiver previously created or reinforced."[7]

Indirect omission liability, captured under (b), sweeps much more broadly. It applies to all offenses that don't explicitly apply to omissions, and that's the vast majority of offenses. Most dramatically, indirect omission liability extends to the most serious offense on the books, homicide. Again and again, courts have upheld manslaughter, even murder, convictions of those who "cause[d] the death of another human being,"[8] to use the Model Code's homicide definition, through inaction rather than through action.[9]

Not just anyone will be liable for criminal offenses she engaged in by doing nothing. I must have been under a duty to do that which I didn't. But where would I find such a duty? On this subject the Code is oddly vague. True, speaking of duties "otherwise imposed by law" excludes duties not imposed by law, and those imposed by morality or religion or some other non-legal system of norms in particular. But law comes in many shapes and sizes, and the

7. § 223.3(3).

8. § 210.1(1).

9. See, e.g., Commonwealth v. Pestinikas, 421 Pa.Super. 371 (1992) (murder); People v. Steinberg, 79 N.Y.2d 673 (1992) (manslaughter).

Code doesn't exclude any as sources of omission duties.

More specifically, the Code does not provide that only *statutorily* defined duties should matter for purposes of indirect omission liability. It's difficult to reconcile this position with the Code's categorical declaration that the legislature holds the monopoly on criminal lawmaking: "No conduct constitutes an offense unless it is a crime or violation under this Code or another statute of this State."[10]

As a result, common law and statute law both qualify as sources of duties the violation of which results in criminal liability, provided that a criminal offense can be found that threatens anyone causing a certain type of harm (death) with criminal punishment (say, homicide). Traditional common law duties include those based on certain "relationships" (parent to child, husband to wife, captain to sailor, employer to employee, and so on), on a specific mutual "contract" to provide assistance (which presumably differs from the general contractual relationship between, say, an employer and an employee), or—most ambiguously—on the one-sided "voluntary assumption of care," the bane of Good Samaritans everywhere (which presumably differs from the voluntary assumption manifested in a mutual contract).

In addition to these non-statutory sources of criminally enforceable duties, there are the duties one can find in the vast array of modern statutes,

10. § 1.05(1).

criminal or not. Some of these duties simply codify traditional common law duties. For instance, the New York Court of Appeals managed to find a statutory source for a father's duty to prevent the death of his daughter.[11] It invoked New York's *Family Court Act* in support of the proposition that "[p]arents have a nondelegable affirmative duty to provide their children with adequate medical care." The section of the Family Court Act, however, established no such duty, though it vaguely referred to one. Instead, it defined "neglected child," as "a child less than eighteen years of age ... whose physical, mental or emotional condition has been impaired or is in imminent danger of becoming impaired as a result of the failure of his parent or other person legally responsible for his care to exercise a minimum degree of care ... in supplying the child with adequate food, clothing, shelter or education ..., or medical, dental, optometrical or surgical care, though financially able to do so or offered financial or other reasonable means to do so...."[12]

Perhaps this case illustrates that limiting criminal omission duties to statutory sources, by itself, wouldn't do much to constrain a court's freewheeling search for duties more felt than specified. A court is likely to find a duty if it looks hard enough, even among statutes. Still, it's odd that the Code didn't at least force courts eager to convict unseemly omitters to jump through this additional hoop. Not every court will play that fast and loose with

11. People v. Steinberg, 79 N.Y.2d 673 (1992).

12. N.Y. Family Court Act § 1012(f)(i)(A).

statutory language, assuming they should find it, as the New York Court of Appeals did. In the end, the court's expansive reading of the Family Court Act didn't make much of a difference, since the parent-child relationship had been long established as a *common law* source of criminally enforceable duties.

The important point is, however, that a system of criminal law concerned about constraining judicial discretion in formulating basic rules of criminal liability, as the Code clearly is, forces courts to find specific identifiable sources of duties, rather than simply postulating them. Without that explicit foundation in positive law, the line between legal and moral duties will be difficult to maintain.

But let's say we've found a bona fide omission duty of one kind or another. Although the Code doesn't say so directly, we can assume that omissions must be voluntary too, just like commissions. The Code's list of "involuntary acts" doesn't easily translate to nonacts (what's a reflex omission, or an omissive reflex?), but it's doubtful that the Code drafters meant to hold us criminally liable for what we don't do while not sleepwalking anymore than for what we do do while sleepwalking.

At this point, it might appear that the Code's commitment to the "act requirement" is about as firm as its sense of what counts as an act is generous. But that's no surprise. One would expect that the Code drafters would hesitate to shackle the act requirement with dogmatic constraints. After all, an omission too can provide convincing evidence of

(D) Possession

The Code's flexible understanding of the act requirement becomes most obvious, however, in its rather cavalier treatment of an offense that was to become the policing tool of choice in the war on crime: possession.[14] Possession might be many things. It might be a status, or perhaps a relationship between a person and an object. But whatever it is, it isn't an act or any other type of conduct.[15] It's a status, a fact. To possess something is *to be* in possession of it.[16]

One would expect that this simple, and universally acknowledged, fact would remove possession offenses from the arsenal of a system of criminal law as emphatically devoted to the act requirement as the Model Penal Code proclaims to be: "A person is not guilty of an offense unless his liability is based on conduct that includes a voluntary act or the omission to perform an act of which he is physically capable."[17] (Perhaps it doth protest too much after all.)

---

13. For more on the Code's treatmentist approach, see supra § 2.

14. See Markus Dirk Dubber, Policing Possession: The War on Crime and the End of Criminal Law, 91 J. Crim. L. & Criminology 829 (2002).

15. See, e.g., Regina v. Dugdale, 1 El. & Bl. 435, 439 (1853) (Coleridge, J.).

16. The nature of possession as an inchoate offense is discussed infra § 5.2(a).

17. § 2.01(1).

But that's not so. Possession offenses play a crucial role in the Code's scheme for identifying and treating dangerous persons. In that scheme, persons who possess certain items, "instruments of crime" or weapons, reveal themselves as suffering from a criminal disposition by the mere fact of possession.[18] For that reason, a preventive system of criminal law is entitled, even required, to step in already at this point, long before dangerous possessions have been put to any use by their presumptively dangerous possessor.

Unwilling to do without this mechanism for early treatment intervention, yet unable simply to ignore the tension between possession offenses and the act requirement, the Code drafters simply cut the Gordian knot by *declaring* that "[p]ossession is an act." Possession is an act, they said, "if the possessor knowingly procured or received the thing possessed or was aware of his control thereof for a sufficient period to have been able to terminate his possession."[19] In other words, possession is an act because acquisition is an act and because non-disposal isn't an act, but an omission, and possession implies both acquisition and non-disposal. (The failure to dispose presumably is criminal because we are all under an—undeclared—duty to get rid of things we're not supposed to possess.) That much, of course, is true; but it's also true of any status acquired after birth, yet no one would describe the *facts of being* over-

18. §§ 5.06 & .07.

19. § 2.01(4); cf. N.Y. Penal Law § 15.00(2) (possession as *voluntary* act).

weight, forgetful, or bald as acts. At any rate, if it's the acquisition or the non-disposal they're after, the drafters might have done better to criminalize these acts directly. They didn't, and neither have other legislatures. It's possessing guns or drugs that's criminal, not buying them or failing to get rid of them.

So much for the actus. But what makes it reus? Perhaps its voluntariness. But that's unlikely; so many voluntary acts are perfectly benign, even saintly. No, what makes an actus reus is what makes conduct criminal: it must match the definition of a criminal offense. The act requirement is a sort of preliminary check that every defendant is subjected to before her conduct is matched against a criminal offense definition. If she flunks the act test, the inquiry into criminal liability is over, and she is—procedurally speaking—acquitted.

§ 4.2 Mens Rea and Offense Elements

Let's assume that the object of our inquiry into criminal liability, the defendant, has met the act requirement. Now we must check if her act satisfies the more specific requirements listed in the definition of a criminal offense. If there's a match, we have *prima facie*, or facial, criminal liability. Facial criminal liability is the topic of the current chapter. Facial liability, however, isn't quite the same as actual liability, or "guilt." Facial liability becomes guilt only if the defendant cannot avail herself of a defense. We will cover defenses, called justifications and excuses, in chapters 2 and 3, respectively.

In the Model Penal Code, as in modern criminal codes generally, the offenses defined in the Code's special part have the job of spelling out the criminal law's general proscription of "conduct that unjustifiably and inexcusably inflicts or threatens substantial harm to individual or public interests."[20] To assemble the multitude of offenses into the edifice of criminal law with the necessary clarity and specificity, code drafters have several building blocks at their disposal. The Model Code calls these building blocks "offense elements." These offense elements are assembled into offenses, which in turn are put together to form the special part of a criminal code.

(A) Element Types

In Model Penal Code language, there are three basic types of offense elements: conduct, attendant circumstance, and result (or CAR, for friends of mnemonic devices).[21] All offenses in the Code are constructed out of these elemental building blocks. With these tools in hand, the drafting possibilities are limitless, or close enough to limitless for purposes of criminal law. An offense could have, but didn't have to have, all three types of elements. It could include no attendant circumstances, or one, or as many as the drafters could think of. It might have a result element. Then again, it might not.

20. § 1.02(1)(a).

21. Note that "conduct" here is used in a slightly different, narrower, sense than it is in § 1.02(1)(a). In its broader, and looser, sense, conduct refers to the entire offense definition. In its narrower sense, it applies only to one element of that definition.

Conduct is a different story. Given the act requirement, every offense has to include at least a conduct element.[22]

Although criminal law doctrine doesn't require this, offense definitions tend to consist of more than a bare conduct element. That's because without an attendant circumstance or a result, the offense may run afoul of the constitutional prohibition against vague criminal statutes.[23]

A crime defined simply as "driving" for example wouldn't give you a lot of notice of what exactly you're prohibited from doing and, even worse, would give police officers a lot of discretion to decide this question for you on the spot. Even if "driving" wasn't too vague, it may well be too broad—unless the state could constitutionally prohibit anyone from driving anything anywhere. "Driving under the influence of alcohol" is another story. The attendant circumstance of "under the influence of alcohol" narrows the reach of the conduct, "driving." The conduct itself might be further specified to include the driving of certain things, like "motor vehicles." An offense like "operating a motor vehicle under the influence of alcohol" would pass constitutional muster—it wouldn't be too vague or too broad.[24]

22. See § 1.13(5) (defining conduct as "an action or omission").

23. On vagueness, see City of Chicago v. Morales, 527 U.S. 41 (1999) (gang loitering); Papachristou v. City of Jacksonville, 405 U.S. 156 (1972) (vagrancy).

24. See, e.g., N.Y. Veh. & Traf. Law § 1192(3).

We could further pinpoint our offense by throwing in a result element, like "serious physical injury." This would transform our *conduct offense* (embellished with an attendant circumstance) into a result offense: "causing serious physical injury while operating a motor vehicle under the influence of alcohol." Note that only *result offenses* have a result element. This will be important later on, when we talk about causation.[25] There's no need to worry about causation unless you're confronted with a result offense, which is a good thing since causation issues can be quite a headache.

It's important to keep in mind that the Code's trichotomy of offense elements is a means to an end, rather than an end in itself. That end is analytic clarity. Don't get bogged down trying to decide whether a particular word, or phrase, in an offense definition counts as one type of element or another. In most cases, it makes no difference whether you're dealing with conduct, attendant circumstance, or result—though, as you might expect, we'll soon turn to an important, if unfortunate, exception to that rule.[26]

In conclusion, here is the Commentaries' sensible take on the point of distinguishing among the various element types:

> The "circumstances" of the offense refer to the objective situation that the law requires to exist,

[25]. See infra § 5.1.

[26]. Another exception, besides the definition of mental states, is the law of attempt, which assigns different mental states to different element types. See infra § 5.2(a).

in addition to the defendant's act or any results that the act may cause. The elements of "nighttime" in burglary, "property of another" in theft, "female not his wife" in rape, and "dwelling" in arson are illustrations. "Conduct" refers to "breaking and entering" in burglary, "taking" in theft, "sexual intercourse" in rape and "burning" in arson. Results, of course, include "death" in homicide. *While these terms are not airtight categories, they have served as a helpful analytical device in the development of the Code.*[27]

So much for the three basic types of offense element (or CAR). There's one more ingredient that's needed to transform a pile of offense definitions into the special part of a criminal code: *mens rea* or, as the Model Code drafters preferred to say, *culpability*.

Culpability in turn comes in four varieties, or five, depending on who's counting: purpose, knowledge, recklessness, negligence, and strict liability. Strict liability is the fifth wheel here. The other kinds of culpability often are referred to as "mental states" or "states of mind." Strictly speaking, however, strict liability isn't a mental state. It's a kind of liability, namely one that's "strict" precisely because it pays no attention to mental state. For purposes of strict liability, it doesn't matter whether the defendant had a mental state of any kind— which is not to say that he didn't, just that it doesn't matter whether he did or not.

27. Commentaries § 5.01, at 301 n.9 (emphasis added).

True, negligence also doesn't quite fit in with the others. That's because negligence really isn't quite a mental state either. It's the *absence* of a mental state: to act negligently means not being aware of a risk of harm. But unlike strict liability, negligence at least makes some reference to a mental state—awareness—even if only *in absentia*. To punish negligence is to punish this absence; it's to say that the defendant *should have* been aware, even though he wasn't. It's his *failure* to recognize that his behavior might cause harm that renders him criminally liable.

In sum, we have three types of offense elements, and four states of mind. Now the Model Code drafters decided that each element of an offense could have attached to it a different state of mind, or one and the same, or none whatever. And if none of the four mental states fits the bill, there was strict liability—at least for minor offenses called "violations." Imagine the mixing and matching options now!

Unfortunately, not only did the drafting possibilities prove endless, so did the fruitless confusion of students trying to make sense of all this. To add insult to injury, the Code drafters went on to define the various kinds of culpability differently, depending on the type of element to which they were attached. So "purposeful" meant one thing when it accompanied a conduct or a result element, and quite another when it was attached to an attendant circumstance. "Knowingly" was one thing for conduct and attendant circumstance, and another for result. The definitions of "reckless" and "negligent" were less differentiated, so undifferentiated in fact that it was unclear whether they were defined at all when they accompanied a conduct element, as opposed to an attendant circumstance or a result.[28]

Countless classroom hours are spent each year on the tedious, and ultimately fruitless, task of making sense of the Code's unnecessarily complicated taxonomy of elements and mental states, and then trying to apply it to particular offenses. (Is this a conduct element? A result? Or perhaps an attendant circumstance?) One is much better off to recognize that the Code drafters might have lost the forest for the trees here and instead to recover the general rationalizing impetus underlying their convoluted scheme.

Let's take a step back, then, and look at the big picture, before zooming in on the details of the Code's mens rea system. The Code drafters were eager to do away with what they saw as the common law's hopelessly confused doctrine of mens rea. They viewed that doctrine as the root of all—certainly most—evil in traditional Anglo-American criminal law. They were not the only ones, nor were they the first, to become exasperated with mens rea. Here's a fairly typical, and roughly contemporaneous, complaint about the looseness—and useless-

---

28. See Paul H. Robinson & Jane A. Grall, Element Analysis in Defining Criminal Liability, 35 Stan. L. Rev. 681 (1983), for in-depth exploration of this point, and the Code's mens rea scheme in general.

ness—of a unitary concept of mens rea, taken from Herbert Packer's classic *The Limits of the Criminal Sanction*:

> When we speak of Arthur's having the *mens rea* of murder, we may mean any one or more of the following things: that he intended to kill Victor; or that he was aware of the risk of his killing Victor but went ahead and shot him anyhow; or (more dubiously) that he ought to have known but didn't that there was a substantial risk of his killing Victor or that he knew it was wrong to kill a fellow human being, or that he ought to have known it; or that he didn't really think that Victor was trying to kill him; or that he did think that, but only a fool would have thought it; or that he was not drunk to the point of unconsciousness when he killed Victor; or that even though he was emotionally disturbed he wasn't grossly psychotic, etc., etc.[29]

So great was the Code drafters' disdain for traditional mens rea that they banned the concept from the realm of enlightened criminal law. Since then it is considered bad taste to speak of mens rea, or its cousin "intent," in the context of the Model Penal Code. (I don't see any reason to adhere to this

---

29. Herbert L. Packer, The Limits of the Criminal Sanction 104–05 (1968). By the time the Model Code drafters and their contemporaries got into the act, railing against the common law's notion of mens rea already had a long, and distinguished, tradition. See, e.g., James Fitzgerald Stephen's opinion in R. v. Tolson, 23 Q.B.D. 168, 185–86 (1889). For a brief historical account of common law mens rea, see Francis B. Sayre, Mens Rea, 45 Harv. L. Rev. 974 (1932).

taboo—talking about criminal law without reference to intention makes about as much sense as talking about criminal law without mentioning punishment.[30])

The Code drafters' attempt to overhaul the law of mens rea was a huge success. The Code's all new, all differentiated, mens rea scheme was widely hailed as a significant advance, and rightly so. The mens rea section, § 2.02, is the heart of the Model Penal Code. For that reason alone it deserves careful attention. It's also the single most influential section in the Code, in MPC-and non-MPC-jurisdictions alike.

The drafters' basic claim, also not new, was that traditional mens rea jurisprudence mistakenly assumed that each offense had only a single mens rea requirement and, even more generally, that there was only one concept of mens rea *in the entire criminal law*. At common law, there was mens rea, period. Criminal liability turned on two questions: one, was there actus reus?, and, two, was there mens rea? In other words, did the defendant engage in the proscribed conduct as defined?, and, did he have the requisite "depravity of the will,"[31] "diabolic malignity,"[32] "abandoned" or "bad heart,"[33]

30. That didn't keep the Model Code drafters from trying. See Markus Dirk Dubber, Penal Panopticon: The Idea of a Modern Model Penal Code, 4 Buff. Crim. L. Rev. 53, 70–73 (2000) (punishment taboo in Model Code).

31. 4 William Blackstone, Commentaries on the Laws of England 21 (1769).

32. General Summary of Crimes, and Their Punishments, in 2 Laws of the Commonwealth of Pennsylvania 558, 568 (1810).

33. 4 William Blackstone, Commentaries on the Laws of England 200 (1769).

"heart regardless of social duty, and fatally bent on mischief,"[34] "wicked heart,"[35] "mind grievously depraved,"[36] or "mischievous vindictive spirit"[37]?

By contrast, the Code drafters decided not only that offenses had different mens rea requirements (rejecting the notion of a single concept of mens rea for all of criminal law), but also that *individual offenses* might have different mens rea requirements attached to their constitutive parts, the aforementioned "elements." And so the Code's "element analysis" of mens rea was born to replace the "offense analysis" of the common law.

That's when things got complicated. The price of lucidity was complexity, and of differentiation, confusion. The common law had known two units of analysis: mens rea and actus reus. The Code recognized seven, and that's not even counting strict (mens-rea-less) liability. The quartet "purpose, knowledge, recklessness, and negligence" took the place of mens rea, and conduct, attendant circumstance, and result, that of actus reus.

If every element of every offense—rather than every offense—can have its very own mental state, an obvious problem arises: how can one tell which

34. General Summary of Crimes, and Their Punishments, in 2 Laws of the Commonwealth of Pennsylvania 558, 562, 573 (1810).

35. Id. at 562.

36. Id. at 562.

37. Id. at 570.

mental state attaches to which offense element? The simplest solution would be to say so in the offense definition. This would lead to offense definitions that would consist more of mental states than of offense elements. So adultery, for instance, might become something like "knowingly engaging in an act one knows to constitute sexual intercourse with another whom one knows to be a person at a time when one is reckless with regard to one's having a spouse and with regard to that spouse's being alive, or when one is virtually certain that the other person has a spouse and where he should have been aware of a substantial likelihood that this spouse is alive."[38]

(B) Rules of Interpretation

To avoid monstrous concoctions of this sort—which are ugly to look at, as well as confusing to the point of vagueness—the Code drafters instead set up rules of statutory interpretation which allowed courts, and law students, to match mental states to offense elements in the case of offense definitions that contained elements unaccompanied by mental states. This is a cumbersome exercise, and becomes no more fruitful for being an entirely preliminary matter that has nothing to do with the substance of criminal law. Unfortunately, it's also a necessary evil; without having figured out precisely what the elements of an offense are and what mental state, if any, attaches to each, we can't proceed to the real

38. Loosely based on N.Y. Penal Law § 255.17 ("engag[ing] in sexual intercourse with another person at a time when he has a living spouse, or the other person has a living spouse").

task: to determine whether the defendant's behavior matches the definition of that offense, and therefore qualifies for facial liability—the topic of the present chapter.

Rule 1. Absence means presence I (default).[39]

If the offense definition doesn't identify the mental state accompanying an offense element, apply recklessness. Example: To commit adultery in New York, i.e., "engage in sexual intercourse with another person at a time when he has a living spouse, or the other person has a living spouse," one would have to have been at least reckless about the fact that the other person was married at the time. In other words, the relevant element of the offense— once filled in by implication—would read "at a time when he was reckless regarding the possibility that the other person has a living spouse." And, since recklessness in the Model Code means conscious disregard of a substantial and unjustifiable risk that the offense element exists,[40] the offense element in full bloom reads something like this: "at a time when he consciously disregarded a substantial and unjustifiable risk that the other person has a living spouse." (Note: Don't confuse this rule of statutory interpretation with a finding of fact. Rule 1 simply provides that a mental state of recklessness should be read into an offense definition in certain circumstances. It doesn't help you determine whether the defendant actually acted with that mental state.

39. § 2.02(3).

40. § 2.02(3)(c).

That's a substantive question of liability, not a preliminary question of interpretation.)

Rule 2. Absence means presence II (one-for-all).[41]

If the offense definition doesn't identify the mental state accompanying an offense element, but lists a mental state with respect to another element, apply that mental state, unless it's clear from the text of the statute that this isn't what the legislature intended. Example: In a famous Supreme Court case, *Morissette v. United States*,[42] the defendant was convicted of having committed the following offense: "Whoever embezzles, steals, purloins, or knowingly converts government property is punishable by fine and imprisonment." Does the mental state "knowingly" apply (a) only to "converts," or (b) to "government property" as well? Under the Model Code's Rule 2, the answer is (b). There is no reason to believe that whoever drafted the offense definition meant to confine the reach of "knowingly" to its immediate successor, "converts." That's also what the Supreme Court decided, though by a far more circuitous route—after all, it didn't have the Model Penal Code to invoke; the Code wasn't finished until ten years later. Though even if the Code already had been around at the time, it's important to see why it wouldn't have resolved the issue for the Court. The Court might have turned to the Code for advice, or at least inspiration, and thereby saved itself a lot of trouble. But the Model Code itself isn't binding on the Court, nor for that matter on any other court.

41. § 2.02(4).
42. 342 U.S. 246 (1952).

Even in jurisdictions that have adopted some version of some parts of the Code, its authority is at best persuasive—never conclusive. This was a federal statute. And, as we know by now, the federal criminal code, Title 18 of the United States Code, is among those American criminal codes that have remained virtually untouched by the Model Code's influence.

Rule 2 also includes an exception to itself. Don't apply one mental state across the board if a "contrary purpose plainly appears." So Rule 2 might not apply to the *Morissette* statute if that statute instead had read: "Whoever knowingly converts, or embezzles, steals, or purloins government property is punishable by fine and imprisonment." And it certainly wouldn't have applied to this statute: "Whoever embezzles, steals, purloins, or knowingly converts government property is punishable by fine and imprisonment. Ignorance of the fact that the property in question is government property is immaterial."

Rule 3. Absence means absence (strict liability).[43]

If the offense definition doesn't identify the mental state accompanying an offense element, it means what it says: no mental state applies. Example: Rule 3 would read the New York adultery statute as a strict liability offense through and through.[44] For

43. § 2.05.

44. In fact, adultery was one of the classic strict liability offenses of the common law. See, e.g., Commonwealth v. Thomp-

instance, it wouldn't matter whether one knew, or even suspected, that "the other person has a living spouse" or not. (Strictly speaking, Rule 3 would also render mental states regarding all other elements irrelevant, including the facts that "the other person" was in fact a person—rather than, say, a hologram—or that what one was engaging in was "sexual intercourse"—rather than, say, a friendly embrace—or that one had a "living spouse"—rather than a dead one, or a living fiancé—of one's own.)

Note, however, that the Code would prevent this reading of our adultery statute for another reason: It limits strict liability to a class of noncriminal offenses called "violations." (Actually, it also allows strict liability for other, criminal, offenses, as long as they're defined outside the criminal code and it's clear that the legislature wanted to create a strict liability offense. This barndoor exception we'll ignore here.[45]) An offense qualifies as a violation if it

son, 6 Allen 591 (Mass.1863) (Thompson I); Commonwealth v. Thompson, 11 Allen 23 (Mass.1865) (Thompson II).

45. § 2.05(1)(b). After opening the door to the barn, the drafters tried to shut it right away, by providing that any strict liability offense found in a statute other than the criminal code would be treated as a violation, no matter how it might be classified in that statute. Id. § (2)(a). Given how many crimes are defined outside codes of crimes in contemporary American law, their treatment was of enormous significance to the drafters' attempt to systematize criminal law. It's even more important today, as the trend to generate these once "supplementary" crimes has only accelerated since the days of the Code. Take federal criminal law. One would learn very little about federal criminal law by reading the so-called "Federal Criminal Code," Title 18 of the U.S. Code. By one recent count, of the approximately 3,300 federal crimes, only about 1,200 appear in Title 18.

is identified as such or if it is punishable only by fine, forfeiture, or some other civil penalty (like disbarment).[46] What counts is the penalty threatened in the code, not that actually sought or imposed in a case. (Note that there are no limits on the amount of the fine.)

Rule 3 thus wouldn't apply to adultery because adultery is, at least in New York, a misdemeanor. (It's designated as a misdemeanor in the New York Penal Law; plus, it's punishable by imprisonment of up to three months.[47]) This limitation works well enough for the Code itself. It doesn't work so well when it's applied to other, real, criminal codes, as these often do not limit the application of the "no (mental state) means no" rule to minor offenses. As a result, there is no interpretative rule that bars courts from reading even the most serious crimes as strict liability offenses. Among the most prominent examples of this practice are strict liability drug possession felonies that impose severe punishments,

The rest, almost two-thirds, are sprinkled throughout the other forty-nine titles of the U.S. Code, not to mention the more than 10,000 administrative regulations carrying criminal penalties strewn about the Code of Federal Regulations. Ronald L. Gainer, Federal Criminal Code Reform: Past and Future, 2 Buff. Crim. L. Rev. 45, 53, 74 (1998). A similar proliferation of crimes outside criminal codes has occurred in the states, where the problem is exacerbated by the criminalization activities of smaller governmental entities within each state, including counties, cities, towns, villages, and so on. See Wayne A. Logan, The Shadow Criminal Law of Municipal Governance, 62 Ohio St. L.J. 1409 (2001).

46. § 1.04(5).

47. N.Y. Penal Law § 70.15(2).

up to and including life imprisonment without the possibility of parole, in the absence of mental state requirements with respect to such elements as the fact of possession, or the nature and the weight of the drug possessed.[48]

At any rate, the same caveat that applies to the use of Rule 2 (one-for-all) in *Morissette* also applies here. The Model Code's rules of interpretation don't control the interpretation of other codes—they apply to the Code itself only. That's not to say that courts won't look to them for inspiration, but they don't have to follow them, or pay any attention to them, for that matter. The New York adultery statute differs from *Morissette* in that the New York Penal Law, unlike the federal criminal code, was fundamentally revised on the basis of the Model Penal Code. But, as in every other MPC jurisdiction, New York didn't adopt the Model Code wholesale. The drafters picked and chose, and often changed what they chose. And among the Code provisions they chose to change was Rule 3. The New York Penal Law does contain a general presumption against strict liability, but it doesn't limit strict liability to noncriminal offenses and, in fact, expressly recognizes strict liability crimes, without limitation, provided the statute clearly shows that the legislature meant to create a strict liability crime.[49] (The New York drafters, rather sensibly, dropped the Code's distinction between offenses de-

48. See, e.g., Harmelin v. Michigan, 501 U.S. 957 (1991) (life without parole for simple possession).

49. N.Y. Penal Law § 15.15(2).

fined in the Code those defined elsewhere. They also changed Rule 1: the default mental state is negligence, not recklessness.[50] Only Rule 2 remained pretty much intact.[51])

A final note on strict liability and statutory interpretation. The Code's move from offense to element analysis, its shift of focus from the offense to its constituent elements, meant not only that different elements could have different mental states attached to them. Now different elements also could have, or *not* have, a mental state attached to them. Strict liability, the *absence* of mens rea, became too a characteristic of elements, rather than of offenses. Strictly speaking, therefore, in Code-speak there is no such thing as a "strict liability offense"; there are only strict liability elements.

So much for rules of interpretation. Here's a chart that shows them all:

Chart 1
Rules of Interpretation (Ambiguous Mental State Requirements)

Rule 1   Recklessness Default
(absence means presence I)

Rule 2   One For All
(absence means presence II)

Rule 3   Strict Liability for Violations
(absence means absence)

[50]. Id. ("mental culpability" as default, which implies at least "criminal negligence").

[51]. Id. § 15.15(1).

(C) The Modes of Culpability

Let's assume we've managed to figure out, with the help of our three rules, what the offense definitions in our criminal code's special part look like, in full bloom, with gaps and ambiguities filled in as needed, keeping in mind that absence can, but need not, mean presence, at least when it comes to mens rea requirements. Now we can proceed to check whether the defendant's behavior matches the definition of an offense, or perhaps more than one. Or can we?

Not quite. For, as noted above, the Model Code drafters were not content to attach—or not—attach mental states to each and every element of an offense. They also defined each mental state differently, depending on which type of element it accompanies. In other words, we're still not quite done filling in the details of the offense definition. But before we know exactly what the requirements for criminal liability under a particular statute are, we can't decide whether the defendant's behavior meets them.

We're still at the preliminary, pre-matching, stage. But at least we're moving closer to criminal law. We're no longer just coloring in the outlines of offense definitions. We're now beginning to figure out what these offense definitions, or at least whatever mental states they may contain, *mean*.

Here are the definitions, arranged by type of offense element, taken from § 2.02(2):[52]

[52]. For a more detailed discussion of this topic and a more detailed chart, see Paul H. Robinson & Jane A. Grall, Element

Chart 2
Modes of Culpability, by Offense Element (Model Penal Code)

	Conduct	Attendant Circumstance	Result
Purpose	conscious object	awareness, belief, hope	conscious object
Knowledge	awareness	awareness	awareness of practical certainty
Recklessness	[not defined]	conscious disregard of substantial & unjustifiable risk[53]	conscious disregard of substantial & unjustifiable risk
Negligence	[not defined]	failure to perceive substantial & unjustifiable risk[54]	failure to perceive substantial & unjustifiable risk

The Model Code drafters may have gotten a little carried away here in their drive for analytic precision. It's best not to get hung up on the fine points of the distinctions within the definition of a given mental state. (The drafters of criminal codes based on the MPC didn't either, as we'll see shortly.[55]) The distinctions *among* the mental states are tough enough to keep track of.

Analysis in Defining Criminal Liability, 35 Stan. L. Rev. 681, 697 (1983).

53. The conscious disregard of the risk constitutes "a gross deviation from the standard of conduct that a law-abiding person would observe in the actor's situation."

54. The failure to perceive the risk constitutes "a gross deviation from the standard of care that a reasonable person would observe in the actor's situation."

55. See, e.g., N.Y. Penal Law § 15.05

One of the problems with taking the drafters too seriously here is that it's hard to classify the elements of living, breathing offenses by type. In the words of the drafters themselves: "[t]he distinction between conduct and attendant circumstance or result is not always a bright one...."[56] The distinction often is difficult to draw in the Model Code itself.[57] And it doesn't get any brighter when one moves into real criminal law, bustling with awkward offense definitions that—to put it mildly—weren't put together by drafters eager to accommodate the Model Code's classification of offense element types.[58] But these very distinctions take on crucial significance as soon as the definition of a mental state varies with the type of offense element it happens to accompany.

Still, the above chart wasn't included just for completeness's sake. It's important to understand what the Code drafters were trying to do when they set up their taxonomy of culpability. And with a little common sense, much of the chart makes pretty good sense. We'll use the simplified chart in the New York Penal Law for comparison.[59] (At its best,

56. Commentaries § 2.02, at 240.

57. Try these questions: What's "conduct" in homicide (§ 210.1)? And "attendant circumstance"? And "result"? How about in causing suicide (§ 210.5(1))? In burglary (§ 221.1)?

58. Here's the example used in the Commentaries, a relatively tame federal statute: "A person is guilty of an offense if, by fire or explosion, he (1) damages a public facility; or (2) damages substantially a building or a public structure." Commentaries § 2.02, at 240.

59. N.Y. Penal Law § 15.05.

CRIMINAL CONDUCT 63

the New York code is a less persnickety version of the MPC.) Inevitably this will lead us to the more interesting topic, the distinctions among the various mental states, rather than those within each.[60]

Chart 3
Modes of Culpability, by Offense Element
(N.Y. Penal Law)

	Conduct	Attendant Circumstance	Result
Purpose[61]	conscious objective	[not defined]	conscious objective
Knowledge	awareness	awareness	[not defined]
Recklessness	[not defined]	awareness & conscious disregard of substantial & unjustifiable risk[62]	awareness & conscious disregard of substantial & unjustifiable risk
Negligence	[not defined]	failure to perceive substantial & unjustifiable risk[63]	failure to perceive substantial & unjustifiable risk

(i) *Purpose.* Starting from the top, with purpose, it's easy to see that what's distinctive about this

60. For a common law precursor of the Code's culpability scheme, balanced precariously on the pin of "intention," see Regina v. Faulkner, 13 Cox Crim. Cas. 550, 557 (1877) (opinion of Fitzgerald, J.).

61. Actually, the New York Penal Law calls purpose "intention," and negligence "criminal negligence."

62. The conscious disregard of the risk constitutes "a gross deviation from the standard of conduct that a reasonable person would observe in the situation."

63. The failure to perceive the risk constitutes "a gross deviation from the standard of care that a reasonable person would observe in the situation."

mental state is the concept of "conscious object" (or objective, in the New York Penal Law). This point can be obscured if one pays too much attention to the Model Code's definition of purpose with respect to attendant circumstances. The reason the Model Code drafters, in their quest for comprehensiveness, defined purpose differently for attendant circumstances (and the New York Penal Law drafters not at all) was presumably that it often doesn't make sense to speak of having the existence of an attendant circumstance as one's conscious object. Attendant circumstances, unlike conduct and result, tend to be out of the actor's control. Take the traditional distinction between ordinary daytime and aggravated nighttime burglary. It's either dark or it isn't when I break into a house, and, absent supernatural powers there is nothing I can do about that.

Similarly, though less clearly, in offenses where the age or status of my victim makes a difference—sometimes between criminal liability and impunity, sometimes between types of crimes or levels of liability—my victim either is old enough (or young enough) or not, or a police officer or not. Actually, in this type of offense, where the attendant circumstance defines the victim, it's not hard to imagine a case where the offender doesn't just *know, believe, or hope* that the victim is of a particular age, status, gender, or race, but that it was his *conscious object* to go after a victim with that particular attendant circumstance. This, arguably, is what hate crimes are all about—unless you think that hate crimes are about *motive*, not purpose.[64]

At any rate, the Model Code's definition of purpose as to an attendant circumstance not only clarifies, but also simplifies, the prosecutor's task. It provides that, whenever purpose attaches to an attendant circumstance, proof of knowledge, belief (much less than knowledge), or hope (even less than belief) will do. There's no need to prove conscious object, provided that would make sense.

(ii) *Knowledge*. Knowledge is next. Here the watchword is awareness. This works well enough for conduct and attendant circumstances. I can be aware (or not) that I am doing something and that I'm doing something under certain conditions, say when it's dark outside. Result is a little different. Once again assuming that I'm blessed with neither omnipotence (allowing me to change day to night) nor prescience (allowing me to see the future), it makes no sense to say that I *know* that what I'm

64. See, e.g., State v. Wyant, 64 Ohio St.3d 566 (1992). It's blackletter law that motive is not a relevant consideration in the analysis of criminal liability, as a matter of substance. Wayne R. LaFave & Austin W. Scott, Jr., Criminal Law § 3.6 (2d ed. 1986). It's not supposed to matter *why* you intentionally killed your brother, only *that* you did. But see § 5.01(4) (no renunciation defense to attempt if "motivated ... by circumstances ... which increase the probability of detection"). By contrast, no one doubts that, as a matter of procedure, motive is helpful—if not essential—when it comes to convincing a factfinder, jury or judge, that a particular defendant did the crime. See, e.g., Commonwealth v. Malone, 354 Pa. 180, 188 (1946). Plus, it's generally conceded that motive may make a difference in sentencing—or the prescription of peno-correctional treatment. Cf. § 210.6(3)(g) ("murder was committed for pecuniary gain" as aggravating circumstance in capital case).

doing will lead to a particular result. That's why the Model Code drafters defined knowledge regarding result not simply as awareness, but as awareness of a practical certainty, i.e., the closest thing we ordinary mortals can come to know anything about the future. (Once again, the New York Penal Law drafters avoided this difficulty by not defining knowledge as to result at all.)

The distinction between purpose and knowledge, then, is that between conscious object(ive) and awareness. It's important to get this distinction straight. It's also important to realize that it makes little difference in the criminal law, generally speaking. As we saw earlier, the default mental state in the Model Code is recklessness. This means that the distinction between purpose and knowledge generally doesn't come up, since recklessness is enough for liability. What's more, most offenses that require more than recklessness with respect to any of their elements don't require purpose, but knowledge. For example, murder generally requires only proof of knowledge that one was causing the death of another person.[65]

Still there are some offenses that do require purpose, rather than "mere" knowledge.[66] The most

65. See § 210.1.

66. Note that the mental states in the Model Code are neatly stacked, so that proof of a "higher" mental state implies proof of any and all "lower" ones. In other words, proof of purpose implies proof of "mere" knowledge, recklessness, and negligence, and so on down the line. Needless to say, proof of any mental state, including negligence, implies proof of none whatever, i.e., strict liability. The prosecution is always free to go beyond the

frequently cited, and least frequent, example is treason, which requires the doing of something with the purpose of aiding the enemy.[67]

(iii) *Recklessness*. Considerably more significant is the distinction between knowledge and recklessness. The gist of recklessness isn't as difficult to make out as that of purpose or knowledge; the Model Code drafters provided only one definition of it (as they did of negligence) for all types of offense elements. One recklessness fits all. Or nearly all. For the Code drafters didn't provide a definition of recklessness (or negligence) for conduct. That's probably a good thing, not only because it makes it easy to see the point of recklessness. It would also have been difficult to figure out just what it would mean to recklessly (or negligently) engage in conduct. Here mens rea bumps up against actus reus. Given that conduct isn't conduct unless it's an act, and that an act isn't criminal unless it's voluntary, what would a voluntary yet reckless or negligent act look like? To pass the voluntariness prong of the act requirement, the defendant's behavior would have to be (or rather, not not to be) "a product of the effort or the determination of the actor, either conscious or habitual."[68] But how could someone engage in an act that's voluntary (or not involuntary) in this sense, and yet engage in it recklessly or negligently, as these mental states are defined in

call of duty and establish a "higher" mental state than is required by statute.

67. See Haupt v. United States, 330 U.S. 631, 641 (1947).

68. § 2.01(2)(d).

the Model Code? Recall that to act recklessly means to consciously disregard the risk that something is the case and to act negligently is to fail to even perceive that risk. If all I'm aware of is the risk that I *might be engaging* in some sort of conduct, it would be odd to classify that conduct as involving a voluntary act. And that goes double if I'm unaware of even the possibility that I might be doing something, as in the case of negligence. In sum, if I'm not actually aware of the fact (not the possibility) that I'm engaging in one type of conduct, rather than another or none at all, it's hard to see how I can be said to engage in it voluntarily. Put differently, nothing less than knowledge (as defined by the Code drafters) will do for conduct, as a matter of actus reus, rather than of mens rea.

The line between knowledge and recklessness is important for several reasons. Most obvious, it's the line that separates many more serious crimes from less serious ones. The prime example is, once again, homicide. In the Model Code scheme of things, the main line between murder and manslaughter is that between knowledge and recklessness. Murder is knowingly (or purposely) causing another's death; manslaughter is recklessly doing it. (We'll get to so-called voluntary manslaughter (or murder plus provocation) later.[69])

The knowledge/recklessness distinction also tracks that between specific and general intent, which in turns affects the availability of certain defenses. Strictly speaking, the distinction between

69. Infra § 16.

specific and general intent is as foreign to the world of the Model Penal Code as is the concept of intent itself. The whole point of the Code's taxonomy of mental states, after all, was to do away with the confused concept of intent. But, despite the Code drafters' best efforts, talk of specific and general intent survives in American courtrooms and criminal codes (and criminal law classes), as does talk of intent and intention. And some of the substance of the distinction between the two types of intent persists even in the Code itself, as we'll see when we get to the intoxication "defense." It turns out that the Code retains, in substance though not in form, the traditional—and somewhat counterintuitive—rule that intoxication is a defense only to specific intent crimes, but not to general intent (and generally *less* serious) ones.[70] Similarly, the drafters insisted that their recklessness default rule of statutory interpretation (our Rule 1 above) not only fought definitional clutter, but also reflected the mens rea requirement of the common law, such as it was, namely, as a sort of general presumption of mens rea, or intent, at least for common law crimes (i.e., those defined by the courts, rather than by statute) and in the absence of contrary legislative intent.[71]

Since the distinction between specific and general intent, and the concept of intent that underlies it, continue to matter, even in the Code, it's useful to see how intent-talk maps onto Model Penal Code

70. See infra § 4.3(a).

71. Commentaries § 2.02, at 244.

talk. This diagram provides an overview of the relationship:

Chart 4
Modes of Culpability (MPC) vs.
Intent(Common Law)

	Model Penal Code			
	Purpose	Knowledge	Recklessness	Negligence
Common Law 1[72]	Intent———————————————————>			Criminal Negligence—>
	Specific—> General————————————>			
Common Law 2[73]	Intent——————————————————————————>			
	Specific—————————> General ——————————>			

The Model Code drafters were right. Intent, specific and general, meant many things to many people—it still does. This chart makes no attempt to capture all, or even most, varieties of intent-talk. (For example, it ignores secondary intent offenses, such as assault with intent to kill, which are often called specific intent crimes.) It does show two of the more common, and recent, varieties, one based on the pre-MPC Louisiana criminal code, the other on a post-MPC New Jersey case. The Model Code drafters of course wouldn't have endorsed either, having sworn off intent-talk entirely. Still, if pressed, they might have acknowledged that both schemes were half right, or at least half not wrong.

72. Based on La. Crim. Code §§ 10–12 (1942) (pre-MPC codification).

73. Based on State v. Cameron, 104 N.J. 42 (1986) (interpreting MPC-based provision).

In differentiating between intent and negligence, the common law scheme no. 1 reflects the drafters' claim that their recklessness default rule codified the common law requirement of mens rea, i.e., of intent, or *scienter*. By contrast, classifying negligence—which implies the *absence* of awareness—as a form of intent (or *scienter*), as in the second scheme, doesn't sound quite right. Scheme no. 2, however, has the advantage of drawing the line between specific and general intent at recklessness, rather than at knowledge. While the common law certainly would provide support for limiting specific intent to purpose (as it would for a host of definitions of intent), expanding it to include knowledge as well fits better with the Model Code's attempt to capture the common law's limitation of the intoxication defense to specific intent offenses. (Recall that intoxication under the Model Code may disprove knowledge (and purpose), but not recklessness.)

Now that we've got an idea of why the distinction between knowledge and recklessness matters—and how it may or may not relate to that between specific and general intent—let's see what that distinction is. Here we might differentiate between two axes of comparison, which I'll call *attitude* and *probability*.[74] Knowledge and recklessness differ most clearly along the probabilistic axis. Knowledge

74. If you like, you can also call them "subjective" and "objective," though these terms tend to bring a lot of excess baggage along, plus probability also has a subjective aspect, if the actor's awareness of (or attitude toward) the risk in question makes a difference.

requires certainty (or practical certainty, when it comes to result). Recklessness requires something less than 100% certainty, namely a substantial risk.[75] What's "substantial" the Code drafters didn't say. They left this decision up to the jury (or the judge, in a bench trial).[76] To illustrate, the difference between murder and (involuntary) manslaughter then is the difference between doing something one knows *will* cause the death of another person and doing something one knows *might* lead to that result.

It's clear enough why knowledge would result in greater criminal liability than recklessness, if one focuses on the issue of probability. It's worse (and more dangerous) to do something knowing it will result in some harm than doing the same thing thinking it might.

That's not to say, however, that culpability (or dangerousness) is directly proportional to probability. Take purpose, for example. Purpose is the "highest" mode of culpability—purposeful action is

75. The Model Code also requires that the risk be "unjustifiable." That issue, however, is best treated in the context of justification defenses generally. See infra ch. 2. The drafters had in mind typical justification situations like a surgeon taking a chance on a dangerous operation when the alternative is almost certain death. Commentaries § 2.02, at 237.

76. Commentaries § 2.02, at 237. Every reference to the jury in the Commentaries, and in this text, should be taken with several grains of salt. The jury in American criminal law for some time has been more a symbol than an institution, and its significance more hypothetical than actual, as the overwhelming majority of criminal cases are disposed of by the juryless process of plea bargaining.

more culpable and punished more severely than any other type of action, including knowing action. Yet along the probabilistic axis, knowledge lies ahead of purpose. Note that purpose, when it comes to conduct and result, is defined without respect to probability.[77] What matters is whether the actor had the "conscious object(ive)" of acting in a certain way or bringing about a certain result. It doesn't matter how likely it is that he will succeed in realizing his conscious object(ive).[78] In the case of treason, for instance, it doesn't matter whether the traitor turning over top secret documents is sure to succeed in "aiding the enemy," or whether there's just a chance that he might. (It would be odd if certainty, or at least practical certainty, were required: the successful traitor is a hero, not a criminal.) Treason is all purpose, and all attitude. Probability of success is irrelevant.[79]

Let's now turn to the attitudinal axis. There knowledge and recklessness look similar enough. Both imply awareness, of a fact in one case, and of a substantial risk in the other. But recklessness requires more than awareness, namely conscious dis-

77. The definition of purpose as to an attendant circumstance mentions, but doesn't require, awareness. Belief or hope will do.

78. Cf. People v. Steinberg, 79 N.Y.2d 673 (1992) (intention regardless of awareness of risk); United States v. United States Gypsum Co., 438 U.S. 422, 445 (1978) (quoting Wayne R. LaFave & Austin W. Scott, Jr., Criminal Law 196 (1972)) (purpose regardless of likelihood of success).

79. We'll talk about impossible attempts later on. The Model Code, by the way, doesn't recognize an impossibility defense in attempts. See infra § 5.2(a).

regard. The New York Penal Law makes this point explicit, by defining recklessness as awareness *plus* conscious disregard of a risk.[80] Arguably, there's a difference between simply being aware of a risk, say that one's behavior might result in someone's death, and consciously disregarding it.

To see this issue more clearly, let's take a look at it from another perspective, that of German criminal law. German criminal law distinguishes sharply between a case in which the actor *hopes* that her behavior will not result in the proscribed harm, or perhaps even that she will be able to *avoid* that result, and a case in which she has no similar qualms and is happy to take her chances, and thus *accepts* the harmful result, should it occur. Even though the risk of harm I'm aware of is the same in both cases, German criminal law treats only the second case as an instance of intentional conduct.[81]

Example: Let's say I'm eager to try out my new high-powered rifle. I drive to a large abandoned lot across town and take aim at the windows of a dilapidated burnt-out building some distance away. I end up shooting and seriously wounding a home-

80. See supra chart 3.

81. German criminal law draws a basic distinction between intention (*dolus*) and a mode of culpability less than intention (*culpa*). Criminal liability requires *dolus* unless otherwise provided by statute. *Dolus* comes in several varieties, and so does *culpa*. In the example above, the second case exemplifies *dolus eventualis*—as opposed to purpose (*Absicht*), or knowledge (*dolus directus*). The first case illustrates conscious *culpa*, or *culpa* with awareness—as opposed to nonconscious *culpa*, which doesn't require awareness of a risk and in this regard resembles negligence.

less person asleep in the building. I was aware all along that this might happen, though I wasn't sure it would. In one case, though, I sincerely hope that the building is unoccupied and that, even if it isn't, I won't end up hitting whomever is in it. In the other, I couldn't care less if someone gets hurt—what was the victim doing trespassing anyway?

Now, under German criminal law, I would have acted intentionally in the second case (with dolus eventualis), but not in the first.[82] The question is whether the Model Penal Code would be able to differentiate between these cases in a similar way. I clearly didn't act knowingly with respect to the proscribed result—I wasn't certain enough that it would come about. Was I reckless? Clearly I was reckless in the second case. I was aware of the risk and then consciously disregarded it. Whether the first case also qualifies as recklessness turns on our reading of "conscious disregard." If conscious disregard adds nothing to the awareness of the risk, then I was reckless in both cases. If conscious disregard, however, requires more, in particular an *acceptance*

82. The Model Code instead attempts to differentiate between cases of this sort by adding a *sui generis*, mens rea-type, element, "circumstances manifesting extreme indifference to the value of human life." § 211.1(2)(a); see also § 210.2(1)(b). The precise status of this clause remains in doubt. See, e.g., People v. Register, 60 N.Y.2d 270, 276 (1983) ("neither the mens rea nor the actus reus"; "not an element in the traditional sense"). Moreover, it applies by definition only to result offenses involving threats to "human life." Finally, differentiating recklessness from recklessness *plus* still wouldn't allow the Code to distinguish recklessness with conscious disregard from recklessness with mere awareness.

of the risk actually manifesting itself, i.e., of the homeless man actually dying, then case one doesn't qualify as an instance of recklessness.

(iv) *Negligence.* Arguably, the line between recklessness and negligence is even more significant than that separating knowledge from recklessness. As a general rule (often broken), criminal liability ends where recklessness ends, and negligence begins. Recklessness is the default mental state in the Model Penal Code and, at least in the interpretation of the Model Code drafters, marks the lower limit of the common law's requirement of mens rea (or intent, or *scienter*). That's not to say that there aren't any crimes that require nothing more than negligence, only that there aren't many. The special part of the Model Code, for example, includes only three: negligent homicide, assault (with a deadly weapon), and criminal mischief (with dangerous means).[83] (The New York Penal Law has four: negligent homicide, assault (with a deadly weapon), vehicular assault, and vehicular manslaughter.[84])

Along the probabilistic axis, negligence occupies the same spot as recklessness; a substantial risk, rather than practical certainty, is enough. The difference between negligence and recklessness is entirely a matter of attitude. Recklessness implies a conscious disregard of the risk; negligence requires neither awareness, nor disregard, of the risk. It's instead the very failure to be aware of the risk that

83. §§ 210.4, 211.1(b), 220.3.
84. N.Y. Penal Law §§ 120.00(3), 120.03(1), 125.10, 125.12.

the Model Code calls negligence.⁸⁵ So it's not just that negligence doesn't require awareness; negligence requires unawareness. I should have been aware, but wasn't. And that's why I'm culpable (and dangerous), and need penal treatment. (Negligence thus is a sort of omission mens rea, the *failure* to have a mental state rather than having one.)

Actually, in the fine print of the Model Code lies buried another distinction between recklessness and negligence. The points of comparison differ. In the case of recklessness, the factfinder is to consider whether the risk was substantial and unjustifiable enough to warrant penal treatment by asking herself whether the defendant's behavior "involves a gross deviation from the standard of conduct that a law-abiding person would observe in the actor's situation." In the case of negligence, the same standard applies, except that now the point of comparison isn't "a law-abiding person," but "a reasonable person."⁸⁶ Not much rides on this distinction; it was ignored by many MPC-based criminal codes, including the New York Penal Law (which uses the reasonableness standard in both cases⁸⁷). Instead of pondering the distinction between a law-abiding and a reasonable person, it's good to keep in mind the point of these clauses. They weren't meant to

85. See People v. Strong, 37 N.Y.2d 568 (1975) (manslaughter vs. negligent homicide).

86. "Reasonable" plays a central role in the Code's approach to the excuse defenses of duress and provocation. See infra §§ 13, 16.

87. N.Y. Penal Law § 15.05(3) & (4).

settle deep questions of criminal law, but to provide some guidance to jurors faced with the difficult task of applying the Code's admittedly amorphous definitions of recklessness and negligence.[88]

At this point it's probably a good idea to pause and review the various ways in which the Code's modes of culpability differ, or not. This diagram tries to do just that:

Chart 5
Modes of Culpability (Mental States)

	Purpose	Knowledge	Recklessness	Negligence
Conduct				
attitude:	conscious object	awareness	[not defined]	[not defined]
probability:	irrelevant	100%	[not defined]	[not defined]
Circumstance				
attitude:	awareness, belief, hope	awareness	conscious disregard	none
probability:	irrelevant	100%	substantial risk	substantial risk
Result				
attitude:	conscious object	awareness	conscious disregard	none
probability:	irrelevant	practical certainty	substantial risk	substantial risk

88. Commentaries § 2.02, at 237, 241. Presumably the requirement of a "gross" deviation, rather than a plain deviation, also represents an attempt to differentiate criminal negligence from civil negligence in tort law. Traditionally, American criminal law has sidestepped this issue in various ways, by simply labeling criminal negligence "*criminal* negligence" (as in the N.Y. Penal Law) or by explaining, no more helpfully, that criminal negligence is "that degree of negligence that is more than the negligence required to impose tort liability." Commentaries § 2.02, at 242 (quoting Jerome Hall, General Principles of Criminal Law 124 (2d ed. 1960)).

(v) *Strict Liability*. The above chart gives a pretty good overview of the various mental states, as defined by the Code. It may be misleading, however, in that it suggests that there is no criminal liability beyond negligence. But negligence isn't the end of the line. There's still strict liability to be contended with, even if strict liability is only an option for the Code's *sui generis* civil offenses, the "violations." This means our linedrawing work still isn't done. Fortunately, the line between negligence and strict liability is bright. Negligence implies the culpable failure to perceive a risk one should have recognized. Strict liability implies neither a mental state (like perception), nor its absence. It is a mode of culpability that imposes criminal liability without regard to mental states. Your attitude toward a result, for example, is as irrelevant as the likelihood of the result actually coming about. Strict liability doesn't show up on either of the axes defining the other four modes of culpability. Here, then is the complete chart of modes of liability (as opposed to mental states):

Chart 6
Modes of Culpability
(including Strict Liability)

	Purpose	Knowledge	Recklessness	Negligence	Strict Liability
Conduct					
attitude:	conscious object	awareness	[not defined]	[not defined]	irrelevant
probability:	irrelevant	100%	[not defined]	[not defined]	irrelevant

	Purpose	Knowledge	Recklessness	Negligence	Strict Liability
Circumstance					
attitude:	awareness, belief, hope	awareness	conscious disregard	none	irrelevant
probability:	irrelevant	100%	substantial risk	substantial risk	irrelevant
Result					
attitude:	conscious object	awareness	conscious disregard	none	irrelevant
probability:	irrelevant	practical certainty	substantial risk	substantial risk	irrelevant

(D) Matching Conduct to Offense

Now, finally, the matching can begin. We started our analysis of criminal liability, in the previous section, by checking whether the defendant passes the general act requirement—whether his behavior qualifies as an *actus*, so to speak. If he doesn't pass, our inquiry ends: the defendant is not liable.

If he does pass, we move on to the next step—to determine whether his *actus* was also *reus*. This we do by inquiring whether his behavior matches any of the offenses defined and categorized in the special part of a given criminal code. As we saw, each offense may consist of elements of various types—thus capturing a particular *actus reus*. Each of these elements in turn may, or may not, have a mental state attached to it—thus adding the *mens rea* ingredient and completing the definition of the crime.

Much of criminal law in action is occupied with this matching exercise: does the defendant's conduct match the definition of an offense? This legal question shouldn't be confused with the factual question of whether the state can *prove* that the defendant's conduct matches the definition of the offense as charged.[89]

This matching procedure is, by and large, a matter for the special part of criminal law. In fact, that's what the special part is all about: specifying which forms of behavior are criminalized. There you'll find discussions of just what it means, in the abstract, to murder, assault, steal, embezzle, and annoy. And once you've figured this out, you can investigate whether a particular behavior, engaged in by a particular person at a particular time in a particular place, matches the ideal type of crimes called murder, assault, theft, embezzlement, and public nuisance.[90]

So much for the actus reus. Questions of mens rea, by contrast, have been largely extracted from the special part and moved into the general part. This is one way of looking at what the Model Code drafters did when they overhauled the law of intent. They replaced a cornucopia of intents that varied

89. Notice that questions of provability usually don't come up in criminal law exams. Ordinarily, you'll be asked to assume certain facts and then run them through the analysis of criminal liability.

90. There *are* a very few offense definitions that appear in the Model Code's general part. I'm thinking here of the inchoate offenses (attempt, solicitation, conspiracy, possession). Except for possession, however, these aren't really freestanding offenses. Instead, they establish a type of criminal liability, and as such, attach to existing offense definitions in the special part. There is no crime of attempt; there is only attempted murder, attempted rape, and so on. These we will take up a little later on, infra § 5.2. (Possession we've already dealt with, in supra § 4.1; at any rate, possession offenses ordinarily aren't defined in a criminal code's general part.)

from offense to offense (and not only from judge to judge) with four modes of culpability. While there were never as many *mentes reae* as there were *actus rei*, there certainly was considerable variety among the mental elements attached to the mass of criminal offenses that has cropped up in the common law over the centuries. After the Model Code, there were only four left. Colorful mental states like "malice aforethought" (murder) and *"animus furandi"* or *"lucri causa"* (larceny) gave way to the quartet of purpose, knowledge, recklessness, and negligence.

So instead of defining mental states in the special part, the Model Code drafters defined them in the general part, once and for all. The special part, for example, defines the actus reus of manslaughter (recklessly causing the death of another human being), and the general part its mens rea (recklessness).

Mens-rea-matching thus is a matter of the general part, and therefore, it is a matter for us. Now the Model Code doesn't just define all modes of culpability in the general part, laying out the abstract concepts against which messy life is to be matched. It also highlights two scenarios that might preclude such a match, no matter what the offense: intoxication and mistake. To these we now turn.

§ 4.3 Intoxication and Mistake

The first thing to notice about the Model Penal Code's provisions on intoxication and mistake is that they are largely superfluous.[91] They mainly serve to illustrate two, particularly common, situations in which the defendant lacked the mens rea required for criminal liability. It's confusing to refer to intoxication and mistake, in this sense, as "defenses," unless you think of a defense as the absence of an offense. If we must call them defenses, we might call them "failure-of-proof"[92] defenses or, following our tripartite analysis of criminality, *level one* defenses.[93]

As their titles suggest, these provisions spell out that a defendant may lack the requisite mental state because she was intoxicated or because she was mistaken about some matter of relevance. Both aren't *entirely* superfluous, but for slightly different reasons. The intoxication section actually does the opposite of what it appears to be doing; rather than establish a defense of intoxication, it sets up what amounts to an intoxication exception to the general rule that criminal liability requires a match be-

91. The Model Code's provision on *consent* is also largely superfluous, but for a different reason. The consent provision is redundant insofar as it clarifies that the presence of consent precludes conviction of an offense that includes the absence of consent as one of its elements. By contrast, the provisions on intoxication and mistake are redundant insofar as they clarify that the absence of a mode of culpability—say, knowledge—precludes conviction for an offense the definition of which includes that mode of culpability. Cf. infra § 11.

92. Paul H. Robinson, Criminal Law Defenses: A Systematic Analysis, 82 Colum. L. Rev. 199, 204–08 (1982).

93. Similarly, the Code provision on *consent*, another level one "defense," is also only *largely* redundant because consent may also be a level *two* defense (i.e., a justification).

tween behavior and offense definition.[94] In other words, the intoxication provision *contracts* the scope of intoxication as a level one defense.

At the same time, the intoxication provision *expands* the scope of the intoxication defense, by recognizing intoxication as a *level three* defense, an excuse.[95] The Code drafters made it clear that, as a general matter, intoxication, no matter how severe, couldn't amount to an excuse in and of itself. *Involuntary* intoxication, however, could qualify as an excuse if it was severe enough to amount to criminal insanity (or rather the inability characteristic of insanity, without the underlying mental defect—a sort of insanity without insanity).[96]

And mistake too can be an excuse. In certain strictly limited circumstances, *ignorance of law* is a defense (notwithstanding the old saw that *ignorantia legis non excusat*).

(A) Intoxication

The Model Code explains that intoxication precludes criminal liability if the defendant lacked the requisite mental state because he was drunk (or high). (Actually, it says—with a characteristic double negative—that intoxication is *not* a defense *unless* it "negatives an element of the offense," i.e., it disproves a mental state requirement.) Nothing out of the ordinary so far. But it then goes on to exempt from this general, self-explanatory, rule any offense that requires a mental state less than knowledge.

94. § 2.08(2).

95. Excuses are discussed infra ch. 3.

96. § 2.08(4). Insanity is discussed infra § 17.

(That's what this means: "When recklessness establishes an element of the offense, if the actor, due to self-induced intoxication, is unaware of a risk of which he would have been aware had he been sober, such unawareness is immaterial.")

Negligence too is not negatived by intoxication. Negligence actually implies unawareness; so saying that you were unaware of a risk because you were drunk doesn't prove that you weren't negligent, it explains *why* you *were* negligent.[97] (You're inculpating, not exculpating, yourself here.)

But no one has ever suggested that intoxication precludes negligence. Recklessness is the sticking point, and it's an important one since so many crimes require recklessness—it's the default mental state, after all. To say that intoxication is irrelevant as to recklessness is to say it's irrelevant for most of criminal law. Here the Code showed uncharacteristic deference to traditional—and underrationalized—criminal law doctrine and simply followed the old common law rule, which had limited the relevance of intoxication to crimes of "specific intent."

---

97. Since it's awareness that matters, intoxication does preclude knowledge and purpose, at least to the extent that they imply awareness. That's obviously the case for knowledge. As we've seen earlier on, to know something means to be aware of it, or to be practically certain that it will come about. Purpose isn't so clear. Recall that the Model Code does not define purpose in terms of awareness. If attached to conduct or result, purpose means conscious object—where consciousness may be said to imply awareness (as in the case of recklessness, which requires a "conscious disregard"). But purpose as to an attendant circumstance needn't involve awareness; the belief or the hope that an attendant circumstance exists is enough. So, at least theoretically, it appears that intoxication doesn't necessarily preclude a finding of purpose as to an attendant circumstance.

Under that rule, a drunk would avoid a murder conviction (which required a showing of "specific intent") but he would still be liable for manslaughter (which required only "general intent").

The hostility toward the intoxication defense in the common law ran deep and wide. Intoxication, after all, was a crime in public and a sin, at least, in private.[98] That hostility persists to this day, as evidenced by a Montana statute providing that voluntary intoxication "may not be taken into consideration in determining the existence of a mental state which is an element of [a criminal] offense."[99] In upholding this statute, the U.S. Supreme Court could quote from an 1820 opinion by Justice Story:

> This is the first time, that I ever remember it to have been contended, that the commission of one crime was an excuse for another. Drunkenness is a gross vice, and in the contemplation of some of our laws is a crime; and I learned in my earlier studies, that so far from its being in law an excuse for murder, it is rather an aggravation of its malignity.[100]

98. Cf. the "public" intoxication statute at issue in Powell v. Texas, 392 U.S. 514 (1968): "Whoever shall get drunk or be found in a state of intoxication in any public place, *or at any private house except his own*, shall be fined not exceeding one hundred dollars." Id. at 517 (quoting Texas Penal Code art. 477 (1952)) (emphasis added).

99. Mont. Code Ann. § 45–2–203 (upheld in Montana v. Egelhoff, 518 U.S. 37 (1996)).

100. Montana v. Egelhoff, 518 U.S. 37, 44 (1996) (quoting United States v. Cornell, 25 F. Cas. 650, 657–58 (No. 14,868)

The Model Code adopts the common law rule, merely substituting "knowledge or purpose" for "specific intent" and "recklessness" for "general intent."[101] In the drafters' view, the lack of awareness at the time of the offense, which ordinarily would preclude recklessness, is irrelevant if caused by intoxication because the original act of excessive drinking "has no affirmative social value." And it's in this very act that the actor's moral culpability—and abnormal dangerousness—lies.[102] It makes no difference that this act isn't itself criminal, and doesn't form part of the definition of the subsequent offense committed while intoxicated.[103]

In sum, voluntary—or what the Code calls self-induced—intoxication matters only to the extent

(C.C.R.I. 1820)); see also 4 William Blackstone, Commentaries on the Laws of England 26 (1769) ("the law of England, considering how easy it is to counterfeit this excuse, and how weak an excuse it is, (though real) will not suffer any man thus to privilege one crime by another").

101. See State v. Cameron, 104 N.J. 42 (1986).

102. Commentaries § 2.08, at 359.

103. It's manslaughter, not "manslaughter after getting drunk," or even "getting drunk with the purpose of committing homicide." In German criminal law, the significance of intoxication turns on the actor's mode of culpability when she got drunk. So, in Model Code terms, if she got drunk with the purpose of committing a crime, say to get up her courage, she is guilty of crimes that require purpose. Analogously, if she got drunk knowing full well that she would commit a crime under the influence, she would be liable for crimes requiring knowledge, and so on down through recklessness (awareness of a good chance that she would do it) and negligence (culpable unawareness of that chance). See Claus Roxin, Strafrecht Allgemeiner Teil 781–90 (3d ed. 1997) ("actio libera in causa").

that it negatives knowledge or purpose. It's irrelevant for crimes that require recklessness or negligence. Given the Code drafters' resistance to make room for voluntary intoxication as a level one, or failure-of-proof, defense, it's no surprise they did not recognize it as an excuse, or level three, defense. Under the Code, voluntary intoxication cannot amount to an irresponsibility defense, even if it is so severe as to render the person incapable of telling right from wrong or of controlling her behavior, i.e., to reduce her to criminal insanity.[104]

The Code is more forgiving, and more consistent, when it comes to what used to be called involuntary intoxication, i.e., intoxication that's not self-induced or "pathological."[105] Flexibility on involuntary intoxication comes cheap, however. Cases of involuntary intoxication are extremely rare, and certainly incomparably rarer than cases of voluntary intoxication. As a level one defense, *involuntary* intoxication applies across the board to all modes of

104. § 2.08(3). German criminal law does recognize an excuse of irresponsibility through intoxication, voluntary or not. § 20 StGB [German Criminal Code] (total incapacity); see also § 21 StGB (diminished capacity). Those who qualify for this excuse, however, don't necessarily escape criminal liability altogether. In case of voluntary intoxication, they are liable for a separate offense, gross intoxication (Vollrausch). § 323a StGB.

105. It may be misleading to speak of involuntary and voluntary intoxication because talk of voluntariness is, in Model Penal Code language, limited to the act requirement. Involuntary intoxication, however, does not imply an involuntary act, at least in the Code's scheme of things. Whether intoxication, voluntary or not, might be so severe as to preclude voluntary action is another question. The Code here deals only with intoxication's (limited) relevance to mens rea, not to actus reus.

culpability, including recklessness and, presumably, negligence.

Moreover, involuntary intoxication can make out a level three defense. Unlike its voluntary cousin, involuntary intoxication is an excuse if it is so severe as to cause an incapacity to tell right from wrong or to keep oneself from doing something one knows to be wrong. Here involuntary intoxication takes the place of a mental disease or defect in the classic excuse defense of insanity. In the case of insanity, as we'll see in greater detail in chapter 3, the same types of incapacity are caused not by intoxication but by some mental disease or defect.

Of the two kinds of involuntary intoxication the Code recognizes, one is more obvious than the other. Most clearly, intoxication is involuntary in the strict sense of "not self-induced" if it's *other*-induced, as when someone forces me to become intoxicated (e.g., by injecting me with heroin while I'm sleeping, or while I'm tied to a chair) or gets me to intoxicate myself without knowing it (e.g., by slipping alcohol into a high school reunion punch). Intoxication can also be involuntary without being other-induced, as when I mistake cocaine for powdered sugar, without anyone having misled me.

But the Code recognizes another form of involuntary intoxication besides intoxication that's "not self-induced," or other-induced. "Pathological" intoxication is supposed to deal with cases in which a person is abnormally sensitive to the effects of an intoxicant she consumes voluntarily.[106] Pathological intoxication "means," to quote the Code, "intoxication grossly excessive in degree, given the amount of the intoxicant, to which the actor does not know he is susceptible." In this case, not only the consumption of the intoxicant is voluntary, as in the case of involuntary self-induced intoxication, so is the intoxication itself. What's involuntary isn't the intoxication, but its degree.

(B) Mistake

As a level one defense, mistake operates much like intoxication. Unlike intoxication, however, the Code doesn't place external—"public policy"—limitations on the scope of mistake as a level one defense.[107] Like *involuntary* intoxication, mistake is a defense if it negatives any mode of culpability identified in the offense definition. So under a statute proscribing the sale of liquor to anyone under twenty-one, if I thought my customer was twenty-one, I didn't "know" he was nineteen. If the statute requires "knowledge" with respect to the attendant circumstance of the purchaser's age, then my mistake regarding his age would constitute a level one, or failure of proof, defense.

What if a different mental state were required? How about recklessness? My mistake wouldn't do me any good as long as I was aware not of *the fact*

---

106. See State v. Sette, 259 N.J.Super. 156 (1992) (not self-induced vs. pathological intoxication).

107. Note, however, that the relevance of mistake is limited to *material* elements, while intoxication is not. Compare § 2.04(1)(a) with § 2.08(1).

that he was under age, but of a substantial chance that he was. Similarly, in the case of negligence, my mistake wouldn't help me if I wasn't, but should have been, aware of that substantial chance.

If no mental state is required—as is likely in our liquor-selling example—then even a non-negligent mistake would be of no use. Even if there is nothing that did, or should have, tipped me off about my customer's age, I would have committed the offense as defined. As in all level one "defenses," mistake is no defense against strict liability; you cannot negative mens rea if there is no mens rea to be negatived.

For that reason, questions of the relevance of mistake as a level one defense often arise in strict liability cases. A defendant argues that he didn't commit some crime because he made a mistake, generally about some attendant circumstance, and often about a specific attendant circumstance, age. The easiest way to dismiss this argument is to hold that the element about which the defendant claims to have been mistaken is a strict liability element.

That's exactly what happened in the most famous mistake/strict liability case of them all, *Regina v. Prince*.[108] Prince was convicted under a statutory rape statute—which actually looks more like larceny of human possessions—making it a misdemeanor to "unlawfully take ... any unmarried girl, being under the age of sixteen years, out of the possession and against the will of her father or mother, or of

108. 1875 L.R. 2 C.C.R. 154.

any person having the lawful care or charge of her." In his defense, Prince argued that "the girl Annie Phillips, though proved by her father to be fourteen years old on April 6, 1875, looked very much older than sixteen, and the jury found upon reasonable evidence that before the defendant took her away she had told him that she was eighteen, that the defendant bona fide believed that statement, and that such belief was reasonable."[109]

The initial question in *Prince* was whether "being under the age of sixteen years" was a strict liability element, or, in traditional common law terms, whether *scienter* was required with respect to it, where *scienter* was roughly equivalent to purpose-or-knowledge-or-recklessness-but-probably-not-negligence-unless-it's-gross. In Model Code terms, if it's a strict liability element, then mistake makes no difference. Is it?

Applying our trusted rules of interpretation, and assuming that the statute appeared as quoted in the Model Code, without more, the answer would be "no." For under Rule 1, recklessness is the default mental state "[w]hen the culpability sufficient to establish a material element of an offense is not prescribed by law." (Rule 2 doesn't apply because no mode of culpability appears anywhere in the definition of the offense, so that none could be applied from one element to all.[110] Rule 3 doesn't

109. Id.

110. Actually, Prince argued that "unlawfully" was just such a mental state. Not so under the Model Code. Cf. §§ 2.02(9) (illegality of conduct not offense element); 3.11(1) (defining un-

apply because the offense appears in the Code itself and is a misdemeanor, which carries a possible sentence of incarceration.) If recklessness applies, then a reckless mistake wouldn't be a defense. Merely mistaking the girl for eighteen wouldn't be enough, provided I thought there was a good chance she might be under sixteen. (If negligence applied instead, being wrong wouldn't help as long as I *should* have thought there was such a chance, and so on.)

But everyone agreed that Prince's mistake was "reasonable," i.e., it wasn't reckless, or even negligent, in Model Code language.[111] The reason he still lost was that the court decided the element about which he was reasonably mistaken—"being under the age of sixteen years"—was a strict liability element, rendering his mistake irrelevant. That, in fact, is what distinguished statutory, from common law, rape—the absence of mens rea, particularly with respect to the victim's age. By classifying stat-

lawful force). Unlawfully is more commonly taken to refer, albeit redundantly, to the absence of justifications. See Regina v. Prince, 1875 L.R. 2 C.C.R. 154 (opinion of Bramwell, B.) ("The word 'unlawfully' means 'not lawfully,' 'otherwise than lawfully,' 'without lawful cause'—such as would exist for instance on a taking by a police officer on a charge of felony or a taking by a father of his child from her school."). Note that "unlawfully" also appears as an attendant circumstance, which may—or may not—have a mental state attached to it. See, e.g., §§ 212.1 (kidnapping) ("unlawfully"), 221.2(2) (trespass) ("not licensed or privileged," "in a manner prescribed by law"), 223.2. (theft by unlawful taking or disposition), 224.3 (fraudulent destruction, removal or concealment of recordable instruments) ("writing for which the law provides public recording").

111. § 1.13(16).

utory rape as, well, statutory, the common law got to hold onto its ironclad mens rea requirement (embodied in the famous maxim that "actus non facit reum nisi mens sit rea," or that "an act doesn't become bad unless the mind is bad"). If Parliament wanted to do away with mens rea, that was their prerogative. But that didn't shake the common law's, and therefore the courts', commitment to the mens rea principle, or so the story went.[112]

The Model Code drafters too went out of their way to stress their commitment to the mens rea requirement; and yet they too kept a version of the statutory rape exception to this requirement. Under the Code, the age element of any sex offense is strict liability if the "critical age" is ten (as in rape, defined as a "male ha[ving] sexual intercourse with a female" who is "less than 10 years old"[113]). If it's an age other—meaning higher—than ten, then it's up to the defendant "to prove by a preponderance of the evidence that he reasonably believed the child to be above the critical age."[114]

This narrow exception to the mens rea rule goes beyond the other two exceptions to the mens rea requirement that we encountered earlier on—per-

112. For a similar move in the law of possession, which was thought to violate actus reus, the common law's other unshakable principle of criminal law, see Markus Dirk Dubber, Policing Possession: The War on Crime and the End of Criminal Law, 91 J. Crim. L. & Criminology 829, 904 (2002) (citing Rex v. Lennard, 1 Leach 90 (1772)).

113. § 213.1(1)(d).

114. § 213.6(1).

mitting strict liability for "violations" as well as for offenses defined outside the criminal code proper.[115] Note that rape under the Code is a serious felony, as it is in all other American criminal codes. The exception may be narrow, but it also has real bite.

There are of course, really, two exceptions here. One is clearcut. If the critical age is ten, then age is a strict liability element—no mens rea needed. But what's supposed to happen if the critical age is over ten isn't so clear. Since only a "reasonable" mistake about the victim's age counts as a defense—and the Code elsewhere defines a "reasonable" mistake as one that's neither reckless nor negligent[116]—we could read at least negligence back into the age element, so that the actor must have been at least negligently wrong regarding the victim's age.

Now we indeed would have a mens rea, and thus would have brought the statute back into line with the Code's commitment to mens rea, even if only a watered-down version thereof—since we would require negligence and not quite the ordinary default of recklessness.

The problem is, though, that the statute now bumps into another Code requirement—since constitutionalized in *In re Winship*[117]—that the state bear the burden of proving, beyond a reasonable doubt, every element of an offense, including mens

115. § 2.05.

116. So that the mistake-maker neither was, nor should have been, aware of a good chance that he might be making a mistake.

117. 397 U.S. 358, 364 (1970) ("every fact necessary to constitute the crime with which [the defendant] is charged").

rea.[118] So how can the Code shift the burden of proof onto the defendant?

The easy, and not particularly helpful, answer is that the Code here transforms mistake about age into an "affirmative defense," procedurally speaking.[119] But surely the Code, simply by transforming the absence of an *offense* element into a *defense*, could not avoid the constraints of *Winship*.[120]

Note also that, even under the Code itself, an affirmative defense ordinarily doesn't place the burden of proof on the defendant. Instead, the defendant only bears the burden of *production* (of "adduc[ing] supporting evidence"), while the burden of *persuasion* (the other half of the burden of proof) remains on the state.[121] Mistake about age thus would be a kind of super-affirmative defense, which shifts the entire burden of proof onto the defendant—like ignorance of law, for instance.[122] And

118. § 1.12(1).

119. Substantively speaking, mistake about age presumably would function as an excuse, i.e., a level three defense, on the assumption that no one would characterize mistake about the victim's age as *justifying* facially criminal conduct, i.e., a level two defense.

120. Actually, it probably could. See Patterson v. New York, 432 U.S. 197 (1977) (provocation); Martin v. Ohio, 480 U.S. 228 (1987) (self-defense).

121. § 1.12(2). Even the burden of production falls on the defendant only if the state doesn't introduce evidence of the defense as part of its case. As long as "there is evidence supporting [the] defense," there's no need for the defendant to produce any. § 1.12(2)(a).

122. § 2.04(4); see also §§ 2.07(5) (due diligence), 2.13(2) (entrapment), 5.07 (temporary possession).

what exactly would be the theory of excuse that could give rise to an affirmative defense of mistake of age—unavoidability, "fairness," lack of self-control, irresponsibility?[123]

Let's assume, however, that we're dealing neither with a strict liability offense nor with a contemporary version of "statutory rape." Let's assume, in other words, that the Code's normal, and normally redundant, mistake provision applies—that any mistake negativing an offense element precludes criminal liability, just as any other level one (or failure-of-proof) defense would. Now, not any mistake will negative any offense element. A reckless mistake with respect to an offense element will preclude conviction of an offense that requires a mens rea above recklessness (purpose or knowledge) regarding that element. But it will not stand in the way of criminal liability for an offense that requires only recklessness, or negligence for that matter.

What's more, the Code provides that, even if my mistake does negative an offense element, and is neither reckless nor negligent (or if it is, there are no offenses that require mere recklessness or negligence), or I managed to carry the burden of proving the super-affirmative defense of reasonable mistake, I may not escape criminal liability altogether. Rather I will be punished (or penally treated) for whatever offense I thought—mistakenly—I was committing, rather than for the one I actually did commit:

123. The Code's approach to excuses is discussed infra § 12.

> Although ignorance or mistake would otherwise afford a defense to the offense charged, the defense is not available if the defendant would be guilty of another offense had the situation been as he supposed. In such case, however, the ignorance or mistake of the defendant shall reduce the grade and degree of the offense of which he may be convicted to those of the offense of which he would be guilty had the situation been as he supposed.[124]

To see how the drafters might have come up with this odd-sounding rule, let's return to the chestnut of *Regina v. Prince*.[125] The opinions in that case laid out various ways of analyzing a mistake claim. We've already discussed one—rejecting the claim as irrelevant to a strict liability element, here the age of the unmarried girl taken out of her father's possession. The others involve the same sort of thought experiment embodied in the Code passage quoted above. Each requires comparing the defendant's imaginary world (the world of fiction), that is the world as the he thought it—mistakenly—to be, with the world of fact. They differ in the question each asks about the world of fiction. In one, the mistake claim would be irrelevant if the defendant, in the world of fiction, had committed a *wrong* (wrongfulness test).[126] In another, mistake doesn't matter if, in the world of fiction, he had committed an *unlawful* act, i.e., an act in violation of civil or

124. § 2.04(2).
125. 1875 L.R. 2 C.C.R. 154.
126. See id. (opinion of Bramwell, B.).

criminal law (illegality test).[127] In yet another, even a wrongful unlawful act in the world of fiction wouldn't preclude the defendant from relying on a mistake:[128] his mistake claim would fall on deaf ears only if he had committed a crime, rather than a civilly illegal act (such as a breach of contract or a tort), in the world of fiction—though obviously not the one he stands accused of in the world of fact (criminality test).

The Model Code takes one step further down this progression from hypothetical wrongfulness to illegality to criminality, with each being a subset of the other. It too disallows a mistake defense *to the crime charged* if the defendant would have committed a crime even in the world of fiction. But the Code doesn't stop here, at the criminality test familiar from *Prince*. Conviction of the crime charged, it turns out, doesn't mean punishment for the crime charged. Instead, the defendant is penally treated according to the crime he thought he had committed, in the world of fiction. So, let's say selling liquor to a fifteen-year-old is a misdemeanor, and selling it to a sixteen-year-old a violation. I am charged with the misdemeanor because the buyer is in fact fifteen, but I mount a successful defense of mistake of fact, that I thought she was sixteen. In that case, the Code would convict me of selling liquor to a fifteen-year-old, but then "reduce the grade and degree of the offense of which he may be convicted to those of the offense of which he would

127. See id. (opinion of Brett, J.).
128. See id. (opinion of Brett, J.).

be guilty had the situation been as he supposed," i.e., reclassify the offense of conviction as a violation, and punish (or rather treat) me accordingly.

The correctional regimen thus is matched to the penological diagnosis of the offender's specific criminal disposition, rather than to the abstract offense she actually committed, once again reconfirming that offense definitions in the Code serve as rough indicators of criminal disposition, which, in certain circumstances, may be disregarded. That's how someone can be convicted of one crime (in fact), but treated as though she had committed another crime (in fiction).

Not surprisingly, holding someone liable for an offense she didn't in fact commit, but only thought she did, isn't that easy, doctrinally speaking. The most obvious way of dealing with this problem would have been to convict the defendant of an *attempt* to commit the offense she thought she was committing, rather than of the one she did commit.[129] Another would have been to convict of the lesser—though fictional—offense, rather than convicting of the more serious—and factual—offense, and then punishing for the lesser one. It was for procedural reasons[130] that the drafters instead opt-

129. This would result in pretty much the same punishment—or penal treatment—as conviction of the consummated offense, because the Code punishes attempts on par with consummated offenses, except if the attempted offense is a first degree felony, in which case the attempt is punished as a second degree felony. See § 5.05(1).

130. Mostly, that it would be unfair to convict a defendant of an offense not charged in the indictment, particularly in cases

ed for the, considerably less elegant, conviction-for-one and punishment-for-the-other solution.

What if the factual offense is *less serious* than the fictional one? What if the defendant, under the circumstances as she supposed them to be, had committed a felony, but it turns out that her conduct amounted to a misdemeanor instead? It would seem that, under the Code, she would be criminally liable for the more serious, fictional, offense. The Model Code's approach to the mistake issue after all rests on the proposition that a person should be held liable for the offense she thought she committed, rather than for the one she did commit. That's not so, however, according to the Code drafters. Mistakes are supposed to mitigate liability, not to aggravate it, even if the world of fiction was worse than the world of fact. Mistakes serve only to "*reduce* the grade and degree of the offense of which he may be convicted to those of the offense of which he would be guilty had the situation been as he supposed."[131] As the Commentaries explain, "an actor should not be held liable for more serious consequences than those for which he had the requisite culpability, *nor should he be held liable for a more serious consummated offense if no such offense has occurred.*"[132] But why?

where there is no lesser included offense of which the defendant would have been guilty had she not been mistaken. See Commentaries § 2.04, at 273–74.

131. § 2.04(2) (emphasis added).

132. Commentaries § 2.04, at 274 (emphasis added).

We can't leave the topic of mistake without at least mentioning the distinction between mistakes of fact and mistakes of law. This distinction, illustrated with varying degrees of success in scores of common law opinions, plays no role in the Model Code's approach to mistake. Under the Code, it makes no difference how a mistake is classified; the only thing that matters is whether or not it negatives an element of the offense. (Hence, section 2.04 speaks of "[i]gnorance or mistake as to a matter of *fact or law*.") Under the common law, classification made all the difference, as is so often the case. Mistakes of fact mattered, mistakes of law didn't.[133] As one might suspect, the problem was telling the two apart. What looked like law from one angle, looked like fact from another (aren't laws facts as well?), and what about mistakes in the application of law to fact, and was interpretation law, or was it fact? The distinction between law and fact has never been able to hold much water—just look at the Sisyphean efforts to distinguish between the tasks of jury and judge in the modern criminal trial (in the U.S. and elsewhere[134]), not to mention the attempt to differentiate legally impossible from factually impossible attempts.

133. Many codes based on the Model Code have retained the traditional limitation to mistakes of fact. See, e.g., N.Y. Penal Law § 15.20(1) ("mistaken belief of fact"); cf. § 15.20(2) (ignorance of law as excuse).

134. Cf. Albert W. Alschuler & Andrew G. Deiss, A Brief History of the Criminal Jury in the United States, 61 U. Chi. L. Rev. 867 (1994); Markus Dirk Dubber, The German Jury and the Metaphysical *Volk*: From Romantic Idealism to Nazi Ideology, 43 Am. J. Comp. L. 227 (1995).

And yet, in effect, if not in doctrine, the distinction between mistakes of fact and mistakes of law persists even in the Model Code. So the bulk of mistakes negativing an offense element—of mistake as a level one (of failure-of-proof) defense—will be mistakes of fact. So the mistake about the girl's age in *Prince* is a mistake of fact which negatives the mens rea, if any, attaching to the age element of the offense. (It turned out, of course, that there was no mens rea to be negatived.) By contrast, a mistake regarding another attendant circumstance element, that the girl was in her father's "possession," for instance, might qualify as a mistake of law, or at least as a hybrid mistake of "legal fact" (or the application of law to a set of facts), if it's based on a misunderstanding of the concept of possession in the domestic law of the time.

At the same time, the paradigmatic mistake as a level three defense—an excuse—is a mistake of law. In the common law, the maxim *ignorantia legis non excusat* was considered an indispensable bulwark against criminal chaos—who after all wouldn't claim not to have known that murder is a crime? This anxiety accounted for much of the hostility toward mistake of law. Holding the line separating mistake of fact and mistake of law thus became essential to maintaining the king's peace—or public order, later on.

The Model Code drafters didn't share this sense of urgency and so were willing to make room for mistake of law in some cases. We've already seen that the Code doesn't categorically preclude mistake of law as a level one defense—as long as the mistake negatives an element of the offense.[135] What's more, the Code provides for a separate level three mistake of law defense. In certain, limited, circumstances, ignorance of the law does excuse after all. We'll discuss this excuse in greater detail later on;[136] for now, let's see how it differs from mistake as a level one defense.

Ignorance of law is a defense, properly speaking. It's not that knowledge of the law is an element of the offense, so that ignorance of it would negative it. Ignorance of the law is an affirmative defense that the defendant must prove by a preponderance of the evidence.[137]

As a level three defense, ignorance of the law should be a defense to all offenses, including strict liability ones. This is so because, unlike level one mistake, it doesn't negative the mens rea attached to a particular offense element, like age.

That's not to say that ignorance of law may not also be a level one defense, but only if the definition of the offense in fact includes awareness of law as one of its elements. That's how some courts have interpreted the very un-MPC mens rea of "wilfulness." Since wilfulness doesn't exactly fit any of the

135. Most obviously in offenses that include "unlawfully" as an attendant circumstance. See supra n. 110; see also Liparota v. United States, 471 U.S. 419 (1985) ("not authorized").

136. Infra § 15.

137. § 2.04(4). In fact it's a super-affirmative defense in that it places the entire burden proof on the defendant, rather than merely the burden of production.

MPC mental states, courts in MPC jurisdictions have tried to squeeze it into the MPC quartet of mental states as best they can—ignoring, by and large, what the MPC itself says about wilfulness (that it's synonymous with knowledge).[138] Ignorance of law—or rather its absence—has helped them do just that.[139] In New York, for instance, wilfulness is knowledge plus awareness of law, though not of the specific criminal statute in question, but of law generally speaking. In other words, the defendant acts wilfully as long as she acts knowingly and is aware of the illegality (or unlawfulness), if not the criminality, of her action.[140]

§ 4.4 Liability for Another's Conduct

To complete our discussion of the "conduct" which, according to section 1.02, may constitute a crime, let's take a look at how the Model Penal

138. § 2.02(8). The Code doesn't use wilfulness in the definition of offenses, by design. At the 1955 ALI meeting, Herbert Wechsler responded to Judge Learned Hand's remark that wilfully is an "awful word": "I agree with Judge Hand, and I promise you unequivocally that the word will never be used in the definition of any offense in the Code. But because it is such a dreadful word and so common in the regulatory statutes, it seemed to me useful to superimpose some norm of meaning on it." ALI Proceedings 160 (1955).

139. So has motive—so that wilfulness would be knowledge plus evil motive, or "ill-will." Cf. Regina v. Cunningham, 1957 2 Q.B. 396 ("maliciously").

140. People v. Coe, 71 N.Y.2d 852 (1988); see also Ratzlaf v. United States, 510 U.S. 135 (1994); Bryan v. United States, 524 U.S. 184 (1998); see generally Sharon L. Davies, The Jurisprudence of Willfulness: An Evolving Theory of Excusable Ignorance, 48 Duke L.J. 341 (1998).

Code handles cases in which one person's conduct becomes that of another.[141] When is one person's conduct—which matches the definition of some crime—treated as though it were also another's person's conduct? When does one person's actual conduct become another's constructive conduct? When may one person's conduct be *imputed* to another?

The Model Code provides two answers to this question:

(1) when "acting with the kind of culpability that is sufficient for the commission of the offense, he causes an innocent or irresponsible person to engage in such conduct," or

(2) "he is an accomplice of such other person in the commission of the offense."[142]

Answer (2) tends to attract the lion's share of doctrinal attention. That makes sense, both because it's more complex than answer (1) (what after all is an accomplice?) and because it applies to more cases. But the law of complicity makes a lot more sense, I think, if one sees it in its doctrinal context, i.e., as but one way in which, as the Code puts it, "a person is legally accountable for the conduct of another person." Keeping in mind that complicity is

141. For a useful discussion of the common law of complicity, including its historical development, see Francis B. Sayre, Criminal Responsibility for the Acts of Another, 43 Harv. L. Rev. 689 (1930).

142. § 2.06(2). That section also contains another answer: whenever the Code says so. § 2.06(2)(b). One example is the crime of "aiding suicide." § 210.5(2).

about conduct may also make distinguishing it from conspiracy a little easier. Complicity is a theory of imputation. Conspiracy is a crime. Complicity is about conduct. Conspiracy is about an agreement. But we're getting ahead of ourselves.[143]

(A) Instruments

The basic idea underlying answer (1) is that the criminal law will treat another person's conduct as my own if I use him as a mere means to my criminal ends. The same principle precludes criminal liability in cases where one person is tossed by another into the path of a third, and thus is used as the means to commit an assault. In that case, the tossee isn't liable because she has not committed a voluntary act. By contrast, the tosser—and only the tosser—is liable because he—and only he—has.

The Code's imputation provision instead deals with situations in which the tool has engaged in a voluntary act, and in this sense engaged in "conduct"—thus raising the question of whether her conduct can be imputed to another. According to the Code, this imputation is permissible under two conditions—causation and innocence or irresponsibility.

From the point of view of causation, the imputation provision is redundant. It says, in effect, that one person is liable for criminal conduct if she caused it. And whether she caused it or not will then be decided according to the law of causation.[144]

143. Cf. infra § 5.2(b).

144. Discussed infra § 5.1.

The difficulty here is, of course, that what's being caused is not some resulting harm—like death—but another person's conduct. That other person, however, presumably is perfectly capable of making up her own mind about whether she wants to go ahead and let her conduct be "caused" by another person or not.

Presumably, yes, but only presumably. That presumption doesn't hold in cases where the person whose conduct is being caused is "innocent or irresponsible." Obviously, I can't make up my own mind about some criminal conduct if I don't even know I'm engaging in that conduct. So if you hand me what I think is cold medicine, which I then feed to my sick child, but which actually turns out—beknownst to you—to be poison, then I might have been the one who engaged in the conduct that fits the definition of homicide—causing the death of another person—but, surely, you were the one who caused me to cause the death.

"Innocence" isn't necessarily limited to cluelessness, though.[145] Suppose I knew full well that you gave me a poison pill, but you held a gun to my head, forcing me to feed it to my coughing eight-year-old. In that case, shouldn't my conduct be imputed to you as well, since your threat transformed me into a mere means to your criminal ends?

145. The concept of "innocence" doesn't quite fit into a criminal code, or so it would seem. Not even the law of criminal procedure recognizes it—instead speaking in terms of guilt ("guilty") or its absence ("not guilty"). Cf. infra § 14 (predisposition in entrapment).

Then again, perhaps this would be a case of using an "irresponsible" person, rather than an innocent one. Depending on one's view of the duress defense—in particular whether it applies to murder—I may be able to excuse my conduct. Under the Model Code—which does permit the defense in murder cases—I would have a good argument that you subjected me to a threat so grave that I couldn't be held responsible for my failure to ignore it, and instead do what you ordered me to do.[146]

What about other excuses? Military orders? Entrapment? Ignorance of law? If one takes a broad view of responsibility, and regards all excuses as addressing the question whether a particular actor in a particular setting could be held responsible for his concededly unlawful actions, then any person who places another person in a position that would excuse that person of criminal liability would be legally accountable for that other person's facially criminally conduct.

The Model Code, however, appears to take a narrower view of responsibility—and therefore of irresponsibility as well. In devotes an entire article of its general part to "responsibility" (article 4), but deals there with only two defenses against criminal liability, insanity and infancy. What we can say with confidence then is that anyone who uses a "madman" or a "child"[147] to commit criminal conduct will be accountable "as if the conduct were his

146. See § 2.09.

147. Commentaries § 2.06, at 302; see, e.g., Johnson v. State, 38 So. 182 (Ala.1905).

own."[148] Just who counts as a madman or a child presumably is to be determined in reference to the Code's treatment of insanity and infancy in article 4.

(B) Complicity

Innocent or irresponsible human instruments are one thing. In fact, they are the exception. The presumption, and the rule, is that the person who actually engages in the facially criminally conduct is neither innocent nor irresponsible. How can that person's conduct be imputed to me? How can my criminal liability derive from his criminal conduct?[149]

This is the challenge of the law of complicity. There is no doubt that the person who commits the act defined in the criminal statute has committed a crime. This person is the principal. The question is whether that criminal liability can be extended to someone else, the would-be-accomplice. Who's an accomplice, then?

That, at any rate, is the question under the Model Code scheme of things. That scheme, however, dramatically simplified the doctrine of complicity (or of

148. Commentaries § 2.06 at 300; see generally Commonwealth v. Tavares, 382 Pa.Super. 317 (1989).

149. That's how assisted suicide differs from complicity—and solicitation. Suicide isn't a crime (anymore), so that aiding or soliciting suicide can't make me an accomplice. Hence the need to create "Aiding or Soliciting Suicide as an Independent Offense." § 210.5(2); but see People v. Duffy, 79 N.Y.2d 611 (1992) (causing suicide as homicide).

"parties to crime") under the common law.[150] The common law set up an intricate set of distinctions so as to capture the various degrees of participation of various parties to a crime. Here is the Supreme Court's pithy summary:

> In felony cases, parties to a crime were divided into four distinct categories: (1) principals in the first degree who actually perpetrated the offense; (2) principals in the second degree who were actually or constructively present at the scene of the crime and aided or abetted its commission; (3) accessories before the fact who aided or abetted the crime, but were not present at its commission; and (4) accessories after the fact who rendered assistance after the crime was complete.[151]

As so often, the Model Code replaced this elaborate set of rules with a single, flexible, standard. The challenge no longer was to figure out who counts as what kind of principal or accessory, but to get right to the heart of the matter—who counts as an accomplice? And the answer is:

> A person is an accomplice of another person in the commission of an offense if ... with the purpose of promoting or facilitating the commission of the offense, he
>
> (i) solicits such other person to commit it; or

---

150. Note, once again, that this differentiation among various participants in a course of criminal conduct is not merely a relic of the old common law. German criminal law recognizes a similar taxonomy of participation, and of culpability.

151. Standefer v. United States, 447 U.S. 10, 15 (1980); see also 4 William Blackstone, Commentaries on the Laws of England 34–35 (1769). In misdemeanors, no such fine distinctions were drawn; everyone was a principal.

(ii) aids or agrees or attempts to aid such other person in planning or committing it.[152]

The Model Code thus retained the substantive core of common law complicity. What the common law had called aiding or abetting, the Model Code called aiding or soliciting. At the same time, the Code drafters tried to improve on the common law in various ways. Most important, they sought to focus doctrinal attention on what they considered the core issue, the relationship between the accomplice's and the principal's conduct, rather than on formal distinctions amongst categories of principals and accessories. In addition to spelling out the obvious (but not necessarily the common law), namely, that omission can constitute complicity, the drafters also tried to put some meat on the bare bones of the notoriously elusive concept of "abetting." And so, in its solicitation section, the Code defined soliciting as "with the purpose of promoting or facilitating its commission ... command[ing], encourag[ing] or request[ing] another person to engage in specific conduct which would constitute such crime or an attempt to commit such crime."[153]

152. § 2.06(3). Subsection (iii), on complicity by omission, is discussed below. Note how the various subsections of § 2.06 hang together. Subsection (1) provides that you can be "legally accountable" for another's conduct. Subsection (2) next explains what "legally accountable" means, including being an "accomplice." And subsection (3) then lays out who counts as an "accomplice."

153. § 5.02(1). The original draft of the complicity provision referred not to solicitation, but spelled out what soliciting meant: "command[ing], request[ing], encourag[ing] or provok[ing]." Tentative Draft No. 1, § 2.04(3).

Moreover, the Code clarified—and arguably expanded—the scope of "aiding," that other form of common law complicity, by extending accomplice liability to mere attempts to aid. The common law didn't require but-for causation for accomplice liability; rather than limiting accomplice liability to cases in which the principal wouldn't have been able to commit the offense without her accomplice's assistance, the common law required merely that the accomplice's assistance was a contributing factor, that it made some difference, rather than the difference.[154] The Code, by contrast, extended accomplice liability even to those cases where the would-be accomplice was of no use to the principal whatsoever. From the perspective of penal treatment, the penological diagnosis of dangerousness is the same regardless whether an actor succeeds in crime, or merely does everything she can to succeed, but then fails in the end, for one reason or another.

At the same time, the Code rejected what had come to be known as the *Pinkerton* rule, according to which conspiracy, by itself, implies complicity. Under *Pinkerton v. United States*,[155] every member of a conspiracy automatically was criminally liable, as an accomplice, for *any* act of a co-conspirator committed in furtherance of the conspiracy. No additional proof of aiding or abetting was required. The conspiracy itself, without more, satisfied the conditions of complicity, even if there was no evidence that the purported accomplice did anything—

154. See, e.g., State v. Tally, 15 So. 722, 738–39 (Ala.1894).

155. 328 U.S. 640 (1946).

or tried to do anything—to aid or abet, or even knew about, the specific offense committed by her co-conspirator.

Since the liability of an accomplice is parasitic on the liability of the principal, through imputing the latter's conduct to the former and treating the accomplice *as if* she herself had committed the offense, the proper focus of inquiry under the Code is on the principal's conduct in committing the offense, rather than on some prior agreement between the principal and another. The question is whether the would-be accomplice in fact solicited the would-be principal to commit the specific offense, or in fact aided, or attempted to aid, her in committing it. Conspiracy, i.e., an agreement to engage in certain criminal conduct, may be sufficient to establish "aiding or abetting," but it needn't be. On the issue of complicity, conspiracy thus is of evidentiary significance. It does not establish complicity as a matter of law.

The Code drafters regarded the rejection of the *Pinkerton* rule—which remains in force in many jurisdictions, including federal criminal law—as "[t]he most important point at which the Model Code formulation diverges from [the common law]."[156] Whether it's of more than doctrinal significance, however, is another question.[157] The practical effect of transforming a legal rule into an evidentiary standard is to give the factfinder (in theory the

156. Commentaries § 2.06, at 307.

157. For a case in which it apparently made a difference, see People v. McGee, 49 N.Y.2d 48 (1979).

jury, in practice the judge, or rather the plea bargaining prosecutor) more wiggle room. Whether he will use that discretion to reach a different result—in this case to find no complicity where *Pinkerton* would have found one as a matter of law—is another question. (The same question arises with respect to the Code drafters' decision to "reject" another categorically harsh common law rule—felony murder—by transforming it into an evidentiary standard.[158])

In the present context, suffice it to note that the drafters went out of their way to compensate for contracting the scope of complicity resulting from their abandonment of *Pinkerton* by broadening the definition of complicity itself. How could one explain a linguistic monstrosity like "aids or agrees or attempts to aid such other person in planning or committing" an offense, if not as a sign that the drafters got cold feet after their brash rejection of *Pinkerton*, or at least that they felt the need to reassure legislators, judges, and prosecutors throughout the land that nothing much had

---

158. See § 210.2(1)(b), defining a type of murder based on a presumption of recklessness and "extreme indifference to the value of human life," which arises from the commission of certain predicate felonies. Unlike in traditional felony murder, the state retains the burden of proving the requisite mens rea for murder, namely, in this case, recklessness and indifference. On the question of whether indifference is a mental state here, see People v. Register, 60 N.Y.2d 270 (1983). For a comprehensive study of the state of the felony murder rule after its "abolition" in the Model Code, see Guyora Binder, Felony Murder and Mens Rea Default Rules: A Study in Statutory Interpretation, 4 Buff. Crim. L. Rev. 399 (2000).

changed and that anyone who was reached by *Pinkerton* would be covered by the Code's complicity provision as well?

So much for the Code's treatment of the actus reus of complicity. On the subject of its mens rea, what the Code almost did is more interesting than what it did. This was one of the few issues on which the Code did not adopt the view of its principal drafter, Herbert Wechsler. Wechsler favored knowledge. Judge Learned Hand, however, preferred purpose. Hand won.[159] A clause that would have based complicity on mere knowledge that one's conduct was aiding another person's commission of an offense was struck from the original draft of the Code's complicity section.[160]

So it's purpose, then, that's needed for complicity under the Code.[161] The line between knowledge and

159. Commentaries § 2.06, at 318–19. Contrast United States v. Peoni, 100 F.2d 401 (2d Cir.1938) (Hand, J.), with Backun v. United States, 112 F.2d 635 (4th Cir.1940) (Parker, J.).

160. Here is what it would have said: "A person is an accomplice of another in commission of a crime if ... acting with knowledge that such other person was committing or had the purpose of committing the crime, substantially facilitated its commission." Tentative Draft No. 1, § 2.04(3). An alternate version would have read: "acting with knowledge that such other person was committing or had the purpose of committing the crime, he knowingly provided means or opportunity for the commission of the crime, substantially facilitating its commission." Id.

161. That's not entirely true. Although purpose is required for the imputation of a principal's conduct to her accomplice, it's not required for the imputation of an *instrument's* conduct to her user under § 2.06(2)(a). Commentaries § 2.06, at 302–03. Inno-

purpose, however, may not be so hard to cross. The law has long recognized various ways in which purpose can be inferred from knowledge in general, and in cases of complicity in particular.[162]

That knowing assistance doesn't qualify for complicity—i.e., for the imputation of one person's conduct to another—doesn't mean that it won't be punished. Unlike the Model Code itself, some of the criminal code revisions it inspired inserted a separate offense of facilitation, which essentially criminalizes the type of conduct captured by the deleted knowledge clause in the Model Code's original complicity provision.[163]

cent or irresponsible persons, in this sense, are treated like inanimate objects—such as a hammer, or a remote control robot—that somehow are capable of voluntary acts, and therefore, conduct. Their user's criminal liability will depend entirely on the mens rea of the offense, if any. To say that he was reckless in causing his human instrument to engage in criminal conduct is just another way of saying that he was reckless in committing the criminal act, and therefore is liable for any offense with a mens rea of recklessness. In the Commentaries' stark example, "[o]ne who recklessly leaves his car keys with an irresponsible agent known to have a penchant for mad driving should ... be accountable for a homicide due to such driving if the irresponsible agent uses the car in that way." Id. at 302.

162. See, e.g., People v. Lauria, 59 Cal.Rptr. 628 (Cal.App. 1967).

163. See, e.g., N.Y. Penal Law § 115.00: "A person is guilty of criminal facilitation in the fourth degree when, believing it probable that he is rendering aid ... to a person who intends to commit a crime, he engages in conduct which provides such person with means or opportunity for the commission thereof and which in fact aids such person to commit a felony." Note that the New York statute requires less than knowledge, but a belief in the probability of assistance. At the same time, it limits

In sum, then, complicity under the Model Code consists of purposely aiding or abetting ("soliciting") the commission of an offense by another person. In that case, that other person becomes my principal and I her accomplice, which means that her conduct will be imputed to me, or that I will be "legally accountable" for her conduct.

Given this basic concept of complicity, the rest of the Code's complicity section pretty much falls into place. Since complicity is imputation of conduct, and conduct may consist of omission or commission, it's no surprise that omission in the face of a duty to act may amount to complicity.[164]

Similarly redundant is the Code's provision dealing with result offenses, i.e., with offenses that contain a result element.[165] Being an accomplice means being held legally accountable for another person's conduct, not necessarily for the results of that person's conduct. Complicity puts me in the shoes of another person, treating his conduct as my own. In other words, it means that my behavior satisfies one of the elements of the offense, namely the conduct element. Whether or not it also satisfies another, the result element, is another question.

If the result element requires some sort of mens rea, including a mens rea other than purpose, then my liability for that result will depend on whether I

facilitation to felonies. Although it is categorized as an inchoate—or incomplete—offense, it betrays its origin in the law of complicity by requiring the actual commission of the facilitated offense. For a discussion of inchoate offenses, see infra § 5.2.

164. § 2.06(3)(iii).
165. § 2.06(4).

had the requisite mens rea with respect to the result. And the answer to that question has nothing to do with the answer to the question of whether the principal had the requisite mens rea or not. This means also that the principal and I may face different criminal liability, that we have committed different result offenses, if these offenses differ in the mens rea they require with respect to their result element. So, to pick everyone's favorite result offense, accomplice and principal may have committed different types of homicides. If the principal acted with the conscious objective of causing death, then he's guilty of murder. If his accomplice acted only with recklessness toward the possibility of death, then she's guilty of manslaughter.

The mens rea of complicity with respect to conduct, then, is purpose. With respect to result, it's whatever it is in the definition of the offense. That leaves attendant circumstances, the third, and last, type of element recognized in the Model Code. What complicity's mens rea requirement is here, i.e., whether it's purpose (like conduct) or whether it's determined by the definition of the offense (like result), the Code doesn't say.[166] That's just as well, since where conduct ends and attendant circumstance begins isn't always easy to tell; plus, recall that acting purposely with respect to attendant circumstances is defined as "being aware of the existence of such circumstances" (which is identical to the definition of knowledge) or "believ[ing] or

166. Commentaries § 2.06, at 311 n.37. See also Commentaries § 5.03, at 408–14 (conspiracy).

hop[ing] that they exist"[167] (which is getting close to recklessness, insofar as belief is awareness of a risk smaller than practical certainty).

But let's assume that one can differentiate between conduct and attendant circumstance in a particular offense and that there is a significant difference between recklessness, and certainly negligence, and purpose with respect to an attendant circumstance. In that case it would seem that the Model Code should treat attendant circumstances like result, so that the mens rea attaching to any attendant circumstance would be that specified in the offense, rather than purpose. That way, the only difference between the principal and the accomplice would be in the mens rea regarding conduct—except of course if the offense itself requires purpose with respect to conduct, in which case here too accomplice and principal would be treated the same. Conduct is different because, as we've seen, conduct is the nexus between principal and accomplice, the conduit through which liability passes from one to the other. Once that nexus is established, each faces the liability to the extent that his mental state fits the requirements of a given criminal statute.[168]

167. § 2.02(2)(a)(ii).

168. For this reason, it's possible under the Code to be an accomplice to a principal who commits a crime that requires less than purpose with respect to one or all of its elements. See, e.g., People v. Flayhart, 72 N.Y.2d 737 (1988) (negligent homicide). While the accomplice's mental state with respect to *her* conduct must be purpose, the principal's mental state with respect to the elements of the offense *he* committed is irrelevant for determin-

Since complicity imputes the principal's conduct to the accomplice, thus putting the accomplice in the principal's shoes, it also makes sense to impose accomplice liability on a person who is incapable of committing the offense herself.[169] So I can be guilty of receiving a bribe as an accomplice, even if I'm not a public official, and therefore couldn't have been guilty of that offense as a principal. My liability is parasitic on the principal's, and so if she committed the crime, so did I.

But what if paying a bribe is also a crime? If my assistance to the bribe recipient consisted in my payment of the bribe, then I would be liable both for receiving the bribe (under an accomplice theory) and for paying it (as a principal).[170] (In fact, if the public official solicited the bribe, she'd be liable twice as well, once as principal in her bribe reception and once as accomplice to my bribe payment.)

ing the accomplice's liability (though it's of course very relevant for figuring out his own liability). The significance of the principal for purposes of the accomplice's liability is only as a stand-in whose actual conduct can be attributed to the accomplice as constructive conduct. That principal and accomplice hang together only by the thread of conduct, and therefore could face different liability, wasn't so clear under the common law, given its talk of "shared intent" between accomplice and principal (or rather among the various types of accessories and principals). See, e.g., Maiorino v. Scully, 746 F.Supp. 331 (S.D.N.Y.1990) (murder and attempted murder for one, manslaughter and assault for the other).

169. § 2.06(5).

170. See, e.g., Standefer v. United States, 447 U.S. 10 (1980). For another example, the relation between seller and buyer (or rather distributor and possessor), of particular importance to drug criminal law, see People v. Manini, 79 N.Y.2d 561 (1992).

To deal with this situation,[171] the Code provides that accomplice liability doesn't extend to conduct "inevitably incident" to the commission of the offense, unless the legislature provides otherwise.[172] Note, however, that the Code drafters don't think of this limitation as implicit in their approach to complicity (or as required by the double jeopardy proscription[173]). Legislatures remain free to criminalize inevitably incident conduct as complicity; they just have to say so.

Now, since complicity liability flows from one person (the principal) to another (the accomplice), how can the accomplice stop the flow? By "terminat[ing] his complicity prior to the commission of the offense."[174] This provision is the analogue to the abandonment (or renunciation) provision in the law of attempt, except that here it's the accomplice who

[171]. But not only with this sort of double-dipping. The Code drafters were also concerned about cases in which a legislature may not want to criminalize accomplice conduct, even if that conduct isn't covered by some other offense which would generate principal liability, as in the case of bribe paying and bribe receiving. The drafters cited "ambivalence in public attitudes" toward extending accomplice liability in cases like that of a woman in a criminal late-term abortion prosecution against a doctor: "if liability is pressed to its logical extent, public support may be wholly lost." Commentaries § 2.06, at 325.

[172]. § 2.06(6). The Code also specifically provides that the conduct of the "victim" cannot generate accomplice liability. § 2.06(6)(a).

[173]. Double jeopardy isn't supposed to be a problem because the Fifth Amendment provides that no one "be subject for the same offense to be twice put in jeopardy of life or limb," and reciprocal offenses aren't "the same."

[174]. § 2.06(6)(c).

changes his mind.[175] Now, while "renunciation of purpose" is enough to avoid attempt liability, something more is required if I'm the accomplice. If it's just me, or if I'm the principal, changing my mind about committing the crime means that the crime won't be committed. By contrast, if I'm an accomplice, I can abandon my criminal scheme and the crime might still be committed, by the principal. So the law of complicity requires not only that I stop doing what I'm doing—i.e., that I stop aiding or abetting—but that I undo what I've done. According to the Model Code, that doesn't mean that I must succeed in preventing the commission of the crime, nor that I do everything possible to prevent it. It instead requires that I "deprive[] [my complicity] of effectiveness in the commission of the offense," which is another way of saying that I eliminate it as a contributing cause—but not as a but-for cause. Just how I might do this depends on the nature of my assistance. If I supplied the means for committing the crime (e.g., weapons or burglary tools), I have to take them back. If all I did was encourage, then discouragement may be enough. Alternatively, I can "make[] proper efforts to prevent the commission of the offense," perhaps by alerting the police, or the victim, or in some other way, though, once again, these efforts needn't be successful.

The renunciation—or "termination"—provision in essence provides for exceptional cases in which purposely aiding or abetting another person to com-

175. See infra § 5.2(d).

mit an offense doesn't render me legally accountable for that person's criminal conduct. If I renounce my criminal purpose and make "proper efforts" to prevent the crime, then the principal's conduct won't be imputed to me after all. This is an exception that proves the rule of imputation by assistance.

The provision in the Model Code's complicity section that fits least comfortably with the Code's general approach to complicity as derivative liability is the very last one, according to which an acquittal of the purported principal doesn't bar conviction of the purported accomplice. But without a principal, how can there be an accomplice, if the accomplice's liability derives from the principal's?[176]

The short answer is: the jury. Juries, alas, have been known to reach inconsistent verdicts. And one wrong acquittal, that of the principal, is enough. Why compound one error by another? In the words of the Commentaries, "[w]hile inconsistent verdicts of this kind present a difficulty, they appear to be a lesser evil than granting immunity to the accomplice because justice has miscarried in the charge against the person who committed the offense."[177] But how would we know which is the miscarriage of justice, the acquittal of the principal, or the conviction of the accomplice? Not to worry, though,

176. See, e.g., People v. Taylor, 12 Cal.3d 686 (1974) ("collateral estoppel" bars conviction of accomplice after acquittal of principal).

177. Commentaries § 2.06, at 328; see also Standefer v. United States, 447 U.S. 10 (1980).

because—as the Commentaries stress—the commission of the offense must still be proved for accomplice liability (even if the person who is supposed to have committed it is acquitted)[178] and this is, at any rate, "a matter of procedure that need not be resolved in the substantive criminal code" (so why did they resolve it?).[179]

Still, some substantive questions remain. What if the principal is acquitted not because she didn't engage in the offense (i.e., because she didn't satisfy level one of the analysis of criminal liability), but because she had a valid defense, either a justification or an excuse? If she is justified, it would seem that her accomplice wouldn't be held criminally liable either, but not because he wasn't an accomplice, but because he too could avail himself of the justification defense—placing him in her shoes. In the case of an excuse, would the instrument theory of imputation apply (see above), or could he still be an accomplice (i.e., an aider or abettor), even if the principal is excused?

(C) Corporations

Before we move on, we need to touch briefly on another corner of criminal law doctrine in which the conduct of one person is imputed to that of another, or even to a "corporate" entity other than a person.[180] In the latter case, the Code holds a corporation (or unincorporated association) legally

---

178. But see § 5.01(3) (attempt liability for aiding crime not committed).

179. Id.

180. § 2.07.

accountable for the conduct of certain persons, its "agents," who act in its behalf. Corporate liability thus resembles complicity in that it requires the imputation of conduct. It differs from complicity in that the target of the imputation isn't another person, but a nonpersonal entity. That nonpersonal entity, the corporation, is incapable of conduct and so the conduct of its agent cannot, strictly speaking, be imputed to it at all. Plus, even if that imputation were possible, since the corporation is also incapable of forming a purpose, the prerequisite for the imputation under the law of complicity, namely purposeful assistance, isn't applicable either. Instead, the corporation's accountability must rest on another basis, the aforementioned agency.[181]

While the Code thus permits the imputation of a person's conduct to a corporation, it does not provide for interpersonal vicarious liability, i.e., for the imputation of one person's conduct to another person within the corporation, such as from a lower level employee to his supervisor. A manager may, of course, be liable as an accomplice for the conduct of her subordinate, provided that she aided or abetted his conduct as specified in the law of complicity. But the mere relationship between the two within the corporation—or between an employer and her employee—does not generate criminal liability of one for the conduct of the other. Under the Model Code,

181. This theory of imputation applies to any conduct of a corporate agent, no matter what the crime. See, e.g., Commonwealth v. Penn Valley Resorts, 343 Pa.Super. 387 (1985) (homicide); People v. Warner–Lambert, 51 N.Y.2d 295 (1980) (same).

respondeat superior does not apply to criminal liability.[182]

§ 5 "... That Inflicts or Threatens ..."

So far, we've covered the first—and traditionally the single most important—component of the definition of crime laid out in section 1.02 of the Model Penal Code: conduct. Recall that this nutshell of criminal liability defines crime as "conduct that inflicts or threatens substantial harm to individual or public interests."

Traditional Anglo–American criminal law concerned itself largely with the two general elements of any crime, actus reus and mens rea. We saw how the Model Code differentiated these two concepts into a taxonomy of offense elements and modes of culpability, complete with rules of statutory interpretation and theories of imputing one person's conduct to another. Let's now take a closer look at the relation between conduct as defined in a criminal statute and the harm it might—or might not—inflict. In the next, and final, section of the current chapter, we will consider the nature of that harm, rather than its relation to conduct.[183]

182. But see United States v. Dotterweich, 320 U.S. 277 (1943) (recognizing vicarious criminal liability); Commonwealth v. Koczwara, 397 Pa. 575 (1959) (same except "in cases involving true crimes").

183. See infra § 6.

§ 5.1 Causation

The doctrinal locus for questions of the connection between conduct and harm, or more specifically the conduct and the result elements of an offense, is the law of causation—the "causal relationship between conduct and result."[184] The first thing to note about causation is that it's only an issue in result offenses, i.e., in offenses that contain a result element. The prime example of these is homicide, which is all result, as the Model Code's definition makes plain: "A person is guilty of criminal homicide if he purposely, knowingly, recklessly or negligently causes the death of another human being."[185] It matters not how the person causes the death of another, just *that* he does. For purposes of homicide liability, poisoning, tripping, stabbing, shooting, pushing, and running over are all the same. Conduct is required to be sure—even if by omission—but it's the connection between the conduct, unspecified in the definition of the offense, and the death that makes all the difference. Causation is not an issue in conduct offenses, like driving while intoxicated or adultery, or status offenses, like drug possession or vagrancy, which are criminalized regardless of whatever harmful consequences they may have had.

The next thing to note about causation is that it consists of two components. First, there's factual (or but-for) cause. For conduct to cause a result for

[184]. § 2.03. See David J. Karp, Note, Causation in the Model Penal Code, 78 Colum. L. Rev. 1249 (1978).

[185]. § 210.1(1).

purposes of the criminal law, it must be a *conditio sine qua non* of the result. Next, there's legal (or proximate) cause. For a cause to be a cause, it must be both, factual and legal. Perhaps the best way to think of legal cause is as whatever the law of causation requires beyond factual cause for conduct to count as a cause, no matter how circular that may sound.[186] The Model Code makes this point straightforwardly at the very outset of its causation section:

(1) Conduct is the cause of a result when:

(a) it is an antecedent but for which the result in question would not have occurred; and

(b) the relationship between the conduct and result satisfies any additional causal requirements imposed by the Code or by the law defining the offense.[187]

Perhaps not surprisingly, most of the law of causation is about legal cause. In fact, the rest of the Code section on causation is about these very "additional causal requirements imposed by the Code." It turns out that these additional causal requirements differ depending on the mode of culpability, if any, that attaches to the result element of the offense in question.

---

186. The concept of "legal cause" in tort law is no less tautological. See Restatement (Second) of Torts § 9 ("the causal sequence by which the actor's tortious conduct has resulted in an invasion of some legally protected interest of another ... such that the law holds the actor responsible for such harm unless there is some defense to liability").

187. § 2.03(1).

But let's briefly deal with factual cause first, before tackling the intricacies of the amorphous concept of legal cause. The Model Code didn't add anything to traditional factual cause analysis, and didn't find new solutions to old factual cause problems. These problems tend to arise in cases with two potential but-for causes. If two actions constitute sufficient concurrent causes of a result, i.e., if either of them would have been sufficient to cause the result, then neither of them is the result's but-for cause. Suppose two people, acting independently, each fire one fatal shot at a third. Neither shot is the but-for cause of the victim's death because the victim would have died even if it hadn't been fired. The only way the victim wouldn't be dead is if neither shot had been fired. And yet, the law of causation treats both shots as but-for causes. How? By stressing that the causation inquiry focuses on the particular harm inflicted at a particular time in a particular way, rather than on the abstract category of harm captured in the statute ("death of another human being"). And the particular harm inflicted at a particular time in a particular way was in fact caused by the two shots. Plus, while each individual shot doesn't make for a but-for cause, they do constitute a single, cumulative, but-for cause. But for *one or the other* being fired, the victim's death wouldn't have occurred.

But for cause doesn't sound like much. To see that it has some bite, compare it with the type of causal connection required for accomplice liability. Recall that for assistance to count as complicity, it's not necessary that it be the *conditio sine qua* the principal couldn't have committed the offense.[188] Here the Model Code follows traditional analysis, as exemplified in this passage from the celebrated case of *State v. Tally*:[189]

> The assistance given ... need not contribute to the criminal result in the sense that but for it the result would not have ensued. It is quite sufficient if it facilitated a result that would have transpired without it. It is quite enough if the aid merely rendered it easier for the principal actor to accomplish the end intended by him and the aider and abettor, though in all human probability the end would have been attained without it.

Not every antecedent is a contributing cause, not every contributing cause is a but-for cause, and—most important—not every but-for cause is a proximate, or legal, cause. Most of the criminal law of causation concerns itself with this third, and final, selection among the myriad of antecedents to a particular harm, the infliction of which is proscribed in a criminal statute.

The law of causation in this sense resembles the law of complicity. Both are about attribution, or imputation. The law of complicity sets out the conditions under which one person's conduct can be imputed to another. The law of causation deter-

---

188. Tort law, too, requires less than but-for cause. Being "a substantial factor in bringing about the harm" is enough. Restatement (Second) of Torts § 431(a).

189. 15 So. 722, 738–39 (Ala.1894).

mines when a particular harm—the "result"—can be attributed to a person's conduct.

There is of course a fairly straightforward way of making the necessary connection between result and conduct, and thereby enabling the imputation of the one to whoever committed the other: one might decide that factual cause, or cause strictly speaking, is enough.[190]

The Model Code, however, doesn't stop there. It makes explicit the normative component of the apparently factual inquiry of traditional common law causation analysis. Rather than speaking in terms of "chains of causations" that are "broken" by intervening causes, as the common law did, the Model Code instead frames the legal cause analysis openly in terms of culpability and fair attribution. The question is not whether some conduct is the cause of some result. The question instead is whether some result can fairly be attributed to the person engaging in that conduct.

Once again, the Code drafters can be seen as replacing common law rules about how to handle particular clusters of causation issues with a general, flexible, standard. Note, however, that the drafters didn't go quite as far in the direction of flexibility and normativity as they might have gone. In the end, they shied away from specifically instructing the factfinder—the hypothetical jury—to disregard results "too remote or accidental in its occurrence to have a *just* bearing on the actor's liability or on

190. Arguably this is true of the law of torts. See Restatement (Second) of Torts § 435 (foreseeability irrelevant).

the gravity of his offense." The open invitation to considerations of justice was instead relegated to non-committal brackets.[191]

Since it's about attribution, Model Code causation resembles complicity. Another way to think about causation in the Code is to place it alongside two other related doctrinal questions: mens rea and attempt. As in the case of complicity, so too in the law of causation, attribution is largely a matter of culpability—and mental states in particular. That's not to say that causation and mens rea are one and the same thing. Think of mens rea as a first cut at the question of culpability at an abstract level—the level of the definition of the offense. If there's no mens rea, here then the question of causation doesn't even come up.

Causation takes the culpability inquiry to a lower, factual, level—the level of what actually happened. Assuming the connection between an actor, the defendant, and a general *type* of result as defined in a statute—say, death—has been established, we next ask ourselves whether a similar connection exists between the actor's particular conduct and the particular way in which the abstract result—death—came about: by stabbing, by firing a gun, by punching, in the head or in the stomach, once, twice or three times, by aiming at one person, but hitting another instead, who dies within three minutes or

191. § 2.03(2)(b) & (3)(b) ("too remote or accidental in its occurrence to have a [just] bearing on the actor's liability or on the gravity of his offense"); see Commentaries § 2.03, at 261. For other uses of this drafting technique, see §§ 4.01(1) (insanity), 210.6 (capital sentencing factors).

five days or two years, after having been run over by a drunk driver, receiving improper medical care, committing suicide in despair over her injuries, and so on. None of these details appears on the face of the criminal statute—in this case, as in the vast majority of causation cases, homicide—and yet it's these details that determine whether a particular result can be attributed, causally, to the particular conduct of a particular person.

And so the Model Code's causation test looks like a particularized, and simplified, version of the Code's mens rea test. The type of result defined in the statute—death—is run through the complex mens rea test; now the specific result that actually occurred—death by strangulation through the use of an electric cord in the dark—is run through the streamlined causation test.

There are five modes of culpability—counting strict liability. There are three causation tests. One for purpose and knowledge (or, more precisely, for offenses in which purpose or knowledge are attached to the result element; murder would be an example). One for recklessness and negligence (manslaughter and negligent homicide, respectively). And one for strict liability.

The basic idea is straightforward. If purpose or knowledge is required with respect to the abstract offense element (death), then "purpose" or "contemplation" is required with respect to the specific result (death by strangulation etc.). If recklessness or negligence is the result mens rea, then the actual result must not have been within the actor's purpose or her contemplation; instead, it must have been "within the risk of which the actor is aware" for recklessness (which, you will recall, is defined as awareness and disregard of a risk), and within the risk of which she "*should* be aware" for negligence (defined in the Code's mens rea provision, section 2.02, as constructive, but not actual, awareness of a risk).

Most interesting causation cases aren't covered by these background rules. They're about the exceptions. The Code specifically deals with two particularly common ones: (a) different victim, and (b) different harm. Differences in the identity of the victim are irrelevant. If the actual result differs from the one contemplated[192] only in that it affected a different victim (a person or piece of property), that result is still causally attributed to the actor. Let's say I aim at Karl's head and pull the trigger, fully contemplating that I will hit and kill him. Karl ducks at the last moment and I hit and kill Melinda instead, who had been standing behind Karl. According to the Code's causation analysis, Melinda's death will be attributed to my conduct (aiming and pulling the trigger) as result to cause, even though the only result I had contemplated was Karl's death.

Differences between actual and contemplated harm may or may not be relevant, depending on

192. Or whatever the requisite mental state might be—e.g., if recklessness is in the statute, rather than purpose or knowledge, then contemplation isn't required, but awareness of the risk that the actual result might come about.

whether the actual harm is more or less serious than the contemplated harm. If I thought I would inflict *greater* harm than I actually managed to inflict, then the actual harm will nonetheless be attributed to my conduct. Not so if, by contrast, I planned to do less harm than I ended up inflicting. Suppose I aim a gun at Richard's stomach and pull the trigger with the intent to kill him. If he pulls through, I'll still be liable for (aggravated) assault, even though—strictly speaking—the particular harm that actually occurred wasn't within my contemplation (I had hoped to kill him, after all, not just to inflict (serious) bodily injury).[193] If, conversely, I try merely to hurt him, but end up killing him instead, I won't be liable for murder. That doesn't mean that I won't be liable for another type of homicide, though. Even if I didn't intend to kill him, I may have been reckless or negligent with respect to his death, if I knew—or should have known—there was a good chance that he'd die from a shot in the stomach.

And so the Code uses causation analysis to dispose of two irksome problems of criminal liability. Or rather, it takes care to explain that strict causation analysis doesn't stand in the way of assigning criminal liability in certain, unobjectionable, cases despite differences between the actual and the contemplated result.

More difficult are cases of a mismatch between actual and contemplated result that don't fall into either category (different victim or contemplated

193. § 211.1(2).

harm more serious than actual harm). What are we to do in cases where the actual harm bears a tolerable resemblance to the harm contemplated (say death), but is "remote or accidental" nonetheless? How, in other words, are we to handle the causation issues most likely to appear in a law school exam (and least likely to appear in real life)? What if I hit my unsuspecting neighbor over the head with a snow shovel in retaliation for the inconsiderate use of his supercharged snowblower in subzero degree weather after a solid week of heavy snowfall, fully intending to kill him? Assume further that, having snapped out of my homicidal rage, I remorsefully drag the lightly bleeding, but still conscious, man into my car and, over snowbanks and through unplowed sidestreets, rush him to the hospital, where he falls into the hands of the inevitably incompetent surgeon/intern/nurse, who naturally misdiagnoses him as suffering from appendicitis, mistakenly removes his left lung, and then, accidentally drops three dollars in small change into his opened chest cavity before sewing him back up. Add, if you like, that he, upon awakening—miraculously—the next morning, rips out the "tubes inserted into his nasal passages and trachea in order to maintain the breathing process"[194] and, for some additional remoteness, that his chance of recovery upon proper treatment would have been 100%.

194. United States v. Hamilton, 182 F.Supp. 548, 549 (D.D.C. 1960).

It's here that the Code drafters threw up their hands and placed the issue squarely in the jury's lap. For the Code explains simply that "remote or accidental" harms are attributable to an actor only if they are not "*too* remote or accidental." How is the jury to tell the difference between remote and too remote? By asking itself whether the harm still had "a [just] bearing on the actor's liability or on the gravity of his offense." In other words, "remote" harms are imputable to a person if they are [justly] imputable to her, in which case they're not "too remote."

Apart from its circularity, the problem with this approach to the most vexing causation problems in the criminal law is that it doesn't provide the factfinder with much guidance to speak of. (It's a standard, not a rule, after all.) The drafters jettisoned the panoply of more or less rigid rules developed by common law judges, which turned on such factors as "intervening or concurrent clauses, natural or human; unexpected physical conditions; distinctions between mortal and nonmortal wounds," and, perhaps most significant, the foreseeability, actual or constructive, of the result.[195] An alternative formulation would have incorporated the latter factor into the causation analysis by asking whether the result "occurs in a manner which the actor knows or should know is rendered substantially

---

195. We might also add the most straightforward, and least attractive, of these rules, the "year-and-a-day rule," which barred the attribution of deaths occurring more than a year after the act in question. Cf. Rogers v. Tennessee, 532 U.S. 451 (2001).

more probable by his conduct."[196] Note, however, that the Code's flexible standard doesn't render the traditional causation factors irrelevant. It merely transforms them from dispositive rules into guidelines for the application of a less artificial standard that exposes the underlying issue of imputation for all the world to see, no matter how uncomfortably vague it might be. And so (actual) foresight and (constructive) foreseeability are alive and well in contemporary causation law, even in MPC jurisdictions such as New York,[197] and so are the other familiar analytic tools such as "supervening causes."[198]

But what about strict liability? If you conceive of causation in terms of attribution, and therefore of culpability, then strict liability crimes (more precisely, crimes with a strict liability result element) will pose a problem. If you're criminally liable even if you lacked mens rea with respect to the abstract result element in the statute, then surely you're criminally liable even if you lacked mens rea with respect to the specific harm that actually occurred.

196. Commentaries § 2.03, at 261 n.17 (quoting Tentative Draft No. 4, at 16 (1955)).

197. See, e.g., People v. Kibbe, 35 N.Y.2d 407 (1974); People v. Warner–Lambert, 51 N.Y.2d 295 (1980). New York did not codify causation. For a similar result in an MPC-jurisdiction that did, see Commonwealth v. Rementer, 410 Pa.Super. 9 (1991).

198. See, e.g., People v. Griffin, 80 N.Y.2d 723 (1993) (medical malpractice). This also means that Hart & Honoré's celebrated—and surprisingly readable—study of causation in (criminal) law, which emphasized the significance of intervention by an autonomous agent, has lost little of its relevance. See H.L.A. Hart & A.M. Honoré, Causation in the Law (1959).

Causation, in other words, would be reduced to factual, but-for, causation. That's how it stood in the original draft of the causation provision.[199] And that's exactly what some courts concluded, even (or perhaps especially) in the most serious of all strict liability crimes, felony murder—which does without mens rea with respect to the result element of "murder," though it may require all sorts of mens rea with respect to any or all elements of its other half, the (predicate) "felony."[200]

Not so according to the final version of the Code. Even for strict liability crimes, there's now a legal cause requirement beyond factual cause, *probability*, objectively speaking—i.e., without any requirement that the actor be, or should be, aware of or contemplate that result, or even the risk that it might come about. Anything else would be, as the Commentaries explain, unjust.[201] But then so is strict liability.

So causation is like complicity in that it's about attribution, though of a particular result to one's conduct, rather than of another's (the principal's) conduct. Like complicity, it's also about mens rea. Attribution for purposes of culpability turns, among other things, upon one's attitude toward the result (or, in the case of complicity, the other person's conduct).

199. Commentaries § 2.03, at 264 n.21.

200. See, e.g., People v. Stamp, 82 Cal.Rptr. 598 (Cal.App. 1969).

201. Commentaries § 2.03, at 264.

CRIMINAL CONDUCT 141

What happens if the "causal relationship between conduct and result"[202] isn't such as to permit attributing one to the other, and therefore to me, the actor? If criminal liability (for result offenses) requires causation, does the absence of causation imply absence of criminal liability? No, because there's always *attempt*.

§ 5.2 Inchoate Offenses

Attempt is one of the Model Code's "inchoate offenses."[203] The others are, in order of appearance, conspiracy, solicitation, and possession.[204] To say that inchoate offenses are inchoate[205] (or "incomplete,"[206] "anticipatory,"[207] or "preparatory"[208]) is a

202. § 2.03.

203. See generally Herbert Wechsler et al., The Treatment of Inchoate Crimes in the Model Penal Code of the ALI: Attempt, Solicitation, and Conspiracy, 61 Colum. L. Rev. 571 (1961).

204. The Model Code does not contain a provision on facilitation, which appears among the inchoate offenses in some criminal codes based on the Code. See, e.g., N.Y. Penal Law § 115.00. Since it requires the commission of the offense, facilitation, however, is best thought of not as an inchoate offense, but as a sort of mini complicity—aiding with less than purpose. See supra § 4.4(b).

205. "1. In an initial or early stage; incipient. 2. Imperfectly formed or developed." American Heritage Dictionary of the English Language: Fourth Edition (2000).

206. See, e.g., Chisler v. State, 553 So.2d 654 (Ala.Crim.App. 1989) (quoting Ala. Code § 13A-2-23 cmt. at 40).

207. See, e.g., N.Y. Penal Law tit. G ("Anticipatory Offenses").

208. See, e.g., Texas Penal Code ch. 15 ("Preparatory Offenses"). "Preparatory" is problematic since "preparation" short of an "attempt" isn't punishable.

polite way of saying that they aren't offenses at all, at least insofar as a criminal offense is conduct (including nonconduct, namely an omission) that matches the statutory definition of a criminal offense. So whatever attempted murder is, it's *not* murder. But in criminal law—at least in modern criminal law—close but no cigar doesn't apply. If you get close enough to the actual commission of a criminal offense, you will be punished even if you came up short.

Inchoate offenses, then, aren't offenses at all, but lay out ways in which criminal law holds someone liable even if she didn't actually commit a criminal offense. So we don't convict people of "attempt," but of attempted murder, not of "conspiracy," but of "conspiracy to distribute drugs," and so on. Inchoate liability, in other words, is parasitic on choate liability[209]—in theory, at least, since the crime never actually was completed.

Note also that the Model Code, as does American criminal law generally, treats inchoate offenses as "offenses of general applicability."[210] Attempting—or conspiring or soliciting another—to commit *any* offense, no matter how minor, is criminal. Inchoacy, in other words, is truly a general theory of criminal

209. Choate being, according to the Oxford English Dictionary, "[a]n erroneous word, framed to mean 'finished', 'complete', as if the *in-* of *inchoate* were the L. negative."

210. The title of the chapter on inchoate offenses in the Proposed New Federal Criminal Code of 1971. Prop. New Fed. Crim. Code ch. 10 (1971).

liability, rather than a doctrinal tool for expanding the reach of particular offense definitions.[211]

Despite their derivative status, and their fairly recent introduction into Anglo–American criminal law, inchoate offenses lie at the very core of the Model Code.[212] The drafters lavished considerable attention on this topic, and so will we. It's here that the Code's treatmentism emerges most clearly. An attempt is punished because—and insofar as—it reveals a person's abnormal criminal disposition.

211. That's not to say that the Code doesn't *also* recognize a host of specific attempt offenses in its special part. For *attempts*, see, e.g., §§ 211.1 (assault), 221.1(2)(a) (burglary), 224.7(3) (deceptive business practices), 241.6(1) (witness tampering); for *solicitations*, see, e.g., §§ 210.5(2) (aiding suicide), 224.8 (commercial bribery), 224.9(2) (rigging publicly exhibited contest), 240.1 (official bribery), 240.3 (compensation for past official action), 240.5 (gifts to public servants), 240.7 (selling political endorsement), 241.6(3) (witness tampering), 251.2(2)(d) & (h) (prostitution), 251.3 (loitering to solicit deviate sexual relations); for *conspiracies*, see, e.g., §§ 224.8 (commercial bribery), 224.9(2) (rigging publicly exhibited contest), 240.1 (official bribery), 240.3 (compensation for past official action), 240.5 (gifts to public servants), 240.6(2) (compensating public servant for assisting private interests), 240.7 (selling political endorsement), 241.6(3) (witness tampering), 251.2(2)(h) (prostitution), 251.4(2) (obscenity).

212. The origin of modern attempt law is generally traced back to the 1784 English case of Rex v. Scofield, Cald. 397 (1784) (opinion of Mansfield, L.). See generally Francis B. Sayre, Criminal Attempts, 41 Harv. L. Rev. 821 (1928). Attempts to commit particular offenses, particularly robbery, were punished long before then. 4 William Blackstone, Commentaries on the Laws of England 241 (1769). In German criminal law, an attempt to commit a felony is always punishable, an attempt to commit a misdemeanor only if the statute specifically so provides. § 23 StGB.

The same goes for the other inchoate offenses. Since criminal disposition is key, there is no reason to retain the old common law rule that attempts should be punished less severely than consummated offenses.[213] A consummated offense and its inchoate version provide the same evidence of criminal disposition. If we're lucky enough to catch the criminal earlier, rather than later, there's no reason why we shouldn't punish him any less than we would have otherwise. His penological diagnosis is the same, so is his need for penal treatment, and so should be his punishment (which is but an outmoded word for treatment).[214] Likewise, impossible attempts (even legally impossible ones) are punishable,[215] along with unilateral "conspiracies"[216] and uncommunicated "solicitations."[217]

(A) Attempt

One way behavior might fall short of a complete offense is by failing to bring about the *result* specified in the criminal statute. If I set out to kill my

213. See § 5.05(1).

214. Equal treatment for equal diagnosis also meant doing away with other rules, (1) that an inchoate offense could be punished *more* harshly than its consummated version and (2) that the inchoate version—specifically conspiracy—and the consummated version of a single crime could be punished cumulatively. See, e.g., Pinkerton v. United States, 328 U.S. 640 (1946); Callanan v. United States, 364 U.S. 587 (1961).

215. See § 5.01 ("conduct which would constitute the crime *if the attendant circumstances were as he believes them to be*") (emphasis added); Commentaries § 5.01, at 307–20.

216. See § 5.04.

217. See § 5.02(2).

roommate by thrusting a steak knife into his rib cage, but succeed only in hurting him, then my behavior matches the definition of murder (purposely or knowingly causing the death of another human being) in every element except the result. He's a human being. He's another human being. I acted with purpose. But I didn't cause the result I intended, namely his death. Since I set out to engage in behavior that would match the definition of the criminal offense of murder in every respect, but failed to do so, I'm not liable for murder, but for attempted murder.

Note the distinction between attempt and causation here. This case doesn't raise a causation question because the abstract result element laid out in the statute (death) did not in fact occur. Since my roommate survived, my behavior cannot be described as causing the death of another human being—or anyone else, for that matter. Without that result element, i.e., without a dead person, the question whether that result could be attributed to me doesn't arise. Hence no causation question.

Now assume that my roommate did die, but only after a sequence of intervening causes and unforeseeable turns of events that would make his death "too remote" to be fairly attributable to me. In other words, let's assume my act of stabbing him doesn't qualify as a legal cause of his death. In that case, I would escape murder liability because even though most of the elements of murder are satisfied (purpose, death, another human being), one isn't: causation. While this time there is a dead person, there's no causal connection between my act and the *corpus delicti*. Nonetheless, since I did my best to satisfy all of the elements, including causation, I'm still liable for attempted murder.[218]

Unlike causation, the question of attempt doesn't arise only in result offenses. An attempt can fall short in as many ways as there are elements in an offense. Failing to bring about an intended result is only one. Consider, for example, the lobbyist who slips an envelope stuffed with cash to a tourist whom she mistakes for a powerful legislator. Here the missing element is an attendant circumstance, i.e., the bribe recipient being a "public servant."[219] Or take the case of the ex-husband whose plan to burn down his gasoline-soaked former family home fails only because he can't get any of the soggy matches in his pocket to strike a flame. Here there's no conduct element (assuming arson requires one to "start[] a fire"[220]).

By attempting to commit a crime, but failing for one reason or another, I have revealed myself as a person in need of peno-correctional treatment. In the words of the New York Court of Appeals, "[t]he ultimate issue is whether an individual's intentions and actions, though failing to achieve a manifest and malevolent criminal purpose, constitute a danger to organized society of sufficient magnitude to warrant the imposition of criminal sanctions."[221]

218. Cf. People v. Dlugash, 41 N.Y.2d 725 (1977).

219. § 240.1(1).

220. § 220.1(1).

221. People v. Dlugash, 41 N.Y.2d 725, 726 (1977).

Or, in the language of the Code Commentaries, "the primary purpose of punishing attempts is to neutralize dangerous individuals."[222] And so attempt law is about diagnosing these human dangers, about detecting the all-important "indication that the actor is disposed toward [criminal] activity, not alone on this occasion but on others."[223]

According to the Model Code, dangerousness is indicated if two symptoms are present: a "substantial step" (the actus reus of attempt) and purpose (the mens rea of attempt). The first symptom, however, collapses into the second since the point of the substantial step requirement is merely evidentiary—a step is substantial if it's "strongly corroborative of the actor's criminal purpose."[224] Purpose, however, is just a stand-in for extreme dangerousness. As we saw in our discussion of the Code's taxonomy of mental states, purpose stands atop the hierarchy of modes of culpability and, as such, calls for the most intensive form of peno-correctional intervention. Purposeful actors, in other words, are the most dangerous of them all. And it's those human dangers that attempt law seeks to identify and eliminate.

222. Commentaries § 5.01, at 323.

223. Commentaries art. 5, at 294 (introduction). The point of attempt law is *not* that even an unsuccessful attempt at committing a crime can inflict harm upon the intended victim (who, for instance, might have escaped death by the skin of her teeth). Unlike in tort law, there is no requirement that the intended victim even be aware of the attempt on her physical or psychological integrity. See Restatement (Second) of Torts § 22.

224. § 5.01(2). Well, actually, the Model Code provides that a step *cannot* be substantial *unless* it's evidence of purpose.

Once again, the Code drafters identify a basic question—the diagnosis of abnormal criminal dangerousness manifesting itself as "purpose"—and then adopt a flexible standard ("substantial step") in the place of a cornucopia of time-honored rules developed by common law courts to carve up nebulous doctrinal territory (the distinction between (nonpunishable) "preparation" and (punishable) "attempt"). These rules are then reclassified as evidentiary factors to be taken into account when addressing the basic question. Unlike in other pockets of doctrine, however, in the case of attempts, the Code drafters actually listed many of the traditional rules for locating the *locus poenitentiae* by differentiating mere "preparation" from "attempt," and—now—differentiating a mere step from that all-important "substantial step:"[225]

(a) lying in wait, searching for or following the contemplated victim of the crime;

(b) enticing or seeking to entice the contemplated victim of the crime to go to the place contemplated for its commission;

(c) reconnoitering the place contemplated for the commission of the crime;

(d) unlawful entry of a structure, vehicle or enclosure in which it is contemplated that the crime will be committed;

225. More precisely, it lists not the rules themselves ("last proximate act," "physical proximity," "dangerous proximity," "indispensable element," "probable desistance," "abnormal step," and of course "*res ipsa loquitur*"), but the factual scenarios driving their application. Cf. Commentaries § 5.01, at 321–29.

(e) possession of materials to be employed in the commission of the crime, which are specially designed for such unlawful use or which can serve no lawful purpose of the actor under the circumstances;

(f) possession, collection or fabrication of materials to be employed in the commission of the crime, at or near the place contemplated for its commission, where such possession, collection or fabrication serves no lawful purpose of the actor under the circumstances;

(g) soliciting an innocent agent to engage in conduct constituting an element of the crime.[226]

It's often said that the Code's approach to the actus reus in attempt focuses not on what the actor hasn't done, but on what she has done instead.[227] It's a "substantial step" that turns preparation into attempt, not the "last proximate act" before the commission of the target offense. That makes perfect sense, of course, since the Code doesn't punish attempt because it's almost a consummated offense. An attempt doesn't just *approximate* a real offense, it's just as good for purposes of the Code's treatmentism. What matters is the actor's abnormal dangerousness, no matter how it might manifest itself.

While keeping the magical line between preparation and attempt firmly in mind, it's worth remind-

226. § 5.01(2)(a)-(g).

227. Commentary § 5.01, at 329; see, e.g., Commonwealth v. Donton, 439 Pa.Super. 406 (1995).

ing ourselves that there is one type of inchoate offense that's even more inchoate than preparation: possession.[228] Possession, unlike the other inchoate offenses in the Code, actually is a self-standing offense. The Code contains two broad possession offenses, which permit the state to identify dangerous persons long before they have engaged in an act that amounts to a preparation, never mind an attempt to commit a specific crime. It's a misdemeanor both to possess "any instrument of crime" and to possess "any offensive weapon."[229]

Possession of a criminal instrument requires "purpose to employ it criminally." Possession of an offensive weapon does not. Criminal purpose, however, is easily found, thanks to a litany of presumptions attaching to the possession of "a firearm or other weapon on or about his person, in a vehicle occupied by him, or otherwise readily available for use." Establishing that possession, which gives rise to the presumption of criminal purpose, is simplified in turn by its very own set of "Presumptions as to Possession of Criminal Instruments in Automobiles."

There's no need to show criminal purpose if the item possessed qualifies as an offensive weapon, rather than merely as an instrument of crime. The definition of offensive weapon, however, is rather generous, including "any bomb, machine gun,

---

228. See supra § 4.1(d). Not only is possession not quite an attempt, the attempt to possess is itself criminal. People v. Ryan, 82 N.Y.2d 497 (1993).

229. §§ 5.06, .07.

sawed-off shotgun, firearm specially made or specially adapted for concealment or silent discharge, any blackjack, sandbag, metal knuckles, dagger, or other implement for the infliction of serious bodily injury which serves no common lawful purpose." Should the item possessed not fit into this broad category of commonly possessed items, it has a yet greater chance of qualifying as an instrument of crime, which includes "(a) anything specially made or specially adapted for criminal use; or (b) anything commonly used for criminal purposes and possessed by the actor under circumstances which do not negative unlawful purpose."

We've already seen, in our discussion of the act requirement, how tenuous my relationship to an object must be to count as "possession." If we add this flexible concept of possession to the broad range of items the possession of which is criminal, we end up with an offense of breathtaking scope. The key, as in all inchoate offenses, is purpose, as a placeholder for criminal dangerousness. Possession is criminal because—and only insofar as—it manifests criminal purpose.[230] Possession is presumptive evidence of that purpose, and will result in a diagnosis of criminal dangerousness with a prescription of peno-correctional treatment unless I can rebut that presumption, or "negative" that purpose.[231]

230. Even more remotely, *proximity* to an item is criminal, as presumptive evidence of possession, unless I can rebut the presumption. See, e.g., § 5.06(3).

231. See §§ 5.06(1)(b), 5.07.

Now let's move on to what attempt law is all about: purpose, and more precisely, purpose as a proxy for dangerousness. Here the Code distinguishes between three modes of attempting—ways in which one might fall short of consummating a crime.[232]

In the first case, covered in (1)(a), the actor does everything she planned on doing (we're dealing with a *complete* attempt, in other words), and thus a completed incomplete offense, if that makes any sense), but nonetheless doesn't quite manage to commit the crime because things aren't what they seemed. An example would be the empty pocket pickpocket. He has done his best to commit "theft by unlawful taking or disposition" under the Code—defined as "unlawfully tak[ing] ... movable property of another with purpose to deprive him thereof")—and yet he failed to satisfy a crucial element of the crime, the taking. Without a taking there's no theft, but given that he slipped his hands into his "victim's" coatpocket *with the purpose of* taking, he is guilty of attempted theft. We're assuming, of course, that he also "act[ed] with the kind of culpability otherwise required for commission of the crime,"[233] i.e., that he had the "purpose to deprive" his victim of whatever "movable property" he might lift out of her pocket. Without that purpose (a remnant of the venerable *animus furandi* of the common law), there would have been no theft, and

232. Cf. Francis B. Sayre, Criminal Attempts, 41 Harv. L. Rev. 821 (1928).

233. § 5.01(1).

therefore could have been no attempted theft either.

The pickpocket case was one of the most popular illustrations of a *factually* impossible attempt. Another way of reading (1)(a) therefore is as a rejection of factual impossibility as a defense against an attempt charge. This wouldn't have been particularly noteworthy; the common law never had much patience for claims of factual impossibility (or with pickpockets, for that matter). Not so for *legal* impossibility, frequently illustrated by Francis Wharton's hypothetical of Lady Eldon's attempt to smuggle French lace into England. That attempt proved futile because the lace turned out to be not French, but English (the bad news), hence cheap and, more important, not subject to duty (the good news).[234]

The Code rejects claims of impossibility unmodified—focusing instead on "the attendant circumstances ... as [the actor] believes them to be," rather than as they are in fact. From the Code's treatmentist perspective, it makes no difference whether the actor's attempt was impossible, since what counts isn't the likelihood of success (or the proximity to consummation), but the actor's dangerousness. And an impossible attempt provides the

234. The classic American case on legal impossibility is *People v. Jaffe*, the first in a string of decisions struggling with the question of whether I can attempt to "receive stolen property" when the property wasn't in fact stolen, I just thought it was. 185 N.Y. 497 (1906) (no); Booth v. State, 398 P.2d 863 (Ct.Crim. App.Okla.1964) (no; recommending adoption of MPC attempt provision); Commonwealth v. Henley, 504 Pa. 408 (1984) (yes; applying MPC attempt provision).

same evidence of dangerousness as a possible one (or, for that matter, a successful one): "the actor's criminal purpose has been clearly demonstrated; he went as far as he could in implementing that purpose; and, as a result, his 'dangerousness' is plainly manifested."[235] Since impossibility doesn't matter, neither does any particular permutation of impossibility, factual, legal, or otherwise.[236] Simply put, "[u]sing impossibility as a guide to dangerousness of personality presents serious difficulties," and therefore should be disregarded by any system of criminal law designed to provide accurate diagnoses

235. Commentaries § 5.01, at 309.

236. It didn't help that the line between factual impossibility (*not* a defense) and legal impossibility (a defense) "has over a long period of time perplexed our courts." Booth v. State, 398 P.2d 863, 870 (Ct.Crim.App.Okla.1964); see also People v. Dlugash, 41 N.Y.2d 725 (1977). The same was true of the common law's distinction between mistake of fact (a defense) and mistake of law (*not* a defense). See supra § 4.3(b). Factually and legally impossible attempts involve *inculpatory* mistakes, of fact or of law (e.g., that the pocket I'm about to pick is filled with diamonds or that my lace is French), in contrast to the "defense" of mistake which, by definition, tries to put mistakes to *exculpatory* use. Mirroring its limited defense of ignorance of law, the Code recognizes a limited exception to the general rule that impossibility doesn't matter. As the mistaken belief that there is *no* criminal statute covering my conduct may excuse my violation of that statute, so the mistaken belief that there *is* a criminal statute where there is none will shield me from being punished for attempting to violate it. Commentary § 5.01, at 318; see Commonwealth v. Henley, 504 Pa. 408 (1984). What after all would I be charged with if the crime I tried my best to commit doesn't exist? Under the Code, attempting to commit a noncrime is no more criminal than conspiring to commit it. See infra § 5.2(b); but see infra n. 264 (conspiracy to commit "corrupt, dishonest, fraudulent, or immoral" act).

of criminal dangerousness.[237]

As in the first attempt scenario spelled out in the Code, the actor in the second has fallen short of her criminal goal after having done everything she thought necessary (i.e., this too counts as a complete attempt). Whereas in (1)(a), she didn't quite manage to engage in the *conduct* proscribed in the Code, in (1)(b) she failed to bring about the *result* element of the object crime. Let's say the problem isn't that I failed to satisfy the conduct element of a particular offense definition—e.g., the "taking" in theft—but that I committed my criminal act as planned, and yet it didn't have the desired effect. To take everyone's favorite result crime, murder, I can load my gun, aim, pull the trigger, fire the bullet, and still miss. (This particular way of failing wouldn't be available to me in a conduct offense, like theft. If, for example, the act of firing a gun at someone were criminal by itself,[238] then my failure to hit the target wouldn't make a difference. I'd be guilty of the offense—rather than the attempt to commit the offense—either way.)

There is nothing particularly interesting about the Model Code's treatment of this type of attempt

237. In extreme cases, where the actor's conduct is "so inherently unlikely to result or culminate in the commission of a crime that neither such conduct nor the actor presents a public danger," the Code authorizes judges to reduce the punishment or even to dismiss the prosecution altogether. § 5.05(2). This makes sense. In these exceptional cases, the actor's attempt to commit a crime, and her criminal purpose, were not symptomatic of criminal dangerousness, present or future.

238. It is, under the Model Code. § 211.2 ("recklessly endangering another person").

case, except that the Code here doesn't require purpose for attempt liability. While purpose to bring about the result that didn't happen is certainly enough, "the belief that [the act] will cause such result" will do just as well. Here the purely evidentiary significance of the general purpose requirement (the "mens rea" of attempt) becomes clear, or clearer still. Purpose as to the result isn't required for attempt liability because if an actor merely believes that her conduct will bring about a certain proscribed result "the manifestation of the actor's dangerousness is just as great—or very nearly as great—as in the case of purposive conduct."[239]

This covers attempts that don't succeed because of deficits in conduct (1(a)) and result (1(b)). What about the other type of offense element recognized in the Code, attendant circumstances? So far we've learned that attempt under the Code requires purpose with respect to conduct (even if the offense definition requires a lesser mental state regarding conduct) and purpose *or belief* with respect to result.[240] For attendant circumstances attempt requires nothing more—or less—than whatever the

239. Commentaries § 5.01, at 305. This assumes that a mens rea *less* than purpose—knowledge or less—would suffice for conviction of the object offense, which is almost always the case. Otherwise the person wouldn't have been "acting with the kind of culpability otherwise required for commission of the crime." § 5.01(1).

240. "Purpose or belief" really means "intent," as a general concept encompassing purpose and knowledge. See Commentaries § 5.01, at 305. In the context of attempt, the Code drafters thus couldn't get around invoking the concept of intent, which they otherwise did so much to avoid.

object crime requires. This means that, for example, if the object offense requires no mens rea whatsoever regarding a particular attendant circumstance—say, the victim's age in statutory rape—then neither does attempt. If an attendant circumstance is a strict liability element in the object offense, then it is one in the attempt to commit the offense as well.[241] Sticking with our homicidal example, what if my friend loads his gun and aims it at his kid's little league umpire, but I manage to knock the gun out of his hand just as he's about to squeeze the trigger? Once again, he failed to bring about the intended result, and thus to fit himself within the definition of the crime of murder. This time, however, he didn't even get to do everything he set out to do with that result in mind (i.e., we're dealing with an *incomplete* attempt). Never having fired, he didn't even get a chance to miss.

Making sure that he would nonetheless be liable for attempted murder is the point of subsection 1(c). In the third, and last, attempt scenario, I haven't taken all the steps I thought would lead to criminal success, but only some. If these steps add up to a "substantial step," then I will qualify for attempt liability. Although we used a result crime (murder) as our example, attempt liability for "substantial step" applies just as well to conduct crimes. So the mathematician in a famous California case who, "while his wife was away on a trip," rented an office above a bank, filled it with "certain equipment," including "drilling tools, two acetylene gas

241. Commentaries § 5.01, at 301–02.

tanks, a blow torch, a blanket, and a linoleum rug," which he then proceeded to put to use by drilling holes into the floor, using the rug to cover them,[242] was eligible for attempted robbery (a conduct offense) under a substantial step theory just as much as the father suffering from homicidal baseball parent rage.

We've already spent a good deal of time on the subject of "substantial steps" in our discussion of the so-called actus reus of attempt. To repeat, a substantial step is any act that provides sufficient evidence of the actor's criminal disposition, or doctrinally speaking, her purpose.

All this talk about purpose raises the question of what to do with offenses that *don't* require purpose with respect to any or all of their elements. Can I attempt those? This question arises most frequently in cases of homicide, and reckless or negligent homicide in particular. Under the Code, it has a straightforward answer: no. As we just learned, to attempt a crime, "when causing a particular result is an element of the crime" (as death is in homicide), I would have to do (or omit) something "with the purpose of causing or with the belief that it will cause" that result.[243] In other words, the mens rea

242. People v. Staples, 85 Cal.Rptr. 589 (Cal.App.1970).

243. Why belief, rather than knowledge? Because knowledge is an accurate belief. If my belief about the occurrence of the result would have been accurate, however, I would have succeeded in bringing it about and thus actually committing the offense, rather than trying but failing. Purpose, defined as "conscious object," doesn't require a similar adjustment as it applies both to

of attempt (here purpose or belief [read "knowledge"])—as opposed to the mens rea of the object offense (here, recklessness or negligence)—determines the mens rea attaching to the result. An attempt to commit reckless or negligent homicide under the Code thus would actually amount to an attempt to commit murder (which requires purpose or knowledge regarding the result, death).[244] Or, put another way, I can't be held liable for "attempted manslaughter" or "attempted negligent homicide," at least insofar as that would imply that I acted only with recklessness or negligence regarding the risk of death. For attempt, I would need purpose or knowledge regarding the result, and that would qualify me for murder liability—or rather *attempted* murder liability since, after all, I didn't succeed in actually causing the death of another human being.

That's not to say, however, that someone who engages in some conduct while recklessly disregarding a good chance of fatal harm to another—say, by shooting "at a pickup truck carrying three teenage girls"[245]—but is lucky enough not to inflict that harm would escape criminal liability altogether. For these cases of "nonintentional attempts,"[246] the successful and to failed attempts—it doesn't matter whether I achieved my object or not.

244. See J.C. Smith, Two Problems in Criminal Attempts, 70 Harv. L. Rev. 422, 434 (1957).

245. See, e.g., State v. Lyerla, 424 N.W.2d 908 (S.D.1988).

246. They're *nonintentional* in that the actor lacks purpose (or belief) regarding the result; they're *attempts* in that the result didn't occur.

drafters inserted a broadsweeping new crime, reckless endangering, which criminalizes any conduct "which places or may place another person in danger of death or serious bodily injury."[247] Reckless endangering, however, doesn't quite fill the hole left by the omission of reckless or negligent attempts. For one, it doesn't cover negligent endangering. Plus, it's only a misdemeanor, a designation that's consistent with its considerable scope (including potentially dangerous conduct, i.e., threats of threats of harm) but doesn't quite fit with the Code's treatmentist approach to attempt law. After all, the reckless endangerer who escapes manslaughter charges by the skin of her teeth because her errant bullet barely misses its target has displayed a significant criminal disposition calling for peno-correctional treatment—in fact, a dangerousness indistinguishable from that found in another person who wasn't so lucky and is marked, and treated, as a manslaughterer instead, and therefore as a felon, rather than as a mere misdemeanant.

Also note that the drafters' decision to do away with attempts to commit nonintentional result crimes—like involuntary manslaughter—wasn't based on considerations of logical impossibility, conceptual essence, etymological origin, or even linguistic awkwardness, all of which can be found in common law opinions, and in scholarly commentary.[248] The problem isn't that it's impossible to

247. § 211.2.

248. Under the Code, it's "impossible" to attempt a reckless or negligent result offense only in the sense that, given the

attempt to bring about results nonintentionally because attempt "implies" or "requires" intent, logically or in any other way.[249] Instead, it's that "the scope of the criminal law would be *unduly extended* if one could be liable for an attempt whenever he recklessly or negligently created a risk of any result whose actual occurrence would lead to criminal responsibility."[250] From the drafters' treatmentist perspective, this exception for result offenses doesn't quite make sense, however. Once again, the lucky almost manslaughterer has displayed the very same dangerousness as the unlucky consummated one, and therefore requires the very same penocorrectional treatment. And, as we know, attempt

purpose or belief requirement for attempt with respect to result, any attempt to commit a reckless or negligent result offense would automatically be an attempt to commit a purposely or knowing result offense.

249. Contrast People v. Campbell, 72 N.Y.2d 602, 605 (1988) ("Because the very essence of a criminal attempt is the defendant's intention to cause the proscribed result, it follows that there can be no attempt to commit a crime which makes the causing of a certain result criminal even though wholly unintended.").

250. Commentaries § 5.01, at 304 (emphasis added). The drafters had no similar qualms about extending attempt liability to offenses that required less than purpose with respect to elements other than the result. For instance, they specifically noted that reckless endangerment—the very crime they had designed to capture conduct that would otherwise qualify as an attempt to commit reckless or negligent result offenses—could be attempted, even though it required less than purpose. Reckless endangerment, they explained, "aimed at the prohibition of particular reckless *behavior*, rather than the prohibition of a particular *result*." Id. n.16 (emphasis added).

law is all about the identification, and diagnosis of the criminally disposed.

(B) Conspiracy

American courts have long marveled, in horror, at the unique danger inherent in the very idea of conspiracy. Here is one example taken from a 1961 opinion by Justice Felix Frankfurter:

> [C]ollective criminal agreement—partnership in crime—presents a greater potential threat to the public than individual delicts. Concerted action both increases the likelihood that the criminal object will be successfully attained and decreases the probability that the individuals involved will depart from their path of criminality. Group association for criminal purposes often, if not normally, makes possible the attainment of ends more complex than those which one criminal could accomplish. Nor is the danger of a conspiratorial group limited to the particular end toward which it has embarked. Combination in crime makes more likely the commission of crimes unrelated to the original purpose for which the group was formed. In sum, the danger which a conspiracy generates is not confined to the substantive offense which is the immediate aim of the enterprise.[251]

It's no surprise, then, that the treatmentist Model Code would find a prominent place for this traditional crime of exceptional human dangerousness:

251. Callanan v. United States, 364 U.S. 587, 593–94 (1961).

There is little doubt ... that as a basis for preventive intervention by the agencies of law enforcement and for the corrective treatment of persons who reveal that they are disposed to criminality, a penal code properly provides that conspiracy to commit crime is itself a criminal offense.[252]

As in the common law, the core of conspiracy under the Code is an agreement.[253] It's this agreement that gives rise to criminal liability, by transforming a lonely criminal thought hatched in the mind of a single, powerless, individual into a criminal plan. By entering into an agreement with another person, I reveal myself as one of those persons who suffer from an abnormal disposition to engage in criminal conduct, by distinguishing myself from those untold millions who harbor criminal thoughts, but never share them with others, never mind act on them in any way. But my decision to seek out likeminded protocriminals, and to join hands with them in the pursuit of a common criminal goal is not only symptomatic of my extraordinary dangerousness. By combining forces with another similarly dangerous person, I multiply my already considerable dangerousness through the magic of cooperation.

So much for what courts like to call the gravamen of conspiracy. If this basic idea is kept in mind, the Model Code's approach to conspiracy falls into place fairly readily. As in the case of attempt, the "actus reus" and "mens rea" of conspiracy amount to a

252. Commentaries § 5.03, at 388.

253. Id. at 421 (§ 5.03 "rests on the primordial conception of agreement as the core of the conspiracy idea").

list of factors relevant to a diagnosis of dangerousness. The actus reus is the agreement. What's an agreement the Code doesn't say. Presumably, any meeting of the minds will do, with no requirement that the agreement take any particular form, written or otherwise. This is nothing new, except that under the Model Code even an *apparent* meeting of the minds will do. The Code adopts what its drafters call the "unilateral" theory of conspiracy, i.e., of a one-sided agreement between two sides.[254] This criminal law version of a tango for one—or, if you prefer, the sound of one hand clapping—makes perfect sense, of course, if the point of conspiracy law is to identify and eliminate dangerous people. From the treatmentist perspective, the person who thinks she is doing something is indistinguishable from the person who actually does it. There were no impossible attempts, and there are no impossible conspiracies now. Even if a particular "conspiracy," say between me and a police informant, poses no danger whatsoever, the Code steps in to assign me the indicated peno-correctional treatment.[255] The "incapacity, irresponsibility, or immunity" of my purported partner in crime is simply irrelevant for purposes of coming up with an individualized assessment of my dangerousness.[256]

[254]. See People v. Berkowitz, 50 N.Y.2d 333 (1980) (acquittal of co-conspirator).

[255]. See People v. Schwimmer, 411 N.Y.S.2d 922 (1978) (undercover officer & confidential informer).

[256]. This much we know from the law of complicity. See § 2.06(7).

Common law traditionally required another act for conspiracy liability: some "overt" act "in furtherance of" the first, central, and alarmingly covert, act of agreement. The Model Code retains the overt act requirement, except in cases of serious conspiracy, i.e., conspiracies to commit a felony.[257] Agreements to commit serious crimes are by themselves sufficiently indicative of exceptional criminal dangerousness to warrant peno-correctional treatment, even without further evidence of criminal purpose in the form of an additional act designed to put them into action.

As in the case of attempt, we have reached the point at which the actus reus of conspiracy reveals itself as purely instrumental. The law of conspiracy requires whatever actus reus is necessary to firm up a diagnosis of mens rea, i.e., of criminal dangerousness. As in the case of attempt, that mens rea is purpose. Only purpose, the "highest" of the Code's modes of culpability, warrants state interference already at the point of inchoacy, even before an offense defined in the Code's special part has been committed. Judge Learned Hand's view that only purpose would do for *complicity*, and knowledge would not, won out in conspiracy as well. As the Commentaries point out, "the Institute at its 1953 meeting adopted Learned Hand's view as to complicity," and "[t]he case for this position seems an even stronger one with respect to the inchoate crime."[258]

257. § 5.03(5).

258. Commentaries § 5.03, at 406.

Note that the Code here means what it says. Conspiracy requires purpose with respect not only to conduct, but also with respect to result.[259] Recall that a look at the fine print reveals that in the case of attempt, the purpose requirement applies in full force only to conduct. In the case of result (the all-important element in homicide), attempt liability would attach even to those who merely believed in the success of their criminal efforts, i.e., they acted with the closest thing to knowledge one could have with respect to future events, but not purpose.

Having figured out that purpose is the mens rea of conspiracy, it's time briefly to see how the Code handles conspiracies to commit non-purpose crimes. If the object of the conspiracy is a *result offense* (like homicide) and the mental state with respect to that result (death) is recklessness or negligence (as in manslaughter and negligent homicide, respectively), then the answer is the same as in the case of attempt: no.[260] Under the Code, I can't attempt to recklessly or negligently cause harm, nor can I

[259]. As to attendant circumstances, attempt requires whatever mental state the definition of the consummated offense requires. Whether this is enough for conspiracy—or if purpose is required for that element type as well—was a question the drafters left open, as they had done in their treatment of complicity. Id. at 413.

[260]. Unlike in the case of attempt, however, the answer would also be no if the object offense requires knowledge as to result. For unlike attempt, conspiracy requires purpose (and not just purpose or knowledge) as to the result. Sticking with homicide, a conspiracy to commit murder (which requires purpose or knowledge as to result) would be possible, but only if the state proves purpose as to the result (death).

conspire to do so. Also, as in attempt, *conduct offenses* are a different story; there's no problem, in the drafters' eyes, with conspiring—or attempting—to commit a conduct offense that requires less than purpose, as long as I engage in purposeful conduct myself in doing the conspiring, or the attempting: in the case of "a crime defined in terms of conduct that creates a risk of harm, such as reckless driving or driving above a certain speed limit," or reckless endangering, we might add, from our discussion of attempt, "it would suffice for guilt of conspiracy that the actor's purpose was to promote or facilitate such conduct—for example, if he urged the driver of the car to go faster and faster."[261]

The Code's focus on individual dangerousness may be difficult to bring into line with the concept of conspiracy as an agreement. It is far preferable, however, to an alternative approach to conspiracy that regards it not as an agreement, but as a *group* (a syndicate, an organization, a gang, a cabala—or a union, or a party). Throughout its relatively brief history as a general inchoate crime, conspiracy has been used to ferret out and destroy "conspiracies" that for one reason or another were considered dangerous by those wielding the power to apply the criminal law.[262] Given its history, and the conceptual ambiguity at its heart, conspiracy law threatens to circumvent one of the vaunted principles of

261. Commentaries § 5.03, at 408.

262. The history of modern American conspiracy law thus is to a large extent a history of its abuse, perhaps most famously against labor unions. See generally Francis B. Sayre, Criminal Conspiracy, 35 Harv. L. Rev 393 (1922).

American criminal law: that guilt is personal.[263] Not only does it impose criminal liability on a group, the "conspiracy," from which the liability of its members is then derived. In addition to *group liability*, it makes room for *vicarious liability*, i.e., one person's liability for the behavior of another. It doesn't help matters that conspiracy as thus understood, by imposing *status liability* on the basis of one's being a conspirator, flaunts another basic principle of American criminal jurisprudence, the act requirement.

The Model Code tries to clean up conspiracy's act in various ways. By limiting conspiracy liability to agreements to commit *crimes*, rather to engage in any act that qualifies as "corrupt, dishonest, fraudulent, or immoral, and in that sense illegal,"[264] the drafters made conspiracy less broad and less vague, at the same time.[265] By stressing the individual dangerousness of each "conspirator" (an unfortunate term, given that it defines the person in terms of her membership in the conspiracy, considered as a group), the Code narrowed the focus of conspiracy from the group to the individual. Even the Code's fiction of a unilateral agreement can be seen in this light. So focused is the Code's conspiracy analysis

263. See, e.g., People v. McGee, 49 N.Y.2d 48, 60 (1979).

264. State v. Kemp, 126 Conn. 60, 78 (1939) (quoting State v. Parker, 114 Conn. 354, 360 (1932)).

265. They did not, however, take the additional step of further limiting objects of conspiracy from only crimes to only *some* crimes. In the Code, conspiracy remains a inchoate crime of general application. See Commentaries § 5.03, at 391–93.

on the individual that it denies the inherent bilateralism of an agreement.

What's more, the Code rejects the so-called *Pinkerton* doctrine, a particularly blatant manifestation of the view that conspiracy liability is unconstrained by the principle of personal guilt. As we noted in our discussion of complicity, this doctrine, which survives in federal law and the law of several states, holds every conspirator liable—as an accomplice—for any criminal offense committed by any co-conspirator "in furtherance" of the conspiracy. *Pinkerton* collapses the distinction between conspiracy and complicity, treating one as a sufficient ground for the other, and thus turning every conspirator into her co-conspirator's accomplice. This approach makes perfect sense if one thinks of conspiracy as a criminal group whose members are vicariously liable for each other's actions as members. The basis of *Pinkerton* conspiracy liability is not the person's connection with the substantive crime, but the connection of the substantive crime with the conspiracy ("furtherance"). Assuming the requisite connection between the crime and the criminal enterprise, liability of each partner in the enterprise follows from her own connection to the enterprise (membership). The conspiracy thus quite literally is at the center of the analysis of criminal liability.

The Model Code instead attempts to differentiate conspiracy from complicity. It insists that conspirators are just like other people, and that therefore the liability of each party to a conspiratorial agreement must be assessed individually. The question is not whether the offense can be functionally connected to the enterprise (furtherance), but whether my conduct in perpetrating the offense can be imputed to another party to the agreement. And we already know how imputation works:

A person is an accomplice of another person in the commission of an offense if

(a) with the purpose of promoting or facilitating the commission of the offense, he

(i) solicits such other person to commit it; or

(ii) aids or agrees or attempts to aid such other person in planning or committing it.[266]

As the second clause makes explicit, an agreement or a common plan may well make out accomplice liability. Conspiracy thus may well imply complicity. One follows from the other, however, only if the agreement is specific enough to count as an agreement entered into "with the purpose of promoting or facilitating" the particular criminal conduct actually committed, rather than some general plan to create criminal mischief, or to form a criminal organization. In other words, the particular scope of the agreement, rather than its mere existence, determines the scope of accomplice liability to which it gives rise, for "law would lose all sense of just proportion [!] if simply because of the conspiracy itself each were held accountable for thousands

[266]. § 2.06(3).

of additional offenses of which he was completely unaware and which he did not influence at all."[267]

In many, perhaps most, cases, the Model Code's analysis will reach the same results as the *Pinkerton* doctrine, particularly if "reasonable foreseeability" is recognized as a limitation on the extension of *Pinkerton* liability among co-conspirators.[268] The analysis, however, remains clearly distinct. In its individualized approach, the Code does its best to contain a notorious uncontainable offense, a crime "so vague that it almost defies definition."[269] Rather than abandon conspiracy altogether, the drafters did their best to tame it, by abandoning *Pinkerton* instead.[270]

Doing away with conspiracy as a general inchoate offense, after all, would have meant disregarding a convenient doctrinal locus for the assessment of the all-important criminal dangerousness. In fact, what initially looks like conspiracy's oppressive weakness is transformed into its penological strength. Its very flexibility makes room for the sort of penological diagnosis that lies at the heart of the Code's theory of inchoacy.

267. Commentaries § 2.06, at 307.

268. See Pinkerton v. United States, 328 U.S. 640, 648 (1946).

269. Krulewitch v. United States, 336 U.S. 440, 446 (1949) (Jackson, J., concurring) (quoted in Commentaries § 5.03, at 402).

270. Commentaries § 2.06, at 307 ("The reason for [abandoning *Pinkerton*] is that there appears to be no other or no better way to confine within reasonable limits the scope of liability to which conspiracy may theoretically give rise.").

Once evinced, the abnormal criminal disposition of the conspirator called for appropriate peno-correctional treatment. And since the dangerousness of the conspirator was identical to that of the perpetrator of the conspiracy's object, the Code provided for identical peno-correctional treatment of both, consistent with its general approach to inchoate offenses. The conspiracy and its object are punished the same. In the law of attempt, treating inchoate and consummated offenses the same meant increasing the punishment for attempt, which traditionally had been less—often significantly less—than that for the substantive offense. In the law of conspiracy, it also meant putting a stop to the practice of punishing conspiracies more *harshly* than, and *in addition to*, their objectives, on the ground that they by themselves posed a danger independent of and beyond that posed by the commission of their object offense.[271]

In fact, however, the dangerousness of one planning an offense was determined by that of one actually committing it. The danger of conspiring to do X was nothing more—and nothing less—than doing X. Conspiring to commit murder evinced the same quantity and quality of criminal dangerousness as committing murder—or attempting to com-

---

271. Since each of the inchoate offenses is but a tool for diagnosing a single condition, abnormal dangerousness, it also makes no sense to permit convictions of more than one inchoate offense per unconsummated crime. § 5.05(3). Any of the inchoate offenses will do for diagnostic purposes. It's the condition that calls for peno-correctional treatment, not its symptom, or symptoms, with the specific degree and nature of dangerousness being determined by the object crime.

mit it, for that matter (or soliciting it, as we'll see shortly).

At the same time, the Code modified another rule found in the common law, which merged the conspiracy into the completed crime. While it made no sense to punish conspiracies more harshly than their objects, cumulative punishment remained appropriate if the conspiracy encompassed offenses other than the one actually committed. A conspiracy to commit murder thus merged in murder. A conspiracy to commit murder and theft didn't. The defendant, after all, had evinced the degree and type of dangerousness associated with murder as well as that associated with theft.[272]

(C) Solicitation

We've already seen that a unilateral agreement can make a conspiracy. From the Code's treatmentist perspective, the person who *thinks* she's conspiring with another to commit a crime is indistinguishable from the person who actually manages to form a conspiracy. In other words, as the inchoate crime is indistinguishable from the consummated crime, so is the inchoate version of the inchoate crime from the inchoate crime itself—problems of infinite regress notwithstanding.

What's more, it turns out that the Code actually recognizes, as a separate offense, just such an inchoate inchoate crime: solicitation, which, as the Commentaries explain, "may, indeed, be thought of as

272. Commentaries § 5.06, at 390.

an attempt to conspire."[273] Treatmentism demands nothing less:

> There should be no doubt on this issue. Purposeful solicitation presents dangers calling for preventive intervention and is sufficiently indicative of a disposition towards criminal activity to call for liability.[274]

Solicitation is meant to provide for the penocorrectional treatment of those abnormally dangerous persons who managed to slip through the already finely woven net of the two main inchoate offenses, attempt and conspiracy—which it combines into a single inchoate inchoate crime, thus extending the sphere of state intervention to reach conduct that would not quite qualify for either.

The most remarkable thing about solicitation in the Code may be its existence, which is testimony to the strength of the drafters' commitment to treatmentism in general, and to the prosecution of inchoate offenses in particular. A close second, however, would be its scope, which is remarkable even for an inchoate offense under the Code. As we know, unilateral conspiracies, or agreements with myself, are just as criminal as actual conspiracies. We also know that solicitation punishes the attempt to form a one-sided agreement. What's more, attempts to solicit—"uncommunicated solicitations"—are treated the same as successful solicitations, i.e., attempts

273. Commentaries § 5.02, at 365–66.
274. Id. at 366.

to enter into a criminal agreement, uni-or multilateral.[275]

Assuming the all-important "purpose," a letter offering $1,000 to an undercover police officer for murdering my ex-husband which I mistakenly slip into the return slot at my local movie-rental place, rather than the mailbox right next to it, will make me criminally liable for solicitation—not for attempted solicitation, but solicitation. It would make no difference to my liability, and my exposure to peno-correctional treatment, whether the letter actually reached its intended reader, whether that reader had any intention of taking me up on my offer, or even of pretending to take me up on it, or even whether there ever was a possibility that she might (agree or pretend to agree, that is);[276] and, if we're dealing with anything other than a first-degree felony, then it wouldn't even make a difference whether she actually went ahead and put that agreement into action, or at least tried to do so. The only thread that holds these widely different scenarios together is my purpose, which we long ago have come to recognize as a proxy for abnormal dangerousness. "The crucial manifestation of dangerous-

275. § 5.02(2); cf. People v. Lubow, 29 N.Y.2d 58, 62 (1971) (exploring the scope of this "new kind of offense, simpler in structure than an attempt or a conspiracy, and resting solely on communication without need for any resulting action").

276. As an attempt to conspire, it's no surprise that impossibility isn't a defense to solicitation, subject to the utter impossibility (pins in voodoo doll) exception also familiar from the law of attempt. Commentaries § 5.02, at 370 (citing § 5.05(2)).

ness lies in the endeavor to communicate the incriminating message to another person, it being wholly fortuitous whether the message was actually received."[277]

Solicitation, however, isn't just an attempt to conspire—a double inchoacy. It's also a familiar foundation for accomplice liability. One way of having another person's conduct imputed to me is by "soliciting" her to engage in it.[278] Imputation of another person's conduct to me, however, presumes that the conduct actually took place. Solicitation, by contrast, does not. And so solicitation turns out to be not only attempted conspiracy, but attempted complicity as well.[279]

277. Commentaries § 5.02, at 381.

278. § 2.06(3).

279. Attempted complicity, i.e., conduct that would qualify as complicity but for the substantive offense not taking place, thus preventing the imputation of the would-be principal's offense to the would-be accomplice, is also dealt with in the attempt provision. § 5.01(3) treats as an attempt "conduct designed to aid another to commit a crime that would establish his complicity ... if the crime were committed," on the by now familiar ground that "the actor who attempts to aid ... manifests the same *dangerousness of character* as the actor who himself attempts to commit the offense." Commentaries § 5.01, at 356 (emphasis added). Solicitation covers failed attempts to *solicit*, rather than to *aid*, the commission of the crime. See § 2.06(3)(i) (soliciting) & (ii) (aiding). So the crooked but hapless police officer who, belatedly, tries to tip off gamblers about a police raid after the raid has occurred, see Commonwealth v. Haines, 147 Pa.Super. 165 (1942), would be guilty of attempt, under § 5.01(3), rather than of solicitation, under § 5.02. Whether differential treatment of these cases is necessary—in fact, whether we need a crime of solicitation if we have an expansive crime of attempt—is, of course, another question.

(D) Renunciation

Each of the inchoate offenses in the Code—attempt, conspiracy, and solicitation—provide for an affirmative defense of renunciation.[280] The renunciation has to be "complete and voluntary," two conditions the Code drafters defined with characteristic indirectness:

> [R]enunciation of criminal purpose is not voluntary if it is motivated, in whole or in part, by circumstances, not present or apparent at the inception of the actor's course of conduct, which increase the probability of detection or apprehension or which make more difficult the accomplishment of the criminal purpose. Renunciation is not complete if it is motivated by a decision to postpone the criminal conduct until a more advantageous time or to transfer the criminal effort to another but similar objective or victim.[281]

280. §§ 5.01(4), 5.02(3), 5.03(6). Recall that an affirmative defense under the Model Code imposes not the burden of proof, but only the burden of production, on the defendant. § 1.12(3). There is no renunciation provision for the remaining inchoate offense codified in the Code's general part, possession—whatever such a provision might look like. It's possible, of course, to discontinue possession of an object or to rebut a presumption of possessing it with a "criminal purpose," thus avoiding a diagnostic inference of dangerousness. There is also an affirmative defense allowing a "defendant to prove by a preponderance of evidence that he possessed or dealt with [an 'offensive weapon'] solely as a curio or in a dramatic performance, or that he possessed it briefly in consequence of having found it or taken it from an aggressor, or under circumstances similarly negativing any purpose." § 5.07.

281. § 5.01(4).

So interrupting a gas station holdup just because the police have arrived doesn't amount to renunciation.[282]

Since inchoate crimes are about dangerousness, so is the defense of renunciation. According to the Commentaries, renunciation "significantly negatives dangerousness of character."[283] Assuming the actor's preparatory conduct evinces criminal purpose, a diagnosis of abnormal dangerousness follows, except if contrary evidence indicates otherwise. Renunciation is that contrary evidence which can rebut the presumption of dangerousness:

> In cases where the actor has gone beyond the line drawn for defining preparation, indicating prima facie sufficient firmness of purpose, he should be allowed to rebut such a conclusion by showing that he has plainly demonstrated his lack of firm purpose by completely renouncing his purpose to commit the crime.[284]

The versions of the renunciation defense don't differ significantly among the various inchoate offenses in the Code.[285] In attempt, renunciation requires that the actor "abandoned his effort to

282. E.g., Stewart v. State, 85 Nev. 388 (1969).

283. Commentaries § 5.01, at 360. The drafters also mention another rationale for the renunciation defense: to give actors an incentive to abandon their criminal plan even at the last minute, i.e., even after evidence of dangerousness has become conclusive. Id. at 359–60.

284. Id. at 359.

285. Cf. supra § 4.4(b), discussing the analogous termination "defense" in complicity. § 2.06(6)(c). Unlike renunciation, termination is not an affirmative defense under the Code.

commit the crime or otherwise prevented its commission,"[286] in solicitation that he "persuaded" the solicitee not to commit the crime "or otherwise prevented the commission of the crime,"[287] and in conspiracy that he "thwarted the success of the conspiracy."[288] Each time, however, what matters is whether the renunciation occurred "under circumstances manifesting a complete and voluntary renunciation of his criminal purpose."

§ 6 "... Substantial Harm to Individual or Public Interests"

We've almost come to the end of our discussion of the first level of the analysis of criminal liability, the question whether a crime has been committed in the formal sense of conduct fitting the definition of a criminal offense. So far, we've teased out what the Code means by "conduct" that "inflicts or threatens" something. We now briefly turn to that something, namely "substantial harm to individual or public interests." We won't spend much time on this aspect of criminal law, not because it's not important, but because it's beyond our scope. The taxonomy of criminal harm is by and large a matter for the special part of criminal law, rather than for the general part, which deals with the principles of criminal liability that apply to the entire cornucopia of crimes.

286. § 5.01(4).
287. § 5.02(3).
288. § 5.03(6).

§ 6.1 Substantial Harm

There is one provision in the general part that does address if not the object (or objects) of criminal harm, then its extent. Section 2.12 assigns to the trial judge extensive authority to dismiss prosecutions even if they allege criminal conduct, i.e., conduct that matches an offense definition and is neither justified nor excuse.[289] Traditionally, the task of weeding out what the Code calls "de minimis infractions" has been left to the discretion of prosecutors. This provision sets up a judicial check in cases where this traditional filter has failed for one reason or another, including excessive prosecutorial zeal or perhaps even vindictiveness.

Most interesting, for our purposes, is the drafters' attempt to guide the discretion to disregard "merely technical violations of law."[290] Traditionally, the discretion to bring to bear the state's machinery of law enforcement in a particular case has been entirely unconstrained by law. American criminal law accepts applicatory discretion as a fact of life, trusting in "the good sense of prosecutors."[291] Continental criminal law, by contrast, has adopted the principle of compulsory prosecution to protect defendants from the bad sense of prosecutors, and other state officials. Prohibiting prosecutorial discretion, however, isn't the same as eliminating it. In fact, more recently, civil law countries have

289. See Stanislaw Pomorski, On Multiculturalism, Concepts of Crime, and the "De Minimis" Defense, 1997 B.Y.U. L. Rev. 51.

290. Commentaries § 5.12, at 399.

291. United States v. Dotterweich, 320 U.S. 277, 285 (1943).

recognized the "opportunity principle" as a counterbalance to compulsory prosecution, allowing dismissal in cases that meet certain criteria, including the seriousness of the crime, the public interest in a criminal prosecution, and the degree of culpability.[292] The Model Code's de minimis provision tries to set out criteria of this sort.

Two of the three grounds for dismissal are mini versions of a justification and an excuse defense. This makes sense. Even de minimis infractions, after all, remain infractions, and "technical violations of law" are still violations. There would be no need for an extraordinary dismissal if the conduct charged didn't match the definition of some criminal offense. One ground for dismissal covers cases of implied consent (a justification) that fall "within a customary license or tolerance, [not] expressly negatived by the person whose interest was infringed."[293] Another, and potentially the broadest,[294] rationale sounds more like a general excuse defense of unavoidability for exceptional and unanticipated cases, involving conduct that "presents such other extenuations that it cannot reasonably be regarded as envisaged by the legislature in forbidding the

292. See, e.g., §§ 153, 153a, 153b StPO [German Code of Criminal Procedure]. These provisions have become a common basis for plea bargaining, or its continental equivalents. See, e.g., Markus Dirk Dubber, American Plea Bargains, German Lay Judges, and the Crisis of Criminal Procedure, 49 Stan. L. Rev. 547 (1997).

293. For our discussion of consent, see infra § 11.

294. Perhaps not surprisingly, dismissal on this ground requires a written justification. § 2.12(3).

offense."[295] Here the court is clearly second-guessing the legislature on the ground that it could not have wanted to punish that which could not be avoided, an application of Blackstone's "Tenth Rule," that "acts of parliament that are impossible to be performed are of no validity."[296]

Only one of the grounds for a de minimis dismissal really is about de minimis infractions, strictly speaking. It authorizes dismissal in cases where the proscribed conduct (1) "did not actually cause or threaten the harm or evil sought to be prevented by the law defining the offense," or (2) "did so only to an extent too trivial to warrant the condemnation of conviction." The Commentaries cast the first clause as a generalization of the utter impossibility (voodoo doll) cases in the law of inchoate crimes.[297] With the second clause, the drafters had in mind everyday occurrences like "unconsented-to contacts" on subways, in ticket lines, or at rock concerts, which might technically count as an assault. A more direct way of dealing with this issue, of course, would be to define the criminal offense more narrowly, thus precluding even "technical" liability for de minimis harm—as the Code drafters did with the crime of assault, for instance.[298]

295. Excuses are discussed infra § 12.

296. Commentaries § 2.12, at 404 n.18.

297. Id. at 403.

298. Id. at 404; see § 211.1 (by requiring at least recklessness in most cases and by limiting relevant harm to bodily injury, defined as "physical pain, illness or any impairment of physical condition" or serious bodily injury, defined as "bodily injury which creates a substantial risk of death or which causes

§ 6.2 Individual or Public Interests

The realm of criminal law isn't defined only by a particular degree of interference—"substantial harm"—but also by a set of objects of that interference—"individual or public interests." These interests structure the special part of the Model Code, a vast improvement over the alphabetical ordering in previous efforts at statutory compilation. The federal criminal code, in Title 18, for instance, to this day begins with chapters on "aircraft and motor vehicles," "animals, birds, fish, and plants," "arson," "assault," "bankruptcy," and "biological weapons," and ends with "terrorism," "trafficking in contraband cigarettes," "treason, sedition, and subversive activities," "transportation for illegal sexual activity," "war crimes," "wire and electronic communications interception and interception of oral communications," and—reflecting a sudden loss of the will to alphabetize—"stored wire and electronic communication and transactional records access," followed by "prohibition on release and use of certain personal information from state motor vehicle records."[299]

The Code instead recognizes the following "private or public interests" as worthy of criminal protection:

serious, permanent disfigurement, or protracted loss or impairment of the function of any bodily member or organ").

299. For a systematic, interest-based, ordering of federal crimes, one must instead refer to the federal sentencing guidelines. See Markus Dirk Dubber, Reforming American Penal Law, 90 J. Crim. L. & Criminology 49, 78 (1999).

existence or stability of the state (art. 200)[300]
person (arts. 210–13)[301]
property (arts. 220–24)
family (art. 230)
public administration (arts. 240–43)
public order and decency (arts. 250–51)
miscellaneous[302]

Although the Code drafters organized their special part around these interests—or at any rate categories that could be translated into interests—it would be a mistake to think that they spent a great deal of time thinking about the nature and types of criminal harm. In fact, as we've seen again and again, they were not particularly interested in the phenomenon of harm. Their focus instead was on the diagnosis of abnormal criminal dangerousness and the prescription of appropriate peno-correctional treatment.

In fact, the formulation "private or public interests" was adopted only as an afterthought. Originally, section 1.02(1)(a) referred to "individual *and* public interests."[303] "And" became "or" only after an article entitled "Logic and Law" had pointed out some possible ambiguities in the original formulation, in a 1962 book entitled, hopefully, "Law and Electronics: The Challenge of a New Era—A Pio-

300. Model Penal Code 241 (Proposed Official Draft 1962).

301. Actually, "offenses involving danger to the person."

302. Model Penal Code 241 (Proposed Official Draft 1962) (narcotics, alcoholic beverages, gambling, tax and trade).

303. See Model Penal Code § 1.02(1)(a) (Tentative Draft No. 4, 1955) (emphasis added).

neer Analysis of the Implications of the New Computer Technology for the Improvement of the Administration of Justice."[304]

304. See Commentaries § 1.02, at 16 n.3 (citing Layman E. Allen, Logic and Law, in Law and Electronics: The Challenge of a New Era—A Pioneer Analysis of the Implications of the New Computer Technology for the Improvement of the Administration of Justice 187–98 (Edgar A. Jones Jr. ed., 1962)).

Chapter 2

"Unjustifiably"—Level Two

Having completed our discussion of what qualifies behavior as a criminal offense, it's now time to consider what else it would take to impose criminal liability on a particular person engaging in that behavior. Everyone would agree that counting as a criminal offense according to some criminal statute or other is a necessary precondition for behavior to be punished. Necessary it certainly is, but sufficient it's not. The question we'll address in the remainder of this book is what else we need for punishability, besides matching the definition of some criminal offense.

§ 7 Defenses in General[1]

Traditionally, Anglo–American law has approached this issue not as a substantive question about the elements of criminal liability, but as a question of procedure, and more specifically, of evidence. Procedurally speaking, our question is one of "defenses." Matching some offense definition makes out a prima facie case of punishability. That presumption of criminality then can be rebutted by

1. See Note, Justification: The Impact of the Model Penal Code on Statutory Reform, 75 Colum. L. Rev. 914 (1975).

the "defendant"—as opposed to, say, the "accused"—raising certain "defenses."

This procedural way of looking at things may reflect the roots of the Anglo–American criminal process in trial by combat. Even today, the American criminal process, not only at trial, remains "adversarial"—rather than "inquisitorial"—and continues to be viewed as a struggle, or at least a contest, between adversaries who deliver blows and launch counterattacks in a constant back-and-forth.

This procedural conception may be a little misleading, however, because it creates the impression that it's up to one side, the "prosecution," to establish the offense and to the other, the "defendant," to establish, well, the defense to that offense. We've already seen that "defenses" like intoxication and mistake (or termination in complicity) aren't for the defendant to prove, but for the prosecution to disprove, insofar as they are inconsistent with the prosecution's claim that the defendant had the requisite mens rea.

Now there *are* claims that count as defenses in the sense that it's up to the defense to raise them, and back them up with some modicum ("scintilla") of evidence, before the burden shifts onto the prosecution to disprove them. The Model Code calls these "affirmative" defenses.[2] Some modern codes, the New York Penal Law being one example, go so far as to place the burden of *proof* as to certain defens-

2. § 1.12. To be precise, the Model Code doesn't require the defense to bear the burden of production even with respect to these issues. Evidence of an affirmative defense may also pop up—presumably unintentionally—in the prosecution's case. It's just that "typically" it's the defense that comes up with it.

es on the defense,[3] even to the point of requiring proof beyond a reasonable doubt.[4]

Still, the substantive question of whether the prerequisites for criminal liability have been met is distinct from the procedural question of who should have to prove that they have (or haven't)—or even who should raise the issue, backed up with at least a shred of evidence, whether they have or not. Unfortunately, in American law the procedural tail tends to wag the substantive dog, with the former question receiving far more attention than the latter. In fact, much of the constitutional law regarding the prerequisites for criminal liability is a branch of the law of evidence, with elaborate judicial dissertations on the distinctions among various types and levels of evidentiary burdens (of production, of persuasion, or proof; beyond a reasonable doubt, clear and convincing evidence, or preponderance of the evidence),[5] their assignment to—and then shifting among—the parties (state, defendant),[6] during different stages of the process (trial,

Commentaries § 3.01, at 6. The important point thus is that even in the case of an affirmative defense, what matters under the Model Code is that "there *is* evidence supporting such defense," not who introduces it. § 1.12(2)(a) (emphasis added).

3. The New York Penal Law calls *these* defenses affirmative, distinguishing them from defenses that are affirmative under the Model Code—in that they re. The latter, in New York, are defenses unmodified. N.Y. Penal Law § 25.00.

4. Leland v. Oregon, 343 U.S. 790 (1952) (insanity).

5. In re Winship, 397 U.S. 358 (1970).

6. Mullaney v. Wilbur, 421 U.S. 684 (1975) (provocation); Patterson v. New York, 432 U.S. 197 (1977) (extreme emotional disturbance); Martin v. Ohio, 480 U.S. 228 (1987) (self-defense).

sentencing),[7] and evidentiary presumptions that might be used to alleviate evidentiary burdens, once assigned, without shifting them altogether (rebuttable, irrebuttable, mandatory, permissive).[8]

The Model Code recognizes two types of defenses—or rather their absence—as substantive prerequisites for criminal liability: justifications and excuses.[9] That's why it includes in its definition of offense element "(i) such conduct or (ii) such attendant circumstances or (iii) such a result of conduct as ... (c) negatives an excuse or justification for such conduct."[10] Since the prosecution must prove every offense element (beyond a reasonable doubt),[11] this means—procedurally speaking—that it must also *disprove*—"negative"—justifications and excuses.[12] All in all, criminal liability thus requires conduct that matches (a) "the description of

7. McMillan v. Pennsylvania, 477 U.S. 79 (1986).

8. Sandstrom v. Montana, 442 U.S. 510 (1979).

9. While the Code drafters refused "to draw a fine line" between justifications and excuses, they did make "a rough analytical distinction" between them. Commentaries art. 3, introduction, at 2. We'll explore that distinction in the context of particular justifications and excuses.

10. § 1.13(9)(c).

11. § 1.12(1).

12. It retains that burden even if the defense is classified as affirmative, once some evidence of the defense has been introduced—ordinarily by the defendant—at trial. § 1.12(2)(a). The only exception to this rule are the super-affirmative defenses that the Code "plainly requires the defendant to prove by a preponderance of the evidence." See, e.g., §§ 2.04(4) (ignorance of law), § 2.07(5) (due diligence), 2.13(2) (entrapment), 5.07 (temporary possession), 213.6(1) (mistake about age).

the forbidden conduct in the definition of the offense," including (b) "the required kind of culpability," and that does *not* match an (c) "an excuse or justification for such conduct."[13]

In this light, the elements of a defense appear like the elements of an offense, only upside down. Set out in the general part, justifications and excuses are invisible attachments to any offense definition. So the offense of murder, for instance, is defined as purposely or knowingly causing the death of another human being. Criminal liability for murder, however, requires that we add "without justification or excuse."

What's more, the Model Code classifies (the absence of) justifications and excuses not merely as offense elements, but as *material* elements.[14] This means that its general culpability provisions apply not only to "the description of the forbidden conduct in the definition of the offense," but also to the justifications and excuses for this conduct. While the prosecution bears the burden of proving any element (beyond a reasonable doubt), it needn't prove any mode of culpability with respect to an element that isn't "material." This is a roundabout way of saying that the general presumption of mens rea doesn't apply to a nonmaterial element like one that "negatives a defense under the statute of limitations" or that "establishes jurisdiction or venue."[15] These nonsubstantive matters shouldn't ap-

13. § 1.13(9)(a)-(c).
14. § 1.13(10).
15. § 1.13(9)(d) & (e).

pear in offense definitions at all, but if they do, then they will be strict liability elements, unless of course the legislature specifically provides that they are not. The distinction between material and nonmaterial elements was introduced largely to accommodate the scores of federal crimes that include a jurisdictional element.[16] So the prosecution still needs to prove that the defendant used the mails or traveled in interstate commerce, but needn't prove that she knew she did—or had some other mode of culpability with respect to these common jurisdictional elements.

Not so for justifications and excuses. Think of justifications and excuses as having modes of culpability attached to their elements. To negative a justification or an excuse then would mean to negative that mental state. For instance, using (otherwise criminal) force in self-defense, as we'll see shortly, is "justifiable when the actor *believes* that such force is immediately necessary for the purpose of protecting himself against the use of unlawful force by such other person on the present occa-

---

16. So the Unabomber, Ted Kaczynski, who killed and injured several people in the 1980s and 1990s, committed the federal crime of "Transportation of an Explosive With Intent to Kill or Injure" because he "knowingly did transport and attempt to transport, and willfully did cause to be transported, in interstate commerce an explosive with the knowledge and intent that it would be used to kill, injure and intimidate an individual, and unlawfully to damage and destroy real and personal property." Indictment, United States v. Kaczynski, No. S–CR–S–96–259 (E.D. Cal. June 18, 1996) (citing 18 U.S.C. §§ 844(d)); see also id. ("Mailing an Explosive Device With Intent to Kill or Injure," 18 U.S.C. § 1716)).

sion."[17] Negativing the justification of self-defense thus requires showing that the actor didn't have the requisite "belief" with respect to the elements of the defense (immediate necessity, unlawful force, etc.).

Note that it says "believes" rather than "knows." Knowledge—that is, an *accurate* belief—isn't required.[18] Mistakes are allowed. On its face, the justification is available even if I turned out to be wrong about any or all of the conditions that I thought gave rise to my right to defend myself (maybe it wasn't strictly "necessary," for example, to bodycheck the skateboarder who raced toward me on the sidewalk).

Mistakes are allowed, but whether they are enough to justify is another question. For it turns out that the Model Code also provides that certain types of mistake make out what's sometimes called an *imperfect* defense, i.e., a defense that limits criminal liability, rather than doing away with it altogether. In particular, if my mistake regarding the elements of a defense was reckless or negligent then I will have a defense against offenses that require more than recklessness or negligence for conviction, i.e., offenses that require purpose or knowledge (like murder). But I will remain criminally liable for

17. § 3.04(1); see also §§ 3.02(1) ("conduct which the actor *believes* to be necessary to avoid a harm or evil to himself"); 3.03(3) ("actor *believes* his conduct to be required or authorized"); 3.06(1) ("actor *believes* that such force is immediately necessary"); 3.07(1) (same).

18. Cf. § 2.02(2)(b)(i) (defining knowledge regarding an attendant circumstance as awareness of its existence).

offenses that require less. If I was reckless in making the mistake, I'll be liable for offenses that require recklessness (like manslaughter). And if I was negligent, I'll still be liable for negligence offenses (like negligent homicide).

Note that the Model Code does not speak, at least not directly, in terms of "reasonable" beliefs, or mistakes. Under the common law, and in many American jurisdictions to this day, beliefs—even mistaken ones—about the conditions of my justification are enough, but only if they're reasonable. If I was unreasonably mistaken about having a right to defend myself, for instance, then I had no defense at all. The common law rule was an either-or, an all-or-nothing, proposition: justified if reasonable, not justified if not.[19]

The Model Code instead differentiates, indirectly, among different types of unreasonable mistakes. A reasonable belief, according to the Code, is "a belief which the actor is not reckless or negligent in holding."[20] But as we just saw, the fact that I was recklessly or negligently mistaken doesn't mean that I have no defense, and thus would be liable for any offense, even one requiring purpose or knowledge (like murder). It means that I will escape liability for such serious offenses, and—assuming they exist—will be liable only for offenses in keeping with the nature of my mistake: recklessness

19. See People v. Goetz, 68 N.Y.2d 96 (1986).
20. § 1.13(16).

offenses if reckless, negligence offenses if negligent.[21]

Now that we have a general understanding of the Model Code's approach to defenses, let's take a closer look at specific defenses, justifications first. It's always a good idea to keep this general approach in mind as we make our way through the Code justification provisions, many of which are quite detailed.

§ 8 Necessity Justification

Necessity is the mother of all justifications, as the title of section 3.02 makes plain: "Justifications Generally: Choice of Evils." It's only right and proper that it appear ahead of all the other justification defenses addressed in article 3 of the Code. It's also the fallback justification that might apply if others fail. why?

The basic idea of necessity as a justification is that there are some circumstances in which conduct

---

21. For an intermediate position, which reduces murder liability to manslaughter in the case of an unreasonable mistake regarding the conditions of self-defense, see Weston v. State, 682 P.2d 1119 (Alaska 1984). This doctrine, often referred to as "imperfect self-defense," resembles the Model Code position in that it doesn't bar the defense altogether in cases of unreasonable mistakes. Unlike the Code, however, it doesn't tailor liability to the nature of the actor's mistake. Reckless or negligent, unreasonable mistakes result in liability for manslaughter. Cf. State v. Bowens, 108 N.J. 622 (1987) (rejecting imperfect self-defense in MPC-jurisdiction). Note also that this defense, like that of provocation, is limited to homicide cases. On provocation, see infra § 16.

that's facially criminal isn't unlawful in fact, in the context of the law generally speaking. Assuming that the—or at least one—purpose of the law is to avert "harm or evil," and that criminal law, as a species of law, has that same purpose, then it's not contrary to law to engage in conduct that violates some criminal statute but advances the overall goals of law. If, in other words, I can avert "harm or evil" by violating a criminal statute designed to avert "harm or evil" then I am justified, assuming that the harm or evil I avert is greater than the harm or evil I commit. If I can save the town by burning down my neighbor's farm, then I am not acting unlawfully.

The necessity defense takes its name from its limitation to situations of necessity, or even "emergency."[22] Ordinarily, the balancing of potential costs and benefits of a given course of conduct occurs prospectively at the legislative level, among representatives of the political community. These—my—representatives have passed a criminal code that contains the criminal statute I have violated—arson, say. For me to second guess their, and therefore my, judgment and act contrary to the norms they have defined in furtherance of the goal of averting "harm or evil," I must face extraordinary circumstances. In short, I must face necessity. Without necessity, I am not entitled to take the law into my own hands, breaking a statute to save the law, so to speak or, to put it more dramatically, violate the law for its own sake.

22. N.Y. Penal Law § 35.05(2).

This sort of balancing in light of the underlying purpose of the law, and, in fact, of government generally, underlies all justification defenses. In necessity, or choice of evils, the rationale of justifications is most explicit, and least constrained. It's no accident that the Code's provision on necessity is so much shorter than those on, say, self-defense or law enforcement. The other justification defenses work out the details of the "choice of evils" in particular, and particularly common, scenarios. In these defenses, the legislature attempts to predict the extraordinary circumstances under which its criminal norms, poured into statutes, generate counterproductive results. Self-defense, for example, describes—in considerable detail—those cases in which the prohibition against harming other persons would cause greater harm than its violation.

The Code provision on necessity is refreshingly straightforward:

> Conduct which the actor believes to be necessary to avoid a harm or evil to himself or to another is justifiable, provided that ... the harm or evil sought to be avoided by such conduct is greater than that sought to be prevented by the law defining the offense charged.[23]

What's more, the Commentaries illustrate the point of the defense in an oft-quoted passage that's worth reciting once more:

> [A] principle of necessity, properly conceived, affords a general justification for conduct that

23. § 3.02(1).

would otherwise constitute an offense. It reflects the judgment that such a qualification on criminal liability, like the general requirements of culpability, is essential to the rationality and justice of the criminal law, and is appropriately addressed in a penal code. Under this section, property may be destroyed to prevent the spread of a fire. A speed limit may be violated in pursuing a suspected criminal. An ambulance may pass a traffic light. Mountain climbers lost in a storm may take refuge in a house or may appropriate provisions. Cargo may be jettisoned or an embargo violated to preserve the vessel. An alien may violate a curfew in order to reach an air raid shelter. A druggist may dispense a drug without the requisite prescription to alleviate grave distress in an emergency.[24]

This passage points out, first, that the very idea of codifying a general necessity defense was something new at the time of the Model Code. Even in legal systems with a long tradition of codification, the necessity defense remained uncodified. German courts, for instance, referred to the balance-of-evils defense as "suprastatutory necessity," precisely because its recognition flew in the face of the relevant criminal statute defining the offense. In this sense, necessity was not only uncodified, but uncodifiable as well.[25]

24. Commentaries § 3.02, at 9–10.

25. In Germany, the necessity defense was first recognized in an abortion case, where the doctor performed the abortion to

Note also that the Commentaries here invoke the requirements of "rationality and justice," which is a far cry from the talk of dangerousness that dominates the article on inchoate offenses, for instance. In fact, in the Commentaries on the Code's justification provisions, one is far more likely to come across references to what would be "unjust,"[26] or what has or hasn't a "place in the penal law."[27] The drafters still don't set out an account of either "justice" or "the penal law" (or "law," for that matter), which would help us understand why one, or both, might require the adoption of a particular doctrinal rule. And yet, even in a Code so thoroughly committed to treatmentism as the Model Code, talk of "justification" naturally slips into talk of justice, talk of "unlawfulness"[28] into talk of law, of "wrongful-

save the life of the mother. RGSt 61, 242. It wasn't codified until 1969. See StGB § 34 (necessity as justification).

26. See, e.g., Commentaries § 3.04, at 36; see also Commentaries § 2.09, at 373, 375 (duress).

27. See, e.g., Commentaries § 3.04, at 39. Similarly, the justification Commentaries are littered with discussions—and frequently adoptions—of the treatment of analogous issues in the law of torts, a body of law concerned with remedying harms, and distinctly unconcerned with eliminating dangerousness. In fact, one entire justification provision in the Code does no more than refer to the law of torts. See § 3.10 (justification in property crimes).

28. See, e.g., Commentaries § 3.04(1) ("unlawful force"); see also §§ 2.09, 2.10 (unlawful order), 3.04(2)(a)(i) & 3.07(4) (unlawful arrest), 3.04(2)(a)(ii)(2) (unlawful dispossession), 3.06(1)(a) (unlawful entry and carrying away), 3.06(3)(c) (unlawful re-entry and recaption), 5.01(2)(d) (unlawful entry), 5.01(2)(e) (unlawful use).

ness"²⁹ into talk of wrong, of "claim of right" into talk of right,³⁰ and of "harm or evil"³¹ into talk of, well, harm and evil.³²

The Code section on necessity isn't just unusually clear, it's also relatively generous. Unlike other statutes, most importantly the New York Penal Law, the Code doesn't include an "imminence" requirement.³³ It's not that imminence, or "urgency," doesn't matter under the Code. It's just that it doesn't matter any more, or less, than any other factor in evaluating the necessity for making a choice, or the rightness of choosing one harm over the other. As an example of a case in which imminence might matter the Commentaries mention the famous maritime cannibalism case of *Regina v. Dudley & Stephens*, in which three shipwrecked sailors killed and ate a fourth, only to be rescued within four days.³⁴ The problem was that they

29. See, e.g., § 3.06(6) ("wrongful obstructor"); see also §§ 2.08(4) & 4.01(1) (wrongfulness of conduct).

30. See, e.g., §§ 3.04(2)(a)(ii) & (b)(ii), 3.06(1)(b)(ii), (2)(c), (3)(d)(i), & (6)(a).

31. See, e.g., § 3.02(1); see also §§ 1.09(1)(c), 1.10(1), 1.13(10), 2.02(6), 2.11(1), 2.12(2).

32. That's not to say that one couldn't couch issues of justification in treatmentist terms, just that the drafters didn't do so as often as one might expect. After all, the woman who burns down a house to save the village from an oncoming firestorm doesn't display the same criminal dangerousness as the woman who sets her neighbor's house on fire without a justification of any kind.

33. In fact, it doesn't even require, unlike other justification defenses in the Code, that the facially criminal conduct be "immediately" necessary. See, e.g., §§ 3.04(1) (self-defense); 3.06(1) (defense of property); 3.07(1) (law enforcement).

34. Commentaries § 3.02, at 16 n.20 (citing Regina v. Dudley & Stephens, 14 Q.B.D. 273 (1884)). Note that the Code generally

might have been able to survive, even if not until their rescue, then at least for some time, without cannibalizing one of their number, and that the eventual victim was so sick that he might have died shortly on his own account, without the need to resort to murder. Under the Code, the absence of imminence wouldn't automatically bar a necessity defense. Necessity thus can justify the prevention of a future harm, provided it is sufficiently likely and serious.

Moreover, a belief in the necessity—including imminence, if relevant—will be enough. The general mistake provisions governing defenses apply here as well, so that a correct assessment of the need for action isn't required.[35] A belief in the necessity will do, with the familiar allowances for imperfect defenses in the case of recklessly or negligently mistaken beliefs. In New York, by contrast, the necessity defense on its face applies only to conduct that "*is* necessary as an emergency measure."[36] So even allows a necessity justification for homicidal arithmetic à la *Dudley*. Commentaries § 3.02, at 15. Without such a "numerical preponderance in the lives saved compared to those sacrificed," however, no justification is available. This is bad news for those who find themselves in the other classic shipwreck scenario—sharing a floating plank that can hold one, but not two. Here I wouldn't be justified in pushing off my fellow sailor to save my own skin. Id. at 17. As it turns out, I don't even have an excuse defense here because, as we'll see shortly, the Code doesn't recognize necessity as an excuse (or circumstantial, as opposed to personal, duress) in cases where I face a necessary choice, but not one in which the balance of evils favors me. See infra § 13.

35. N.Y. Penal Law § 35.05(2); Commentaries § 3.02, at 19–22.

36. See People v. Craig, 78 N.Y.2d 616 (1991) (necessity defense "objective only").

JUSTIFICATION

if Dudley and Stephens were wrong in assessing the necessity of killing the cabin boy, and the imminence of their death, they would not be liable for murder, which under the Code requires purpose or knowledge. Depending on the nature of their mistake, however, they may be liable for manslaughter or negligent homicide.

Note, however, that the Code's necessity provision does contain one objective element. A mistaken belief in the necessity of taking facially criminal action doesn't preclude the defense, but a mistaken "choice of evils" will.[37] This crucial limitation was meant to keep the necessity defense from justifying defendants like the one who "genuinely believes that the life of another is less valuable than his own financial security."[38] The Commentaries distinguish mistakes about balancing from mistakes about necessity in that the former are about questions of law, and the latter about questions of fact:

> What is involved may be described as an interpretation of the law of the offense, in light of the submission that the special situation calls for an exception to the criminal prohibition that the legislature could not reasonably have intended to exclude, given the competing values to be weighed.[39]

---

37. See Commentaries § 3.02, at 12; § 3.02(1)(a) ("harm or evil sought to be avoided by such conduct *is* greater than that sought to be prevented by the law defining the offense") (emphasis added).

38. Commentaries § 3.02, at 12.

39. Id.; cf. § 2.12(3) (de minimis).

Finally, the Code does not completely bar the defense if the actor had some fault, no matter how small, in bringing about the situation giving rise to the necessity.[40] In keeping with its general treatment of mistakes as to defense elements, the Code instead differentiates between types of causation: recklessly bringing about and negligently doing so.[41] While purposefully or knowingly setting up the necessity to violate the law won't do, recklessly or negligently creating the situation gives rise only to liability for recklessness or negligence offenses.

§ 9 Defense of Persons (Self and Others) and of Property[42]

The Code's treatment of self-defense distinguishes two types of cases, those that don't involve the use of "deadly force" and those that do. Initially, both are governed by the same general standard, which is simple enough:

40. Contrast N.Y. Penal Law § 35.05(2) (specifically limiting defense to "situation occasioned or developed through no fault of the actor"). On forfeiture in the law of self-defense, see infra § 9.3.

41. Cf. § 3.09(2).

42. This cluster of defenses (of persons and property) are the only "defenses" in the true sense of the word. While any justification or excuse may count as a defense in some *procedural* sense, self-defense, defense of another, and defense of property (mine and another's) are defenses in the *substantive* sense. More specifically, these defenses are defenses in the procedural sense because they are defenses in the substantive sense—at their common core lies my right to defend my rights and those of another against rightless attack.

[T]he use of force upon or toward another person is justifiable when the actor believes that such force is immediately necessary for the purpose of protecting himself against the use of unlawful force by such other person on the present occasion.[43]

So far, the self-defense provision looks a lot like that on necessity, simple and to the point. That's how it should be, in form and in substance, since self-defense is but one instance of necessity. As the provision makes clear, using force in self-defense is justified only if (1) it's *necessary* and (2) it fits a general situation where the "harm or evil" of a certain type of criminal conduct (assault, imprisonment, homicide) is *outweighed* by the "harm or evil" of another type of criminal conduct (assault, imprisonment, kidnapping, rape, or homicide), namely when I have to use the former to protect myself against an unlawful instance of the latter.

The drafters, however, couldn't leave well enough alone. They decided that if I want to claim a self-defense justification for using "deadly force," rather than just any "force," I will have to jump through some additional hoops, which they then proceeded to specify in considerable detail.

§ 9.1 Self–Defense[44]

But let's look at the basic requirements for self-

43. § 3.04(1).

44. For a historical essay on self-defense, which itself is of more than historical interest, see Joseph H. Beale, Retreat from a Murderous Assault, 16 Harv. L. Rev. 567 (1903).

defense first, especially since the provisions on deadly force tend to get all the attention.

(A) Use of Force Upon or Toward Another Person

The first thing to notice is that this provision—as every other justification provision, with two exceptions—deals only with offenses involving the use of *force*, and more particularly of force against another person (codified in articles 210–213 of the Code's special part). The two exceptions are sections 3.02, on necessity, which we just discussed, and section 3.10, on justification in property crimes, which we won't discuss. As its title suggests, section 3.10 deals with defenses to crimes involving harm not to persons, but to property (codified in articles 220–224). The Code drafters weren't particularly interested in this issue, dealing with it by a simple nod in the direction of the law of torts, equating "a defense of privilege in a civil action" with a justification in a criminal case. Here's how the Second Restatement of Torts illustrates the privilege "intentionally to invade interests in present and future possession of chattels": "A, while visiting in B's house, is assaulted by B, who seizes a valuable vase to hurl at him. To protect himself, A picks up B's umbrella, and with it knocks the vase out of B's hands and breaks it and the umbrella. A is not liable to B for the value of either the umbrella or the vase."[45] And, under section 3.10, A wouldn't be *criminally* liable either, say for criminal mischief.[46]

45. Restatement (Second) of Torts § 261.

46. § 220.3; see also N.Y. Penal Law § 145.00.

The justification of all other crimes, not involving harm either to persons or to property, presumably is covered only by the general necessity provision, which isn't limited to any particular type of crime.

(B) Belief

Next we find the familiar reference to belief, with the similarly familiar consequences for the treatment of mistakes. If they're reckless or negligent—and therefore unreasonable—then there can only be liability for recklessness or negligence offenses, respectively. If they're neither reckless nor negligent—and therefore reasonable—then they don't stand in the way of a justification for the use of force.[47]

When it comes to the unlawfulness of the force against which I'm defending myself, however, the Code clarifies that a mistake about un*law*fulness doesn't count if it's "due to ignorance or mistake as to the provisions of the Code [or] any other provision of the criminal *law*."[48] So if I use force to protect myself against your attempt to wrest your wallet out of my hand, firmly[49] believing that it's never lawful to use even moderate force to recover stolen property, that belief wouldn't do me any

---

47. It's here, in assessing the nature of the defendant's belief regarding the conditions for the justified use of self-defensive force, that the Code would accommodate evidence of battered woman syndrome. See State v. Leidholm, 334 N.W.2d 811 (N.D. 1983); see also State v. Kelly, 97 N.J. 178 (1984).

48. § 3.09(1) (emphasis added).

49. But wrongly. § 3.06(1); Commonwealth v. Donahue, 148 Mass. 529 (1889) (assault to reclaim property).

good. By contrast, mistakes of *noncriminal* law count, in analogy to the Code's general mistake provision, which, as we know by now, doesn't differentiate between mistakes of fact and of (noncriminal) law.[50]

(C) Necessity

Like necessity, self-defense covers the use of force only if it's "necessary." Plus it requires a mental state of "purpose" with respect to its conduct element ("protecting himself"), much as necessity requires that the actor "sought to" avoid greater harm by engaging in facially criminal conduct. As we just saw, "belief" is enough with respect to its attendant circumstances ("immediately necessary," "unlawful")—once again echoing necessity ("necessary"[51]). So conduct that only turns out later to have met the conditions for self-defense (say, because the assailant had, unbeknownst to the person claiming self-defense, concealed a bowie knife in her coat pocket) won't qualify as self-defense. On the flipside, however, conduct that turns out later *not* to have met the conditions for self-defense, but appeared to meet them to the actor at the time, will qualify, subject to the familiar provisions regarding reckless and negligent mistakes.

50. § 2.04(1)(a). Presumably, a mistake of law wouldn't preclude a justification if it meets the conditions set out in the Code's ignorance of law provision, § 2.04(3).

51. Except, once again, regarding the balancing element, that the "harm or evil sought to be avoided by such conduct is greater than that sought to be prevented by the law defining the offense charged." Commentaries § 3.02, at 12.

Unlike necessity, however, self-defense doesn't require a balance of evils, at least not explicitly. That balance has been struck in the abstract by the legislature in framing the conditions for self-defense. In a homicide case, for example, necessity would balance lives saved against lives sacrificed. So killing three to save one could never be justified on grounds of necessity. By contrast, killing three (or more) to save one in self-defense may well be justified. In effect, the lives of those who engage in "unlawful" conduct are not weighted as heavily as those who don't.

I have the right to use force in defending myself against one or more persons only if they use "unlawful" force. There is no similar limitation on the right to use force—or to engage in any other criminal conduct—in the name of necessity. To stick with homicide, I may throw Jill overboard to save myself and my friend Jack, even if she engaged in no unlawful conduct of any kind—on grounds of necessity. But I couldn't throw her overboard just to save myself—on grounds of self-defense—since her life counts as much as mine, unless she threatened to use unlawful force against me, say, by trying to throw me overboard herself.[52]

52. Blackstone, without the concept of unlawfulness, would find self-defense here since "their both remaining on the same weal plank is a mutual, though innocent, attempt upon, and an endangering of, each other's life." 4 William Blackstone, Commentaries on the Laws of England 186 (1769). Dudley and Stephens tried a similar argument a century later, but failed. Regina v. Dudley & Stephens, 14 Q.B.D. 273 (1884)

(D) Unlawfulness

Since so much in self-defense—and, as we'll see later on, in duress as well[53]—turns on the "unlawfulness" of the aggressor's force, it's no surprise that the Code drafters took care to define just what they considered "unlawful force" to be. Unfortunately, their definition is not a model of clarity:

> "[U]nlawful force" means force, including confinement, which is employed without the consent of the person against whom it is directed and the employment of which constitutes an offense or actionable tort or would constitute such offense or tort except for a defense (such as the absence of intent, negligence, or mental capacity; duress; youth; or diplomatic status) not amounting to a privilege to use the force.[54]

One might have expected the drafters simply to say that unlawful force meant justified force, since after all conduct is justified if it doesn't violate the law, generally speaking, even if it's facially criminal in the sense of matching the definition of a criminal offense. Under this formulation, self-defense would be justified only against unjustified force or, alternatively, self-defense would be lawful only against unlawful force. (So, for instance, using self-defensive force against force used in self-defense could not be justified.) Instead of referring to justification in general, the drafters make reference to one spe-

53. See infra § 13.
54. § 3.11(1).

cific justification ("consent")[55] and to the rough tort analogue of a justification ("privilege"), so that unlawful force is defined so as not to include force that's consented to or privileged.[56]

The Code formulation also makes clear that, while *justified* conduct may not be resisted by self-defensive force, conduct that's merely *excused* may. Once more, the drafters listed particular excuse defenses, rather than speaking of excuses in general; unlawful force includes force committed under circumstances giving rise to a defense of "mental capacity; duress; youth."[57]

The differential treatment of justified and excused attacks makes sense. Justified conduct means not unlawful conduct. Excused conduct, by contrast, bars criminal liability but doesn't challenge the unlawfulness of the conduct. My killing Roger under duress may be excused, but it cannot be justified. For that reason, Roger may use self-defensive force against my attempt to kill him. More dramatically, I would be justified in using self-defensive force, even deadly force, against attacks by an in-

55. Originally, the section on consent was slated to appear in article 3 of the Code, on "general principles of justification." See Tentative Draft No. 8, § 3.11 (1958). In the final version, it was placed in article 2, as § 2.11. For more on consent, see infra § 11.

56. According to the drafters, however, justifications don't match up perfectly with the analogous privileges. Sometimes they are broader, and sometimes narrower. Commentaries art. 3, introduction, at 2. A further complication is that consent for purposes of determining the unlawfulness of force differs from consent as a defense to criminal liability. Commentaries, § 3.11, 157–59.

57. On the excuses of duress, insanity, and infancy, see infra §§ 13 & 17.

sane person (i.e., someone who qualifies for the excuse of mental disease or defect[58]) or a child (i.e., someone excused by reason of immaturity[59]).

Note that the Code here allows, in fact justifies, the use of self-defensive force against conduct that would not be punishable. In other words, I may kill someone in self-defense with impunity whom the state could not subject to any punishment whatsoever, however slight. In fact, the Code justifies the use of self-defensive force even against conduct that's not punishable because it isn't even facially criminal (as opposed to facially criminal, but excused). For unlawful force—and therefore force against which I am justified in defending myself—includes not only force that "constitutes an offense," but also force that "would constitute such offense ... except for a defense ... such as the absence of intent [or] negligence." In other words, I am justified in using self-defensive force even if the person threatening me lacks the requisite mental state to match the definition of a criminal offense. As long as the "attacker" engaged in the proscribed *conduct*, even if without mens rea of any kind, not even negligence, I am justified in using self-defensive force, including deadly force where appropriate. So, for instance, I may shoot the driver of a car that is about to hit me at high speed, even if I know the driver wasn't negligent in any way, and obeyed the traffic laws to the letter: "Whatever may be thought in tort, it cannot be regarded as a crime to safeguard an innocent person, whether the actor or

58. § 4.01.
59. § 4.10.

another, against threatened death or injury that is unprivileged, even though the source of the threat is *free from fault*."[60] In this case, perfectly lawful conduct is treated as unlawful. Commenting on this sleight of hand, the drafters remarked with characteristic pragmatism that "[i]f the resulting concept is an awkward one, the difficulty is outweighed by the drafting advantages that it entails."[61]

Note also that the Code justifies self-defense against tortious, but noncriminal, force. Force is unlawful as long as it "constitutes an ... actionable tort," or—once again—"*would* constitute such ... tort except for a defense ... such as the absence of intent ... or negligence." Including tortious, and not only criminal, conduct in the definition of "unlawful force" would make sense if one thinks of unlawfulness as violation of the law, generally speaking, rather than merely of the criminal law. This is a useful way of making sense of unlawfulness, and of justifications, as it places the criminal statute violated within the context of the criminal law, which is in turn assigned its place within law. Justified conduct then would be conduct that violates a criminal statute, but does not conflict with the purposes of law, including the prevention of certain types of harm, criminal or not. Such an

60. Commentaries § 3.11, at 159 (emphasis added).

61. Id. The alternative of treating this scenario as a case of necessity wasn't available because the balance of evils wouldn't come out in my favor—I would sacrifice the driver's life for my own. Necessity as an excuse also wouldn't apply since the Code steadfastly denies a defense in cases of circumstantial, rather than personal, duress. See infra § 13.

account of justification, and unlawfulness, however, would have required a general theory of law, and of the criminal law within it, which the Code drafters, perhaps wisely, did not set out.

By limiting self-defense to unlawful force, rather than unjustified force, the Code drafters avoided the need to draw a sharp line between justification and excuse. The problem of demarcating the boundaries of self-defense, however, is thereby merely shifted from the definition of justification to that of unlawfulness. And that definition in the Code is so broad, and so non-committal, including cryptic references to the law of torts (and even the concept of "intent," shunned elsewhere in the Code), that it cannot bear the doctrinal weight the drafters assigned to it, or at least can bear it no better than an attempt to differentiate justification from excuse.

The need for clarity on the issue of unlawfulness—or justification—comes into focus, for instance, when we consider whether I am justified in using self-(or other-) defensive force against someone who mistakenly believes in her right to use self-defensive force against me or another person, i.e., someone who acts in "putative" self-defense. Under the Code's approach, if the use of force in putative self-defense is not "unlawful," then I wouldn't be justified in defending myself against it. So if my friend, mistaking me for my evil twin, and so my hugging him for an assault, punches me in self-defense, would I be justified in protecting myself against his attack?

JUSTIFICATION

The definition of "unlawful force" asks whether my friend's assault on me is entitled to "a privilege to use the force." The closest thing to a "privilege" in criminal law is a justification. Was my friend justified? That's not clear. While the Code "treats in *justification* sections those cases in which an actor mistakenly perceives the circumstances or the necessity for force," the drafters also recognized that in some cases of putative self-defense, "the actor is really offering an *excuse* for his conduct rather than a full-fledged justification."[62]

The Code's treatment of justifications thus isn't much help. Since privilege is a tort law concept, perhaps we should turn to the law of torts instead. And indeed, leaving the Code and its commentaries behind altogether, we learn that the Restatement of Torts extends a "privilege" even to cases of putative self-defense, provided the mistake about the conditions for the use of self-defensive force was "reasonable."[63] What does reasonable mean here? Should we stick with the law of torts, or shift our inquiry back to the law of crimes? According to the Restatement of Torts, "reasonably believes" means "that the actor believes that a given fact or combination of facts exists, and that the circumstances

---

62. Commentaries art. 3, introduction, at 2–3 (emphases added). Note that the drafters of the MPC-based proposed new federal criminal code classified every case of putative self-defense as an excuse, along with any other case involving a mistake regarding the conditions of a justification or excuse. Proposed New Fed. Crim. Code § 608 (1971); see also State v. Leidholm, 334 N.W.2d 811 (N.D.1983) (interpreting N.D. Crim. Code § 12.1–05–08, based on § 608).

63. Restatement (Second) of Torts § 890, cmt. f.

which he knows, or should know, are such as to cause a reasonable man so to believe."[64] Under the Model Code, "reasonably believes" refers to "a belief which the actor is not reckless or negligent in holding."[65]

So, even if we're not clear on whether my friend's putative self-defense amounted to a justification under the Model Code, it would appear that I would not be justified in protecting myself by force against his attack. He would have been entitled to a tort privilege, and therefore would not have used "unlawful force" against me.[66]

We've noted above that the Code's definition of unlawfulness, rather than referring to justifications generally, instead cites a specific example, consent, and a general tort analogue, privilege. Other examples would include not only obvious candidates—like the "justifications" listed in the Code itself, necessity, public duty, defense of self, others, or property, law enforcement, and special responsibility—but also the concept of "claim of right," which pops up at crucial points throughout the Code's

64. Id. § 11.

65. § 1.13(16).

66. My saving grace, however, would be that it would now be my turn to rely on putative self-defense. For now *I* could claim that I believed that my friend was the one using unlawful force against *me*, since his assault in response to my hug came as a total—and unpleasant—surprise to me, so that I was now justified in protecting myself. For what matters in the end, at least under the Code, is not whether the force that I matched with force in self-defense *was* unlawful, but whether I believed it was.

sections on defense of self, other, and property.[67]

Before we move on to another condition for self-defense, it's important to note an exception to the general rule that protective force is justified against "unlawful force." When the justification of self-defense collides with that of law enforcement, the latter takes precedence. Contrary to the law of torts, the Code does not recognize a justification for the use of force against an unlawful arrest.[68] An arrestee's belief in the unlawfulness of an arrest is simply irrelevant. He will not be justified in defending himself against it either way.[69]

(E) Immediacy and Protection

By abandoning the explicit requirement of choosing the lesser of two evils, the self-defense justifica-

67. In general, protective force is not justified against force used by another person acting under a claim of right, i.e., under the claim that she is acting lawfully in protection of her right to property. See §§ 3.04(2)(a)(ii) (self-defense); 3.06(1)(b)(ii), (2)(c), (3)(d)(i), (6)(a) (protection of property).

68. § 3.04(2)(a)(i); Commentaries § 3.04, at 42 (citing Restatement (Second) of Torts § 67). On the flipside, the Code also exempts police attempting to make an arrest from the general retreat requirement imposed upon the use of *deadly* self-defensive force, even if the arrest is unlawful. The tort privilege, by contrast, is limited to lawful arrests. § 3.04(2)(b)(ii)(B); Commentaries § 3.04, at 57 (citing Restatement (Second) of Torts § 65(2)(c)).

69. The *arrester's* criminal liability for making an arrest *she* doesn't believe to be lawful is another matter. Cf. §§ 3.07(1) ("lawful arrest"); 3.09(1)(a) (mistake as to lawfulness of arrest). Plus, the separate offense of "resisting arrest" under the Code still requires a "lawful arrest." § 242.2; cf. People v. Peacock, 68 N.Y.2d 675 (1986).

tion exceeds the bounds of the necessity defense. At the same time, the Code restricts the scope of self-defense by limiting it to protection against *unlawful* attacks. Also, unlike the necessity provision, self-defense is limited to *immediate* necessity, presumably to exclude preventive strikes under the guise of self-*defense*. One of the distinctions between self-defense and necessity is, after all, that the former is *only* defensive, whereas the former may be, and often is, offensive.[70]

Defensive, however, doesn't mean retrospective. Self-defensive force is by nature preventive, and therefore prospective. The point is to *protect* one's self, or someone else's self, or one's property, against future harm, not to retaliate for past harm, or even for past threats of harm. As Blackstone already explained, "if the person assaulted does not fall upon the aggressor till the affray is over, or when he is running away, this is revenge and not defence."[71] Fear is justifiable, anger not.[72]

70. Note, however, that the Code does not limit the use of force to immediate (or "imminent") threats of violence. Instead the attack must occur, or be feared to occur, on the "present occasion." This formulation is meant to be more generous than the traditional imminence requirement, by justifying the use of self-defensive force, for instance, "to prevent an assailant from going to summon reinforcements, given a belief that it is necessary to disable him to prevent an attack by overwhelming numbers." Commentaries § 3.04, at 39–40. Whether cases of this sort couldn't also be reached under a flexible reading of an imminence requirement is another question.

71. 4 William Blackstone, Commentaries on the Laws of England 185 (1769).

72. See Weston v. State, 682 P.2d 1119 (Alaska 1984).

(F) Self– and Other–Defense

Self-defense is limited to force used by a person to protect "himself" (or herself), rather than someone, or something, else. The right to protect someone or something else is handled in separate provisions, which we won't spend much time discussing. Section 3.05, dealing with protection of some*one* else doesn't require separate attention because the drafters decided, wisely, to treat the issue of other-defense in analogy to that of self-defense. In the succinct phrase of the Commentaries, "the rules are the same as those that govern self-defense."[73] That is, I'll be justified in defending another against a third person if I, placing myself in the other's shoes, would have been justified in defending myself against that third person. Tricky cases involving Good—but mistaken—Samaritans who come to the aid of the wrong party in a dispute are handled just as any other mistake about the conditions of justification. If they're reasonable, they make a complete defense. If they're not, they make at least an incomplete defense against crimes that require more than recklessness or negligence, but don't work against crimes that don't.[74]

It's perhaps noteworthy, however, that the Code abandons any attempt to limit the class of third persons whom one would be justified in defending. Unlike the common law, which limited it to certain

73. Commentaries § 3.05, at 62–63.

74. Id. at 65–66. The common law wasn't always so kind. See, e.g., Wood v. State, 128 Ala. 27 (1900) (third-party defender "enter[s] combat at his own peril").

individuals who stand in a special relationship to the actor—relatives, superiors, subordinates[75]—the justification of vicarious self-defense under the Code applies to any person whatsoever ("person of another").

§ 9.2 Defense of Property

The connection between self-defense and defense of property isn't quite as obvious as that between defense of self and defense of other persons. Still, a connection exists. The most important point about the Code's treatment of the right to use force in protection of property is that the right to property cannot trump the right to life.[76] As the Commentaries explain:

> [T]he general principle of the section is quite easy to state, though the drafting of it proved complex. The basic judgment that is reflected is that "the preservation of life has such moral and ethical standing in our culture and society, that the deliberate sacrifice of life merely for the protection of property ought not to be sanctioned by law."[77]

Pouring this "general principle" into statutory form turned out to be so "complex," and the result-

---

75. 4 William Blackstone, Commentaries on the Laws of England 186 (1769) ("the principal civil and natural relations"); see also Restatement (Second) of Torts § 76, cmt. (e).

76. Defense of property tracks defense of person in another way. Just as defense of another's person is handled analogously to defense of my person, so defense of another's property is handled analogously to defense of my property. There is, however, no separate section dealing with defense of another's property. § 3.06 (1)(a); Commentaries § 3.06, at 79.

77. Commentaries § 3.06, at 72 (quoting ALI Proceedings 285–86 (1958)) (statement of Herbert Wechsler).

JUSTIFICATION 219

ing section so convoluted, because the principle proved less universal than the drafters, and Herbert Wechsler in particular, had thought.[78] Several ALI members stressed the need to draft a Code that did not drift too far afield of "basic sentiments of the community"[79] and "popular sentiment"[80] reflected in a string of precedent clearly recognizing a basic right of every "householder"[81] to defend himself and "the members of his household"[82] against the paradigmatic nighttime burglar. Criminal law could not deny a man the right to "protection of his person and of his family,"[83] when confronted with blatant attacks on his home, or so the criticism went.

In response, Wechsler could do little more than reassert the contested principle. When pressed to provide arguments in its support, he replied, with uncharacteristic resignation: "I suppose that this is a kind of proposition that cannot be demonstrated, that involves in the end one's convictions. And one either holds convictions or one does not."[84] Appar-

78. The controversy at the ALI annual meeting on this section is documented in a student note from the time, Note, The Use of Deadly Force in the Protection of Property Under the Model Penal Code, 59 Colum. L. Rev. 1212 (1959).

79. Id. at 1223.

80. Id. at 1224 n.64.

81. Id. at 1223 n.56.

82. Id. at 1216.

83. Id. at 1216 n.19.

84. Id. at 1222 n.54 (quoting ALI Proceedings 285–86 (1958)).

ently, many ALI members did not. Just what changes the critics advocated, however, was less than obvious. An exacerbated Wechsler remarked at the end of the meeting, "I can only say on behalf of the Reporter that I hope the transcript will indicate to me what it is that I am supposed to do."[85]

What Wechsler ended up doing was to make some changes to the section while retaining the "general principle." The Commentaries neatly summarize the doctrinal core of the section on defense of property, in its proposed as well as in its final form:

> The general principle of the section is that moderate but not deadly force may be used to defend property against caption or trespass, with specific exceptions allowing the use of deadly force in certain instances.[86]

Most significant for our purposes, the revised section included a provision specifically dedicated to the "use of deadly force" in defense of property, laying out the two "specific exceptions" to the general rule that life could not be sacrificed for property:

> Use of Deadly Force. The use of deadly force is not justifiable under this Section unless the actor believes that:
>
> (i) the person against whom the force is used is attempting to dispossess him of his dwelling otherwise than under a claim of right to its possession; or

---

85. Id. at 1223 n.59 (quoting ALI Proceedings 325 (1958)).

86. Commentaries § 3.06, at 72.

(ii) the person against whom the force is used is attempting to commit or consummate arson, burglary, robbery or other felonious theft or property destruction and either:

(1) has employed or threatened deadly force against or in the presence of the actor; or

(2) the use of force other than deadly force to prevent the commission or the consummation of the crime would expose the actor or another in his presence to substantial danger of serious bodily harm.[87]

Subsection (d)(i), dealing with the use of deadly force to prevent being kicked out of one's own home by anyone not acting under a claim of right, already appeared in the first draft of the section.[88]

Subsection (d)(ii) was new, but added nothing. Although it extends the right to use deadly force to prevent property crimes with one hand, it limits it to cases of personal threat with the other.[89] The right to use deadly force in the protection of persons, however, had never been in doubt, and is spelled out in the two preceding sections, 3.04 (self-defense) and, by analogy, 3.05 (other-defense).[90] As the Mississippi Supreme Court explained already in 1883:

87. § 3.06(3)(d).

88. See Tentative Draft No. 8, § 3.06(2)(b) (1958).

89. See generally Commentaries § 3.06, at 91–97.

90. Contrast N.Y. Penal Law § 35.20 (right to use deadly force to prevent arson or burglary without showing of personal threat); see N.Y. Penal Law § 35.25 (no right to use deadly force to prevent larceny or criminal mischief).

No man is required by law to yield possession of his property to the unlawful claim of another. He may defend his possession; and while he may not kill to prevent the trespass, he may kill to protect his own person against a deadly assault made by the trespasser on him. In other words, one who assaults a trespasser to prevent the injury threatened is the actor but not the aggressor in the difficulty, and he does not lose the right of self-defence because he makes the attack.[91]

The Code's approach to the use of force, and deadly force in particular, in defense of property is exemplified by its handling of spring guns and similar devices. Their use is justifiable under Code only if they do not amount to the use of deadly force against intruders.[92] Given the general principle that life cannot be sacrificed for the sake of property, this comes as no surprise. As subsection (d)(ii) makes clear, using deadly force against an intruder is justifiable only to prevent death or serious bodily harm to one or more persons. A machine, however, is not a person, nor can it assess whether, under the circumstances, a person interfering with, or threatening to interfere with, my right to property also poses a threat to myself or others.[93] In fact, insofar as spring guns and the like are set up to protect property in the absence of its possessor, devices of this kind are by their nature inconsistent with the

91. Ayers v. State, 60 Miss. 709 (1883):

92. Compare § 3.06(5)(a) with § 3.11(2).

93. Cf. People v. Ceballos, 12 Cal.3d 470 (1974).

Code's limitation of deadly force to the defense of possessors, rather than of their possessions.

§ 9.3 Deadly Force

The use of deadly force against attacks on myself or another is justified if certain additional requirements, beyond those imposed on self-defensive force generally speaking, are met. In other words, there is no general principle prohibiting the sacrifice of one life to save another, or to protect myself—or another—against certain nonlethal harm, including "serious bodily harm, kidnapping or sexual intercourse compelled by force or threat."

The deadly force issue is central to the law of self-defense. In fact, the recognition of self-defense as a general defense applicable to any offense is a fairly recent development. Historically, self-defense was an issue not for the general part, but for the special part of Anglo–American criminal law. More specifically, self-defense was an issue in the law of homicide.[94] Self-defense was a defense *only* in cases involving the use of deadly force. Even today, the vast bulk of self-defense cases—and law school hypotheticals—deal with self-defense as a defense against homicide, and yet more specifically, against murder.

Having said that, it's important to note that the Model Penal Code defines deadly force more broadly than homicidal force. Deadly force under the Code also includes the purposeful, knowing, or reckless (but not negligent) use of force that, if applied

---

94. Self-defense's excuse analogue, provocation, has remained there to this day. See infra § 16.

successfully, would result not in death but in "serious bodily harm," and therefore in liability for aggravated assault,[95] rather than for homicide.[96]

The basic rule governing the use of deadly force is that it may be used if, in addition to the general conditions for self-defense already discussed, "the actor believes that such force is necessary to protect himself against death, serious bodily harm, kidnapping or sexual intercourse compelled by force or threat." The nature of the threat thus determines the nature of the justified response. The response must be proportional to the threat, but it need not be equivalent. I may use deadly force to prevent not only death, but also lesser—though still serious—harm to myself, or another.

The general requirement of proportionality between threat and response is familiar from the common law, though the requirement was looser than it is in the Model Code, requiring the threat of force, rather than of deadly force. Blackstone, for instance, stressed that homicide—the successful use of deadly force—is justified if "committed for the *prevention* of any forcible and atrocious *crime*," though not of "any crime unaccompanied with force."[97] In fact, Blackstone claimed that "the one

95. § 211.1(2).

96. § 3.11(2). Aggravated assault, not simple assault, because the potential of nonserious physical harm isn't enough, nor is the threat of serious physical harm.

97. 4 William Blackstone, Commentaries on the Laws of England 180 (1769). Examples of forcible and atrocious crimes include robbery, murder, burglary (at night), arson, and rape. Id. at 180–81. Other cases of self-defense, not "calculated to hinder

uniform principle that runs through our own, and all other laws, seems to be this: that where a crime, in itself capital, is endeavoured to be committed by force, it is lawful to repel that force by the death of the party attempting."[98]

Elsewhere, however, Blackstone suggests a different proportionality requirement altogether, namely that between *punishment*—not threat—and response, thus highlighting the connection between self-defense and what we now call the justification of law enforcement, to be discussed shortly: "the law of England, like that of every other well-regulated community, is too tender of the public peace, too careful of the lives of the subjects, to ... suffer with impunity any crime to be *prevented* by death, unless the same, if committed, would also be *punished* by death."[99] In this reading, self-defense would be private law enforcement, i.e., law enforcement without the necessary involvement of a "peace officer."[100]

In addition to the general, if implicit, requirement of proportionality between serious threat and deadly response, the Code imposes several other constraints on the use of deadly force. It's important to

the perpetration of a capital crime," constituted not justifiable, but merely excusable, homicide. The paradigm of homicide *se defendendo* was the "*chance-medley*," featuring "a man [who] may protect himself from an assault, or the like, in the course of a sudden brawl or quarrel, by killing him who assaults him." Id. at 183–84.

98. Id. at 181.
99. Id. at 181–82.
100. § 3.07.

keep in mind that these additional limitations, just like the general limitation on the nature of the threat, apply to the use of deadly force only. They do not apply to the use of nondeadly self-defensive force.

The first provision denies the right to use deadly force to anyone who, "with the purpose of causing death or serious bodily harm, provoked the use of force against himself in the same encounter." Note that the Code does more than restate the traditional initial aggressor limitation on the right to use deadly force in self-defense. As in the case of necessity, the Code rejects the idea that anyone who is not without fault in creating the conditions giving rise to a justification thereby forfeits that justification.[101] So if I should pick a fight with a fellow driver over a traffic incident, I would not automatically be precluded from claiming the right to self-defense later in the encounter. If, at some point, my fellow motorist raises the stakes by pulling a gun out of his pants pocket and firing it at me, I will be justified in using deadly force—by retrieving my very own firearm from the glove compartment—to protect myself, *unless* I started the altercation "with the purpose of causing death or serious bodily harm," rather than, say, of punching the victim of my road rage in the nose.

If the victim of my initial aggression escalates the struggle to the level of deadly force, I will be justified, under the Code, in using deadly force in re-

[101]. See supra § 8. Cf. 4 William Blackstone, Commentaries on the Laws of England 186 (1769).

sponse. Because now it's he who is the one using unlawful force by responding, excessively, with deadly force to nondeadly force. He's now using not only unlawful force, but unlawful *deadly* force against me, which turns the justificatory tables entirely by putting me in the position of being authorized to use not just force, but *deadly* force, in response.[102] I'm now the victim, and he the aggressor; I'm now in the right, and he's in the wrong.[103]

The initial aggressor (or forfeiture) rule in this way supplements the other exception to the justifiability of deadly force in self-defense, the retreat rule.[104] I cannot with justification use deadly force if I "know that [I] can avoid the necessity of using such force with complete safety by retreating." If, in our example, I could avoid having to return fire by speeding away, I wouldn't be justified in shoot-

102. I was entitled to use nondeadly, or "moderate," force from the beginning because the initial aggressor exception applies only to the use of deadly force. I can use moderate force to defend myself against an attack that I provoked, provided of course the attack is unlawful, as for instance a punch thrown in anger over a verbal insult.

103. See the classic case of Rowe v. United States, 164 U.S. 546 (1896). There the eventual homicide victim, a white man named Frank Bozeman, provoked a Cherokee by the name of David Cul Rowe by a racial slur into a minor assault (which was concededly unlawful and wrongful, however understandable), to which Bozeman responded with the use of deadly force, prompting the use of deadly force by Rowe in turn, resulting in Bozeman's death. The Court held that Rowe, though the initial aggressor, was not precluded from justifying his use of deadly force on grounds of self-defense.

104. See generally Joseph H. Beale, Retreat from a Murderous Assault, 16 Harv. L. Rev. 567 (1903).

ing even after having been shot at, provided I could get away "with complete safety," and I knew I could. The flipside of the retreat rule now is that, once I *have* retreated as far as I could ("to the wall," in the language of the common law), I'm justified in using deadly force. This is so, under the Model Code, even if I was the original aggressor—once again, in deviation from much common law authority.[105]

It being a general rule, however, also means that the retreat requirement applies to anyone wishing to justify the use of deadly force in self-defense, not just to initial aggressors. It's a familiar rule from the common law, which—once again concerned with the paradigmatic case of "combat"—required that anyone claiming self-defense "must show, that before a mortal stroke given, he had declined any farther combat, and retreated as far as he could with safety."[106]

Just what the retreat rule adds to the necessity requirement, which is all over the Code's section on self-defense, isn't clear. If a person can "protect[] himself against the use of unlawful force by [an]other person on the present occasion" by retreating, then "the use of force upon or toward another person" is *not* "immediately necessary." And if no force of any kind would be necessary, then *deadly*

[105]. Cf. Stoffer v. State, 15 Ohio St. 47 (1864); Rowe v. United States, 164 U.S. 546 (1896).

[106]. General Summary of Crimes, and Their Punishments, in 2 Laws of the Commonwealth of Pennsylvania 558, 571 (1810).

force certainly wouldn't be necessary either. The drafters, however, preferred to view the possibility of safe retreat as distinct from necessity, partly because "all agree" that the use of *nondeadly* force can be "necessary" even though safe retreat would be possible, allowing the actor to "stand his ground and estimate necessity upon that basis."[107] Not so in the case of deadly self-defensive force, however. Here necessity still doesn't require the absence of retreat options as a matter of "logic"; the retreat requirement instead flows from the Code's placing "a high value on the preservation of life."[108] Joseph Beale, in 1903, expressed the basic sentiment underlying the duty to retreat with unusual force, and even a touch of pathos:

> A really honorable man, a man of truly refined and elevated feeling, would perhaps always regret the apparent cowardice of a retreat, but he would regret ten times more, after the excitement of the contest was past, the thought that he had the blood of a fellow-being on his hands. It is undoubtedly distasteful to retreat; but it is ten times more distasteful to kill.[109]

Even in deadly force cases, however, the retreat rule is not without its exceptions. The first excep-

107. Commentaries § 3.04, at 53.

108. Id. at 55.

109. Joseph H. Beale, Retreat from a Murderous Assault, 16 Harv. L. Rev. 567, 581 (1903). Beale went on to favorably compare these sentiments of a cultivated gentleman (like himself) with the "talk of dishonor and cowardice" by "the border-ruffian, who walks about the earth with one hand on his hip-pocket." Id. at 582.

tion to the retreat exception to the justifiability of deadly force in defense against "death, serious bodily harm, kidnapping or sexual intercourse compelled by force or threat" is the house-or-work exception. There's no need to retreat if I'm attacked at home,[110] or at work. This exception, however, has its own set of exceptions: (1) I have to retreat at home *or* at work if I was the initial aggressor[111] and (2) I have to retreat at work if I was attacked by someone I recognize as a coworker (but, unlike in some jurisdictions, not if I was attacked at home by a cohabitant).[112]

Besides the house-or-work exception—with its various sub-exceptions—to the retreat requirement, there is the police (or "public officer") exception. So, for instance, a police officer may kill someone who resists arrest, rather than abandoning her efforts and leaving the arrest for another, better, day, even if safe retreat is possible.[113] Note, however, that the other constraints on the use of deadly force remain; the police exception is only an exception to the retreat exception to the familiar rule justifying the use of deadly force under certain, limited, cir-

110. More precisely, in my "dwelling," defined generously as "any building or structure, though movable or temporary, or a portion thereof, that is for the time being the actor's home or place of lodging." § 3.11(3).

111. Which one would have thought to be covered by the initial aggressor exception, § 3.04(2)(b)(i).

112. See, e.g., N.D. Crim. Code § 12.1–05–07(2)(b) (discussed in State v. Leidholm, 334 N.W.2d 811 (N.D.1983)).

113. And even if she is making an unlawful arrest. Commentaries § 3.04, at 57.

cumstances. Even a police officer, and his private helper, therefore can use deadly force against an arrest resister only if he "believes that such force is necessary to protect himself against death, serious bodily harm, kidnapping or sexual intercourse."[114]

§ 10 Law Enforcement

The general justification for the use of force in making an arrest appears in section 3.07. Arrests, after all, generally imply the use of force, even in the absence of affirmative resistance by the arrestee and beyond the right of the arrester to use force in self-defense, which is handled in section 3.04.[115] Viewed in this light, the Code provision on law enforcement resembles other justification sections dealing with types of conduct that are as commonplace as they are facially criminal, "Execution of Public Duty"[116] and "Use of Force by Persons with

114. For a case that nicely illustrates the interplay of the rules governing the use of force, deadly and moderate, in defense of one's property and of one's person, including the initial aggressor rule and the duty to retreat, see United States v. Peterson, 483 F.2d 1222 (D.C.Cir.1973).

115. The arrest itself, which constitutes facially criminal conduct even if made without force (e.g., kidnapping (§ 212.1), false imprisonment (§ 212.3)), is justifiable under section 3.03, execution of public duty.

116. Justifying "the policeman who exceeds posted speed limits in apprehending a fugitive, the marshal who trespasses to execute a warrant, the sheriff who seizes property to satisfy the judgment of a court," Commentaries § 3.03, at 23, and, to cite the typical case invoked in common law sources, the executioner, who "in the *execution* of public justice, ... put[s] a malefactor to death, who hath forfeited his life by the laws and verdict of his

Special Responsibility for Care, Discipline or Safety of Others."[117]

The first thing the law enforcement section does then is explain why—and ensure that—arrests are justified, and therefore not punishable, even though they may formally constitute an assault.[118] Note here, once again, that an arrest is justified—and thus not unlawful—even if it's in fact unlawful.[119] I'm justified in using force incident to an arrest even if the arrest turns out to have been unlawful (because I lack probable cause, in case of a warrantless arrest, or because the warrant turns out to be no good), as long as I believe in the lawfulness of the arrest. Armed with this belief—subject to the familiar provisos regarding reckless and negligent mistakes, and the irrelevance of mistakes of law[120] —I can use force (that I believe to be) "immediately necessary" to make the arrest. The justification for using force is complete when the (belief in the) immediate necessity of using it and the (belief in the) lawfulness of the arrest are joined by the

country." 4 William Blackstone, Commentaries on the Laws of England 178 (1769) (emphasis added). On the Code's ambiguous stance on capital punishment, see supra § 2.2 n.27.

117. Justifying, among others, parents who punish their children, and wardens their inmates, as well as surgeons who slice open their patients, all facial assaults, simple or aggravated. § 3.08.

118. Under a suitably broad definition of assault as any touching, every arrest is an assault. The Code's definition is more narrow. See § 211.1.

119. Commentaries § 3.07, at 107–09.

120. § 3.09(1); but see § 2.04(3).

arrestee's actual, or constructive, notice of "the purpose of the arrest," i.e., my reason for subjecting her to otherwise criminal conduct, particularly assault. This notice requirement too is phrased broadly, requiring me to inform the suspect of the purpose of her arrest, unless I believe that purpose "is otherwise known" or "cannot reasonably be made known" to her.[121]

Before we get to the details, two characteristics of the Code's law enforcement provision are worth noting. First, it deals with "law enforcement," not with law enforcement officials, or, put another way, with law enforcement as an activity rather than as an institution. It applies to anyone, any "actor," police officer or not. The justification for the use of force in an arrest springs not from the occupation, or special status, or the person using it, but from the purpose for which it is used—namely law enforcement. This point is as crucial as it is easily forgotten.

Second, the law enforcement section deals almost exclusively with arrests.[122] It thus focuses on defin-

121. § 3.09(2)(a)(i).

122. Other facially criminal conduct by state officials—including the use of force unrelated to an arrest, or criminal conduct not involving the use of force (such as searches and seizures of property)—is justified under use of force in crime prevention (§ 3.07(5)), the other topic addressed in the section on law enforcement, and execution of public duty (§ 3.03). State officials of course also are entitled to the same justifications available to all persons, most importantly self-defense (and defense of another). Plus, the Model Code section on self-defense includes certain special—and more generous—provisions applicable to state officials. See, e.g., § 3.04(2)(a)(ii)(1) & (2)(b)(ii)(2)

ing the justificatory limits placed upon the use of force in a particular, and particularly central, aspect of law enforcement, one that involves the use of force almost by definition and raises the specter of additional force by experience, given the tendency of many suspects to resist becoming arrestees, triggering the need to subdue them in return.

Defining the justifiability of using force to arrest in terms of "immediate necessity" is familiar from the Code's self-defense provision, and so is the two-pronged layout of the provision on "the use of force in law enforcement," one dealing with force, the other with deadly force. Also, as in self-defense, things don't really get interesting until the second prong, the one dealing with the use of deadly force.

Like self-defense, law enforcement places additional constraints on the use of deadly force, supplementing the general limitation on the use of force, period—that the actor believe the force to be "immediately necessary to effect a lawful arrest," plus actual, or constructive, notice. These supplemental constraints are straightforward, and eminently quotable:

(i) the arrest is for a felony; and

(ii) the person effecting the arrest is authorized to act as a peace officer or is assisting a person whom he believes to be authorized to act as a peace officer; and

(iii) the actor believes that the force employed creates no substantial risk of injury to innocent persons; and

(iv) the actor believes that:

(1) the crime for which the arrest is made involved conduct including the use or threatened use of deadly force; or

(2) there is a substantial risk that the person to be arrested will cause death or serious bodily harm if his apprehension is delayed.[123]

These constraints on the use of deadly force to make an arrest have since been constitutionalized, in *Tennessee v. Garner*.[124] The Model Code, and *Garner*, did away with the old common law rule which permitted the use of deadly force to arrest any felon, where felony in turn was (often) defined in terms of its prescribed punishment, death.[125] Using death to arrest a felon, then, was justifiable because it merely accelerated the criminal process.[126] Whatever sense this rule made at a time

123. § 3.07(2)(b). As the Commentaries stress, the use of deadly force by the arrester may be justified on other grounds, including self-defense or defense of others. This provision deals only with cases where no justification for using deadly force other than law enforcement, and more specifically, law enforcement through an arrest, is available. The question is when a police officer may use deadly force to effect an arrest, period.

124. 471 U.S. 1 (1985).

125. Blackstone disagreed, instead defining felony in terms of another punishment, forfeiture, and thereby making room for non-capital felonies. 4 William Blackstone, Commentaries on the Laws of England 94–97 (1769).

126. Provided, of course, the felon was indeed a felon. In the common law, greater authority to kill fleeing felons tended to go along with greater liability for killing a nonfelon. See, e.g., Petrie v. Cartwright, 70 S.W. 297 (Ky.App.1902) (officer using deadly

when all (or most) felonies were capital, it made even less sense when all (or most) felonies were no longer capital.

Still, the Code retains the limitation of deadly force to felonies. The commission, or suspected commission, of a felony is no longer a sufficient condition for the use of deadly force to arrest, but it's still necessary. The only difference is that, in the Code, the commission of a felony, without more, is an insufficient indicator of the offender's criminal disposition, or dangerousness, the central factor in the justifiability of deadly force:

> [T]he character of the offender as it can be inferred from the available information, rather than from an abstract classification of the offense he is thought to have committed, should be determinative as to the use of deadly force. Specifically, the judgment is that the use of deadly force should be sanctioned only in cases where the offender is thought to pose such a danger to life or limb that his immediate apprehension overrides competing considerations.[127]

So the Code limits the justifiability of deadly force to certain felonies, namely those which "involved conduct including the use or threatened use of deadly force." In this way, the Code maintains a certain proportionality, but now—as in the case of self-defense—between the act to be justified and the offense, rather than the *punishment* for the offense.

force to arrest suspected felon "does so at his peril" and "must proceed very cautiously").

127. Commentaries § 3.07, at 119–20.

Alternatively, even if no fatal, or potentially, fatal felony was committed, the Code permits the use of deadly force as an incapacitative measure if—in the absence of evidence in the form of a suspected crime already committed—there "is a substantial risk that the person to be arrested will cause death or serious bodily harm if his apprehension is delayed."

Note that when it comes to deadly force, the distinction between police ("law enforcement") and others becomes decisive. Only a "peace officer,"[128] or someone (who believes she is) assisting a peace officer, may use deadly force to arrest.

And, finally, the Code denies even a peace officer the right to use deadly force to arrest unless she believes doing so won't create a substantial risk of "injury" to innocent bystanders. This means that she will have no defense if she believed that using deadly force would in fact create such a risk (i.e., she acted recklessly)[129] or held no particular belief on the matter, perhaps because she was unaware of the risk (i.e., she may have acted negligently). This provision is meant to "emphasiz[e] and articulat[e] the priority that law enforcement personnel ought to accord to safeguarding innocent persons against injury from deadly force directed against persons fleeing from arrest."[130] It sends this message by

---

128. The Code doesn't define peace officer. Just who counts as a peace officer isn't necessarily a simple matter. See People v. Marrero, 69 N.Y.2d 382 (1987).

129. Cf. N.Y. Penal Law § 35.30(2); see People v. Pena, 169 Misc.2d 75 (N.Y.Sup.Ct.1996).

130. Commentaries § 3.07, at 118.

compromising the general principle that anyone who acts with recklessness or negligence under conditions that otherwise would make out a justification be liable only for crimes of recklessness or negligence.

§ 11 Consent

The last justification that deserves a closer look before we turn our attention to the next, and final, level of analysis—excuses—is consent. Unlike the other justifications we've discussed up to this point, consent is not codified in article 3 of the Code, expressly dedicated to "General Principles of Justification." It appears in article 2 instead, dedicated to "General Principles of Liability," which includes not only provisions dealing with the first level of analysis (offense definition)—such as actus reus, mens rea, causation, complicity, and the like—but, as we'll see shortly, also codifies several level three defenses (excuses)—such as duress, military orders, and entrapment—as well as defenses that straddle two levels of analysis—such as mistake and intoxication, which, as we've seen already, appear both as level one (failure of proof) and level three defenses.

Consent finds a home in article 2 because, like mistake and intoxication, it stands with one foot in level one, the subject of the bulk of article 2. Unlike mistake and intoxication, however, its other foot rests in level two, rather than in level three. In other (Model Code) words, consent either "negatives an element of the offense" or it "precludes the infliction of the harm or evil sought to be prevented by the law defining the offense." Given consent's dual status as a failure of proof defense and a justification, it's no surprise that it started out in the article on justification (as section 3.11), but ended up in the article on principles of liability (as section 2.11).[131]

The provision on consent as a level one defense is as straightforward, and as redundant, as are the analogous provisions on mistake and intoxication. It should go without saying that consent would bar even facial criminal liability if it negatived an element of the offense: if the offense definition included the absence of consent, then the presence of consent would mean that the offense hadn't been committed. So, for instance, the Code defines joyriding as "operat[ing] another's automobile, airplane, motorcycle, motorboat, or other motor-propelled vehicle *without consent* of the owner,"[132] cruelty to animals as "kill[ing] or injur[ing] any animal belonging to another *without ... consent* of the owner,"[133] and violation of privacy as "install[ing] in any private place, *without the consent* of the person or persons entitled to privacy there, any device for observing, photographing, recording, amplifying or broadcasting sounds or events in such place, or uses any such unauthorized installation."[134] Similarly, rape traditionally has been defined as sexual inter-

131. See Tentative Draft No. 8, § 3.11 (1958).

132. § 223.9 (emphasis added).

133. § 250.11(3) (emphasis added).

134. § 250.12(1)(b) (emphasis added).

course "by force or threat of force against the will and *without the consent* of the other person."[135]

More interesting are cases where consent operates as a justification, rather than as a failure of proof defense.[136] The justificatory aspect of consent shines through in the reference to "the harm or evil sought to be prevented by the law defining the offense," which echoes the Code's formulation of the necessity defense as a justification for facially criminal conduct if "the harm or evil sought to be avoided by such conduct is greater than that sought to be prevented by the law defining the offense charged."[137]

Other traces of consent's justificationness are strewn about the Code.[138] Perhaps most important, consent occupies a central role in the Code's provision on the justification of the use of force in

135. Md. Crim. Code § 463(a)(1) (emphasis added). The Code defines rape as sexual intercourse by a male with "a female not his wife ... if he compels her to submit by force or by threat of imminent death, serious bodily injury, extreme pain or kidnapping, to be inflicted on anyone." (Yes, the Code retained the "marriage exemption," long since abandoned. See, e.g., People v. Liberta, 64 N.Y.2d 152 (1984).)

136. Rape, as defined in the Code, appears to be an example. Although the absence of consent doesn't appear in the Code's definition of rape, the Commentaries explain that "it is essential to the commission of the crime that there be an unwilling victim of the actor's conduct." Commentaries § 2.11, at 394.

137. § 3.02(1)(a).

138. So consent precludes a finding of unlawfulness, not only because the Code's definition of "unlawful force" says so, but also because it's a key "privilege," the tort analogue to a criminal justification. See supra § 9.1(d).

medical treatment, which requires, among other things, that the treatment be administered

> with the consent of the patient or, if the patient is a minor or an incompetent person, with the consent of his parent or guardian or other person legally competent to consent in his behalf, or the treatment is administered in an emergency when the actor believes that no one competent to consent can be consulted and that a reasonable person, wishing to safeguard the welfare of the patient, would consent.[139]

Just when the victim's consent "precludes the infliction of the harm of evil sought to be prevented by the law defining the offense" of course depends on one's view of the point of criminal law. If criminal law is designed to prevent harm inflicted on individuals, then consent would justify any facially criminal conduct. For if individuals are to be protected, then individuals should be entitled to waive that protection as well.

American criminal law, however, isn't only, or even primarily, about protecting persons against suffering harm or, if that fails, about punishing those who inflicted it. Recall that the Model Code defines crime as "conduct that unjustifiably and inexcusably inflicts or threatens substantial harm to individual *or public interests*," with a distinct emphasis on "public."[140] Of the interests recognized

139. § 3.08(4)(b).

140. This emphasis is nothing new. The vast bulk of Blackstone's discussion of substantive criminal law, the law of "public wrongs," is dedicated to offenses against public interests. Here is

by the Code drafters, only one, "the person" qualifies unequivocally as an individual interest. Even "property" the Code treats as a public interest, or a "system."[141] The remaining interests protected by the criminal law against harm are clearly public: "the existence or stability of the state,"[142] "the family," "public administration," "public order and decency," as well as the interests safeguarded by "miscellaneous offenses,"[143] such as those involving "narcotics," "alcoholic beverages," "gambling," and "offenses against tax and trade laws."

And so the consent defense in American criminal law, and in the Model Code, is not really a general defense. Having announced the general principle of consent as a justification, the Model Code proceeds to exclude cases involving the infliction of serious bodily injury.[144] The leading American criminal law

Blackstone's list of public wrongs, in order: Offences against God and Religion; Offences against the Law of Nations; High Treason; Felonies, injurious to the King's Prerogative; Praemunire ("maintaining the papal power"); Misprisions and Contempts, affecting the King and Government; Offences against Public Justice; Offences against the Public Peace; Offences against Public Trade; Offences against the Public Health, and the Public Police or Oeconomy; Homicide; Offences against the Persons of Individuals; Offences against Private Property. 4 William Blackstone, Commentaries on the Laws of England (1769).

141. Commentaries § 223.1, at 157 ("[p]ersons who take only property to which they believe themselves entitled *constitute no significant threat to the property system*") (emphasis added).

142. Model Penal Code 241 (Proposed Official Draft 1962).

143. Id.

144. The main exception to this exception is the boxing/hockey rule—"joint participation in a lawful athletic contest or competitive sport." § 2.11(2)(b). Some states have added a

treatise goes even farther, declaring that "[c]onsent by the victim is not a defense in a criminal prosecution."[145] The reason generally cited for limiting, or even rejecting, consent as a justification is that the criminal law, unlike torts, is about "public wrongs," not "private wrongs," a distinction familiar since at least Blackstone.[146] A "criminal offense is," we are told, "a wrong affecting the general public, at least indirectly, and consequently cannot be licensed by the individual directly harmed."[147] Similarly, we learn that "[t]he interest of the state is paramount and controls prosecutions ... [f]or it is the public, not a complainant, that is injured by the commission of a crime."[148]

Assuming that consent matters, either as a level one or as a level three defense, in a particular case, considerable doctrinal attention has been devoted to the secondary question of whether consent actually was present. The *law* on this central issue of *fact*—

potentially farreaching exception covering "reasonably foreseeable hazards of ... [t]he victim's occupation or profession." Rev. Stat. Mo. § 565.080 (1986); see State v. George, 937 S.W.2d 251 (Mo.App.1996) (hospital security guard).

145. Wayne R. LaFave & Austin W. Scott, Jr., Criminal Law 477 (2d ed. 1986).

146. See 4 William Blackstone, Commentaries on the Laws of England 5 ("public wrongs, or crimes and misdemeanors, are a breach and violation of the public rights and duties, due to the whole community, considered as a community, in its social aggregate capacity").

147. Wayne R. LaFave & Austin W. Scott, Jr., Criminal Law 477 (2d ed. 1986).

148. Id. at 481 (quoting People v. Brim, 199 N.Y.S.2d 744 (1960)).

was it *really* consent, or was it just "assent," or, alternatively, if it was consent, was that consent "effective"?—is fairly tedious, and the Code does a nice job of summarizing it. Not surprisingly, consent by those who aren't authorized to give it doesn't count; third-party consent isn't effective except in very few circumstances—such as in the cases of medical emergency mentioned above. Consent by those incapable of consenting, for one reason or another, is likewise irrelevant. Interestingly, the Code includes not only "youth, mental disease or defect"—that is, conditions that would make out the incapacity excuses of infancy or insanity[149]— among the reasons for an incapacity to consent, but intoxication as well.[150] Recall that intoxication does not make out an incapacity excuse unless it is not self-induced.[151] In other words, voluntary intoxication can make me incapable of consenting to someone else's crime, but not of committing a crime myself.

As one might expect, consent obtained by force or duress (another inability excuse) also won't do. Then there is consent induced by deception, more precisely by "deception of a kind sought to be prevented by the law defining the offense." This is the Code's attempt to make room for the common law distinction between, in good Law Latin, "fraud

149. See infra § 17.

150. "Improvident" consent is also ineffective. Here the drafters had in mind statutory rape. Commentaries § 2.11, at 398.

151. See supra § 4.3(a).

in the factum" and "fraud in the inducement." In short, consent obtained by fraud in the factum counts, consent induced by fraud in the inducement doesn't. If I get you to agree to let me install in your apartment what you think is a smoke detector, but which actually is a surveillance camera, then I'm still guilty of "violation of privacy," as defined by the Code as "install[ing] in any private place, without the consent of the person or persons entitled to privacy there, any device for observing, photographing, recording, amplifying or broadcasting sounds or events in such place."[152] That's because I perpetrated a fraud in the factum—I deceived you about a fact relevant to an element of the offense to which I claim you consented. You consented not to the installation of a "device for observing, photographing, recording, amplifying or broadcasting sounds or events," but of a smoke detector. Now imagine that I'm up front about installing a surveillance camera, but tell you—falsely—that I'm doing this as part of a science experiment at school. This time, I fooled you into consenting to what I was doing, as opposed to fooling you about what I was doing. I lied not about an element of the offense, but about a "collateral matter," a reason for committing the offense.

Instead of excluding consent obtained by a fraud in the factum—but not in the inducement—the Code excludes any "deception of a kind sought to be prevented by the law defining the offense." This provision isn't particularly helpful, however. There

152. § 250.12(1)(b).

are of course many offenses that aim to prevent all manner of deception, but presumably the drafters didn't just have those in mind.[153] It would seem that consent based on a fraud in the factum still wouldn't count, but not because it's a "deception of a kind sought to be prevented by the law defining the offense," but because the victim didn't really consent to the offense at all, since she wasn't aware of the fact that she was consenting to it, and in fact thought she was consenting to something different altogether.

153. See, e.g., § 210.5(1) (causing suicide), § 212.1 (kidnapping), § 220.3(1)(c) (criminal mischief), § 223.3 (theft by deception), § 223.7(1) (theft of services), art. 224 (forgery and fraudulent practices), § 241.6(1) (witness tampering).

Chapter 3

"Inexcusably"—Level Three

We have now arrived at the third, and last, step in our stroll through the analysis of criminal liability. To make it to this point in the inquiry, a case (hypothetical or real) already would have to clear two previous hurdles—facial criminality and unlawfulness. In Model Penal Code terms, the behavior in question would have to qualify as "conduct that inflicts or threatens substantial harm to individual or public interests" (level one). Put yet another way, the conduct would have to match the face of some criminal statute, satisfying each element in the offense definition it contains. Moreover, stepping outside the confines of the universe of offense definitions that constitutes the criminal law, we must have decided that this instance of prima facie criminality also qualified as unlawful, within the context of the law—criminal, civil, public, private—generally speaking (level two).

§ 12 Excuses in the Model Penal Code

Before we can impose criminal liability on the person who engaged in this concededly criminal and unlawful conduct, however, we need to check one more thing. We need to see if she can be held responsible for her conduct—whether she is blameworthy—taking into account her relevant personal characteristics as well as the relevant circumstances of her behavior in this particular case.

Here, as in its treatment of justifications, the Model Code speaks far more in terms of justice, and morality, than one might expect, given its single-minded effort to transform the criminal law into a system for the identification, diagnosis, and treatment of those displaying criminal dispositions of various of types and degrees. Consider, for instance, the following passage from the Commentaries on the duress excuse, which in no uncertain terms gives precedence to considerations of justice over those of deterrence, or of incapacitation for that matter:

> [L]aw is ineffective in the deepest sense, indeed that it is hypocritical, if it imposes on the actor who has the misfortune to confront a dilemmatic choice, a standard that his judges are not prepared to affirm that they should and could comply with if their turn to face the problem should arise. Condemnation in such a case is bound to be an ineffective threat; *what is, however, more significant is that it is divorced from any moral base and is unjust.*[1]

This much is true, but a reference to moral foundations and justice, without more, doesn't a theory of excuses make. There is no such theory in

1. Commentaries § 2.09, at 374–75 (emphasis added).

the Code, or the Commentaries, just as there is no theory of justifications. Perhaps the most that could be said about the Code's view of excuses in general is that they aren't justifications. So the Commentaries dismiss a provision in the Criminal Code of Western Australia recognizing a necessity defense under "such circumstances of sudden or extraordinary emergency that an ordinary person possessing ordinary power of self-control could not reasonably be expected to act otherwise" with the remark that it "deals with the matter as one rather of excuse than of justification."[2]

As the Commentaries explain, "[t]o say that someone's conduct is 'justified' ordinarily connotes that the conduct is thought to be right, or at least not undesirable." By contrast, "to say that someone's conduct is 'excused' ordinarily connotes that the conduct is thought to be undesirable but that *for some reason the actor is not to be blamed for it.*"[3] And all the Code's excuse provisions do is set out those reasons, one by one, without trying to reduce them to some common principle, except perhaps for the general, and unexplored, notion of blameworthiness. One promising candidate, the notion of avoidability, isn't recognized as such in the Code. The Code also makes occasional reference to fairness and responsibility.

Like justifications, excuses have an article of their own, article 4, entitled "responsibility." That article, however, is more underinclusive than its justifi-

2. Commentaries § 3.02, at 11 n.2.
3. Commentaries art. 3, introduction, at 3 (emphasis added).

cation analogue, article 3, which includes every justification other than consent. Article 4 instead deals with only two excuses, insanity and infancy. Other excuses appear in article 2, including ignorance of law and intoxication (which we already discussed), as well as duress, military orders, and entrapment.[4] Another excuse, provocation or extreme emotional disturbance, in Model Code language, doesn't appear in the general part at all. Limited to homicide, it is codified in the section of the special part dealing with that crime. Finally, the Commentaries acknowledge that, despite their treatment in the article on justifications, cases of putative self-defense—or of mistaken beliefs regarding the conditions of a justification generally—"might more precisely be labeled excuses" insofar as "in some of the cases, at least, it might be said that the actor is really offering an excuse for his conduct rather than a full-fledged justification."[5]

4. Of these three, only duress clearly qualifies as an excuse. Military orders can be a justification or an excuse, depending on whether one views the defense as a way to advance some general interest in the smooth functioning of the military (in which case it would appear as a justification) or on the uniquely coercive power a military order exerts upon its recipient (in which case it would look more like an excuse). Compare § 2.10 with Rules for Courts–Martial 916(d) (justification); United States v. Calley, 22 U.S.C.M.A. 534 (1973). Entrapment, as we'll see, won't be mistaken for a justification. Some jurisdictions instead appear to treat it as a level one defense relating to mens rea, akin to mistake, see, e.g., Jacobson v. United States, 503 U.S. 540 (1992) (state bears burden of disproving entrapment beyond a reasonable doubt), while the Model Code frames it in objective terms, entirely unrelated to the actor's culpability, or blameworthiness.

5. Commentaries art. 3, introduction, at 2–3.

Excuses in the Code thus are a disparate lot, as they are in criminal law generally, and are best treated one at a time.

§ 13 Duress

One way of thinking about duress in the Model Penal Code is to view it as the excuse analogue to the justification of necessity. If with necessity you don't succeed, try duress. In a sense, duress is more about necessity than is the necessity defense. It's choice of evils without the choice of evils. Necessity is all there is in duress, without any claim of right, or lawfulness. The person under duress is forced to commit criminal harm without preventing harm, other than to himself or to another. The person acting under the justification of necessity has done the right thing, or at least not the wrong thing. The person acting under duress has done the wrong thing, and yet cannot be blamed for doing what she did. The person justified under necessity made the right choice. The person excused under duress was forced to make the wrong choice, and in this sense made no choice at all. One is justified by her choice, the other excused by the absence of choice. One made the right choice, the other had no choice.

Duress, however, also shares much with self-defense, and defense of others (though not with defense of property[6]). Force used under duress, for instance, is self-defensive force directed not against

6. Commentaries § 2.09, at 375 ("perils to property" insufficient).

the source of the threat—as in self-defense—but against a third, innocent, person. To protect myself, I harm not the person who threatens me with harm, but someone else altogether.[7] Duress also resembles self-defense in that it comes in a direct and in a vicarious version. I'm excused under duress to prevent harm to myself and to "the person of another," just as I'm justified in using force to protect myself or "the person of another" against an attacker. Here, as in self-defense, the traditional limitation to members of my household has been replaced by a universal reference to all persons.[8]

Note also that, like self-defense but unlike necessity, duress requires "the use of, or a threat to use, *unlawful* force." This reference to unlawfulness is confusing, since duress, unlike the justification of self-defense (or necessity, for that matter), does not

[7]. There's no requirement that I harm anyone, of course. The Code's specifically recognizes the applicability of duress to escape, for instance. The prison escape cases, which for some reason tend to be regarded as the paradigm of duress in American criminal law, are problematic, in that no one ever coerces the defendant to commit the offense he's charged with, escape. Instead, the defendant claims to have escaped to avoid some other harm, usually physical or sexual abuse by fellow inmates or prison guards. The Code makes clear that even if the balance of harms doesn't come out in his favor, so that a necessity justification is unavailable, the escapee wouldn't be precluded from claiming duress simply because "the crime committed by the victim of coercion is [not] one the author of coercion demands." Commentaries § 2.09, at 377 (citing People v. Lovercamp, 43 Cal.App.3d 823 (1974)).

[8]. German criminal law, by contrast, retains this limitation in the case of duress, but not self-defense (or necessity). Contrast § 35 StGB (duress; "relative or other person close to him") with §§ 32 (self-defense; "another") & 34 (necessity; "another").

render facially criminal conduct lawful. The threatened force in self-defense must be unlawful, so that my use of self-protective force against it can be lawful. I cannot lawfully use force against force lawfully used against me. As an excuse, duress lays no such claim. The foundation of duress is not the right to respond to unlawful force, it's the inevitability of responding to any force, lawful or not, provided it is great enough to force my hand.

The point of the reference to "unlawful force" appears to have been to clarify that duress is limited to coercion caused by persons (personal duress), and not to compulsion by natural causes or circumstances (circumstantial duress). That point, however, could have been made without reference to unlawfulness, for instance, by specifically requiring a personal threat.[9] The reason, in turn, for excluding natural compulsion, or coercion by circumstance, appears to have been that, in the case of a personal threat, "the basic interests of the law may be satisfied by prosecution of the agent of unlawful force." Natural causes, however, cannot be punished—or penally treated—so that, "if the actor is excused, no one is subject to the law's application."[10] Just what "the basic interests of the law" might be in this context, other than an apparent need to "apply" itself as widely as possible, remains unclear.

9. See, e.g., the alternative statutory formulations listed in Commentaries § 2.09, at 383 n.59 ("another's threat," "threats by another," "compulsion by another").

10. Commentaries § 2.09, at 379.

Since the Code rejects duress from circumstances, it must resolve cases like *Dudley & Stephens* (the cannibalism on the high seas case) under the rubric of choice of evils. Even in extreme emergencies, facing almost certain death, the Code thus allows a defense only if the actor balanced the potential harms of action and inaction, to herself and others, and then chooses the less harmful course of action (or inaction). This means also that in the yet more dramatic case of the floating plank meant for one but grabbed by two—in a situation, in other words, where I must take your life to save my own—the Code would not allow a defense, because your life is worth as much as mine, no matter how dire my (and your) straits might be. It's never the direness of the straits that matters; only a lesser harm will do, except, of course, if the direness has a personal, rather than a natural, cause.

When the Code drafters speak of prosecuting the source of the threat, they have two things in mind. To begin with, the coercer would be held accountable for the coerced's conduct. Recall that the Code specifically provides, in its "complicity" section, that a "person is legally accountable for the conduct of another person when ... acting with the kind of culpability that is sufficient for the commission of the offense, he causes an innocent or irresponsible person to engage in such conduct.... "[11]

Here, the duress defense is usefully contrasted not to a level two defense—like self-defense or necessity—but to a level one "defense" instead: ne-

11. § 2.06(2)(a).

gativing actus reus. In the eyes of the Code drafters, duress stands to involuntariness as "psychological incapacity" stands to "physical incapacity."[12] Just as mistake and intoxication (and consent, where appropriate) make out a defense by negativing a crime's mens rea element, so certain types of coercion negative a crime's actus reus requirement. For instance, if I toss you over my neighbor's fence into her backyard, it may appear that you have committed a criminal trespass (defined as "enter[ing] ... any place as to which notice against trespass is given by ... fencing"[13]), except of course that you wouldn't have committed the requisite voluntary act. In fact, your entering would have been distinctly involuntary, as "a bodily movement that ... is not a product of the effort or determination of the actor."[14]

In the absence of a voluntary act, there wouldn't even be facial criminality—i.e., you wouldn't even make it past the first level of analysis. Instead, I would be the one who would have done a voluntary act, merely using you as a tool. It's as though I had tossed myself over the fence.

By contrast, if I merely chased you over the fence with a pitchfork, you would have committed a voluntary act, and to escape criminal liability, would have to raise the excuse of duress. Since you were the person who committed the relevant act, I couldn't be straightforwardly liable as the one who "really" did it. Instead, I would have to have *your* act imputed to me; in other words, I would have to

12. Commentaries § 2.09, at 373–74.
13. § 221.2.
14. § 2.01(2)(d).

be held accountable for your act, under the Code's complicity provision.

More interestingly, if the attempt at duress falls flat, the coercer *manqué* would qualify for the aptly named, and broadly framed, offense of "criminal coercion."[15] In fact, criminal coercion can be thought of as the offensive side of the coercion coin, with duress on the other, defensive, side. Duress consists of being "coerced" by another to commit a crime; criminal coercion is doing the coercing. The fit isn't perfect, because criminal coercion covers threats "to commit any criminal offense" and duress only "the use of, or a threat to use, unlawful *force*." It's closer, however, than it was before the Code; the Code drafters rejected a further limitation of the nature of the threat in duress to death, seriously bodily injury, or other violent crimes.[16]

The duress provision places no limitations on the severity, or immediacy, of the threat, even if the defense is raised to excuse the use of deadly force.[17] For the drafters also rejected the categorical exclusion of homicide from the class of offenses against which a duress defense could be raised.[18]

15. § 212.5.

16. Commentaries § 2.09, at 369.

17. When the drafters stressed that "long and wasting pressure may break down resistance more effectively than a threat of immediate destruction," they were thinking specifically of the "brainwashing" of American prisoners of war during the Korean war. Commentaries § 2.09, at 376.

18. Commentaries § 2.09, at 371; but see State v. Toscano, 74 N.J. 421 (1977) (N.J. Code Crim. Just. § 2C:2–9).

The Code's duress provision, in other words, contains no specific, and additional, constraints on the use of deadly force under duress. Unlike in the case of the self-defense justification, there is no requirement, for instance, that threatened force match defensive force, so that only a threat of deadly force could excuse the use of deadly force against another. Nor is there an explicit retreat requirement, with its very own set of exceptions and sub-exceptions.

In the absence of specific rules, the duress provision instead appeals to a single standard, or rather a single thought experiment: what "a person of reasonable firmness" would have done, or not done, in the defendant's "situation." The basic idea here is to inject some objectivity into the duress defense, without requiring any type of proportionality or other principle. It's not enough that a particular person have been overwhelmed by threats, as a matter of fact. Instead, we are to be held to a higher standard of fortitude, not actual but "reasonable firmness." Just what reasonable firmness is, and whether I displayed whatever it is, would be left up to the jury, the general receptacle of reasonableness in American criminal law.

Having imagined the "person of reasonable firmness," the jury is then to place that construct—but not themselves—into the defendant's "situation," to see how she (or he[19]) might have fared. As the Commentaries, but not the Code itself, tell us, the

19. Note that gender is not among the relevant characteristics listed.

"situation" includes certain circumstances, but not others:

> Stark, tangible factors that differentiate the actor from another, like his size, strength, age, or health, would be considered in making the exculpatory judgment. Matters of temperament would not.[20]

In the Commentaries we also learn that there are certain threats that are categorically declared irrelevant to the inquiry into "reasonable firmness": "[W]hen the claimed excuse is that duress was irresistible, threats to property or even reputation cannot exercise sufficient power over persons of 'reasonable firmness' to warrant consideration in these terms."[21] The excuse of duress thus deviates from the justification of defensive force against unlawful attack, codified in sections 3.04–.06, by requiring a threat against the person (mine or another's), while disregarding threats to property.[22]

The Code drafters further restricted the scope of the duress defense, by declaring that recklessly placing myself "in a situation in which it was probable that [I] would be subjected to duress" bars the defense entirely, rather than mitigating liability to recklessness offenses. Recall that, in the case of the

20. Commentaries § 2.09, at 375.

21. Id. The Commentaries suggest that the categorical irrelevance of threats to property or reputation is implied by the reference to threats "against [the defendant's] person or the person of another."

22. Attacks on one's reputation are never grounds for self-defense.

justification defense of necessity, recklessness in this regard did not render the defense inapplicable, but instead reduced liability to a recklessness offense, as negligence reduced liability to a negligence offense. In the case of duress, this general rule of mitigation to match the actual mode of culpability applies only to negligence; if I'm reckless in creating the probability of coercion, such as by "connect[ing myself] with criminal activities," I cannot use that coercion to defend against any crime, including one that requires purpose or knowledge.[23] The Commentaries justify, or rather explain, this "deliberate departure" from the principle that liability match culpability by pointing to "the exceptional nature of the defense."[24]

§ 14 Entrapment

Think of entrapment as official duress, or as the carrot to duress's stick.[25] In duress, a private person "coerce[s]" me through "the use of, or a threat to use, unlawful force" to commit a crime. In entrapment, a "public law enforcement official ... induces or encourages" me to do the same through other improper, though not necessarily "unlawful," means:

23. Commentaries § 2.09, at 379 & n.48.

24. Id.

25. Cf. People v. Calvano, 30 N.Y.2d 199, 205 (1972) (entrapment and duress "differ only in respect of the pressures exerted").

(a) making knowingly false representations designed to induce the belief that such conduct is not prohibited; or

(b) employing methods of persuasion or inducement which create a substantial risk that such an offense will be committed by persons other than those who are ready to commit it.[26]

Entrapment (a) amounts to an attempt to induce a mistake of law. If successful, this attempt may make out an independent mistake of law defense.[27] Success, however, isn't required for entrapment; the attempt is enough because the Code opted for entrapment of the objective variety. Objective entrapment has nothing to do with the defendant, and everything to do with the police. It's designed, exclusively, "to deter wrongful conduct on the part of the government."[28] The innocence of the defendant is entirely irrelevant: "the defendant is just as guilty, with or without the entrapment."[29]

By contrast, the defendant's innocence is all that matters for purposes of subjective entrapment. In its subjective version, entrapment is only available to the innocent, or more precisely to those not

26. § 2.13(1).

27. If the defendant acted "in reasonable reliance upon an official statement of the law ... contained in ... an official interpretation of the public officer or body charged by law with responsibility for the ... enforcement of the law defining the offense." § 2.04(3)(b). Note also the entrapper's potential liability for the offense she induced under a complicity theory. Cf. § 2.06.

28. Commentaries § 2.13, at 406.

29. Id. at 412.

"predisposed" to commit the offense without government inducement.[30] In fact, it's this very limitation to the innocent that induced the Code drafters to opt for objective, and only objective, entrapment. Here the drafters quote Justice Felix Frankfurter:

> Permissible police activity does not vary according to the particular defendant concerned; surely if two suspects have been solicited at the same time in the same manner, one should not go to jail simply because he has been convicted before and is said to have a criminal predisposition.[31]

The drafters' choice of objective entrapment also explains why entrapment (b) requires only the use of tactics that "create a substantial risk" that a crime will be committed by someone who isn't "ready to commit it." Entrapment seeks to deter "unsavory police tactics,"[32] and these tactics are just as unsavory when they succeed as when they don't.

The Code's entrapment standard thus does away with the traditional inquiry into the defendant's "predisposition" to commit an offense. The entrap-

30. See, e.g., Jacobson v. United States, 503 U.S. 540 (1992) (detailed inquiry into defendant's predisposition).

31. Commentaries § 2.13, at 412 (quoting Sherman v. United States, 356 U.S. 369, 383 (1958) (Frankfurter, J., concurring)). Justice Frankfurter notwithstanding, objective entrapment hangs on in federal criminal law only by the thinnest of constitutional threads, as a due process defense of "outrageous governmental misconduct." Compare United States v. Mosley, 965 F.2d 906 (10th Cir.1992) (defense exists) with United States v. Boyd, 55 F.3d 239, 241 (7th Cir.1995) (defense doesn't exist).

32. Commentaries § 2.13, at 412.

ment defense is available to all defendants, predisposed or nonpredisposed.[33]

For that reason, however, entrapment under the Code also doesn't count as an excuse, really. Subjective entrapment would be a different story. As the Commentaries note in passing, after all, "it is *unfair* to prosecute a person persuaded or deceived into criminality by the state."[34]

§ 15 Ignorance of Law

Under the Code, successful "entrapment by estoppel" (also known as "executive estoppel") is an ignorance of law problem, rather than a matter of entrapment. As we noted in our discussion of mistake as a level one defense, the Code makes room for a limited excuse of ignorance of law, the venerated maxim *ignorantia legis non excusat* notwithstanding.[35] That excuse comes in two varieties, "reasonable reliance upon an official statement of the law, afterward determined to be invalid or erroneous"[36] being one, and nonpublication of the law

---

33. As long as they aren't charged with an offense that includes "causing or threatening bodily injury" as an element. Punishing someone entrapped into an assault, say, would "not seem generally unfair," according to the Commentaries. Commentaries § 2.12, at 420.

34. Id. (emphasis added).

35. See supra § 4.3(b).

36. An "invalid" statement would include a statute later determined to be unconstitutional. See State v. Godwin, 123 N.C. 697 (1898) (cited in Commentaries § 2.04, at 278 n.28). For a

the other, and far less important, one.[37]

Note, however, that the Model Code version of the ignorance of law excuse doesn't require a *knowing* misstatement, never mind an intentional one specifically "designed to induce the belief that such conduct is not prohibited," as entrapment would require. The Code does limit the defense to "official" misstatements of the law, thus excluding reliance, no matter how reasonable, on my—or any other—lawyer's nonofficial advice that, by a subsequent official statement, turns out to have been bad, or at least wrong.[38] Needless to say, reliance on the actor's own interpretation of the law, "afterward determined to be ... erroneous," won't do either.[39] "Official" statements of the law encompass statements issued by members of any branch of government, legislature ("a statute or other enactment"), judiciary ("a judicial decision, opinion or judgment"), and executive ("an administrative order or grant of permission"; "an official interpretation of the public officer or body charged by law with responsibility for the interpretation, administration or enforcement of the law defining the offense").

case interpreting an MPC-based ignorance provision, see People v. Studifin, 132 Misc.2d 326 (N.Y.Sup.Ct.1986).

37. The question of publicity wasn't always of little practical relevance. See, e.g., The Cotton Planter, 6 F. Cas. 620 (Cir.Ct. D.N.Y.1810). Lambert v. California, 355 U.S. 225 (1957), has done little to revive the issue.

38. Commentaries § 2.04, at 279–80.

39. See People v. Marrero, 69 N.Y.2d 382 (1987) (good-faith (mis)reading of ambiguous statute not enough).

That ignorance of law is an excuse, rather than a level one "defense" is clear enough.[40] Why this should be so isn't quite so obvious. Unlike duress, provocation, diminished capacity, infancy, and insanity—and perhaps even entrapment, at least in its subjective form—ignorance of law doesn't involve a loss of self-control, however partial. In the case of ignorance, the "reason the actor is not to be blamed for"[41] her concededly "undesirable" conduct may be thought instead to lie in its *unavoidability*. If the actor didn't know, or couldn't reasonably have known, of the criminal statute she is charged with violating, she couldn't have avoided violating it. Similarly, if she did everything she could to determine the meaning of a statute familiar to her, and thus to avoid violating it, it would be unfair to blame her for finding out, after the fact, that she failed.

Perhaps the idea of unavoidability might be seen as undergirding the inability and incapacity excuses like duress, insanity, and so on. In the case of duress, giving in to the coercion was as unavoidable under the circumstances as was succumbing to the inducement of entrapment. Provocation and diminished capacity, too, would appear as unavoidability defenses, though what was unavoidable—or at least too difficult to avoid—here was the violent response triggered by the provocation.

40. Cf. § 2.02(9) (knowledge of illegality no offense element).

41. Commentaries art. 3, introduction, at 3 (emphasis added).

§ 16 Provocation and Diminished Capacity

"Provocation," or "extreme mental or emotional disturbance" in Model Code language, differs from duress and other excuses because it's not a general defense. It's a defense to murder, and to murder only. That's why it doesn't appear in the Code's general part (part I), but in its special part, more specifically, in the article dealing with homicide, and still more specifically, in the section defining manslaughter.

Yet an excuse it clearly is, at least in the Model Code's scheme of things. Provocation carries its excuseness on its sleeve; it covers acts committed "under the influence of extreme mental or emotional disturbance for which there is reasonable explanation or *excuse*." But before we get to provocation as a mini excuse, we need to take a quick detour into the special part's homicide provisions.

What the common law called "voluntary manslaughter" is murder plus provocation, or rather murder minus malice aforethought, or premeditation, on account of provocation. Voluntary manslaughter is still murder in that it's still intentional, however—and in that misleading sense, "voluntary." The provocation, no matter how outrageous, didn't change the fact that the defendant hit the victim over the head with a club with the conscious object of killing him (to speak in Model Code terms). It instead explained why he might have had that conscious object. *Involuntary* manslaughter, by contrast, was manslaughter, period, or nonintentional homicide, homicide that was committed with neither desire nor awareness that death would result.

The Code, probably wisely, jettisons talk of voluntary and involuntary manslaughter (just like it doesn't like speaking of voluntary and involuntary intoxication, voluntariness being reserved for questions of actus reus, not mens rea[42]). It instead sets out two types of manslaughter, without naming them: reckless homicide (recklessly causing the death of another human being)—the Code's version of involuntary manslaughter, which doesn't interest us here—and its version of voluntary manslaughter, which does interest us:

> [A] homicide which would otherwise be murder is committed under the influence of extreme mental or emotional disturbance for which there is reasonable explanation or excuse. The reasonableness of such explanation or excuse shall be determined from the viewpoint of a person in the actor's situation under the circumstances as he believes them to be.[43]

Since it appears in the definition of a criminal offense, and a serious one at that (manslaughter is a second degree felony in the Code), provocation differs from duress, and other excuses, in another way: not only does it apply only to a single offense,

42. On intoxication, see supra § 4.3(a).
43. § 210.3(1)(b).

it's not even a complete defense to that offense.[44] Provocation turns murder into manslaughter, that's it.

Still it's important to see why disturbance works as an excuse. It's clearly not a justification. The person who kills under the influence of extreme mental or emotional disturbance cannot claim a right to kill. If she could, she would qualify for self-defense. Disturbance isn't a level one (or failure of proof) defense, either. The point of the disturbance is to provide an "explanation or excuse" for purposeful or knowing conduct, to wit murder, rather than to deny that it was purposeful or knowing. That, again, is why provocation manslaughter is voluntary; it's intentional, but excusable.

Provocation is a partial, rather than a complete, excuse because it mitigates the actor's blameworthiness, rather than precluding it. It amounts to a "disturbance," however "extreme," rather than to an "inability" (as in the case of duress) or an "incapacity" (as in insanity). Disturbance doesn't negate the inference of "moral depravity"[45] from facially criminal conduct, it reduces the grade of the "depravity" inferred, from that ordinarily associated with purposeful or knowing homicide (murder)

44. In fact, it's not even clear that it's a defense of any kind, rather than being an element of the offense of manslaughter. This was the issue in Patterson v. New York, 432 U.S. 197 (1977). There, the Supreme Court held that the federal constitution doesn't preclude a legislature from classifying provocation not only as a defense, but as an affirmative defense upon which the defendant bears the burden of proof.

45. Commentaries § 210.3, at 61.

to that ordinarily associated with reckless homicide (manslaughter). In short, disturbance requires a downward adjustment in the diagnosis of the actor's criminal disposition, and therefore of her need for peno-correctional treatment.

Doctrinally, provocation falls somewhere in between self-defense, duress, and insanity. As you might think of duress as the excuse alternative to the justification of necessity, so provocation can be seen as the excuse alternative to the justification of self-defense. Unlike self-defense, it's not limited to the use of force against unlawful attacks, nor does it require a showing that my use of force was (nor even that it was believed to be) immediately necessary, never mind the initial aggressor or retreat constraints on the use of deadly force in self-defense. Like self-defense, provocation too has a vicarious analogue; as self-defense has defense of others, so provocation isn't limited to cases where I'm the target of the provocation: "the Code does not require that the actor's emotional distress arise from some injury, affront, or other provocative act perpetrated upon him by the deceased."[46] This also means that, unlike self-defense (or other-defense)—but like duress—I can use provocation as a defense against inflicting harm (deadly harm, in fact) on someone other than the person who's doing the provoking, as "where [I] strike[] out in a blinding rage and kill[] an innocent bystander."[47]

46. Commentaries § 210.3, at 60–61.

47. Id. The victim thus need have engaged in neither unlawful, nor even provocative conduct. This is one reason why the

Like duress, provocation is defined in terms of reasonableness. It's not enough for duress that I was unable to withstand the threats, nor is it enough for provocation that I was so disturbed that I couldn't control myself after being provoked. To inject some objectivity into the inquiry, the Code limits both excuses to cases where it was "reasonable" for me to behave as I did. Once again, this apparently objective inquiry into what "the hypothetical reasonable man"[48] might have done is then tailored to my "situation." As in duress, this means that the factfinder gets to take into account certain, but not all, of my characteristics or "personal handicaps," including "blindness, shock from traumatic injury, and extreme grief," but not "idiosyncratic moral values" like something "as integral a part of moral depravity as a belief in the rightness of killing."[49]

The Code's flexible reasonableness standard sweeps away a host of more or less hard and fast common law rules defining the scope of the provocation defense. So the common law barred provocation in the face of sufficient opportunity to "cool off" and regain self-control after a provocation, and declared that words alone could never provoke. The Code instead throws these considerations, along with anything else that might be relevant to the actor's "situation," into the pot of reasonableness.

Code refers to emotional disturbance rather than provocation. See id. at 61.

48. Id. at 62.

49. Id.

So no particular temporal connection between provocative cause and effect is required, nor is any type (or source or target) of provocation excluded, not even attacks on "property or ... reputation,"[50] which were declared categorically irrelevant to the reasonableness inquiry in cases of duress.

As we've seen, provocation under the Code isn't really—or just—provocation, but "extreme emotional or mental disturbance." While the reference to *emotional* disturbance covers all cases of provocation, and then some, the reference to *mental* disturbance highlights the connection between provocation and insanity. That connection consists of a multifaceted defense called "diminished capacity," or diminished responsibility as the Model Code prefers to call it.

Diminished responsibility, like so many other defenses, comes in two varieties. On one hand, it's a level one defense. Evidence of mental incapacity or abnormality short of full-fledged insanity is relevant to mens rea. This straightforward, evidentiary, aspect of diminished responsibility—familiar from other failure of proof defenses like mistake or intoxication—is codified, however redundantly, in section 4.02 of the Code, immediately following the definition of insanity.[51]

50. Commentaries § 2.09, at 375. The Commentaries suggest that the categorical irrelevance of threats to property or reputation is implied by the reference to threats "against [the defendant's] person or the person of another."

51. See State v. Breakiron, 108 N.J. 591 (1987).

On the other hand, diminished responsibility can be construed as a level three defense, an excuse. No Code section is specifically dedicated to diminished responsibility as an excuse. Instead, this aspect of the defense is covered by the "mental disturbance" language in the Code's provocation provision. Diminished responsibility as an excuse thus functions like provocation as an excuse—in fact, it *is* provocation as an excuse. It reduces the actor's liability from murder to manslaughter, rather than leading to an outright acquittal (as a successful level one defense might), and it applies to no offense other than murder.

Note, however, that diminished responsibility is not an independent defense. It's relevant only insofar as the "mental abnormalities" giving rise to it are relevant to the jury's general reasonableness inquiry and, more specifically, to the "actor's situation" defining that inquiry. Whether it is relevant in a particular case is an open question according to the Commentaries: "Mental disorder clearly does not preclude moral depravity, and there surely will be cases where the actor's mental condition, although recognized as disturbed or abnormal, should be regarded as having no just bearing on his liability for intentional homicide."[52]

§ 17 Insanity and Infancy

The Code drafters devoted a great deal of time and effort to the insanity defense. In their view,

52. Commentaries § 210.3, at 72.

"[n]o problem in the drafting of a penal code presents greater intrinsic difficulty than that of determining when individuals whose conduct would otherwise be criminal ought to be exculpated on the ground that they were suffering from mental disease or defect when they acted as they did."[53] The importance of the insanity defense to the Code project did not reflect its practice significance; as is well known, the insanity defense is very rarely invoked, and almost never successful. The problem instead was a systematic, or "intrinsic" one. Having reformed criminal law from an atavistic ritual of punishment to a scientific system of treatment, the Code drafters struggled to make room for the insanity defense. If all of criminal law is about identifying, diagnosing, and treating persons suffering from some penological abnormality, what's the point of excusing certain persons from punishment on account of some mental abnormality, and subjecting them to treatment instead? If all criminals are mentally abnormal, what's so special about the criminally insane?

In a system of criminal law as punishment—rather than as "peno-correctional treatment"—the question of insanity has a straightforward answer. The criminally insane are those persons to whom the general presumption of sanity—of normality—doesn't apply. Deprived of the mental or affective capacities necessary for choice and therefore for wrongful conduct, they cannot be proper objects of blame. Without blame, they must be without punishment. Instead of deserving punishment, they require treatment.

53. Commentaries § 4.01, at 164.

Given their treatmentist view of criminal law, which excised punishment from its vocabulary, the Model Code drafters instead were forced to frame the problem of insanity in a different, and more roundabout, way. The difference between the sane and the insane, the normal and the abnormal, was not that between punishment and treatment, but between different "modes of disposition" through treatment, and, more specifically, between different administrators of treatment. As the drafters saw it, "the problem is to etch a decent working line between the areas assigned to the authorities responsible for public health and those responsible for the correction of offenders."[54]

The result of the drafters' extended struggle to craft a treatment exception to their treatmentist vision of punishment was a long and highly detailed article entitled "responsibility" (article 4). Despite its broad title, this article is devoted entirely to the defense of insanity, except for one brief section at the very end, disposing of the traditional excuse of infancy (or "immaturity," in Model Code terms).

At common law, infancy worked very much like insanity; it was a substantive defense in a criminal proceeding. The infant, along with the "idiot" or "lunatic," was exempt from criminal liability because he was not among the "persons capable of committing crimes."[55] By the time of the Code,

54. Commentaries § 4.01, at 165.

55. 4 William Blackstone, Commentaries on the Laws of England ch. 2 (1769).

infancy had, for at least half a century, been a procedural, and more precisely a jurisdictional, issue, rather than a substantive one. And so, rather than addressing the conditions under which—and the general reasons why—immaturity might work as an excuse for otherwise criminal conduct, the Code sets up some general jurisdictional rules regarding the "transfer of proceedings to juvenile court."[56]

Immaturity, however, is an excuse for the same reason that insanity is. A child is not responsible for her conduct, or at least not sufficiently responsible for it, to warrant blame. Like the insane person, the child "lacks substantial capacity either to appreciate the criminality [wrongfulness] of his conduct or to conform his conduct to the requirements of law."[57] The difference between immaturity and insanity is that the cause of the incapacity is age, and therefore both presumably temporary and normal, rather than a "mental disease or defect." Plus, modern criminal law treats a certain age—or lack thereof—as an irrebuttable presumption of irresponsibility. So the Model Code, for example, categorically declares that a "person shall not be tried for or convicted of an offense," rather than be acquitted after a trial, "if ... at the time of the conduct charged to constitute the offense he was less than sixteen years of age."[58] In other cases, the presumption of irresponsibility is rebuttable, and

56. § 4.10.
57. § 4.01(1).
58. § 4.10(1)(a).

may even flip over into a presumption of responsibility, as when the actor falls in a gray zone between clear infancy and clear adulthood (say, during the ages of sixteen and seventeen, as under the Code[59]) or when the offense charged is particularly serious. Much of the reform of juvenile law since the Code's publication in 1962 has amounted to a downward extension of that gray zone.[60]

By contrast, the presumption of sanity is universal and it's upon each individual defendant to rebut it. And so insanity under the Code is an affirmative defense, though it should be remembered that affirmative defenses in the Code place only the burden of production upon the defendant, while the burden of persuasion remains on the state.[61]

In a way, it's misleading to say that article 4 on responsibility is entirely—or almost entirely—devoted to the defense of insanity. In fact, the defense is codified in a single section at the outset of the article, section 4.01. The remainder of the article, in sections 4.02 through 4.09, addresses, in often excruciating detail, various procedural issues related to the insanity defense, including—in rough order

---

59. § 4.10(1)(b).

60. For a discussion of the common law's inquiry into the responsibility of a particular defendant raising the defense of infancy, see 4 William Blackstone, Commentaries on the Laws of England 22–24 (1769).

61. § 4.03. Note that the U.S. Supreme Court has found no constitutional fault with placing the burden of *persuasion* on the defendant as well, even to the point of requiring defendants to prove their insanity beyond a reasonable doubt. Leland v. Oregon, 343 U.S. 790 (1952).

276 EXCUSE

of appearance—the relevance of evidence of mental disease, the classification of insanity as an affirmative defense, the requirement of notifying the state of one's intention to raise an insanity defense, the form of the verdict if the defense is successful, incompetence to stand trial, psychiatric examinations of the defendant by state and defense experts, the inadmissibility of incriminating statements made during these examinations, and, eventually, the effect of a verdict of not guilty by reason of insanity ("commit[ment] to the custody of the Commissioner of Mental Hygiene [Public Health] to be placed in an appropriate institution for custody, care and treatment").[62] The vast bulk of the insanity provisions in the Code, in other words, is devoted not to defining the defense of insanity, but to an elaborate, even anxious, attempt to control its implementation, largely with the help of expert testimony.

Luckily, the insanity defense itself is remarkably short and to the point:

> A person is not responsible for criminal conduct if at the time of such conduct as a result of mental disease or defect he lacks substantial capacity either to appreciate the criminality [wrongfulness] of his conduct or to conform his conduct to the requirements of law.[63]

Its main features are quickly identified. The incapacity that matters is incapacity "at the time of"

62. § 4.08(1).
63. § 4.01(1).

the crime, not before or after, most relevantly, at the time of trial. Mental disease or defect at trial—incompetence to stand trial—is measured by a different, procedural, standard ("capacity to understand the proceedings against him or to assist in his own defense") and affects not my responsibility for the crime, but only my "fitness to proceed," which matters only "as long as such incapacity endures."[64]

Insanity requires a different sort of incapacity, or rather incapacities: The *cognitive* incapacity to "appreciate the criminality [wrongfulness] of [my] conduct," and the *volitional* one to "conform [my] conduct to the requirements of the law." The Code drafters here responded to what they perceived as the shortcomings of the then-dominant insanity test, first set out in an advisory English opinion from 1843, *M'Naghten's Case*.[65] And so it's best to place their insanity defense side-by-side with *M'Naghten's*.[66]

64. § 4.03.

65. 1 C. & K. 130, 4 St. Tr. N.S. 847 (1843). M'Naghten set out to assassinate Prime Minister Sir Robert Peel, convinced that spies were following him "night and day." He killed Peel's private secretary instead, mistaking him for Peel. After M'Naghten's acquittal on grounds of insanity, the House of Lords asked for clarification of the law of insanity. *M'Naghten* was the judges' response. See generally Richard Moran, Knowing Right from Wrong: The Insanity Defense of Daniel McNaughtan (1981).

66. The drafters rejected as too ambiguous another contemporary attempt to replace *M'Naghten*, the "product" test set out in *Durham v. United States*, 214 F.2d 862, 874–75 (D.C.Cir.1954) ("accused is not criminally responsible if his unlawful act was the product of mental disease or mental defect"). Commentaries § 4.01, at 173. Also rejected was Wechsler's proposed formula-

Improving *M'Naghten* meant expanding it. Unlike *M'Naghten*, at least as it had entered American criminal law, the Code test doesn't require complete incapacity—lacking a "substantial" capacity will do. Similarly, Code insanity doesn't require that I be incapable merely of "*knowing* right from wrong," as *M'Naghten* had.[67] Under the Code, I may be criminally insane even if I technically "know" the difference between right and wrong, as long as I can't be said to "appreciate" that difference. Here the Code drafters were thinking of someone who suffers from certain "emotional abnormalities" that prevent her "largely detached or abstract awareness" of the wrongfulness of her conduct from "penetrat[ing] to the affective level."[68] So I can be insane, and therefore irresponsible, if I know what I'm doing is wrong, but don't know what that means, exactly. I might know the difference between right and wrong, without understanding it.[69]

More interesting, just *what* I'm supposed to understand (or not understand) had been unclear after *M'Naghten*. Was I insane if I didn't understand that

tion: "A person is not responsible for criminal conduct if at the time of such conduct as a result of mental disease or defect his capacity either to appreciate the criminality of his conduct or to conform his conduct to the requirements of law is *so substantially impaired that he cannot justly be held responsible.*" Tentative Draft No. 4, § 4.01(1)(a) (1955) (emphasis added); see generally United States v. Brawner, 471 F.2d 969 (D.C.Cir.1972) (en banc) (abandoning product test for MPC test).

67. Id. (emphasis added).

68. Commentaries § 4.01, at 166.

69. Id. at 169 ("broader sense of understanding than simple cognition").

what I was doing was illegal (or, yet more specifically, criminal), or was it enough (or required) that I didn't understand that what I was doing was wrong?[70] The Code doesn't resolve the ambiguity, referring equivocally to the conduct's "criminality [wrongfulness]." Now awareness of criminality and of wrongfulness tend to amount to the same thing since criminality and wrongfulness tend to coincide—what's criminal is often wrong, and vice versa (though less frequently). The formulation would make a difference, however, in cases of criminality without wrongfulness. If I can't be insane as long as I appreciate the *criminality* of my conduct, then insane, and mistaken, beliefs in the rightfulness of concededly criminal conduct, perhaps prompted by hearing "the voice of God calling upon [me] to kill the woman as a sacrifice and atonement,"[71] wouldn't count.[72]

To say that I fail to appreciate the criminality or the wrongfulness of my conduct is of course but another way of saying that I am *mistaken* about its criminality or wrongfulness. In yet other words, I am committing a level one mistake (about criminality), in thinking that I'm committing no crime at all,

70. See, e.g., People v. Schmidt, 216 N.Y. 324 (1915).

71. Id. at 324.

72. Command hallucinations can also be viewed as impeding one's *volitional* capacity to control one's conduct, rather than as a mistaken belief in the rightfulness (or at least nonwrongfulness) of the conduct. In that case, they wouldn't be an insane mistake about a justification, but about an excuse—superior orders or, perhaps, duress. Cf. §§ 2.09 (duress) & 2.10 (military orders).

280 *EXCUSE*

or a level two mistake (about unlawfulness), in thinking that I'm justified in committing a crime. And indeed the excuses of insanity—in its cognitive prong—and of ignorance of law are closely related. As we've seen earlier, mere ignorance of law doesn't provide an excuse, absent a failure to publicize or reasonable reliance on an official misstatement of the law.[73] Ignorance of the law, however, does provide an excuse if it is the manifestation of an incapacity to understand the law by applying it to a particular situation, brought on by a mental disease or defect.[74] Then it's called insanity.

Note, once again, that neither the incapacity nor the mental disease or defect is sufficient to make for insanity. The incapacity to tell right from wrong—or to keep oneself from doing wrong—by itself may be unfortunate, but it's no excuse. Likewise, and perhaps more important, a mental disease or defect might be relevant as evidence negativing mens rea, as explained in section 4.02, but it doesn't make for an excuse. Insanity is no defense; irresponsibility brought on by insanity is.

The biggest difference between Model Code insanity and *M'Naghten* insanity, however, lies not in its cognitive prong, but in its volitional prong. *M'Naghten* had no volitional prong—the question of insanity was one of cognition (or knowledge) exclusively. Over the decades since *M'Naghten*, courts,

73. Supra § 15.

74. The Code doesn't define mental disease or defect, instead leaving these terms "open to accommodate developing medical understanding." Commentaries § 4.01, at 164.

however, had grafted onto its cognitive test an "irresistible impulse" addendum that extended the insanity excuse to those who couldn't keep themselves from doing what they knew to be wrong (or criminal).

The Model Code elevated the irresistible impulse supplement to an alternative type of excuse by reason of insanity.[75] Under the volitional prong, the "reason the actor is not to be blamed for" her concededly "undesirable"[76] conduct is that it was unavoidable on account of her mental disease or defect—in other words, her insanity made her do it. Under the cognitive prong, her conduct was unavoidable, and thus excusable, because her insanity prevented her from realizing that she was engaging in criminal, or undesirable, conduct in the first place—in other words, her insanity kept her from *not* doing it.

75. Note that the Code frames the volitional prong in strictly legal terms, referring to the incapacity of conforming one's conduct to "the requirements of law," rather than of refraining from wrongful (or more specifically criminal) conduct.

76. Commentaries art. 3, introduction, at 3 (emphasis added).

Conclusion

Surely the best way to recapitulate, and condense, the overview presented in this book is in a chart, an annotated and slightly modified version of the table of contents at the beginning of the book, which lay out the roadmap for what was then to follow, and which has now followed in fact. This time around, the roadmap is a systematic summary of the analysis of criminal liability, with citations to the relevant Model Penal Code sections every step along the way.

The conceptual flowchart should be useful not only in analyzing a case (hypothetical or not) under the Model Code, but also under American criminal law generally speaking—to the extent such a thing exists, given that there are at least as many American criminal laws as there American criminal jurisdictions. The Model Code, after all, is of interest not only because it lays out an internally consistent doctrine of criminal law—or at least the most internally consistent doctrine we have—but also because it constitutes something like a common denominator of contemporary American criminal law in all of its dizzying variety and idiosyncracy, a conceptual backbone to a diverse body of more or less local rules.

Here then is an analytic guideline for answering the central question in American criminal law teaching and practice: who is liable for what? The basic question of liability is divided into three subquestions, which in turn fall into various sub-sub-, and even subsubsub-, questions. While every question must be answered in every case, no case has nonobvious answers to all. This analytic guideline won't help you pick out the questions with nonobvious answers, nor how to answer them (for that you'll have to consult the discussion in the book). It will, however, make it less likely that you will fail to consider a question, or that you will address a question in the "wrong" doctrinal context—unless, of course, you have a good reason to do so.

§ 18 Analysis of Criminal Liability

1. Criminality (arts. 1–2, 5): Does the behavior constitute criminal conduct?

   A. What are the elements of the offense as defined? (§ 1.13(9))

   1. Conduct (§ 1.13(5))
   2. Circumstances
   3. Result
   4. Mode of Culpability (as to each element)

   – purpose, knowledge, recklessness, negligence (§ 2.02)
   – none (strict liability, § 2.05)
   – rules of interpretation (§§ 2.02(3), (4), 2.05)

   B. Does the behavior satisfy each element of the offense?

   1. Conduct

   – act (§ 2.01)
   – voluntariness (§ 2.01)
   – omission (§ 2.01)
   – complicity (§ 2.06)

   2. Circumstances

   – consent (§ 2.11)

   3. Result

   – causation (§ 2.03)
   – but for (§ 2.03(1)(a))
   – proximate (§ 2.03(1)(b)-(4))

4. Mode of Culpability (as to each element)

- mistake (§ 2.04(1))
- intoxication (§ 2.08)
- diminished capacity (§ 4.02(1))

5. Inchoate Crimes (art. 5)

- attempt (§ 5.01)
- solicitation (§ 5.02)
- conspiracy (§ 5.03)

2. <u>Illegality (Justification) (art. 3)</u>: Is the criminal conduct unlawful generally speaking?

  A. Necessity (choice of evils) (§ 3.02)
  B. Self-defense (§ 3.04); defense of another (§ 3.05); defense of property (§ 3.06)
  C. Law enforcement (§ 3.07)
  D. Public duty (§ 3.03)
  E. Special responsibility (§ 3.08)
  F. Consent (§ 2.11)

3. <u>Guilt (Excuse) (arts. 2, 4)</u>: Is the accused blameworthy for her criminal and unlawful conduct?

  A. Duress (§ 2.09)
  B. Military orders (§ 2.10)
  C. Entrapment (§ 2.13)
  D. Ignorance of law (§ 2.04(3))
  E. Provocation and diminished capacity (§ 210.3(1)(b))
  F. Insanity and infancy (§§ 4.01, .10)

     – involuntary intoxication (§ 2.08(4))

APPENDIX
MODEL PENAL CODE

[Copyright © 1962 by the American Law Institute. Reprinted with permission of the American Law Institute.]

PART I. GENERAL PROVISIONS
ARTICLE 1. PRELIMINARY
Section 1.01. Title and Effective Date.

(1) This Act is called the Penal and Correctional Code and may be cited as P.C.C. It shall become effective on ——.

(2) Except as provided in Subsections (3) and (4) of this Section, the Code does not apply to offenses committed prior to its effective date and prosecutions for such offenses shall be governed by the prior law, which is continued in effect for that purpose, as if this Code were not in force. For the purposes of this Section, an offense was committed prior to the effective date of the Code if any of the elements of the offense occurred prior thereto.

(3) In any case pending on or after the effective date of the Code, involving an offense committed prior to such date:

(a) procedural provisions of the Code shall govern, insofar as they are justly applicable and their application does not introduce confusion or delay;

(b) provisions of the Code according a defense or mitigation shall apply, with the consent of the defendant;

(c) the Court, with the consent of the defendant, may impose sentence under the provisions of the Code applicable to the offense and the offender.

(4) Provisions of the Code governing the treatment and the release or discharge of prisoners, probationers and parolees shall apply to persons under sentence for offenses committed prior to the effective date of the Code, except that the minimum or maximum period of their detention or supervision shall in no case be increased.

Section 1.02. Purposes; Principles of Construction.

(1) The general purposes of the provisions governing the definition of offenses are:

(a) to forbid and prevent conduct that unjustifiably and inexcusably inflicts or threatens substantial harm to individual or public interests;

(b) to subject to public control persons whose conduct indicates that they are disposed to commit crimes;

(c) to safeguard conduct that is without fault from condemnation as criminal;

(d) to give fair warning of the nature of the conduct declared to constitute an offense;

(e) to differentiate on reasonable grounds between serious and minor offenses.

(2) The general purposes of the provisions governing the sentencing and treatment of offenders are:

(a) to prevent the commission of offenses;

(b) to promote the correction and rehabilitation of offenders;

(c) to safeguard offenders against excessive, disproportionate or arbitrary punishment;

(d) to give fair warning of the nature of the sentences that may be imposed on conviction of an offense;

(e) to differentiate among offenders with a view to a just individualization in their treatment;

(f) to define, coordinate and harmonize the powers, duties and functions of the courts and of administrative officers and agencies responsible for dealing with offenders;

(g) to advance the use of generally accepted scientific methods and knowledge in the sentencing and treatment of offenders;

(h) to integrate responsibility for the administration of the correctional system in a State Department of Correction [or other single department or agency].

(3) The provisions of the Code shall be construed according to the fair import of their terms but when the language is susceptible of differing constructions it shall be interpreted to further the general purposes stated in this Section and the special purposes of the particular provision involved. The discretionary powers conferred by the Code shall be exercised in accordance with the criteria stated in the Code and, insofar as such criteria are not decisive, to further the general purposes stated in this Section.

Section 1.03. Territorial Applicability.

(1) Except as otherwise provided in this Section, a person may be convicted under the law of this State of an offense committed by his own conduct or the conduct of another for which he is legally accountable if:

(a) either the conduct which is an element of the offense or the result which is such an element occurs within this State; or

(b) conduct occurring outside the State is sufficient under the law of this State to constitute an attempt to commit an offense within the State; or

(c) conduct occurring outside the State is sufficient under the law of this State to constitute a conspiracy to commit an offense within the State and an overt act in furtherance of such conspiracy occurs within the State; or

(d) conduct occurring within the State establishes complicity in the commission of, or an attempt, solicitation or conspiracy to commit, an offense in another jurisdiction which also is an offense under the law of this State; or

(e) the offense consists of the omission to perform a legal duty imposed by the law of the State with respect to domicile, residence or a relationship to a person, thing or transaction in the State; or

(f) the offense is based on a statute of this State which expressly prohibits conduct outside the State, when the conduct bears a reasonable relation to a legitimate interest of this State and the actor knows or should know that his conduct is likely to affect that interest.

(2) Subsection (1)(a) does not apply when either causing a specified result or a purpose to cause or danger of causing such a result is an element of an offense and the result occurs or is designed or likely to occur only in another jurisdiction where the conduct charged would not constitute an offense, unless a legislative purpose plainly appears to declare the conduct criminal regardless of the place of the result.

(3) Subsection (1)(a) does not apply when causing a particular result is an element of an offense and the result is caused by conduct occurring outside the State which would not constitute an offense if the result had

occurred there, unless the actor purposely or knowingly caused the result within the State.

(4) When the offense is homicide, either the death of the victim or the bodily impact causing death constitutes a "result," within the meaning of Subsection (1)(a) and if the body of a homicide victim is found within the State, it is presumed that such result occurred within the State.

(5) This State includes the land and water and the air space above such land and water with respect to which the State has legislative jurisdiction.

Section 1.04. Classes of Crimes; Violations.

(1) An offense defined by this Code or by any other statute of this State, for which a sentence of [death or of] imprisonment is authorized, constitutes a crime. Crimes are classified as felonies, misdemeanors or petty misdemeanors.

(2) A crime is a felony if it is so designated in this Code or if persons convicted thereof may be sentenced [to death or] to imprisonment for a term which, apart from an extended term, is in excess of one year.

(3) A crime is a misdemeanor if it is so designated in this Code or in a statute other than this Code enacted subsequent thereto.

(4) A crime is a petty misdemeanor if it is so designated in this Code or in a statute other than this Code enacted subsequent thereto or if it is defined by a statute other than this Code which now provides that persons convicted thereof may be sentenced to imprisonment for a term of which the maximum is less than one year.

(5) An offense defined by this Code or by any other statute of this State constitutes a violation if it is so designated in this Code or in the law defining the offense or if no other sentence than a fine, or fine and forfeiture or other civil penalty is authorized upon conviction or if it is defined by a statute other than this Code which now

provides that the offense shall not constitute a crime. A violation does not constitute a crime and conviction of a violation shall not give rise to any disability or legal disadvantage based on conviction of a criminal offense.

(6) Any offense declared by law to constitute a crime, without specification of the grade thereof or of the sentence authorized upon conviction, is a misdemeanor.

(7) An offense defined by any statute of this State other than this Code shall be classified as provided in this Section and the sentence that may be imposed upon conviction thereof shall hereafter be governed by this Code.

Section 1.05. All Offenses Defined by Statute; Application of General Provisions of the Code.

(1) No conduct constitutes an offense unless it is a crime or violation under this Code or another statute of this State.

(2) The provisions of Part I of the Code are applicable to offenses defined by other statutes, unless the Code otherwise provides.

(3) This Section does not affect the power of a court to punish for contempt or to employ any sanction authorized by law for the enforcement of an order or a civil judgment or decree.

Section 1.06. Time Limitations.

(1) A prosecution for murder may be commenced at any time.

(2) Except as otherwise provided in this Section, prosecutions for other offenses are subject to the following periods of limitation:

(a) a prosecution for a felony of the first degree must be commenced within six years after it is committed;

(b) a prosecution for any other felony must be commenced within three years after it is committed;

(c) a prosecution for a misdemeanor must be commenced within two years after it is committed;

(d) a prosecution for a petty misdemeanor or a violation must be commenced within six months after it is committed.

(3) If the period prescribed in Subsection (2) has expired, a prosecution may nevertheless be commenced for:

(a) any offense a material element of which is either fraud or a breach of fiduciary obligation within one year after discovery of the offense by an aggrieved party or by a person who has legal duty to represent an aggrieved party and who is himself not a party to the offense, but in no case shall this provision extend the period of limitation otherwise applicable by more than three years; and

(b) any offense based upon misconduct in office by a public officer or employee at any time when the defendant is in public office or employment or within two years thereafter, but in no case shall this provision extend the period of limitation otherwise applicable by more than three years.

(4) An offense is committed either when every element occurs, or, if a legislative purpose to prohibit a continuing course of conduct plainly appears, at the time when the course of conduct or the defendant's complicity therein is terminated. Time starts to run on the day after the offense is committed.

(5) A prosecution is commenced either when an indictment is found [or an information filed] or when a warrant or other process is issued, provided that such warrant or process is executed without unreasonable delay.

(6) The period of limitation does not run:

(a) during any time when the accused is continuously absent from the State or has no reasonably ascertainable place of abode or work within the State, but in no case shall this provision extend the period of limitation otherwise applicable by more than three years; or

(b) during any time when a prosecution against the accused for the same conduct is pending in this State.

Section 1.07. Method of Prosecution When Conduct Constitutes More Than One Offense.

(1) *Prosecution for Multiple Offenses; Limitation on Convictions.* When the same conduct of a defendant may establish the commission of more than one offense, the defendant may be prosecuted for each such offense. He may not, however, be convicted of more than one offense if:

(a) one offense is included in the other, as defined in Subsection (4) of this Section; or

(b) one offense consists only of a conspiracy or other form of preparation to commit the other; or

(c) inconsistent findings of fact are required to establish the commission of the offenses; or

(d) the offenses differ only in that one is defined to prohibit a designated kind of conduct generally and the other to prohibit a specific instance of such conduct; or

(e) the offense is defined as a continuing course of conduct and the defendant's course of conduct was uninterrupted, unless the law provides that specific periods of such conduct constitute separate offenses.

(2) *Limitation on Separate Trials for Multiple Offenses.* Except as provided in Subsection (3) of this Section, a defendant shall not be subject to separate trials for multiple offenses based on the same conduct or arising from the same criminal episode, if such offenses are known to the appropriate prosecuting officer at the time of the

PART I. GENERAL PROVISIONS

commencement of the first trial and are within the jurisdiction of a single court.

(3) *Authority of Court to Order Separate Trials.* When a defendant is charged with two or more offenses based on the same conduct or arising from the same criminal episode, the Court, on application of the prosecuting attorney or of the defendant, may order any such charge to be tried separately, if it is satisfied that justice so requires.

(4) *Conviction of Included Offense Permitted.* A defendant may be convicted of an offense included in an offense charged in the indictment [or the information]. An offense is so included when:

(a) it is established by proof of the same or less than all the facts required to establish the commission of the offense charged; or

(b) it consists of an attempt or solicitation to commit the offense charged or to commit an offense otherwise included therein; or

(c) it differs from the offense charged only in the respect that a less serious injury or risk of injury to the same person, property or public interest or a lesser kind of culpability suffices to establish its commission.

(5) *Submission of Included Offense to Jury.* The Court shall not be obligated to charge the jury with respect to an included offense unless there is a rational basis for a verdict acquitting the defendant of the offense charged and convicting him of the included offense.

Section 1.08. When Prosecution Barred by Former Prosecution for the Same Offense.

When a prosecution is for a violation of the same provision of the statutes and is based upon the same facts as a former prosecution, it is barred by such former prosecution under the following circumstances:

(1) The former prosecution resulted in an acquittal. There is an acquittal if the prosecution resulted in a finding of not guilty by the trier of fact or in a determination that there was insufficient evidence to warrant a conviction. A finding of guilty of a lesser included offense is an acquittal of the greater inclusive offense, although the conviction is subsequently set aside.

(2) The former prosecution was terminated, after the information had been filed or the indictment found, by a final order or judgment for the defendant, which has not been set aside, reversed, or vacated and which necessarily required a determination inconsistent with a fact or a legal proposition that must be established for conviction of the offense.

(3) The former prosecution resulted in a conviction. There is a conviction if the prosecution resulted in a judgment of conviction which has not been reversed or vacated, a verdict of guilty which has not been set aside and which is capable of supporting a judgment, or a plea of guilty accepted by the Court. In the latter two cases failure to enter judgment must be for a reason other than a motion of the defendant.

(4) The former prosecution was improperly terminated. Except as provided in this Subsection, there is an improper termination of a prosecution if the termination is for reasons not amounting to an acquittal, and it takes place after the first witness is sworn but before verdict. Termination under any of the following circumstances is not improper:

(a) The defendant consents to the termination or waives, by motion to dismiss or otherwise, his right to object to the termination.

(b) The trial court finds that the termination is necessary because:

(1) it is physically impossible to proceed with the trial in conformity with law; or

(2) there is a legal defect in the proceedings which would make any judgment entered upon a verdict reversible as a matter of law; or

(3) prejudicial conduct, in or outside the courtroom, makes it impossible to proceed with the trial without injustice to either the defendant or the State; or

(4) the jury is unable to agree upon a verdict; or

(5) false statements of a juror on voir dire prevent a fair trial.

Section 1.09. When Prosecution Barred by Former Prosecution for Different Offense.

Although a prosecution is for a violation of a different provision of the statutes than a former prosecution or is based on different facts, it is barred by such former prosecution under the following circumstances:

(1) The former prosecution resulted in an acquittal or in a conviction as defined in Section 1.08 and the subsequent prosecution is for:

(a) any offense of which the defendant could have been convicted on the first prosecution; or

(b) any offense for which the defendant should have been tried on the first prosecution under Section 1.07, unless the Court ordered a separate trial of the charge of such offense; or

(c) the same conduct, unless (i) the offense of which the defendant was formerly convicted or acquitted and the offense for which he is subsequently prosecuted each requires proof of a fact not required by the other and the law defining each of such offenses is intended to prevent a substantially different harm or evil, or (ii) the second offense was not consummated when the former trial began.

(2) The former prosecution was terminated, after the information was filed or the indictment found, by an acquittal or by a final order or judgment for the defendant which has not been set aside, reversed or vacated and which acquittal, final order or judgment necessarily required a determination inconsistent with a fact which must be established for conviction of the second offense.

(3) The former prosecution was improperly terminated, as improper termination is defined in Section 1.08, and the subsequent prosecution is for an offense of which the defendant could have been convicted had the former prosecution not been improperly terminated.

Section 1.10. Former Prosecution in Another Jurisdiction: When a Bar.

When conduct constitutes an offense within the concurrent jurisdiction of this State and of the United States or another State, a prosecution in any such other jurisdiction is a bar to a subsequent prosecution in this State under the following circumstances:

(1) The first prosecution resulted in an acquittal or in a conviction as defined in Section 1.08 and the subsequent prosecution is based on the same conduct, unless (a) the offense of which the defendant was formerly convicted or acquitted and the offense for which he is subsequently prosecuted each requires proof of a fact not required by the other and the law defining each of such offenses is intended to prevent a substantially different harm or evil or (b) the second offense was not consummated when the former trial began; or

(2) The former prosecution was terminated, after the information was filed or the indictment found, by an acquittal or by a final order or judgment for the defendant which has not been set aside, reversed or vacated and which acquittal, final order or judgment necessarily required a determination inconsistent with a fact which

must be established for conviction of the offense of which the defendant is subsequently prosecuted.

Section 1.11. Former Prosecution Before Court Lacking Jurisdiction or When Fraudulently Procured by the Defendant.

A prosecution is not a bar within the meaning of Sections 1.08, 1.09 and 1.10 under any of the following circumstances:

(1) The former prosecution was before a court which lacked jurisdiction over the defendant or the offense; or

(2) The former prosecution was procured by the defendant without the knowledge of the appropriate prosecuting officer and with the purpose of avoiding the sentence which might otherwise be imposed; or

(3) The former prosecution resulted in a judgment of conviction which was held invalid in a subsequent proceeding on a writ of habeas corpus, coram nobis or similar process.

Section 1.12. Proof Beyond a Reasonable Doubt; Affirmative Defenses; Burden of Proving Fact When Not an Element of an Offense; Presumptions.

(1) No person may be convicted of an offense unless each element of such offense is proved beyond a reasonable doubt. In the absence of such proof, the innocence of the defendant is assumed.

(2) Subsection (1) of this Section does not:

(a) require the disproof of an affirmative defense unless and until there is evidence supporting such defense; or

(b) apply to any defense which the Code or another statute plainly requires the defendant to prove by a preponderance of evidence.

(3) A ground of defense is affirmative, within the meaning of Subsection (2)(a) of this Section, when:

   (a) it arises under a section of the Code which so provides; or

   (b) it relates to an offense defined by a statute other than the Code and such statute so provides; or

   (c) it involves a matter of excuse or justification peculiarly within the knowledge of the defendant on which he can fairly be required to adduce supporting evidence.

(4) When the application of the Code depends upon the finding of a fact which is not an element of an offense, unless the Code otherwise provides:

   (a) the burden of proving the fact is on the prosecution or defendant, depending on whose interest or contention will be furthered if the finding should be made; and

   (b) the fact must be proved to the satisfaction of the Court or jury, as the case may be.

(5) When the Code establishes a presumption with respect to any fact which is an element of an offense, it has the following consequences:

   (a) when there is evidence of the facts which give rise to the presumption, the issue of the existence of the presumed fact must be submitted to the jury, unless the Court is satisfied that the evidence as a whole clearly negatives the presumed fact; and

   (b) when the issue of the existence of the presumed fact is submitted to the jury, the Court shall charge that while the presumed fact must, on all the evidence, be proved beyond a reasonable doubt, the law declares that the jury may regard the facts giving rise to the presumption as sufficient evidence of the presumed fact.

(6) A presumption not established by the Code or inconsistent with it has the consequences otherwise accorded it by law.

Section 1.13. General Definitions.

In this Code, unless a different meaning plainly is required:

(1) "statute" includes the Constitution and a local law or ordinance of a political subdivision of the State;

(2) "act" or "action" means a bodily movement whether voluntary or involuntary;

(3) "voluntary" has the meaning specified in Section 2.01;

(4) "omission" means a failure to act;

(5) "conduct" means an action or omission and its accompanying state of mind, or, where relevant, a series of acts and omissions;

(6) "actor" includes, where relevant, a person guilty of an omission;

(7) "acted" includes, where relevant, "omitted to act";

(8) "person," "he" and "actor" include any natural person and, where relevant, a corporation or an unincorporated association;

(9) "element of an offense" means (i) such conduct or (ii) such attendant circumstances or (iii) such a result of conduct as

(a) is included in the description of the forbidden conduct in the definition of the offense; or

(b) establishes the required kind of culpability; or

(c) negatives an excuse or justification for such conduct; or

(d) negatives a defense under the statute of limitations; or

(e) establishes jurisdiction or venue;

(10) "material element of an offense" means an element that does not relate exclusively to the statute of limitations, jurisdiction, venue or to any other matter similarly unconnected with (i) the harm or evil, incident to conduct, sought to be prevented by the law defining the offense, or (ii) the existence of a justification or excuse for such conduct;

(11) "purposely" has the meaning specified in Section 2.02 and equivalent terms such as "with purpose," "designed" or "with design" have the same meaning;

(12) "intentionally" or "with intent" means purposely;

(13) "knowingly" has the meaning specified in Section 2.02 and equivalent terms such as "knowing" or "with knowledge" have the same meaning;

(14) "recklessly" has the meaning specified in Section 2.02 and equivalent terms such as "recklessness" or "with recklessness" have the same meaning;

(15) "negligently" has the meaning specified in Section 2.02 and equivalent terms such as "negligence' " or "with negligence" have the same meaning;

(16) "reasonably believes" or "reasonable belief" designates a belief which the actor is not reckless or negligent in holding.

ARTICLE 2. GENERAL PRINCIPLES OF LIABILITY

Section 2.01. Requirement of Voluntary Act; Omission as Basis of Liability; Possession as an Act.

(1) A person is not guilty of an offense unless his liability is based on conduct which includes a voluntary act or the omission to perform an act of which he is physically capable.

(2) The following are not voluntary acts within the meaning of this Section:

(a) a reflex or convulsion;

(b) a bodily movement during unconsciousness or sleep;

(c) conduct during hypnosis or resulting from hypnotic suggestion;

(d) a bodily movement that otherwise is not a product of the effort or determination of the actor, either conscious or habitual.

(3) Liability for the commission of an offense may not be based on an omission unaccompanied by action unless:

(a) the omission is expressly made sufficient by the law defining the offense; or

(b) a duty to perform the omitted act is otherwise imposed by law.

(4) Possession is an act, within the meaning of this Section, if the possessor knowingly procured or received the thing possessed or was aware of his control thereof for a sufficient period to have been able to terminate his possession.

Section 2.02. General Requirements of Culpability.

(1) *Minimum Requirements of Culpability.* Except as provided in Section 2.05, a person is not guilty of an offense unless he acted purposely, knowingly, recklessly or negligently, as the law may require, with respect to each material element of the offense.

(2) *Kinds of Culpability Defined.*

(a) *Purposely.*

> A person acts purposely with respect to a material element of an offense when:

(i) if the element involves the nature of his conduct or a result thereof, it is his conscious object to engage in conduct of that nature or to cause such a result; and

(ii) if the element involves the attendant circumstances, he is aware of the existence of such circumstances or he believes or hopes that they exist.

(b) *Knowingly.*

A person acts knowingly with respect to a material element of an offense when:

(i) if the element involves the nature of his conduct or the attendant circumstances, he is aware that his conduct is of that nature or that such circumstances exist; and

(ii) if the element involves a result of his conduct, he is aware that it is practically certain that his conduct will cause such a result.

(c) *Recklessly.*

A person acts recklessly with respect to a material element of an offense when he consciously disregards a substantial and unjustifiable risk that the material element exists or will result from his conduct. The risk must be of such a nature and degree that, considering the nature and purpose of the actor's conduct and the circumstances known to him, its disregard involves a gross deviation from the standard of conduct that a law-abiding person would observe in the actor's situation.

(d) *Negligently.*

A person acts negligently with respect to a material element of an offense when he should be aware of a substantial and unjustifiable risk that the material element exists or will result from his conduct. The risk must be of such a nature and degree that the actor's failure to perceive it, considering the nature and purpose of his conduct and the circumstances known to him, involves a gross deviation from the standard of care that a reasonable person would observe in the actor's situation.

(3) *Culpability Required Unless Otherwise Provided.* When the culpability sufficient to establish a material element of an offense is not prescribed by law, such element is established if a person acts purposely, knowingly or recklessly with respect thereto.

(4) *Prescribed Culpability Requirement Applies to All Material Elements.* When the law defining an offense prescribes the kind of culpability that is sufficient for the commission of an offense, without distinguishing among the material elements thereof, such provision shall apply to all the material elements of the offense, unless a contrary purpose plainly appears.

(5) *Substitutes for Negligence, Recklessness and Knowledge.* When the law provides that negligence suffices to establish an element of an offense, such element also is established if a person acts purposely, knowingly or recklessly. When recklessness suffices to establish an element, such element also is established if a person acts purposely or knowingly. When acting knowingly suffices to establish an element, such element also is established if a person acts purposely.

(6) *Requirement of Purpose Satisfied if Purpose Is Conditional.* When a particular purpose is an element of an offense, the element is established although such purpose is conditional, unless the condition negatives the harm or evil sought to be prevented by the law defining the offense.

(7) *Requirement of Knowledge Satisfied by Knowledge of High Probability.* When knowledge of the existence of a particular fact is an element of an offense, such knowledge is established if a person is aware of a high probabil-

ity of its existence, unless he actually believes that it does not exist.

(8) *Requirement of Wilfulness Satisfied by Acting Knowingly.* A requirement that an offense be committed wilfully is satisfied if a person acts knowingly with respect to the material elements of the offense, unless a purpose to impose further requirements appears.

(9) *Culpability as to Illegality of Conduct.* Neither knowledge nor recklessness or negligence as to whether conduct constitutes an offense or as to the existence, meaning or application of the law determining the elements of an offense is an element of such offense, unless the definition of the offense or the Code so provides.

(10) *Culpability as Determinant of Grade of Offense.* When the grade or degree of an offense depends on whether the offense is committed purposely, knowingly, recklessly or negligently, its grade or degree shall be the lowest for which the determinative kind of culpability is established with respect to any material element of the offense.

Section 2.03. Causal Relationship Between Conduct and Result; Divergence Between Result Designed or Contemplated and Actual Result or Between Probable and Actual Result.

(1) Conduct is the cause of a result when:

(a) it is an antecedent but for which the result in question would not have occurred; and

(b) the relationship between the conduct and result satisfies any additional causal requirements imposed by the Code or by the law defining the offense.

(2) When purposely or knowingly causing a particular result is an element of an offense, the element is not established if the actual result is not within the purpose or the contemplation of the actor unless:

(a) the actual result differs from that designed or contemplated, as the case may be, only in the respect that a different person or different property is injured or affected or that the injury or harm designed or contemplated would have been more serious or more extensive than that caused; or

(b) the actual result involves the same kind of injury or harm as that designed or contemplated and is not too remote or accidental in its occurrence to have a [just] bearing on the actor's liability or on the gravity of his offense.

(3) When recklessly or negligently causing a particular result is an element of an offense, the element is not established if the actual result is not within the risk of which the actor is aware or, in the case of negligence, of which he should be aware unless:

(a) the actual result differs from the probable result only in the respect that a different person or different property is injured or affected or that the probable injury or harm would have been more serious or more extensive than that caused; or

(b) the actual result involves the same kind of injury or harm as the probable result and is not too remote or accidental in its occurrence to have a [just] bearing on the actor's liability or on the gravity of his offense.

(4) When causing a particular result is a material element of an offense for which absolute liability is imposed by law, the element is not established unless the actual result is a probable consequence of the actor's conduct.

Section 2.04. Ignorance or Mistake.

(1) Ignorance or mistake as to a matter of fact or law is a defense if:

(a) the ignorance or mistake negatives the purpose, knowledge, belief, recklessness or negligence required to establish a material element of the offense; or

(b) the law provides that the state of mind established by such ignorance or mistake constitutes a defense.

(2) Although ignorance or mistake would otherwise afford a defense to the offense charged, the defense is not available if the defendant would be guilty of another offense had the situation been as he supposed. In such case, however, the ignorance or mistake of the defendant shall reduce the grade and degree of the offense of which he may be convicted to those of the offense of which he would be guilty had the situation been as he supposed.

(3) A belief that conduct does not legally constitute an offense is a defense to a prosecution for that offense based upon such conduct when:

(a) the statute or other enactment defining the offense is not known to the actor and has not been published or otherwise reasonably made available prior to the conduct alleged; or

(b) he acts in reasonable reliance upon an official statement of the law, afterward determined to be invalid or erroneous, contained in (i) a statute or other enactment; (ii) a judicial decision, opinion or judgment; (iii) an administrative order or grant of permission; or (iv) an official interpretation of the public officer or body charged by law with responsibility for the interpretation, administration or enforcement of the law defining the offense.

(4) The defendant must prove a defense arising under Subsection (3) of this Section by a preponderance of evidence.

Section 2.05. When Culpability Requirements Are Inapplicable to Violations and to Offenses Defined by Other Statutes; Effect of Absolute Liability in Reducing Grade of Offense to Violation.

(1) The requirements of culpability prescribed by Sections 2.01 and 2.02 do not apply to:

(a) offenses which constitute violations, unless the requirement involved is included in the definition of the offense or the Court determines that its application is consistent with effective enforcement of the law defining the offense; or

(b) offenses defined by statutes other than the Code, insofar as a legislative purpose to impose absolute liability for such offenses or with respect to any material element thereof plainly appears.

(2) Notwithstanding any other provision of existing law and unless a subsequent statute otherwise provides:

(a) when absolute liability is imposed with respect to any material element of an offense defined by a statute other than the Code and a conviction is based upon such liability, the offense constitutes a violation; and

(b) although absolute liability is imposed by law with respect to one or more of the material elements of an offense defined by a statute other than the Code, the culpable commission of the offense may be charged and proved, in which event negligence with respect to such elements constitutes sufficient culpability and the classification of the offense and the sentence that may be imposed therefor upon conviction are determined by Section 1.04 and Article 6 of the Code.

Section 2.06. Liability for Conduct of Another; Complicity.

(1) A person is guilty of an offense if it is committed by his own conduct or by the conduct of another person for which he is legally accountable, or both.

(2) A person is legally accountable for the conduct of another person when:

(a) acting with the kind of culpability that is sufficient for the commission of the offense, he causes an innocent or irresponsible person to engage in such conduct; or

(b) he is made accountable for the conduct of such other person by the Code or by the law defining the offense; or

(c) he is an accomplice of such other person in the commission of the offense.

(3) A person is an accomplice of another person in the commission of an offense if:

    (a) with the purpose of promoting or facilitating the commission of the offense, he

        (i) solicits such other person to commit it; or

        (ii) aids or agrees or attempts to aid such other person in planning or committing it; or

        (iii) having a legal duty to prevent the commission of the offense, fails to make proper effort so to do; or

    (b) his conduct is expressly declared by law to establish his complicity.

(4) When causing a particular result is an element of an offense, an accomplice in the conduct causing such result is an accomplice in the commission of that offense, if he acts with the kind of culpability, if any, with respect to that result that is sufficient for the commission of the offense.

(5) A person who is legally incapable of committing a particular offense himself may be guilty thereof if it is committed by the conduct of another person for which he is legally accountable, unless such liability is inconsistent with the purpose of the provision establishing his incapacity.

(6) Unless otherwise provided by the Code or by the law defining the offense, a person is not an accomplice in an offense committed by another person if:

(a) he is a victim of that offense; or

(b) the offense is so defined that his conduct is inevitably incident to its commission; or

(c) he terminates his complicity prior to the commission of the offense and

> (i) wholly deprives it of effectiveness in the commission of the offense; or
>
> (ii) gives timely warning to the law enforcement authorities or otherwise makes proper effort to prevent the commission of the offense.

(7) An accomplice may be convicted on proof of the commission of the offense and of his complicity therein, though the person claimed to have committed the offense has not been prosecuted or convicted or has been convicted of a different offense or degree of offense or has an immunity to prosecution or conviction or has been acquitted.

Section 2.07. Liability of Corporations, Unincorporated Associations and Persons Acting, or Under a Duty to Act, in Their Behalf.

(1) A corporation may be convicted of the commission of an offense if:

(a) the offense is a violation or the offense is defined by a statute other than the Code in which a legislative purpose to impose liability on corporations plainly appears and the conduct is performed by an agent of the corporation acting in behalf of the corporation within the scope of his office or employment, except that if the law defining the offense designates the agents for whose conduct the corporation is accountable or the circumstances under which it is accountable, such provisions shall apply; or

(b) the offense consists of an omission to discharge a specific duty of affirmative performance imposed on corporations by law; or

(c) the commission of the offense was authorized, requested, commanded, performed or recklessly tolerated by the board of directors or by a high managerial agent acting in behalf of the corporation within the scope of his office or employment.

(2) When absolute liability is imposed for the commission of an offense, a legislative purpose to impose liability on a corporation shall be assumed, unless the contrary plainly appears.

(3) An unincorporated association may be convicted of the commission of an offense if:

(a) the offense is defined by a statute other than the Code which expressly provides for the liability of such an association and the conduct is performed by an agent of the association acting in behalf of the association within the scope of his office or employment, except that if the law defining the offense designates the agents for whose conduct the association is accountable or the circumstances under which it is accountable, such provisions shall apply; or

(b) the offense consists of an omission to discharge a specific duty of affirmative performance imposed on associations by law.

(4) As used in this Section:

(a) "corporation" does not include an entity organized as or by a governmental agency for the execution of a governmental program;

(b) "agent" means any director, officer, servant, employee or other person authorized to act in behalf of the corporation or association and, in the case of an unincorporated association, a member of such association;

(c) "high managerial agent" means an officer of a corporation or an unincorporated association, or, in the case of a partnership, a partner, or any other agent of a corporation or association having duties of such responsibility that his conduct may fairly be assumed to represent the policy of the corporation or association.

(5) In any prosecution of a corporation or an unincorporated association for the commission of an offense included within the terms of Subsection (1)(a) or Subsection (3)(a) of this Section, other than an offense for which absolute liability has been imposed, it shall be a defense if the defendant proves by a preponderance of evidence that the high managerial agent having supervisory responsibility over the subject matter of the offense employed due diligence to prevent its commission. This paragraph shall not apply if it is plainly inconsistent with the legislative purpose in defining the particular offense.

(6)(a) A person is legally accountable for any conduct he performs or causes to be performed in the name of the corporation or an unincorporated association or in its behalf to the same extent as if it were performed in his own name or behalf.

(b) Whenever a duty to act is imposed by law upon a corporation or an unincorporated association, any agent of the corporation or association having primary responsibility for the discharge of the duty is legally accountable for a reckless omission to perform the required act to the same extent as if the duty were imposed by law directly upon himself.

(c) When a person is convicted of an offense by reason of his legal accountability for the conduct of a corporation or an unincorporated association, he is subject to the sentence authorized by law when a natural person is convicted of an offense of the grade and the degree involved.

Section 2.08. Intoxication.

(1) Except as provided in Subsection (4) of this Section, intoxication of the actor is not a defense unless it negatives an element of the offense.

(2) When recklessness establishes an element of the offense, if the actor, due to self-induced intoxication, is unaware of a risk of which he would have been aware had he been sober, such unawareness is immaterial.

(3) Intoxication does not, in itself, constitute mental disease within the meaning of Section 4.01.

(4) Intoxication which (a) is not self-induced or (b) is pathological is an affirmative defense if by reason of such intoxication the actor at the time of his conduct lacks substantial capacity either to appreciate its criminality [wrongfulness] or to conform his conduct to the requirements of law.

(5) *Definitions.* In this Section unless a different meaning plainly is required:

(a) "intoxication" means a disturbance of mental or physical capacities resulting from the introduction of substances into the body;

(b) "self-induced intoxication" means intoxication caused by substances which the actor knowingly introduces into his body, the tendency of which to cause intoxication he knows or ought to know, unless he introduces them pursuant to medical advice or under such circumstances as would afford a defense to a charge of crime;

(c) "pathological intoxication" means intoxication grossly excessive in degree, given the amount of the intoxicant, to which the actor does not know he is susceptible.

Section 2.09. Duress.

(1) It is an affirmative defense that the actor engaged in the conduct charged to constitute an offense because he was coerced to do so by the use of, or a threat to use, unlawful force against his person or the person of another, which a person of reasonable firmness in his situation would have been unable to resist.

(2) The defense provided by this Section is unavailable if the actor recklessly placed himself in a situation in which it was probable that he would be subjected to duress. The defense is also unavailable if he was negligent in placing himself in such a situation, whenever negligence suffices to establish culpability for the offense charged.

(3) It is not a defense that a woman acted on the command of her husband, unless she acted under such coercion as would establish a defense under this Section. [The presumption that a woman, acting in the presence of her husband, is coerced is abolished.]

(4) When the conduct of the actor would otherwise be justifiable under Section 3.02, this Section does not preclude such defense.

Section 2.10. Military Orders.

It is an affirmative defense that the actor, in engaging in the conduct charged to constitute an offense, does no more than execute an order of his superior in the armed services which he does not know to be unlawful.

Section 2.11. Consent.

(1) *In General.* The consent of the victim to conduct charged to constitute an offense or to the result thereof is a defense if such consent negatives an element of the offense or precludes the infliction of the harm or evil sought to be prevented by the law defining the offense.

(2) *Consent to Bodily Harm.* When conduct is charged to constitute an offense because it causes or threatens bodily harm, consent to such conduct or to the infliction of such harm is a defense if:

(a) the bodily harm consented to or threatened by the conduct consented to is not serious; or

(b) the conduct and the harm are reasonably foreseeable hazards of joint participation in a lawful athletic contest or competitive sport; or

(c) the consent establishes a justification for the conduct under Article 3 of the Code.

(3) *Ineffective Consent.* Unless otherwise provided by the Code or by the law defining the offense, assent does not constitute consent if:

(a) it is given by a person who is legally incompetent to authorize the conduct charged to constitute the offense; or

(b) it is given by a person who by reason of youth, mental disease or defect or intoxication is manifestly unable or known by the actor to be unable to make a reasonable judgment as to the nature or harmfulness of the conduct charged to constitute the offense; or

(c) it is given by a person whose improvident consent is sought to be prevented by the law defining the offense; or

(d) it is induced by force, duress or deception of a kind sought to be prevented by the law defining the offense.

Section 2.12. De Minimis Infractions.

The Court shall dismiss a prosecution if, having regard to the nature of the conduct charged to constitute an offense and the nature of the attendant circumstances, it finds that the defendant's conduct:

(1) was within a customary license or tolerance, neither expressly negatived by the person whose interest was infringed nor inconsistent with the purpose of the law defining the offense; or

(2) did not actually cause or threaten the harm or evil sought to be prevented by the law defining the offense or did so only to an extent too trivial to warrant the condemnation of conviction; or

(3) presents such other extenuations that it cannot reasonably be regarded as envisaged by the legislature in forbidding the offense.

The Court shall not dismiss a prosecution under Subsection (3) of this Section without filing a written statement of its reasons.

Section 2.13. Entrapment.

(1) A public law enforcement official or a person acting in cooperation with such an official perpetrates an entrapment if for the purpose of obtaining evidence of the commission of an offense, he induces or encourages another person to engage in conduct constituting such offense by either:

(a) making knowingly false representations designed to induce the belief that such conduct is not prohibited; or

(b) employing methods of persuasion or inducement which create a substantial risk that such an offense will be committed by persons other than those who are ready to commit it.

(2) Except as provided in Subsection (3) of this Section, a person prosecuted for an offense shall be acquitted if he proves by a preponderance of evidence that his conduct occurred in response to an entrapment. The issue of entrapment shall be tried by the Court in the absence of the jury.

(3) The defense afforded by this Section is unavailable when causing or threatening bodily injury is an element of the offense charged and the prosecution is based on conduct causing or threatening such injury to a person other than the person perpetrating the entrapment.

ARTICLE 3. GENERAL PRINCIPLES OF JUSTIFICATION

Section 3.01. Justification an Affirmative Defense; Civil Remedies Unaffected.

(1) In any prosecution based on conduct which is justifiable under this Article, justification is an affirmative defense.

(2) The fact that conduct is justifiable under this Article does not abolish or impair any remedy for such conduct which is available in any civil action.

Section 3.02. Justification Generally: Choice of Evils.

(1) Conduct which the actor believes to be necessary to avoid a harm or evil to himself or to another is justifiable, provided that:

(a) the harm or evil sought to be avoided by such conduct is greater than that sought to be prevented by the law defining the offense charged; and

(b) neither the Code nor other law defining the offense provides exceptions or defenses dealing with the specific situation involved; and

(c) a legislative purpose to exclude the justification claimed does not otherwise plainly appear.

(2) When the actor was reckless or negligent in bringing about the situation requiring a choice of harms or evils or in appraising the necessity for his conduct, the justification afforded by this Section is unavailable in a prosecution for any offense for which recklessness or negligence, as the case may be, suffices to establish culpability.

Section 3.03. Execution of Public Duty.

(1) Except as provided in Subsection (2) of this Section, conduct is justifiable when it is required or authorized by:

(a) the law defining the duties or functions of a public officer or the assistance to be rendered to such officer in the performance of his duties; or

(b) the law governing the execution of legal process; or

(c) the judgment or order of a competent court or tribunal; or

PART I. GENERAL PROVISIONS

(d) the law governing the armed services or the lawful conduct of war; or

(e) any other provision of law imposing a public duty.

(2) The other sections of this Article apply to:

(a) the use of force upon or toward the person of another for any of the purposes dealt with in such sections; and

(b) the use of deadly force for any purpose, unless the use of such force is otherwise expressly authorized by law or occurs in the lawful conduct of war.

(3) The justification afforded by Subsection (1) of this Section applies:

(a) when the actor believes his conduct to be required or authorized by the judgment or direction of a competent court or tribunal or in the lawful execution of legal process, notwithstanding lack of jurisdiction of the court or defect in the legal process; and

(b) when the actor believes his conduct to be required or authorized to assist a public officer in the performance of his duties, notwithstanding that the officer exceeded his legal authority.

Section 3.04. Use of Force in Self-Protection.

(1) *Use of Force Justifiable for Protection of the Person.* Subject to the provisions of this Section and of Section 3.09, the use of force upon or toward another person is justifiable when the actor believes that such force is immediately necessary for the purpose of protecting himself against the use of unlawful force by such other person on the present occasion.

(2) *Limitations on Justifying Necessity for Use of Force.*

(a) The use of force is not justifiable under this Section:

(i) to resist an arrest which the actor knows is being made by a peace officer, although the arrest is unlawful; or

(ii) to resist force used by the occupier or possessor of property or by another person on his behalf, where the actor knows that the person using the force is doing so under a claim of right to protect the property, except that this limitation shall not apply if:

(1) the actor is a public officer acting in the performance of his duties or a person lawfully assisting him therein or a person making or assisting in a lawful arrest; or

(2) the actor has been unlawfully dispossessed of the property and is making a re-entry or recaption justified by Section 3.06; or

(3) the actor believes that such force is necessary to protect himself against death or serious bodily harm.

(b) The use of deadly force is not justifiable under this Section unless the actor believes that such force is necessary to protect himself against death, serious bodily harm, kidnapping or sexual intercourse compelled by force or threat; nor is it justifiable if:

(i) the actor, with the purpose of causing death or serious bodily harm, provoked the use of force against himself in the same encounter; or

(ii) the actor knows that he can avoid the necessity of using such force with complete safety by retreating or by surrendering possession of a thing to a person asserting a claim of right thereto or by complying with a demand that he abstain from any action which he has no duty to take, except that:

(1) the actor is not obliged to retreat from his dwelling or place of work, unless he was the

initial aggressor or is assailed in his place of work by another person whose place of work the actor knows it to be; and

(2) a public officer justified in using force in the performance of his duties or a person justified in using force in his assistance or a person justified in using force in making an arrest or preventing an escape is not obliged to desist from efforts to perform such duty, effect such arrest or prevent such escape because of resistance or threatened resistance by or on behalf of the person against whom such action is directed.

(c) Except as required by paragraphs (a) and (b) of this Subsection, a person employing protective force may estimate the necessity thereof under the circumstances as he believes them to be when the force is used, without retreating, surrendering possession, doing any other act which he has no legal duty to do or abstaining from any lawful action.

(3) *Use of Confinement as Protective Force.* The justification afforded by this Section extends to the use of confinement as protective force only if the actor takes all reasonable measures to terminate the confinement as soon as he knows that he safely can, unless the person confined has been arrested on a charge of crime.

Section 3.05. Use of Force for the Protection of Other Persons.

(1) Subject to the provisions of this Section and of Section 3.09, the use of force upon or toward the person of another is justifiable to protect a third person when:

(a) the actor would be justified under Section 3.04 in using such force to protect himself against the injury he believes to be threatened to the person whom he seeks to protect; and

(b) under the circumstances as the actor believes them to be, the person whom he seeks to protect would be justified in using such protective force; and

(c) the actor believes that his intervention is necessary for the protection of such other person.

(2) Notwithstanding Subsection (1) of this Section:

(a) when the actor would be obliged under Section 3.04 to retreat, to surrender the possession of a thing or to comply with a demand before using force in self-protection, he is not obliged to do so before using force for the protection of another person, unless he knows that he can thereby secure the complete safety of such other person; and

(b) when the person whom the actor seeks to protect would be obliged under Section 3.04 to retreat, to surrender the possession of a thing or to comply with a demand if he knew that he could obtain complete safety by so doing, the actor is obliged to try to cause him to do so before using force in his protection if the actor knows that he can obtain complete safety in that way; and

(c) neither the actor nor the person whom he seeks to protect is obliged to retreat when in the other's dwelling or place of work to any greater extent than in his own.

Section 3.06. Use of Force for the Protection of Property.

(1) *Use of Force Justifiable for Protection of Property.* Subject to the provisions of this Section and of Section 3.09, the use of force upon or toward the person of another is justifiable when the actor believes that such force is immediately necessary:

(a) to prevent or terminate an unlawful entry or other trespass upon land or a trespass against or the unlawful carrying away of tangible, movable property, provided that such land or movable property is, or is believed by the actor to be, in his possession or in the possession of another person for whose protection he acts; or

(b) to effect an entry or re-entry upon land or to retake tangible movable property, provided that the actor believes that he or the person by whose authority he acts or a person from whom he or such other person derives title was unlawfully dispossessed of such land or movable property and is entitled to possession, and provided, further, that:

(i) the force is used immediately or on fresh pursuit after such dispossession; or

(ii) the actor believes that the person against whom he uses force has no claim of right to the possession of the property and, in the case of land, the circumstances, as the actor believes them to be, are of such urgency that it would be an exceptional hardship to postpone the entry or re-entry until a court order is obtained.

(2) *Meaning of Possession.* For the purposes of Subsection (1) of this Section:

(a) a person who has parted with the custody of property to another who refuses to restore it to him is no longer in possession, unless the property is movable and was and still is located on land in his possession;

(b) a person who has been dispossessed of land does not regain possession thereof merely by setting foot thereon;

(c) a person who has a license to use or occupy real property is deemed to be in possession thereof except against the licensor acting under claim of right.

(3) *Limitations on Justifiable Use of Force.*

(a) *Request to Desist.* The use of force is justifiable under this Section only if the actor first requests the person against whom such force is used to desist from his interference with the property, unless the actor believes that:

(i) such request would be useless; or

(ii) it would be dangerous to himself or another person to make the request; or

(iii) substantial harm will be done to the physical condition of the property which is sought to be protected before the request can effectively be made.

(b) *Exclusion of Trespasser.* The use of force to prevent or terminate a trespass is not justifiable under this Section if the actor knows that the exclusion of the trespasser will expose him to substantial danger of serious bodily harm.

(c) *Resistance of Lawful Re-entry or Recaption.* The use of force to prevent an entry or re-entry upon land or the recaption of movable property is not justifiable under this Section, although the actor believes that such re-entry or recaption is unlawful, if:

(i) the re-entry or recaption is made by or on behalf of a person who was actually dispossessed of the property; and

(ii) it is otherwise justifiable under paragraph (1)(b) of this Section.

(d) *Use of Deadly Force.* The use of deadly force is not justifiable under this Section unless the actor believes that:

(i) the person against whom the force is used is attempting to dispossess him of his dwelling otherwise than under a claim of right to its possession; or

(ii) the person against whom the force is used is attempting to commit or consummate arson, burglary, robbery or other felonious theft or property destruction and either:

(1) has employed or threatened deadly force against or in the presence of the actor; or

(2) the use of force other than deadly force to prevent the commission or the consummation of the crime would expose the actor or another in his presence to substantial danger of serious bodily harm.

(4) *Use of Confinement as Protective Force.* The justification afforded by this Section extends to the use of confinement as protective force only if the actor takes all reasonable measures to terminate the confinement as soon as he knows that he can do so with safety to the property, unless the person confined has been arrested on a charge of crime.

(5) *Use of Device to Protect Property.* The justification afforded by this Section extends to the use of a device for the purpose of protecting property only if:

(a) the device is not designed to cause or known to create a substantial risk of causing death or serious bodily harm; and

(b) the use of the particular device to protect the property from entry or trespass is reasonable under the circumstances, as the actor believes them to be; and

(c) the device is one customarily used for such a purpose or reasonable care is taken to make known to probable intruders the fact that it is used.

(6) *Use of Force to Pass Wrongful Obstructor.* The use of force to pass a person whom the actor believes to be purposely or knowingly and unjustifiably obstructing the actor from going to a place to which he may lawfully go is justifiable, provided that:

(a) the actor believes that the person against whom he uses force has no claim of right to obstruct the actor; and

(b) the actor is not being obstructed from entry or movement on land which he knows to be in the possession or custody of the person obstructing him, or in the possession or custody of another person by whose authority the obstructor acts, unless the circumstances, as the actor believes them to be, are of such urgency that it would not be reasonable to postpone the entry or movement on such land until a court order is obtained; and

(c) the force used is not greater than would be justifiable if the person obstructing the actor were using force against him to prevent his passage.

Section 3.07. Use of Force in Law Enforcement.

(1) *Use of Force Justifiable to Effect an Arrest.* Subject to the provisions of this Section and of Section 3.09, the use of force upon or toward the person of another is justifiable when the actor is making or assisting in making an arrest and the actor believes that such force is immediately necessary to effect a lawful arrest.

(2) *Limitations on the Use of Force.*

(a) The use of force is not justifiable under this Section unless:

(i) the actor makes known the purpose of the arrest or believes that it is otherwise known by or cannot reasonably be made known to the person to be arrested; and

(ii) when the arrest is made under a warrant, the warrant is valid or believed by the actor to be valid.

(b) The use of deadly force is not justifiable under this Section unless:

(i) the arrest is for a felony; and

(ii) the person effecting the arrest is authorized to act as a peace officer or is assisting a person whom he believes to be authorized to act as a peace officer; and

(iii) the actor believes that the force employed creates no substantial risk of injury to innocent persons; and

(iv) the actor believes that:

(1) the crime for which the arrest is made involved conduct including the use or threatened use of deadly force; or

(2) there is a substantial risk that the person to be arrested will cause death or serious bodily harm if his apprehension is delayed.

(3) *Use of Force to Prevent Escape from Custody.* The use of force to prevent the escape of an arrested person from custody is justifiable when the force could justifiably have been employed to effect the arrest under which the person is in custody, except that a guard or other person authorized to act as a peace officer is justified in using any force, including deadly force, which he believes to be immediately necessary to prevent the escape of a person from a jail, prison, or other institution for the detention of persons charged with or convicted of a crime.

(4) *Use of Force by Private Person Assisting an Unlawful Arrest.*

(a) A private person who is summoned by a peace officer to assist in effecting an unlawful arrest, is justified in using any force which he would be justified in using if the arrest were lawful, provided that he does not believe the arrest is unlawful.

(b) A private person who assists another private person in effecting an unlawful arrest, or who, not being summoned, assists a peace officer in effecting an unlawful arrest, is justified in using any force which he would be justified in using if the arrest were lawful, provided that (i) he believes the arrest is lawful, and (ii) the arrest would be lawful if the facts were as he believes them to be.

(5) *Use of Force to Prevent Suicide or the Commission of a Crime.*

(a) The use of force upon or toward the person of another is justifiable when the actor believes that such force is immediately necessary to prevent such other person from committing suicide, inflicting serious bodily harm upon himself, committing or consummating the commission of a crime involving or threatening bodily harm, damage to or loss of property or a breach of the peace, except that:

(i) any limitations imposed by the other provisions of this Article on the justifiable use of force in self-protection, for the protection of others, the protection of property, the effectuation of an arrest or the prevention of an escape from custody shall apply notwithstanding the criminality of the conduct against which such force is used; and

(ii) the use of deadly force is not in any event justifiable under this Subsection unless:

(1) the actor believes that there is a substantial risk that the person whom he seeks to prevent from committing a crime will cause death or serious bodily harm to another unless the commission or the consummation of the crime is prevented and that the use of such force presents no substantial risk of injury to innocent persons; or

(2) the actor believes that the use of such force is necessary to suppress a riot or mutiny after the rioters or mutineers have been ordered to disperse and warned, in any particular manner that the law may require, that such force will be used if they do not obey.

(b) The justification afforded by this Subsection extends to the use of confinement as preventive force only if the actor takes all reasonable measures to terminate the confinement as soon as he knows that he safely can, unless the person confined has been arrested on a charge of crime.

Section 3.08. Use of Force by Persons with Special Responsibility for Care, Discipline or Safety of Others.

The use of force upon or toward the person of another is justifiable if:

(1) the actor is the parent or guardian or other person similarly responsible for the general care and supervision of a minor or a person acting at the request of such parent, guardian or other responsible person and:

(a) the force is used for the purpose of safeguarding or promoting the welfare of the minor, including the prevention or punishment of his misconduct; and

(b) the force used is not designed to cause or known to create a substantial risk of causing death, serious bodily harm, disfigurement, extreme pain or mental distress or gross degradation; or

(2) the actor is a teacher or a person otherwise entrusted with the care or supervision for a special purpose of a minor and:

(a) the actor believes that the force used is necessary to further such special purpose, including the maintenance of reasonable discipline in a school, class or other group, and that the use of such force is consistent with the welfare of the minor; and

(b) the degree of force, if it had been used by the parent or guardian of the minor, would not be unjustifiable under Subsection (1)(b) of this Section; or

(3) the actor is the guardian or other person similarly responsible for the general care and supervision of an incompetent person; and:

(a) the force is used for the purpose of safeguarding or promoting the welfare of the incompetent person, including the prevention of his misconduct, or, when such incompetent person is in a hospital or other institution for his care and custody, for the maintenance of reasonable discipline in such institution; and

(b) the force used is not designed to cause or known to create a substantial risk of causing death, serious bodily harm, disfigurement, extreme or unnecessary pain, mental distress, or humiliation; or

(4) the actor is a doctor or other therapist or a person assisting him at his direction, and:

(a) the force is used for the purpose of administering a recognized form of treatment which the actor believes to be adapted to promoting the physical or mental health of the patient; and

(b) the treatment is administered with the consent of the patient or, if the patient is a minor or an incompetent person, with the consent of his parent or guardian or other person legally competent to consent in his behalf, or the treatment is administered in an emergency when the actor believes that no one competent to consent can be consulted and that a reasonable person, wishing to safeguard the welfare of the patient, would consent; or

(5) the actor is a warden or other authorized official of a correctional institution, and:

(a) he believes that the force used is necessary for the purpose of enforcing the lawful rules or procedures of the institution, unless his belief in the lawfulness of the rule or procedure sought to be enforced is erroneous and his error is due to ignorance or mistake as to the provisions of the Code, any other provision of the criminal law or the law governing the administration of the institution; and

(b) the nature or degree of force used is not forbidden by Article 303 or 304 of the Code; and

(c) if deadly force is used, its use is otherwise justifiable under this Article; or

(6) the actor is a person responsible for the safety of a vessel or an aircraft or a person acting at his direction, and

(a) he believes that the force used is necessary to prevent interference with the operation of the vessel or aircraft or obstruction of the execution of a lawful order, unless his belief in the lawfulness of the order is erroneous and his error is due to ignorance or mistake as to the law defining his authority; and

(b) if deadly force is used, its use is otherwise justifiable under this Article; or

(7) the actor is a person who is authorized or required by law to maintain order or decorum in a vehicle, train or other carrier or in a place where others are assembled, and:

(a) he believes that the force used is necessary for such purpose; and

(b) the force used is not designed to cause or known to create a substantial risk of causing death, bodily harm, or extreme mental distress.

Section 3.09. Mistake of Law as to Unlawfulness of Force or Legality of Arrest; Reckless or Negligent Use of Otherwise Justifiable Force; Reckless or Negligent Injury or Risk of Injury to Innocent Persons.

(1) The justification afforded by Sections 3.04 to 3.07, inclusive, is unavailable when:

(a) the actor's belief in the unlawfulness of the force or conduct against which he employs protective force or his belief in the lawfulness of an arrest which he endeavors to effect by force is erroneous; and

(b) his error is due to ignorance or mistake as to the provisions of the Code, any other provision of the criminal law or the law governing the legality of an arrest or search.

(2) When the actor believes that the use of force upon or toward the person of another is necessary for any of the purposes for which such belief would establish a justification under Sections 3.03 to 3.08 but the actor is reckless or negligent in having such belief or in acquiring or failing to acquire any knowledge or belief which is material to the justifiability of his use of force, the justification afforded by those Sections is unavailable in a prosecution for an offense for which recklessness or negligence, as the case may be, suffices to establish culpability.

(3) When the actor is justified under Sections 3.03 to 3.08 in using force upon or toward the person of another but he recklessly or negligently injures or creates a risk of injury to innocent persons, the justification afforded by those Sections is unavailable in a prosecution for such recklessness or negligence towards innocent persons.

Section 3.10. Justification in Property Crimes.

Conduct involving the appropriation, seizure or destruction of, damage to, intrusion on or interference with property is justifiable under circumstances which would establish a defense of privilege in a civil action based thereon, unless:

(1) the Code or the law defining the offense deals with the specific situation involved; or

(2) a legislative purpose to exclude the justification claimed otherwise plainly appears.

Section 3.11. Definitions.

In this Article, unless a different meaning plainly is required:

(1) "unlawful force" means force, including confinement, which is employed without the consent of the person against whom it is directed and the employment of which constitutes an offense or actionable tort or would constitute such offense or tort except for a defense (such as the absence of intent, negligence, or mental capacity; duress; youth; or diplomatic status) not amounting to a privilege to use the force. Assent constitutes consent, within the meaning of this Section, whether or not it otherwise is legally effective, except assent to the infliction of death or serious bodily harm.

(2) "deadly force" means force which the actor uses with the purpose of causing or which he knows to create a substantial risk of causing death or serious bodily harm. Purposely firing a firearm in the direction of another person or at a vehicle in which another person is believed to be constitutes deadly force. A threat to cause death or serious bodily harm, by the production of a weapon or otherwise, so long as the actor's purpose is limited to creating an apprehension that he will use deadly force if necessary, does not constitute deadly force;

(3) "dwelling" means any building or structure, though movable or temporary, or a portion thereof, which is for the time being the actor's home or place of lodging.

ARTICLE 4. RESPONSIBILITY

Section 4.01. Mental Disease or Defect Excluding Responsibility.

(1) A person is not responsible for criminal conduct if at the time of such conduct as a result of mental disease or defect he lacks substantial capacity either to appreciate the criminality [wrongfulness] of his conduct or to conform his conduct to the requirements of law.

(2) As used in this Article, the terms "mental disease or defect" do not include an abnormality manifested only by repeated criminal or otherwise anti-social conduct.

Section 4.02. Evidence of Mental Disease or Defect Admissible When Relevant to Element of the Offense; [Mental Disease or Defect Impairing Capacity as Ground for Mitigation of Punishment in Capital Cases].

(1) Evidence that the defendant suffered from a mental disease or defect is admissible whenever it is relevant to prove that the defendant did or did not have a state of mind which is an element of the offense.

[(2) Whenever the jury or the Court is authorized to determine or to recommend whether or not the defendant shall be sentenced to death or imprisonment upon conviction, evidence that the capacity of the defendant to appreciate the criminality [wrongfulness] of his conduct or to conform his conduct to the requirements of law was impaired as a result of mental disease or defect is admissible in favor of sentence of imprisonment.]

Section 4.03. Mental Disease or Defect Excluding Responsibility Is Affirmative Defense; Requirement of Notice; Form of Verdict and Judgment When Finding of Irresponsibility Is Made.

(1) Mental disease or defect excluding responsibility is an affirmative defense.

(2) Evidence of mental disease or defect excluding responsibility is not admissible unless the defendant, at the time of entering his plea of not guilty or within ten days thereafter or at such later time as the Court may for good cause permit, files a written notice of his purpose to rely on such defense.

(3) When the defendant is acquitted on the ground of mental disease or defect excluding responsibility, the verdict and the judgment shall so state.

Section 4.04. Mental Disease or Defect Excluding Fitness to Proceed.

No person who as a result of mental disease or defect lacks capacity to understand the proceedings against him or to assist in his own defense shall be tried, convicted or sentenced for the commission of an offense so long as such incapacity endures.

Section 4.05. Psychiatric Examination of Defendant with Respect to Mental Disease or Defect.

(1) Whenever the defendant has filed a notice of intention to rely on the defense of mental disease or defect excluding responsibility, or there is reason to doubt his fitness to proceed, or reason to believe that mental disease or defect of the defendant will otherwise become an issue in the cause, the Court shall appoint at least one qualified psychiatrist or shall request the Superintendent of the ___ Hospital to designate at least one qualified psychiatrist, which designation may be or include himself, to examine and report upon the mental condition of the defendant. The Court may order the defendant to be committed to a hospital or other suitable facility for the purpose of the examination for a period of not exceeding sixty days or such longer period as the Court determines to be necessary for the purpose and may direct that a qualified psychiatrist retained by the defendant be permitted to witness and participate in the examination.

(2) In such examination any method may be employed which is accepted by the medical profession for the examination of those alleged to be suffering from mental disease or defect.

(3) The report of the examination shall include the following: (a) a description of the nature of the examination; (b) a diagnosis of the mental condition of the defendant; (c) if the defendant suffers from a mental disease or defect, an opinion as to his capacity to understand the

proceedings against him and to assist in his own defense; (d) when a notice of intention to rely on the defense of irresponsibility has been filed, an opinion as to the extent, if any, to which the capacity of the defendant to appreciate the criminality [wrongfulness] of his conduct or to conform his conduct to the requirements of law was impaired at the time of the criminal conduct charged; and (e) when directed by the Court, an opinion as to the capacity of the defendant to have a particular state of mind which is an element of the offense charged.

If the examination can not be conducted by reason of the unwillingness of the defendant to participate therein, the report shall so state and shall include, if possible, an opinion as to whether such unwillingness of the defendant was the result of mental disease or defect.

The report of the examination shall be filed [in triplicate] with the clerk of the Court, who shall cause copies to be delivered to the district attorney and to counsel for the defendant.

Section 4.06. Determination of Fitness to Proceed; Effect of Finding of Unfitness; Proceedings if Fitness is Regained [; Post–Commitment Hearing].

(1) When the defendant's fitness to proceed is drawn in question, the issue shall be determined by the Court. If neither the prosecuting attorney nor counsel for the defendant contests the finding of the report filed pursuant to Section 4.05, the Court may make the determination on the basis of such report. If the finding is contested, the Court shall hold a hearing on the issue. If the report is received in evidence upon such hearing, the party who contests the finding thereof shall have the right to summon and to cross-examine the psychiatrists who joined in the report and to offer evidence upon the issue.

(2) If the Court determines that the defendant lacks fitness to proceed, the proceeding against him shall be

suspended, except as provided in Subsection (3) [Subsections (3) and (4)] of this Section, and the Court shall commit him to the custody of the Commissioner of Mental Hygiene [Public Health or Correction] to be placed in an appropriate institution of the Department of Mental Hygiene [Public Health or Correction] for so long as such unfitness shall endure. When the Court, on its own motion or upon the application of the Commissioner of Mental Hygiene [Public Health or Correction] or the prosecuting attorney, determines, after a hearing if a hearing is requested, that the defendant has regained fitness to proceed, the proceeding shall be resumed. If, however, the Court is of the view that so much time has elapsed since the commitment of the defendant that it would be unjust to resume the criminal proceeding, the Court may dismiss the charge and may order the defendant to be discharged or, subject to the law governing the civil commitment of persons suffering from mental disease or defect, order the defendant to be committed to an appropriate institution of the Department of Mental Hygiene [Public Health].

(3) The fact that the defendant is unfit to proceed does not preclude any legal objection to the prosecution which is susceptible of fair determination prior to trial and without the personal participation of the defendant.

[Alternative: (3) At any time within ninety days after commitment as provided in Subsection (2) of this Section, or at any later time with permission of the Court granted for good cause, the defendant or his counsel or the Commissioner of Mental Hygiene [Public Health or Correction] may apply for a special post-commitment hearing. If the application is made by or on behalf of a defendant not represented by counsel, he shall be afforded a reasonable opportunity to obtain counsel, and if he lacks funds to do so, counsel shall be assigned by the Court. The application shall be granted only if the counsel for the defendant satisfies the Court by affidavit or otherwise that as an attorney he has reasonable grounds for a good faith belief that his client has, on the facts and the law, a defense to the charge other than mental disease or defect excluding responsibility.]

[(4) If the motion for a special post-commitment hearing is granted, the hearing shall be by the Court without a jury. No evidence shall be offered at the hearing by either party on the issue of mental disease or defect as a defense to, or in mitigation of, the crime charged. After hearing, the Court may in an appropriate case quash the indictment or other charge, or find it to be defective or insufficient, or determine that it is not proved beyond a reasonable doubt by the evidence, or otherwise terminate the proceedings on the evidence or the law. In any such case, unless all defects in the proceedings are promptly cured, the Court shall terminate the commitment ordered under Subsection (2) of this Section and order the defendant to be discharged or, subject to the law governing the civil commitment of persons suffering from mental disease or defect, order the defendant to be committed to an appropriate institution of the Department of Mental Hygiene [Public Health].]

Section 4.07. Determination of Irresponsibility on Basis of Report; Access to Defendant by Psychiatrist of His Own Choice; Form of Expert Testimony When Issue of Responsibility Is Tried.

(1) If the report filed pursuant to Section 4.05 finds that the defendant at the time of the criminal conduct charged suffered from a mental disease or defect which substantially impaired his capacity to appreciate the criminality [wrongfulness] of his conduct or to conform his conduct to the requirements of law, and the Court, after a hearing if a hearing is requested by the prosecuting attorney or the defendant, is satisfied that such impairment was sufficient to exclude responsibility, the Court on motion of the defendant shall enter judgment of ac-

quittal on the ground of mental disease or defect excluding responsibility.

(2) When, notwithstanding the report filed pursuant to Section 4.05, the defendant wishes to be examined by a qualified psychiatrist or other expert of his own choice, such examiner shall be permitted to have reasonable access to the defendant for the purposes of such examination.

(3) Upon the trial, the psychiatrists who reported pursuant to Section 4.05 may be called as witnesses by the prosecution, the defendant or the Court. If the issue is being tried before a jury, the jury may be informed that the psychiatrists were designated by the Court or by the Superintendent of the ___ Hospital at the request of the Court, as the case may be. If called by the Court, the witness shall be subject to cross-examination by the prosecution and by the defendant. Both the prosecution and the defendant may summon any other qualified psychiatrist or other expert to testify, but no one who has not examined the defendant shall be competent to testify to an expert opinion with respect to the mental condition or responsibility of the defendant, as distinguished from the validity of the procedure followed by, or the general scientific propositions stated by, another witness.

(4) When a psychiatrist or other expert who has examined the defendant testifies concerning his mental condition, he shall be permitted to make a statement as to the nature of his examination, his diagnosis of the mental condition of the defendant at the time of the commission of the offense charged and his opinion as to the extent, if any, to which the capacity of the defendant to appreciate the criminality [wrongfulness] of his conduct or to conform his conduct to the requirements of law or to have a particular state of mind which is an element of the offense charged was impaired as a result of mental disease or defect at that time. He shall be permitted to make any explanation reasonably serving to clarify his diagno-

sis and opinion and may be cross-examined as to any matter bearing on his competency or credibility or the validity of his diagnosis or opinion.

Section 4.08. Legal Effect of Acquittal on the Ground of Mental Disease or Defect Excluding Responsibility; Commitment; Release or Discharge.

(1) When a defendant is acquitted on the ground of mental disease or defect excluding responsibility, the Court shall order him to be committed to the custody of the Commissioner of Mental Hygiene [Public Health] to be placed in an appropriate institution for custody, care and treatment.

(2) If the Commissioner of Mental Hygiene [Public Health] is of the view that a person committed to his custody, pursuant to paragraph (1) of this Section, may be discharged or released on condition without danger to himself or to others, he shall make application for the discharge or release of such person in a report to the Court by which such person was committed and shall transmit a copy of such application and report to the prosecuting attorney of the county [parish] from which the defendant was committed. The Court shall thereupon appoint at least two qualified psychiatrists to examine such person and to report within sixty days, or such longer period as the Court determines to be necessary for the purpose, their opinion as to his mental condition. To facilitate such examination and the proceedings thereon, the Court may cause such person to be confined in any institution located near the place where the Court sits, which may hereafter be designated by the Commissioner of Mental Hygiene [Public Health] as suitable for the temporary detention of irresponsible persons.

(3) If the Court is satisfied by the report filed pursuant to paragraph (2) of this Section and such testimony of the reporting psychiatrists as the Court deems necessary that the committed person may be discharged or released on

PART I. GENERAL PROVISIONS 341

condition without danger to himself or others, the Court shall order his discharge or his release on such conditions as the Court determines to be necessary. If the Court is not so satisfied, it shall promptly order a hearing to determine whether such person may safely be discharged or released. Any such hearing shall be deemed a civil proceeding and the burden shall be upon the committed person to prove that he may safely be discharged or released. According to the determination of the Court upon the hearing, the committed person shall thereupon be discharged or released on such conditions as the Court determines to be necessary, or shall be recommitted to the custody of the Commissioner of Mental Hygiene [Public Health], subject to discharge or release only in accordance with the procedure prescribed above for a first hearing.

(4) If, within [five] years after the conditional release of a committed person, the Court shall determine, after hearing evidence, that the conditions of release have not been fulfilled and that for the safety of such person or for the safety of others his conditional release should be revoked, the Court shall forthwith order him to be recommitted to the Commissioner of Mental Hygiene [Public Health], subject to discharge or release only in accordance with the procedure prescribed above for a first hearing.

(5) A committed person may make application for his discharge or release to the Court by which he was committed, and the procedure to be followed upon such application shall be the same as that prescribed above in the case of an application by the Commissioner of Mental Hygiene [Public Health]. However, no such application by a committed person need be considered until he has been confined for a period of not less than [six months] from the date of the order of commitment, and if the determination of the Court be adverse to the application, such person shall not be permitted to file a further application

until [one year] has elapsed from the date of any preceding hearing on an application for his release or discharge.

Section 4.09. Statements for Purposes of Examination or Treatment Inadmissible Except on Issue of Mental Condition.

A statement made by a person subjected to psychiatric examination or treatment pursuant to Sections 4.05, 4.06 or 4.08 for the purposes of such examination or treatment shall not be admissible in evidence against him in any criminal proceeding on any issue other than that of his mental condition but it shall be admissible upon that issue, whether or not it would otherwise be deemed a privileged communication [, unless such statement constitutes an admission of guilt of the crime charged].

Section 4.10. Immaturity Excluding Criminal Convictions; Transfer of Proceedings to Juvenile Court.

(1) A person shall not be tried for or convicted of an offense if:

(a) at the time of the conduct charged to constitute the offense he was less than sixteen years of age [, in which case the Juvenile Court shall have exclusive jurisdiction*]; or

(b) at the time of the conduct charged to constitute the offense he was sixteen or seventeen years of age, unless:

(i) the Juvenile Court has no jurisdiction over him, or,

(ii) the Juvenile Court has entered an order waiving jurisdiction and consenting to the institution of criminal proceedings against him.

(2) No court shall have jurisdiction to try or convict a person of an offense if criminal proceedings against him are barred by Subsection (1) of this Section. When it appears that a person charged with the commission of an

offense may be of such an age that criminal proceedings may be barred under Subsection (1) of this Section, the Court shall hold a hearing thereon, and the burden shall be on the prosecution to establish to the satisfaction of the Court that the criminal proceeding is not barred upon such grounds. If the Court determines that the proceeding is barred, custody of the person charged shall be surrendered to the Juvenile Court, and the case, including all papers and processes relating thereto, shall be transferred.

* The bracketed words are unnecessary if the Juvenile Court Act so provides or is amended accordingly.

ARTICLE 5. INCHOATE CRIMES

Section 5.01. Criminal Attempt.

(1) *Definition of Attempt.* A person is guilty of an attempt to commit a crime if, acting with the kind of culpability otherwise required for commission of the crime, he:

(a) purposely engages in conduct which would constitute the crime if the attendant circumstances were as he believes them to be; or

(b) when causing a particular result is an element of the crime, does or omits to do anything with the purpose of causing or with the belief that it will cause such result without further conduct on his part; or

(c) purposely does or omits to do anything which, under the circumstances as he believes them to be, is an act or omission constituting a substantial step in a course of conduct planned to culminate in his commission of the crime.

(2) *Conduct Which May Be Held Substantial Step Under Subsection (1)(c).* Conduct shall not be held to constitute a substantial step under Subsection (1)(c) of this Section unless it is strongly corroborative of the actor's criminal purpose. Without negativing the sufficiency of

other conduct, the following, if strongly corroborative of the actor's criminal purpose, shall not be held insufficient as a matter of law:

(a) lying in wait, searching for or following the contemplated victim of the crime;

(b) enticing or seeking to entice the contemplated victim of the crime to go to the place contemplated for its commission;

(c) reconnoitering the place contemplated for the commission of the crime;

(d) unlawful entry of a structure, vehicle or enclosure in which it is contemplated that the crime will be committed;

(e) possession of materials to be employed in the commission of the crime, which are specially designed for such unlawful use or which can serve no lawful purpose of the actor under the circumstances;

(f) possession, collection or fabrication of materials to be employed in the commission of the crime, at or near the place contemplated for its commission, where such possession, collection or fabrication serves no lawful purpose of the actor under the circumstances;

(g) soliciting an innocent agent to engage in conduct constituting an element of the crime.

(3) *Conduct Designed to Aid Another in Commission of a Crime.* A person who engages in conduct designed to aid another to commit a crime which would establish his complicity under Section 2.06 if the crime were committed by such other person, is guilty of an attempt to commit the crime, although the crime is not committed or attempted by such other person.

(4) *Renunciation of Criminal Purpose.* When the actor's conduct would otherwise constitute an attempt under Subsection (1)(b) or (1)(c) of this Section, it is an affirmative defense that he abandoned his effort to com-

mit the crime or otherwise prevented its commission, under circumstances manifesting a complete and voluntary renunciation of his criminal purpose. The establishment of such defense does not, however, affect the liability of an accomplice who did not join in such abandonment or prevention.

Within the meaning of this Article, renunciation of criminal purpose is not voluntary if it is motivated, in whole or in part, by circumstances, not present or apparent at the inception of the actor's course of conduct, which increase the probability of detection or apprehension or which make more difficult the accomplishment of the criminal purpose. Renunciation is not complete if it is motivated by a decision to postpone the criminal conduct until a more advantageous time or to transfer the criminal effort to another but similar objective or victim.

Section 5.02. Criminal Solicitation.

(1) *Definition of Solicitation.* A person is guilty of solicitation to commit a crime if with the purpose of promoting or facilitating its commission he commands, encourages or requests another person to engage in specific conduct which would constitute such crime or an attempt to commit such crime or which would establish his complicity in its commission or attempted commission.

(2) *Uncommunicated Solicitation.* It is immaterial under Subsection (1) of this Section that the actor fails to communicate with the person he solicits to commit a crime if his conduct was designed to effect such communication.

(3) *Renunciation of Criminal Purpose.* It is an affirmative defense that the actor, after soliciting another person to commit a crime, persuaded him not to do so or otherwise prevented the commission of the crime, under circumstances manifesting a complete and voluntary renunciation of his criminal purpose.

Section 5.03. Criminal Conspiracy.

(1) *Definition of Conspiracy.* A person is guilty of conspiracy with another person or persons to commit a crime if with the purpose of promoting or facilitating its commission he:

(a) agrees with such other person or persons that they or one or more of them will engage in conduct which constitutes such crime or an attempt or solicitation to commit such crime; or

(b) agrees to aid such other person or persons in the planning or commission of such crime or of an attempt or solicitation to commit such crime.

(2) *Scope of Conspiratorial Relationship.* If a person guilty of conspiracy, as defined by Subsection (1) of this Section, knows that a person with whom he conspires to commit a crime has conspired with another person or persons to commit the same crime, he is guilty of conspiring with such other person or persons, whether or not he knows their identity, to commit such crime.

(3) *Conspiracy With Multiple Criminal Objectives.* If a person conspires to commit a number of crimes, he is guilty of only one conspiracy so long as such multiple crimes are the object of the same agreement or continuous conspiratorial relationship.

(4) *Joinder and Venue in Conspiracy Prosecutions.*

(a) Subject to the provisions of paragraph (b) of this Subsection, two or more persons charged with criminal conspiracy may be prosecuted jointly if:

(i) they are charged with conspiring with one another; or

(ii) the conspiracies alleged, whether they have the same or different parties, are so related that they constitute different aspects of a scheme of organized criminal conduct.

(b) In any joint prosecution under paragraph (a) of this Subsection:

(i) no defendant shall be charged with a conspiracy in any county [parish or district] other than one in which he entered into such conspiracy or in which an overt act pursuant to such conspiracy was done by him or by a person with whom he conspired; and

(ii) neither the liability of any defendant nor the admissibility against him of evidence of acts or declarations of another shall be enlarged by such joinder; and

(iii) the Court shall order a severance or take a special verdict as to any defendant who so requests, if it deems it necessary or appropriate to promote the fair determination of his guilt or innocence, and shall take any other proper measures to protect the fairness of the trial.

(5) *Overt Act.* No person may be convicted of conspiracy to commit a crime, other than a felony of the first or second degree, unless an overt act in pursuance of such conspiracy is alleged and proved to have been done by him or by a person with whom he conspired.

(6) *Renunciation of Criminal Purpose.* It is an affirmative defense that the actor, after conspiring to commit a crime, thwarted the success of the conspiracy, under circumstances manifesting a complete and voluntary renunciation of his criminal purpose.

(7) *Duration of Conspiracy.* For purposes of Section 1.06(4):

(a) conspiracy is a continuing course of conduct which terminates when the crime or crimes which are its object are committed or the agreement that they be committed is abandoned by the defendant and by those with whom he conspired; and

(b) such abandonment is presumed if neither the defendant nor anyone with whom he conspired does any overt act in pursuance of the conspiracy during the applicable period of limitation; and

(c) if an individual abandons the agreement, the conspiracy is terminated as to him only if and when he advises those with whom he conspired of his abandonment or he informs the law enforcement authorities of the existence of the conspiracy and of his participation therein.

Section 5.04. Incapacity, Irresponsibility or Immunity of Party to Solicitation or Conspiracy.

(1) Except as provided in Subsection (2) of this Section, it is immaterial to the liability of a person who solicits or conspires with another to commit a crime that:

(a) he or the person whom he solicits or with whom he conspires does not occupy a particular position or have a particular characteristic which is an element of such crime, if he believes that one of them does; or

(b) the person whom he solicits or with whom he conspires is irresponsible or has an immunity to prosecution or conviction for the commission of the crime.

(2) It is a defense to a charge of solicitation or conspiracy to commit a crime that if the criminal object were achieved, the actor would not be guilty of a crime under the law defining the offense or as an accomplice under Section 2.06(5) or 2.06(6)(a) or (b).

Section 5.05. Grading of Criminal Attempt, Solicitation and Conspiracy; Mitigation in Cases of Lesser Danger; Multiple Convictions Barred.

(1) *Grading.* Except as otherwise provided in this Section, attempt, solicitation and conspiracy are crimes of the same grade and degree as the most serious offense which is attempted or solicited or is an object of the conspiracy. An attempt, solicitation or conspiracy to commit a [capital crime or a] felony of the first degree is a felony of the second degree.

(2) *Mitigation.* If the particular conduct charged to constitute a criminal attempt, solicitation or conspiracy is so inherently unlikely to result or culminate in the commission of a crime that neither such conduct nor the actor presents a public danger warranting the grading of such offense under this Section, the Court shall exercise its power under Section 6.12 to enter judgment and impose sentence for a crime of lower grade or degree or, in extreme cases, may dismiss the prosecution.

(3) *Multiple Convictions.* A person may not be convicted of more than one offense defined by this Article for conduct designed to commit or to culminate in the commission of the same crime.

Section 5.06. Possessing Instruments of Crime; Weapons.

(1) *Criminal Instruments Generally.* A person commits a misdemeanor if he possesses any instrument of crime with purpose to employ it criminally. "Instrument of crime" means:

(a) anything specially made or specially adapted for criminal use; or

(b) anything commonly used for criminal purposes and possessed by the actor under circumstances which do not negative unlawful purpose.

(2) *Presumption of Criminal Purpose from Possession of Weapon.* If a person possesses a firearm or other weapon on or about his person, in a vehicle occupied by him, or otherwise readily available for use, it is presumed that he had the purpose to employ it criminally, unless:

(a) the weapon is possessed in the actor's home or place of business;

(b) the actor is licensed or otherwise authorized by law to possess such weapon; or

(c) the weapon is of a type commonly used in lawful sport.

"Weapon" means anything readily capable of lethal use and possessed under circumstances not manifestly appropriate for lawful uses which it may have; the term includes a firearm which is not loaded or lacks a clip or other component to render it immediately operable, and components which can readily be assembled into a weapon.

(3) *Presumptions as to Possession of Criminal Instruments in Automobiles.* Where a weapon or other instrument of crime is found in an automobile, it shall be presumed to be in the possession of the occupant if there is but one. If there is more than one occupant, it shall be presumed to be in the possession of all, except under the following circumstances:

(a) where it is found upon the person of one of the occupants;

(b) where the automobile is not a stolen one and the weapon or instrument is found out of view in a glove compartment, car trunk, or other enclosed customary depository, in which case it shall be presumed to be in the possession of the occupant or occupants who own or have authority to operate the automobile;

(c) in the case of a taxicab, a weapon or instrument found in the passengers' portion of the vehicle shall be presumed to be in the possession of all the passengers, if there are any, and, if not, in the possession of the driver.

Section 5.07. Prohibited Offensive Weapons.

A person commits a misdemeanor if, except as authorized by law, he makes, repairs, sells, or otherwise deals in, uses, or possesses any offensive weapon. "Offensive weapon" means any bomb, machine gun, sawed-off shotgun, firearm specially made or specially adapted for concealment or silent discharge, any blackjack, sandbag, metal knuckles, dagger, or other implement for the infliction of serious bodily injury which serves no common lawful purpose. It is a defense under this Section for the defendant to prove by a preponderance of evidence that he possessed or dealt with the weapon solely as a curio or in a dramatic performance, or that he possessed it briefly in consequence of having found it or taken it from an aggressor, or under circumstances similarly negativing any purpose or likelihood that the weapon would be used unlawfully. The presumptions provided in Section 5.06(3) are applicable to prosecutions under this Section.

ARTICLE 6. AUTHORIZED DISPOSITION OF OFFENDERS

Section 6.01. Degrees of Felonies.

(1) Felonies defined by this Code are classified, for the purpose of sentence, into three degrees, as follows:

(a) felonies of the first degree;

(b) felonies of the second degree;

(c) felonies of the third degree.

A felony is of the first or second degree when it is so designated by the Code. A crime declared to be a felony, without specification of degree, is of the third degree.

(2) Notwithstanding any other provision of law, a felony defined by any statute of this State other than this Code shall constitute for the purpose of sentence a felony of the third degree.

Section 6.02. Sentence in Accordance with Code; Authorized Dispositions.

(1) No person convicted of an offense shall be sentenced otherwise than in accordance with this Article.

[(2) The Court shall sentence a person who has been convicted of murder to death or imprisonment, in accordance with Section 210.6.]

(3) Except as provided in Subsection (2) of this Section and subject to the applicable provisions of the Code, the

Court may suspend the imposition of sentence on a person who has been convicted of a crime, may order him to be committed in lieu of sentence, in accordance with Section 6.13, or may sentence him as follows:

(a) to pay a fine authorized by Section 6.03; or

(b) to be placed on probation [, and, in the case of a person convicted of a felony or misdemeanor to imprisonment for a term fixed by the Court not exceeding thirty days to be served as a condition of probation]; or

(c) to imprisonment for a term authorized by Sections 6.05, 6.06, 6.07, 6.08, 6.09, or 7.06; or

(d) to fine and probation or fine and imprisonment, but not to probation and imprisonment [, except as authorized in paragraph (b) of this Subsection].

(4) The Court may suspend the imposition of sentence on a person who has been convicted of a violation or may sentence him to pay a fine authorized by Section 6.03.

(5) This Article does not deprive the Court of any authority conferred by law to decree a forfeiture of property, suspend or cancel a license, remove a person from office, or impose any other civil penalty. Such a judgment or order may be included in the sentence.

Section 6.03. Fines.

A person who has been convicted of an offense may be sentenced to pay a fine not exceeding:

(1) $10,000, when the conviction is of a felony of the first or second degree;

(2) $5,000, when the conviction is of a felony of the third degree;

(3) $1,000, when the conviction is of a misdemeanor;

(4) $500, when the conviction is of a petty misdemeanor or a violation;

(5) any higher amount equal to double the pecuniary gain derived from the offense by the offender;

(6) any higher amount specifically authorized by statute.

Section 6.04. Penalties Against Corporations and Unincorporated Association; Forfeiture of Corporate Charter or Revocation of Certificate Authorizing Foreign Corporation to Do Business in the State.

(1) The Court may suspend the sentence of a corporation or an unincorporated association which has been convicted of an offense or may sentence it to pay a fine authorized by Section 6.03.

(2)(a) The [prosecuting attorney] is authorized to institute civil proceedings in the appropriate court of general jurisdiction to forfeit the charter of a corporation organized under the laws of this State or to revoke the certificate authorizing a foreign corporation to conduct business in this State. The Court may order the charter forfeited or the certificate revoked upon finding (i) that the board of directors or a high managerial agent acting in behalf of the corporation has, in conducting the corporation's affairs, purposely engaged in a persistent course of criminal conduct and (ii) that for the prevention of future criminal conduct of the same character, the public interest requires the charter of the corporation to be forfeited and the corporation to be dissolved or the certificate to be revoked.

(b) When a corporation is convicted of a crime or a high managerial agent of a corporation, as defined in Section 2.07, is convicted of a crime committed in the conduct of the affairs of the corporation, the Court, in sentencing the corporation or the agent, may direct the [prosecuting attorney] to institute proceedings authorized by paragraph (a) of this Subsection.

(c) The proceedings authorized by paragraph (a) of this Subsection shall be conducted in accordance with the procedures authorized by law for the involuntary dissolution of a corporation or the revocation of the certificate authorizing a foreign corporation to conduct business in this State. Such proceedings shall be deemed additional to any other proceedings authorized by law for the purpose of forfeiting the charter of a corporation or revoking the certificate of a foreign corporation.

Section 6.05. Young Adult Offenders.

(1) *Specialized Correctional Treatment.* A young adult offender is a person convicted of a crime who, at the time of sentencing, is sixteen but less than twenty-two years of age. A young adult offender who is sentenced to a term of imprisonment which may exceed thirty days [alternatives: (1) ninety days; (2) one year] shall be committed to the custody of the Division of Young Adult Correction of the Department of Correction, and shall receive, as far as practicable, such special and individualized correctional and rehabilitative treatment as may be appropriate to his needs.

(2) *Special Term.* A young adult offender convicted of a felony may, in lieu of any other sentence of imprisonment authorized by this Article, be sentenced to a special term of imprisonment without a minimum and with a maximum of four years, regardless of the degree of the felony involved, if the Court is of the opinion that such special term is adequate for his correction and rehabilitation and will not jeopardize the protection of the public.

[(3) *Removal of Disabilities; Vacation of Conviction.*

(a) In sentencing a young adult offender to the special term provided by this Section or to any sentence other than one of imprisonment, the Court may order that so long as he is not convicted of another felony, the judgment shall not constitute a conviction for the purposes of any disqualification or disability imposed by law upon conviction of a crime.

(b) When any young adult offender is unconditionally discharged from probation or parole before the expiration of the maximum term thereof, the Court may enter an order vacating the judgment of conviction.]

[(4) *Commitment for Observation.* If, after pre-sentence investigation, the Court desires additional information concerning a young adult offender before imposing sentence, it may order that he be committed, for a period not exceeding ninety days, to the custody of the Division of Young Adult Correction of the Department of Correction for observation and study at an appropriate reception or classification center. Such Division of the Department of Correction and the [Young Adult Division of the] Board of Parole shall advise the Court of their findings and recommendations on or before the expiration of such ninety-day period.]

Section 6.06. Sentence of Imprisonment for Felony; Ordinary Terms.

A person who has been convicted of a felony may be sentenced to imprisonment, as follows:

(1) in the case of a felony of the first degree, for a term the minimum of which shall be fixed by the Court at not less than one year nor more than ten years, and the maximum of which shall be life imprisonment;

(2) in the case of a felony of the second degree, for a term the minimum of which shall be fixed by the Court at not less than one year nor more than three years, and the maximum of which shall be ten years;

(3) in the case of a felony of the third degree, for a term the minimum of which shall be fixed by the Court at not less than one year nor more than two years, and the maximum of which shall be five years.

Alternate Section 6.06. Sentence of Imprisonment for Felony; Ordinary Terms.

A person who has been convicted of a felony may be sentenced to imprisonment, as follows:

(1) in the case of a felony of the first degree, for a term the minimum of which shall be fixed by the Court at not less than one year nor more than ten years, and the maximum at not more than twenty years or at life imprisonment;

(2) in the case of a felony of the second degree, for a term the minimum of which shall be fixed by the Court at not less than one year nor more than three years, and the maximum at not more than ten years;

(3) in the case of a felony of the third degree, for a term the minimum of which shall be fixed by the Court at not less than one year nor more than two years, and the maximum at not more than five years.

No sentence shall be imposed under this Section of which the minimum is longer than one-half the maximum, or, when the maximum is life imprisonment, longer than ten years.

Section 6.07. Sentence of Imprisonment for Felony; Extended Terms.

In the cases designated in Section 7.03, a person who has been convicted of a felony may be sentenced to an extended term of imprisonment, as follows:

(1) in the case of a felony of the first degree, for a term the minimum of which shall be fixed by the Court at not less than five years nor more than ten years, and the maximum of which shall be life imprisonment;

(2) in the case of a felony of the second degree, for a term the minimum of which shall be fixed by the Court at not less than one year nor more than five years, and the maximum of which shall be fixed by the Court at not less than ten nor more than twenty years;

(3) in the case of a felony of the third degree, for a term the minimum of which shall be fixed by the Court at not less than one year nor more than three years, and the maximum of which shall be fixed by the Court at not less than five nor more than ten years.

Section 6.08. Sentence of Imprisonment for Misdemeanors and Petty Misdemeanors; Ordinary Terms.

A person who has been convicted of a misdemeanor or a petty misdemeanor may be sentenced to imprisonment for a definite term which shall be fixed by the Court and shall not exceed one year in the case of a misdemeanor or thirty days in the case of a petty misdemeanor.

Section 6.09. Sentence of Imprisonment for Misdemeanors and Petty Misdemeanors; Extended Terms.

(1) In the cases designated in Section 7.04, a person who has been convicted of a misdemeanor or a petty misdemeanor may be sentenced to an extended term of imprisonment, as follows:

(a) in the case of a misdemeanor, for a term the minimum of which shall be fixed by the Court at not more than one year and the maximum of which shall be three years;

(b) in the case of a petty misdemeanor, for a term the minimum of which shall be fixed by the Court at not more than six months and the maximum of which shall be two years.

(2) No such sentence for an extended term shall be imposed unless:

(a) the Director of Correction has certified that there is an institution in the Department of Correction, or in a county, city [or other appropriate political subdivision of the State] which is appropriate for the detention and correctional treatment of such misdemeanants or petty misdemeanants, and that such institution is available to receive such commitments; and

(b) the [Board of Parole] [Parole Administrator] has certified that the Board of Parole is able to visit such institution and to assume responsibility for the release of such prisoners on parole and for their parole supervision.

Section 6.10. First Release of All Offenders on Parole; Sentence of Imprisonment Includes Separate Parole Term; Length of Parole Term; Length of Recommitment and Reparole After Revocation of Parole; Final Unconditional Release.

(1) *First Release of All Offenders on Parole.* An offender sentenced to an indefinite term of imprisonment in excess of one year under Section 6.05, 6.06, 6.07, 6.09 or 7.06 shall be released conditionally on parole at or before the expiration of the maximum of such term, in accordance with Article 305.

(2) *Sentence of Imprisonment Includes Separate Parole Term; Length of Parole Term.* A sentence to an indefinite term of imprisonment in excess of one year under Section 6.05, 6.06, 6.07, 6.09 or 7.06 includes as a separate portion of the sentence a term of parole or of recommitment for violation of the conditions of parole which governs the duration of parole or recommitment after the offender's first conditional release on parole. The minimum of such term is one year and the maximum is five years, unless the sentence was imposed under Section 6.05(2) or Section 6.09, in which case the maximum is two years.

(3) *Length of Recommitment and Reparole After Revocation of Parole.* If an offender is recommitted upon revocation of his parole, the term of further imprisonment upon such recommitment and of any subsequent reparole or recommitment under the same sentence shall

be fixed by the Board of Parole but shall not exceed in aggregate length the unserved balance of the maximum parole term provided by Subsection (2) of this Section.

(4) *Final Unconditional Release.* When the maximum of his parole term has expired or he has been sooner discharged from parole under Section 305.12, an offender shall be deemed to have served his sentence and shall be released unconditionally.

Section 6.11. Place of imprisonment.

(1) When a person is sentenced to imprisonment for an indefinite term with a maximum in excess of one year, the Court shall commit him to the custody of the Department of Correction [or other single department or agency] for the term of his sentence and until released in accordance with law.

(2) When a person is sentenced to imprisonment for a definite term, the Court shall designate the institution or agency to which he is committed for the term of his sentence and until released in accordance with law.

Section 6.12. Reduction of Conviction by Court to Lesser Degree of Felony or to Misdemeanor.

If, when a person has been convicted of a felony, the Court, having regard to the nature and circumstances of the crime and to the history and character of the defendant, is of the view that it would be unduly harsh to sentence the offender in accordance with the Code, the Court may enter judgment of conviction for a lesser degree of felony or for a misdemeanor and impose sentence accordingly.

Section 6.13. Civil Commitment in Lieu of Prosecution or of Sentence.

(1) When a person prosecuted for a [felony of the third degree,] misdemeanor or petty misdemeanor is a chronic alcoholic, narcotic addict [or prostitute] or person suffer-

ing from mental abnormality and the Court is authorized by law to order the civil commitment of such person to a hospital or other institution for medical, psychiatric or other rehabilitative treatment, the Court may order such commitment and dismiss the prosecution.

The order of commitment may be made after conviction, in which event the Court may set aside the verdict or judgment of conviction and dismiss the prosecution.

(2) The Court shall not make an order under Subsection (1) of this Section unless it is of the view that it will substantially further the rehabilitation of the defendant and will not jeopardize the protection of the public.

ARTICLE 7. AUTHORITY OF COURT IN SENTENCING

Section 7.01. Criteria for Withholding Sentence of Imprisonment and for Placing Defendant on Probation.

(1) The Court shall deal with a person who has been convicted of a crime without imposing sentence of imprisonment unless, having regard to the nature and circumstances of the crime and the history, character and condition of the defendant, it is of the opinion that his imprisonment is necessary for protection of the public because:

(a) there is undue risk that during the period of a suspended sentence or probation the defendant will commit another crime; or

(b) the defendant is in need of correctional treatment that can be provided most effectively by his commitment to an institution; or

(c) a lesser sentence will depreciate the seriousness of the defendant's crime.

(2) The following grounds, while not controlling the discretion of the Court, shall be accorded weight in favor of withholding sentence of imprisonment:

PART I. GENERAL PROVISIONS 361

(a) the defendant's criminal conduct neither caused nor threatened serious harm;

(b) the defendant did not contemplate that his criminal conduct would cause or threaten serious harm;

(c) the defendant acted under a strong provocation;

(d) there were substantial grounds tending to excuse or justify the defendant's criminal conduct, though failing to establish a defense;

(e) the victim of the defendant's criminal conduct induced or facilitated its commission;

(f) the defendant has compensated or will compensate the victim of his criminal conduct for the damage or injury that he sustained;

(g) the defendant has no history of prior delinquency or criminal activity or has led a law-abiding life for a substantial period of time before the commission of the present crime;

(h) the defendant's criminal conduct was the result of circumstances unlikely to recur;

(i) the character and attitudes of the defendant indicate that he is unlikely to commit another crime;

(j) the defendant is particularly likely to respond affirmatively to probationary treatment;

(k) the imprisonment of the defendant would entail excessive hardship to himself or his dependents.

(3) When a person who has been convicted of a crime is not sentenced to imprisonment, the Court shall place him on probation if he is in need of the supervision, guidance, assistance or direction that the probation service can provide.

Section 7.02. Criteria for Imposing Fines.

(1) The Court shall not sentence a defendant only to pay a fine, when any other disposition is authorized by

law, unless having regard to the nature and circumstances of the crime and to the history and character of the defendant, it is of the opinion that the fine alone suffices for protection of the public.

(2) The Court shall not sentence a defendant to pay a fine in addition to a sentence of imprisonment or probation unless:

(a) the defendant has derived a pecuniary gain from the crime; or

(b) the Court is of opinion that a fine is specially adapted to deterrence of the crime involved or to the correction of the offender.

(3) The Court shall not sentence a defendant to pay a fine unless:

(a) the defendant is or will be able to pay the fine; and

(b) the fine will not prevent the defendant from making restitution or reparation to the victim of the crime.

(4) In determining the amount and method of payment of a fine, the Court shall take into account the financial resources of the defendant and the nature of the burden that its payment will impose.

Section 7.03. Criteria for Sentence of Extended Term of Imprisonment; Felonies.

The Court may sentence a person who has been convicted of a felony to an extended term of imprisonment if it finds one or more of the grounds specified in this Section. The finding of the Court shall be incorporated in the record.

(1) The defendant is a persistent offender whose commitment for an extended term is necessary for protection of the public.

The Court shall not make such a finding unless the defendant is over twenty-one years of age and has previously been convicted of two felonies or of one felony and two misdemeanors, committed at different times when he was over [insert Juvenile Court age] years of age.

(2) The defendant is a professional criminal whose commitment for an extended term is necessary for protection of the public.

The Court shall not make such a finding unless the defendant is over twenty-one years of age and:

(a) the circumstances of the crime show that the defendant has knowingly devoted himself to criminal activity as a major source of livelihood; or

(b) the defendant has substantial income or resources not explained to be derived from a source other than criminal activity.

(3) The defendant is a dangerous, mentally abnormal person whose commitment for an extended term is necessary for protection of the public.

The Court shall not make such a finding unless the defendant has been subjected to a psychiatric examination resulting in the conclusions that his mental condition is gravely abnormal; that his criminal conduct has been characterized by a pattern of repetitive or compulsive behavior or by persistent aggressive behavior with heedless indifference to consequences; and that such condition makes him a serious danger to others.

(4) The defendant is a multiple offender whose criminality was so extensive that a sentence of imprisonment for an extended term is warranted.

The Court shall not make such a finding unless:

(a) the defendant is being sentenced for two or more felonies, or is already under sentence of imprisonment for felony, and the sentences of imprisonment involved will run concurrently under Section 7.06; or

(b) the defendant admits in open court the commission of one or more other felonies and asks that they be taken into account when he is sentenced; and

(c) the longest sentences of imprisonment authorized for each of the defendant's crimes, including admitted crimes taken into account, if made to run consecutively would exceed in length the minimum and maximum of the extended term imposed.

Section 7.04. Criteria for Sentence of Extended Term of Imprisonment; Misdemeanors and Petty Misdemeanors.

The Court may sentence a person who has been convicted of a misdemeanor or petty misdemeanor to an extended term of imprisonment if it finds one or more of the grounds specified in this Section. The finding of the Court shall be incorporated in the record.

(1) The defendant is a persistent offender whose commitment for an extended term is necessary for protection of the public.

The Court shall not make such a finding unless the defendant has previously been convicted of two crimes, committed at different times when he was over [insert Juvenile Court age] years of age.

(2) The defendant is a professional criminal whose commitment for an extended term is necessary for protection of the public.

The Court shall not make such a finding unless:

(a) the circumstances of the crime show that the defendant has knowingly devoted himself to criminal activity as a major source of livelihood; or

(b) the defendant has substantial income or resources not explained to be derived from a source other than criminal activity.

PART I. GENERAL PROVISIONS 365

(3) The defendant is a chronic alcoholic, narcotic addict, prostitute or person of abnormal mental condition who requires rehabilitative treatment for a substantial period of time.

The Court shall not make such a finding unless, with respect to the particular category to which the defendant belongs, the Director of Correction has certified that there is a specialized institution or facility which is satisfactory for the rehabilitative treatment of such persons and which otherwise meets the requirements of Section 6.09, Subsection (2).

(4) The defendant is a multiple offender whose criminality was so extensive that a sentence of imprisonment for an extended term is warranted.

The Court shall not make such a finding unless:

(a) the defendant is being sentenced for a number of misdemeanors or petty misdemeanors or is already under sentence of imprisonment for crime of such grades, or admits in open court the commission of one or more such crimes and asks that they be taken into account when he is sentenced; and

(b) maximum fixed sentences of imprisonment for each of the defendant's crimes, including admitted crimes taken into account, if made to run consecutively, would exceed in length the maximum period of the extended term imposed.

Section 7.05. Former Conviction in Another Jurisdiction; Definition and Proof of Conviction; Sentence Taking Into Account Admitted Crimes Bars Subsequent Conviction for Such Crimes.

(1) For purposes of paragraph (1) of Section 7.03 or 7.04, a conviction of the commission of a crime in another jurisdiction shall constitute a previous conviction. Such conviction shall be deemed to have been of a felony if sentence of death or of imprisonment in excess of one

year was authorized under the law of such other jurisdiction, of a misdemeanor if sentence of imprisonment in excess of thirty days but not in excess of a year was authorized and of a petty misdemeanor if sentence of imprisonment for not more than thirty days was authorized.

(2) An adjudication by a court of competent jurisdiction that the defendant committed a crime constitutes a conviction for purposes of Sections 7.03 to 7.05 inclusive, although sentence or the execution thereof was suspended, provided that the time to appeal has expired and that the defendant was not pardoned on the ground of innocence.

(3) Prior conviction may be proved by any evidence, including fingerprint records made in connection with arrest, conviction or imprisonment, that reasonably satisfies the Court that the defendant was convicted.

(4) When the defendant has asked that other crimes admitted in open court be taken into account when he is sentenced and the Court has not rejected such request, the sentence shall bar the prosecution or conviction of the defendant in this State for any such admitted crime.

Section 7.06. Multiple Sentences; Concurrent and Consecutive Terms.

(1) *Sentences of Imprisonment for More Than One Crime.* When multiple sentences of imprisonment are imposed on a defendant for more than one crime, including a crime for which a previous suspended sentence or sentence of probation has been revoked, such multiple sentences shall run concurrently or consecutively as the Court determines at the time of sentence, except that:

   (a) a definite and an indefinite term shall run concurrently and both sentences shall be satisfied by service of the indefinite term; and

   (b) the aggregate of consecutive definite terms shall not exceed one year; and

(c) the aggregate of consecutive indefinite terms shall not exceed in minimum or maximum length the longest extended term authorized for the highest grade and degree of crime for which any of the sentences was imposed; and

(d) not more than one sentence for an extended term shall be imposed.

(2) *Sentences of Imprisonment Imposed at Different Times.* When a defendant who has previously been sentenced to imprisonment is subsequently sentenced to another term for a crime committed prior to the former sentence, other than a crime committed while in custody:

(a) the multiple sentences imposed shall so far as possible conform to Subsection (1) of this Section; and

(b) whether the Court determines that the terms shall run concurrently or consecutively, the defendant shall be credited with time served in imprisonment on the prior sentence in determining the permissible aggregate length of the term or terms remaining to be served; and

(c) when a new sentence is imposed on a prisoner who is on parole, the balance of the parole term on the former sentence shall be deemed to run during the period of the new imprisonment.

(3) *Sentence of Imprisonment for Crime Committed While on Parole.* When a defendant is sentenced to imprisonment for a crime committed while on parole in this State, such term of imprisonment and any period of reimprisonment that the Board of Parole may require the defendant to serve upon the revocation of his parole shall run concurrently, unless the Court orders them to run consecutively.

(4) *Multiple Sentences of Imprisonment in Other Cases.* Except as otherwise provided in this Section, multiple terms of imprisonment shall run concurrently or consecu-

tively as the Court determines when the second or subsequent sentence is imposed.

(5) *Calculation of Concurrent and Consecutive Terms of Imprisonment.*

(a) When indefinite terms run concurrently, the shorter minimum terms merge in and are satisfied by serving the longest minimum term and the shorter maximum terms merge in and are satisfied by discharge of the longest maximum term.

(b) When indefinite terms run consecutively, the minimum terms are added to arrive at an aggregate minimum to be served equal to the sum of all minimum terms and the maximum terms are added to arrive at an aggregate maximum equal to the sum of all maximum terms.

(c) When a definite and an indefinite term run consecutively, the period of the definite term is added to both the minimum and maximum of the indefinite term and both sentences are satisfied by serving the indefinite term.

(6) *Suspension of Sentence or Probation and Imprisonment; Multiple Terms of Suspension and Probation.* When a defendant is sentenced for more than one offense or a defendant already under sentence is sentenced for another offense committed prior to the former sentence:

(a) the Court shall not sentence to probation a defendant who is under sentence of imprisonment [with more than thirty days to run] or impose a sentence of probation and a sentence of imprisonment [, except as authorized by Section 6.02(3)(b)]; and

(b) multiple periods of suspension or probation shall run concurrently from the date of the first such disposition; and

(c) when a sentence of imprisonment is imposed for an indefinite term, the service of such sentence shall satisfy a suspended sentence on another count or a prior suspended sentence or sentence to probation; and

(d) when a sentence of imprisonment is imposed for a definite term, the period of a suspended sentence on another count or a prior suspended sentence or sentence to probation shall run during the period of such imprisonment.

(7) *Offense Committed While Under Suspension of Sentence or Probation.* When a defendant is convicted of an offense committed while under suspension of sentence or on probation and such suspension or probation is not revoked:

(a) if the defendant is sentenced to imprisonment for an indefinite term, the service of such sentence shall satisfy the prior suspended sentence or sentence to probation; and

(b) if the defendant is sentenced to imprisonment for a definite term, the period of the suspension or probation shall not run during the period of such imprisonment; and

(c) if sentence is suspended or the defendant is sentenced to probation, the period of such suspension or probation shall run concurrently with or consecutively to the remainder of the prior periods, as the Court determines at the time of sentence.

Section 7.07. Procedure on Sentence; Pre-sentence Investigation and Report; Remand for Psychiatric Examination; Transmission of Records to Department of Correction.

(1) The Court shall not impose sentence without first ordering a pre-sentence investigation of the defendant and according due consideration to a written report of such investigation where:

(a) the defendant has been convicted of a felony; or

(b) the defendant is less than twenty-two years of age and has been convicted of a crime; or

(c) the defendant will be [placed on probation or] sentenced to imprisonment for an extended term.

(2) The Court may order a pre-sentence investigation in any other case.

(3) The pre-sentence investigation shall include an analysis of the circumstances attending the commission of the crime, the defendant's history of delinquency or criminality, physical and mental condition, family situation and background, economic status, education, occupation and personal habits and any other matters that the probation officer deems relevant or the Court directs to be included.

(4) Before imposing sentence, the Court may order the defendant to submit to psychiatric observation and examination for a period of not exceeding sixty days or such longer period as the Court determines to be necessary for the purpose. The defendant may be remanded for this purpose to any available clinic or mental hospital or the Court may appoint a qualified psychiatrist to make the examination. The report of the examination shall be submitted to the Court.

(5) Before imposing sentence, the Court shall advise the defendant or his counsel of the factual contents and the conclusions of any pre-sentence investigation or psychiatric examination and afford fair opportunity, if the defendant so requests, to controvert them. The sources of confidential information need not, however, be disclosed.

(6) The Court shall not impose a sentence of imprisonment for an extended term unless the ground therefor has been established at a hearing after the conviction of the defendant and on written notice to him of the ground proposed. Subject to the limitation of Subsection (5) of this Section, the defendant shall have the right to hear

and controvert the evidence against him and to offer evidence upon the issue.

(7) If the defendant is sentenced to imprisonment, a copy of the report of any pre-sentence investigation or psychiatric examination shall be transmitted forthwith to the Department of Correction [or other state department or agency] or, when the defendant is committed to the custody of a specific institution, to such institution.

Section 7.08. Commitment for Observation; Sentence of Imprisonment for Felony Deemed Tentative for Period of One Year; Re-sentence on Petition of Commissioner of Correction.

(1) If, after pre-sentence investigation, the Court desires additional information concerning an offender convicted of a felony or misdemeanor before imposing sentence, it may order that he be committed, for a period not exceeding ninety days, to the custody of the Department of Correction, or, in the case of a young adult offender, to the custody of the Division of Young Adult Correction, for observation and study at an appropriate reception or classification center. The Department and the Board of Parole, or the Young Adult Divisions thereof, shall advise the Court of their findings and recommendations on or before the expiration of such ninety-day period. If the offender is thereafter sentenced to imprisonment, the period of such commitment for observation shall be deducted from the maximum term and from the minimum, if any, of such sentence.

(2) When a person has been sentenced to imprisonment upon conviction of a felony, whether for an ordinary or extended term, the sentence shall be deemed tentative, to the extent provided in this Section, for the period of one year following the date when the offender is received in custody by the Department of Correction [or other state department or agency].

(3) If, as a result of the examination and classification by the Department of Correction [or other state department or agency] of a person under sentence of imprisonment upon conviction of a felony, the Commissioner of Correction [or other department head] is satisfied that the sentence of the Court may have been based upon a misapprehension as to the history, character or physical or mental condition of the offender, the Commissioner, during the period when the offender's sentence is deemed tentative under Subsection (2) of this Section shall file in the sentencing Court a petition to re-sentence the offender. The petition shall set forth the information as to the offender that is deemed to warrant his re-sentence and may include a recommendation as to the sentence to be imposed.

(4) The Court may dismiss a petition filed under Subsection (3) of this Section without a hearing if it deems the information set forth insufficient to warrant reconsideration of the sentence. If the Court is of the view that the petition warrants such reconsideration, a copy of the petition shall be served on the offender, who shall have the right to be heard on the issue and to be represented by counsel.

(5) When the Court grants a petition filed under Subsection (3) of this Section, it shall re-sentence the offender and may impose any sentence that might have been imposed originally for the felony of which the defendant was convicted. The period of his imprisonment prior to re-sentence and any reduction for good behavior to which he is entitled shall be applied in satisfaction of the final sentence.

(6) For all purposes other than this Section, a sentence of imprisonment has the same finality when it is imposed that it would have if this Section were not in force.

(7) Nothing in this Section shall alter the remedies provided by law for vacating or correcting an illegal sentence.

Section 7.09. Credit for Time of Detention Prior to Sentence; Credit for Imprisonment Under Earlier Sentence for the Same Crime.

(1) When a defendant who is sentenced to imprisonment has previously been detained in any state or local correctional or other institution following his [conviction of] [arrest for] the crime for which such sentence is imposed, such period of detention following his [conviction] [arrest] shall be deducted from the maximum term, and from the minimum, if any, of such sentence. The officer having custody of the defendant shall furnish a certificate to the Court at the time of sentence, showing the length of such detention of the defendant prior to sentence in any state or local correctional or other institution, and the certificate shall be annexed to the official records of the defendant's commitment.

(2) When a judgment of conviction is vacated and a new sentence is thereafter imposed upon the defendant for the same crime, the period of detention and imprisonment theretofore served shall be deducted from the maximum term, and from the minimum, if any, of the new sentence. The officer having custody of the defendant shall furnish a certificate to the Court at the time of sentence, showing the period of imprisonment served under the original sentence, and the certificate shall be annexed to the official records of the defendant's new commitment.

PART II. DEFINITION OF SPECIFIC CRIMES

OFFENSES AGAINST EXISTENCE OR STABILITY OF THE STATE[1]

[This category of offenses, including treason, sedition, espionage and like crimes, was excluded from the scope of the Model Penal Code. These offenses are peculiarly the concern of the federal government. The Constitution itself defines treason: "Treason against the United States shall consist of levying War against them, or in adhering to their Enemies, giving the Aid and Comfort...." Article III, Section 3; cf. Pennsylvania v. Nelson, 350 U.S. 497 (supersession of state sedition legislation by federal law). Also, the definition of offenses against the stability of the state is inevitably affected by special political considerations. These factors militated against the use of the Institute's limited resources to attempt to draft "model" provisions in this area. However we provide at this point in the Plan of the Model Penal Code for an Article 200, where definitions of offenses against the existence of stability of the state may be incorporated.]

OFFENSES INVOLVING DANGER TO THE PERSON

ARTICLE 210. CRIMINAL HOMICIDE

Section 210.0. Definitions.

In Articles 210–213, unless a different meaning plainly is required:

(1) "human being" means a person who has been born and is alive;

---

1. Model Penal Code 123 (Proposed Official Draft 1962).

(2) "bodily injury" means physical pain, illness or any impairment of physical condition;

(3) "serious bodily injury" means bodily injury which creates a substantial risk of death or which causes serious, permanent disfigurement, or protracted loss or impairment of the function of any bodily member or organ;

(4) "deadly weapon" means any firearm, or other weapon, device, instrument, material or substance, whether animate or inanimate, which in the manner it is used or is intended to be used is known to be capable of producing death or serious bodily injury.

Section 210.1. Criminal Homicide.

(1) A person is guilty of criminal homicide if he purposely, knowingly, recklessly or negligently causes the death of another human being.

(2) Criminal homicide is murder, manslaughter or negligent homicide.

Section 210.2. Murder.

(1) Except as provided in Section 210.3(1)(b), criminal homicide constitutes murder when:

(a) it is committed purposely or knowingly; or

(b) it is committed recklessly under circumstances manifesting extreme indifference to the value of human life. Such recklessness and indifference are presumed if the actor is engaged or is an accomplice in the commission of, or an attempt to commit, or flight after committing or attempting to commit robbery, rape or deviate sexual intercourse by force or threat of force, arson, burglary, kidnapping or felonious escape.

(2) Murder is a felony of the first degree [but a person convicted of murder may be sentenced to death, as provided in Section 210.6].

Section 210.3. Manslaughter.

(1) Criminal homicide constitutes manslaughter when:

(a) it is committed recklessly; or

(b) a homicide which would otherwise be murder is committed under the influence of extreme mental or emotional disturbance for which there is reasonable explanation or excuse. The reasonableness of such explanation or excuse shall be determined from the viewpoint of a person in the actor's situation under the circumstances as he believes them to be.

(2) Manslaughter is a felony of the second degree.

Section 210.4. Negligent Homicide.

(1) Criminal homicide constitutes negligent homicide when it is committed negligently.

(2) Negligent homicide is a felony of the third degree.

Section 210.5. Causing or Aiding Suicide.

(1) *Causing Suicide as Criminal Homicide.* A person may be convicted of criminal homicide for causing another to commit suicide only if he purposely causes such suicide by force, duress or deception.

(2) *Aiding or Soliciting Suicide as an Independent Offense.* A person who purposely aids or solicits another to commit suicide is guilty of a felony of the second degree if his conduct causes such suicide or an attempted suicide, and otherwise of a misdemeanor.

[Section 210.6. Sentence of Death for Murder; Further Proceedings to Determine Sentence].

(1) *Death Sentence Excluded.* When a defendant is found guilty of murder, the Court shall impose sentence for a felony of the first degree if it is satisfied that:

(a) none of the aggravating circumstances enumerated in Subsection (3) of this Section was established by the evidence at the trial or will be established if further proceedings are initiated under Subsection (2) of this Section; or

PART II. DEFINITION OF SPECIFIC CRIMES 377

(b) substantial mitigating circumstances, established by the evidence at the trial, call for leniency; or

(c) the defendant, with the consent of the prosecuting attorney and the approval of the Court, pleaded guilty to murder as a felony of the first degree; or

(d) the defendant was under 18 years of age at the time of the commission of the crime; or

(e) the defendant's physical or mental condition calls for leniency; or

(f) although the evidence suffices to sustain the verdict, it does not foreclose all doubt respecting the defendant's guilt.

(2) *Determination by Court or by Court and Jury.* Unless the Court imposes sentence under Subsection (1) of this Section, it shall conduct a separate proceeding to determine whether the defendant should be sentenced for a felony of the first degree or sentenced to death. The proceeding shall be conducted before the Court alone if the defendant was convicted by a Court sitting without a jury or upon his plea of guilty or if the prosecuting attorney and the defendant waive a jury with respect to sentence. In other cases it shall be conducted before the Court sitting with the jury which determined the defendant's guilt or, if the Court for good cause shown discharges that jury, with a new jury empanelled for the purpose.

In the proceeding, evidence may be presented as to any matter that the Court deems relevant to sentence, including but not limited to the nature and circumstances of the crime, the defendant's character, background, history, mental and physical condition and any of the aggravating or mitigating circumstances enumerated in Subsections (3) and (4) of this Section. Any such evidence, not legally privileged, which the Court deems to have probative force, may be received, regardless of its admissibility under the exclusionary rules of evidence, provided that the defendant's counsel is accorded a fair opportunity to rebut such evidence. The prosecuting attorney and the defendant or his counsel shall be permitted to present argument for or against sentence of death.

The determination whether sentence of death shall be imposed shall be in the discretion of the Court, except that when the proceeding is conducted before the Court sitting with a jury, the Court shall not impose sentence of death unless it submits to the jury the issue whether the defendant should be sentenced to death or to imprisonment and the jury returns a verdict that the sentence should be death. If the jury is unable to reach a unanimous verdict, the Court shall dismiss the jury and impose sentence for a felony of the first degree.

The Court, in exercising its discretion as to sentence, and the jury, in determining upon its verdict, shall take into account the aggravating and mitigating circumstances enumerated in Subsections (3) and (4) and any other facts that it deems relevant, but it shall not impose or recommend sentence of death unless it finds one of the aggravating circumstances enumerated in Subsection (3) and further finds that there are no mitigating circumstances sufficiently substantial to call for leniency. When the issue is submitted to the jury, the Court shall so instruct and also shall inform the jury of the nature of the sentence of imprisonment that may be imposed, including its implication with respect to possible release upon parole, if the jury verdict is against sentence of death.

Alternative formulation of Subsection (2):

(2) *Determination by Court.* Unless the Court imposes sentence under Subsection (1) of this Section, it shall conduct a separate proceeding to determine whether the defendant should be sentenced for a felony of the first degree or sentenced to death. In the proceeding, the Court, in accordance with Section 7.07, shall consider the report of the pre-sentence investigation and, if a psychiat-

ric examination has been ordered, the report of such examination. In addition, evidence may be presented as to any matter that the Court deems relevant to sentence, including but not limited to the nature and circumstances of the crime, the defendant's character, background, history, mental and physical condition and any of the aggravating or mitigating circumstances enumerated in Subsections (3) and (4) of this Section. Any such evidence, not legally privileged, which the Court deems to have probative force, may be received, regardless of its admissibility under the exclusionary rules of evidence, provided that the defendant's counsel is accorded a fair opportunity to rebut such evidence. The prosecuting attorney and the defendant or his counsel shall be permitted to present argument for or against sentence of death.

The determination whether sentence of death shall be imposed shall be in the discretion of the Court. In exercising such discretion, the Court shall take into account the aggravating and mitigating circumstances enumerated in Subsections (3) and (4) and any other facts that it deems relevant but shall not impose sentence of death unless it finds one of the aggravating circumstances enumerated in Subsection (3) and further finds that there are no mitigating circumstances sufficiently substantial to call for leniency.

(3) *Aggravating Circumstances.*

(a) The murder was committed by a convict under sentence of imprisonment.

(b) The defendant was previously convicted of another murder or of a felony involving the use or threat of violence to the person.

(c) At the time the murder was committed the defendant also committed another murder.

(d) The defendant knowingly created a great risk of death to many persons.

[Fel Murder]

(e) The murder was committed while the defendant was engaged or was an accomplice in the commission of, or an attempt to commit, or flight after committing or attempting to commit robbery, rape or deviate sexual intercourse by force or threat of force, arson, burglary or kidnapping.

(f) The murder was committed for the purpose of avoiding or preventing a lawful arrest or effecting an escape from lawful custody.

(g) The murder was committed for pecuniary gain.

(h) The murder was especially heinous, atrocious or cruel, manifesting exceptional depravity.

(4) *Mitigating Circumstances.*

(a) The defendant has no significant history of prior criminal activity.

[provocation] (b) The murder was committed while the defendant was under the influence of extreme mental or emotional disturbance.

(c) The victim was a participant in the defendant's homicidal conduct or consented to the homicidal act.

(d) The murder was committed under circumstances which the defendant believed to provide a moral justification or extenuation for his conduct.

(e) The defendant was an accomplice in a murder committed by another person and his participation in the homicidal act was relatively minor.

(f) The defendant acted under duress or under the domination of another person.

(g) At the time of the murder, the capacity of the defendant to appreciate the criminality [wrongfulness] of his conduct or to conform his conduct to the requirements of law was impaired as a result of mental disease or defect or intoxication.

PART II. DEFINITION OF SPECIFIC CRIMES

(h) The youth of the defendant at the time of the crime.]

ARTICLE 211. ASSAULT; RECKLESS ENDANGERING; THREATS

Section 211.0. Definitions.

In this Article, the definitions given in Section 210.0 apply unless a different meaning plainly is required.

Section 211.1. Assault.

(1) *Simple Assault.* A person is guilty of assault if he:

(a) attempts to cause or purposely, knowingly or recklessly causes bodily injury to another; or

(b) negligently causes bodily injury to another with a deadly weapon; or

(c) attempts by physical menace to put another in fear of imminent serious bodily injury.

Simple assault is a misdemeanor unless committed in a fight or scuffle entered into by mutual consent, in which case it is a petty misdemeanor.

(2) *Aggravated Assault.* A person is guilty of aggravated assault if he:

(a) attempts to cause serious bodily injury to another, or causes such injury purposely, knowingly or recklessly under circumstances manifesting extreme indifference to the value of human life; or

(b) attempts to cause or purposely or knowingly causes bodily injury to another with a deadly weapon.

Aggravated assault under paragraph (a) is a felony of the second degree; aggravated assault under paragraph (b) is a felony of the third degree.

Section 211.2. Recklessly Endangering Another Person.

A person commits a misdemeanor if he recklessly engages in conduct which places or may place another person in danger of death or serious bodily injury. Recklessness and danger shall be presumed where a person knowingly points a firearm at or in the direction of another, whether or not the actor believed the firearm to be loaded.

Section 211.3. Terroristic Threats.

A person is guilty of a felony of the third degree if he threatens to commit any crime of violence with purpose to terrorize another or to cause evacuation of a building, place of assembly, or facility of public transportation, or otherwise to cause serious public inconvenience, or in reckless disregard of the risk of causing such terror or inconvenience.

ARTICLE 212. KIDNAPPING AND RELATED OFFENSES; COERCION

Section 212.0. Definitions.

In this Article, the definitions given in Section 210.0 apply unless a different meaning plainly is required.

Section 212.1. Kidnapping.

A person is guilty of kidnapping if he unlawfully removes another from his place of residence or business, or a substantial distance from the vicinity where he is found, or if he unlawfully confines another for a substantial period in a place of isolation, with any of the following purposes:

(a) to hold for ransom or reward, or as a shield or hostage; or

(b) to facilitate commission of any felony or flight thereafter; or

(c) to inflict bodily injury on or to terrorize the victim or another; or

PART II. DEFINITION OF SPECIFIC CRIMES 383

(d) to interfere with the performance of any governmental or political function.

Kidnapping is a felony of the first degree unless the actor voluntarily releases the victim alive and in a safe place prior to trial, in which case it is a felony of the second degree. A removal or confinement is unlawful within the meaning of this Section if it is accomplished by force, threat or deception, or, in the case of a person who is under the age of 14 or incompetent, if it is accomplished without the consent of a parent, guardian or other person responsible for general supervision of his welfare.

Section 212.2. Felonious Restraint.

A person commits a felony of the third degree if he knowingly:

(a) restrains another unlawfully in circumstances exposing him to risk of serious bodily injury; or

(b) holds another in a condition of involuntary servitude.

Section 212.3. False Imprisonment.

A person commits a misdemeanor if he knowingly restrains another unlawfully so as to interfere substantially with his liberty.

Section 212.4. Interference with Custody.

(1) *Custody of Children.* A person commits an offense if he knowingly or recklessly takes or entices any child under the age of 18 from the custody of its parent, guardian or other lawful custodian, when he has no privilege to do so. It is an affirmative defense that:

(a) the actor believed that his action was necessary to preserve the child from danger to its welfare; or

(b) the child, being at the time not less than 14 years old, was taken away at its own instigation without enticement and without purpose to commit a criminal offense with or against the child.

Proof that the child was below the critical age gives rise to a presumption that the actor knew the child's age or acted in reckless disregard thereof. The offense is a misdemeanor unless the actor, not being a parent or person in equivalent relation to the child, acted with knowledge that his conduct would cause serious alarm for the child's safety, or in reckless disregard of a likelihood of causing such alarm, in which case the offense is a felony of the third degree.

(2) *Custody of Committed Persons.* A person is guilty of a misdemeanor if he knowingly or recklessly takes or entices any committed person away from lawful custody when he is not privileged to do so. "Committed person" means, in addition to anyone committed under judicial warrant, any orphan, neglected or delinquent child, mentally defective or insane person, or other dependent or incompetent person entrusted to another's custody by or through a recognized social agency or otherwise by authority of law.

Section 212.5. Criminal Coercion.

(1) *Offense Defined.* A person is guilty of criminal coercion if, with purpose unlawfully to restrict another's freedom of action to his detriment, he threatens to:

(a) commit any criminal offense; or

(b) accuse anyone of a criminal offense; or

(c) expose any secret tending to subject any person to hatred, contempt or ridicule, or to impair his credit or business repute; or

(d) take or withhold action as an official, or cause an official to take or withhold action.

It is an affirmative defense to prosecution based on paragraphs (b), (c) or (d) that the actor believed the accusation or secret to be true or the proposed official action justified and that his purpose was limited to compelling the other to behave in a way reasonably related to the circumstances which were the subject of the accusation, exposure or proposed official action, as by desisting from further misbehavior, making good a wrong done, refraining from taking any action or responsibility for which the actor believes the other disqualified.

(2) *Grading.* Criminal coercion is a misdemeanor unless the threat is to commit a felony or the actor's purpose is felonious, in which cases the offense is a felony of the third degree.

ARTICLE 213. SEXUAL OFFENSES

Section 213.0. Definitions.

In this Article, unless a different meaning plainly is required:

(1) the definitions given in Section 210.0 apply;

(2) "Sexual intercourse" includes intercourse per os or per anus, with some penetration however slight; emission is not required;

(3) "Deviate sexual intercourse" means sexual intercourse per os or per anus between human beings who are not husband and wife, and any form of sexual intercourse with an animal.

Section 213.1. Rape and Related Offenses.

(1) *Rape.* A male who has sexual intercourse with a female not his wife is guilty of rape if:

(a) he compels her to submit by force or by threat of imminent death, serious bodily injury, extreme pain or kidnapping, to be inflicted on anyone; or

(b) he has substantially impaired her power to appraise or control her conduct by administering or employing without her knowledge drugs, intoxicants or other means for the purpose of preventing resistance; or

(c) the female is unconscious; or

(d) the female is less than 10 years old.

Rape is a felony of the second degree unless (i) in the course thereof the actor inflicts serious bodily injury upon anyone, or (ii) the victim was not a voluntary social companion of the actor upon the occasion of the crime and had not previously permitted him sexual liberties, in which cases the offense is a felony of the first degree.

(2) *Gross Sexual Imposition.* A male who has sexual intercourse with a female not his wife commits a felony of the third degree if:

(a) he compels her to submit by any threat that would prevent resistance by a woman of ordinary resolution; or

(b) he knows that she suffers from a mental disease or defect which renders her incapable of appraising the nature of her conduct; or

(c) he knows that she is unaware that a sexual act is being committed upon her or that she submits because she mistakenly supposes that he is her husband.

Section 213.2. Deviate Sexual Intercourse by Force or Imposition.

(1) *By Force or Its Equivalent.* A person who engages in deviate sexual intercourse with another person, or who causes another to engage in deviate sexual intercourse, commits a felony of the second degree if:

(a) he compels the other person to participate by force or by threat of imminent death, serious bodily injury, extreme pain or kidnapping, to be inflicted on anyone; or

(b) he has substantially impaired the other person's power to appraise or control his conduct, by administering or employing without the knowledge of the other person drugs, intoxicants or other means for the purpose of preventing resistance; or

(c) the other person is unconscious; or

(d) the other person is less than 10 years old.

(2) *By Other Imposition.* A person who engages in deviate sexual intercourse with another person, or who causes another to engage in deviate sexual intercourse, commits a felony of the third degree if:

(a) he compels the other person to participate by any threat that would prevent resistance by a person of ordinary resolution; or

(b) he knows that the other person suffers from a mental disease or defect which renders him incapable of appraising the nature of his conduct; or

(c) he knows that the other person submits because he is unaware that a sexual act is being committed upon him.

Section 213.3. Corruption of Minors and Seduction.

(1) *Offense Defined.* A male who has sexual intercourse with a female not his wife, or any person who engages in deviate sexual intercourse or causes another to engage in deviate sexual intercourse, is guilty of an offense if:

(a) the other person is less than [16] years old and the actor is at least [4] years older than the other person; or

(b) the other person is less than 21 years old and the actor is his guardian or otherwise responsible for general supervision of his welfare; or

(c) the other person is in custody of law or detained in a hospital or other institution and the actor has supervisory or disciplinary authority over him; or

(d) the other person is a female who is induced to participate by a promise of marriage which the actor does not mean to perform.

(2) *Grading.* An offense under paragraph (a) of Subsection (1) is a felony of the third degree. Otherwise an offense under this section is a misdemeanor.

Section 213.4. Sexual Assault.

A person who has sexual contact with another not his spouse, or causes such other to have sexual contact with him, is guilty of sexual assault, a misdemeanor, if:

(1) he knows that the contact is offensive to the other person; or

(2) he knows that the other person suffers from a mental disease or defect which renders him or her incapable of appraising the nature of his or her conduct; or

(3) he knows that the other person is unaware that a sexual act is being committed; or

(4) the other person is less than 10 years old; or

(5) he has substantially impaired the other person's power to appraise or control his or her conduct, by administering or employing without the other's knowledge drugs, intoxicants or other means for the purpose of preventing resistance; or

(6) the other person is less than [16] years old and the actor is at least [4] years older than the other person; or

(7) the other person is less than 21 years old and the actor is his guardian or otherwise responsible for general supervision of his welfare; or

(8) the other person is in custody of law or detained in a hospital or other institution and the actor has supervisory or disciplinary authority over him.

Sexual contact is any touching of the sexual or other intimate parts of the person for the purpose of arousing or gratifying sexual desire.

Section 213.5. Indecent Exposure.

A person commits a misdemeanor if, for the purpose of arousing or gratifying sexual desire of himself or of any person other than his spouse, he exposes his genitals under circumstances in which he knows his conduct is likely to cause affront or alarm.

Section 213.6. Provisions Generally Applicable to Article 213.

(1) *Mistake as to Age.* Whenever in this Article the criminality of conduct depends on a child's being below the age of 10, it is no defense that the actor did not know the child's age, or reasonably believed the child to be older than 10. When criminality depends on the child's being below a critical age other than 10, it is a defense for the actor to prove by a preponderance of the evidence that he reasonably believed the child to be above the critical age.

(2) *Spouse Relationships.* Whenever in this Article the definition of an offense excludes conduct with a spouse, the exclusion shall be deemed to extend to persons living as man and wife, regardless of the legal status of their relationship. The exclusion shall be inoperative as respects spouses living apart under a decree of judicial separation. Where the definition of an offense excludes conduct with a spouse or conduct by a woman, this shall not preclude conviction of a spouse or woman as accomplice in a sexual act which he or she causes another person, not within the exclusion, to perform.

(3) *Sexually Promiscuous Complainants.* It is a defense to prosecution under Section 213.3 and paragraphs (6), (7) and (8) of Section 213.4 for the actor to prove by a preponderance of the evidence that the alleged victim had, prior to the time of the offense charged, engaged promiscuously in sexual relations with others.

(4) *Prompt Complaint.* No prosecution may be instituted or maintained under this Article unless the alleged offense was brought to the notice of public authority

within [3] months of its occurrence or, where the alleged victim was less than [16] years old or otherwise incompetent to make complaint, within [3] months after a parent, guardian or other competent person specially interested in the victim learns of the offense.

(5) *Testimony of Complainants.* No person shall be convicted of any felony under this Article upon the uncorroborated testimony of the alleged victim. Corroboration may be circumstantial. In any prosecution before a jury for an offense under this Article, the jury shall be instructed to evaluate the testimony of a victim or complaining witness with special care in view of the emotional involvement of the witness and the difficulty of determining the truth with respect to alleged sexual activities carried out in private.

OFFENSES AGAINST PROPERTY

ARTICLE 220. ARSON, CRIMINAL MISCHIEF, AND OTHER PROPERTY DESTRUCTION

Section 220.1. Arson and Related Offenses.

(1) *Arson.* A person is guilty of arson, a felony of the second degree, if he starts a fire or causes an explosion with the purpose of:

(a) destroying a building or occupied structure of another; or

(b) destroying or damaging any property, whether his own or another's, to collect insurance for such loss. It shall be an affirmative defense to prosecution under this paragraph that the actor's conduct did not recklessly endanger any building or occupied structure of another or place any other person in danger of death or bodily injury.

(2) *Reckless Burning or Exploding.* A person commits a felony of the third degree if he purposely starts a fire or causes an explosion, whether on his own property or another's, and thereby recklessly:

(a) places another person in danger of death or bodily injury; or

(b) places a building or occupied structure of another in danger of damage or destruction.

(3) *Failure to Control or Report Dangerous Fire.* A person who knows that a fire is endangering life or a substantial amount of property of another and fails to take reasonable measures to put out or control the fire, when he can do so without substantial risk to himself, or to give a prompt fire alarm, commits a misdemeanor if:

(a) he knows that he is under an official, contractual, or other legal duty to prevent or combat the fire; or

(b) the fire was started, albeit lawfully, by him or with his assent, or on property in his custody or control.

(4) *Definitions.* "Occupied structure" means any structure, vehicle or place adapted for overnight accommodation of persons, or for carrying on business therein, whether or not a person is actually present. Property is that of another, for the purposes of this section, if anyone other than the actor has a possessory or proprietary interest therein. If a building or structure is divided into separately occupied units, any unit not occupied by the actor is an occupied structure of another.

Section 220.2. Causing or Risking Catastrophe.

(1) *Causing Catastrophe.* A person who causes a catastrophe by explosion, fire, flood, avalanche, collapse of building, release of poison gas, radioactive material or other harmful or destructive force or substance, or by any other means of causing potentially widespread injury or damage, commits a felony of the second degree if he does so purposely or knowingly, or a felony of the third degree if he does so recklessly.

(2) *Risking Catastrophe.* A person is guilty of a misdemeanor if he recklessly creates a risk of catastrophe in

the employment of fire, explosives or other dangerous means listed in Subsection (1).

(3) *Failure to Prevent Catastrophe.* A person who knowingly or recklessly fails to take reasonable measures to prevent or mitigate a catastrophe commits a misdemeanor if:

(a) he knows that he is under an official, contractual or other legal duty to take such measures; or

(b) he did or assented to the act causing or threatening the catastrophe.

Section 220.3. Criminal Mischief.

(1) *Offense Defined.* A person is guilty of criminal mischief if he:

(a) damages tangible property of another purposely, recklessly, or by negligence in the employment of fire, explosives, or other dangerous means listed in Section 220.2(1); or

(b) purposely or recklessly tampers with tangible property of another so as to endanger person or property; or

(c) purposely or recklessly causes another to suffer pecuniary loss by deception or threat.

(2) *Grading.* Criminal mischief is a felony of the third degree if the actor purposely causes pecuniary loss in excess of $5,000, or a substantial interruption or impairment of public communication, transportation, supply of water, gas or power, or other public service. It is a misdemeanor if the actor purposely causes pecuniary loss in excess of $100, or a petty misdemeanor if he purposely or recklessly causes pecuniary loss in excess of $25. Otherwise criminal mischief is a violation.

ARTICLE 221. BURGLARY AND OTHER CRIMINAL INTRUSION

Section 221.0. Definitions.

In this Article, unless a different meaning plainly is required:

(1) "occupied structure" means any structure, vehicle or place adapted for overnight accommodation of persons, or for carrying on business therein, whether or not a person is actually present.

(2) "night" means the period between thirty minutes past sunset and thirty minutes before sunrise.

Section 221.1. Burglary.

(1) *Burglary Defined.* A person is guilty of burglary if he enters a building or occupied structure, or separately secured or occupied portion thereof, with purpose to commit a crime therein, unless the premises are at the time open to the public or the actor is licensed or privileged to enter. It is an affirmative defense to prosecution for burglary that the building or structure was abandoned.

(2) *Grading.* Burglary is a felony of the second degree if it is perpetrated in the dwelling of another at night, or if, in the course of committing the offense, the actor:

(a) purposely, knowingly or recklessly inflicts or attempts to inflict bodily injury on anyone; or

(b) is armed with explosives or a deadly weapon.

Otherwise, burglary is a felony of the third degree. An act shall be deemed "in the course of committing" an offense if it occurs in an attempt to commit the offense or in flight after the attempt or commission.

(3) *Multiple Convictions.* A person may not be convicted both for burglary and for the offense which it was his purpose to commit after the burglarious entry or for an attempt to commit that offense, unless the additional offense constitutes a felony of the first or second degree.

Section 221.2. Criminal Trespass.

(1) *Buildings and Occupied Structures.* A person commits an offense if, knowing that he is not licensed or privileged to do so, he enters or surreptitiously remains in any building or occupied structure, or separately secured or occupied portion thereof. An offense under this Subsection is a misdemeanor if it is committed in a dwelling at night. Otherwise it is a petty misdemeanor.

(2) *Defiant Trespasser.* A person commits an offense if, knowing that he is not licensed or privileged to do so, he enters or remains in any place as to which notice against trespass is given by:

(a) actual communication to the actor; or

(b) posting in a manner prescribed by law or reasonably likely to come to the attention of intruders; or

(c) fencing or other enclosure manifestly designed to exclude intruders.

An offense under this Subsection constitutes a petty misdemeanor if the offender defies an order to leave personally communicated to him by the owner of the premises or other authorized person. Otherwise it is a violation.

(3) *Defenses.* It is an affirmative defense to prosecution under this Section that:

(a) a building or occupied structure involved in an offense under Subsection (1) was abandoned; or

(b) the premises were at the time open to members of the public and the actor complied with all lawful conditions imposed on access to or remaining in the premises; or

(c) the actor reasonably believed that the owner of the premises, or other person empowered to license access thereto, would have licensed him to enter or remain.

ARTICLE 222. ROBBERY

Section 222.1. Robbery.

(1) *Robbery Defined.* A person is guilty of robbery if, in the course of committing a theft, he:

(a) inflicts serious bodily injury upon another; or

(b) threatens another with or purposely puts him in fear of immediate serious bodily injury; or

(c) commits or threatens immediately to commit any felony of the first or second degree.

An act shall be deemed "in the course of committing a theft" if it occurs in an attempt to commit theft or in flight after the attempt or commission.

(2) *Grading.* Robbery is a felony of the second degree, except that it is a felony of the first degree if in the course of committing the theft the actor attempts to kill anyone, or purposely inflicts or attempts to inflict serious bodily injury.

ARTICLE 223. THEFT AND RELATED OFFENSES

Section 223.0. Definitions.

In this Article, unless a different meaning plainly is required:

(1) "deprive" means: (a) to withhold property of another permanently or for so extended a period as to appropriate a major portion of its economic value, or with intent to restore only upon payment of reward or other compensation; or (b) to dispose of the property so as to make it unlikely that the owner will recover it.

(2) "financial institution" means a bank, insurance company, credit union, building and loan association, investment trust or other organization held out to the public as a place of deposit of funds or medium of savings or collective investment.

(3) "government" means the United States, any State, county, municipality, or other political unit, or any department, agency or subdivision of any of the foregoing, or any corporation or other association carrying out the functions of government.

(4) "movable property" means property the location of which can be changed, including things growing on, affixed to, or found in land, and documents although the rights represented thereby have no physical location. "Immovable property" is all other property.

(5) "obtain" means: (a) in relation to property, to bring about a transfer or purported transfer of a legal interest in the property, whether to the obtainer or another; or (b) in relation to labor or service, to secure performance thereof.

(6) "property" means anything of value, including real estate, tangible and intangible personal property, contract rights, choses-in-action and other interests in or claims to wealth, admission or transportation tickets, captured or domestic animals, food and drink, electric or other power.

(7) "property of another" includes property in which any person other than the actor has an interest which the actor is not privileged to infringe, regardless of the fact that the actor also has an interest in the property and regardless of the fact that the other person might be precluded from civil recovery because the property was used in an unlawful transaction or was subject to forfeiture as contraband. Property in possession of the actor shall not be deemed property of another who has only a security interest therein, even if legal title is in the creditor pursuant to a conditional sales contract or other security agreement.

Section 223.1. Consolidation of Theft Offenses; Grading; Provisions Applicable to Theft Generally.

(1) *Consolidation of Theft Offenses.* Conduct denominated theft in this Article constitutes a single offense. An accusation of theft may be supported by evidence that it was committed in any manner that would be theft under this Article, notwithstanding the specification of a different manner in the indictment or information, subject only to the power of the Court to ensure fair trial by granting a continuance or other appropriate relief where the conduct of the defense would be prejudiced by lack of fair notice or by surprise.

(2) *Grading of Theft Offenses.*

(a) Theft constitutes a felony of the third degree if the amount involved exceeds $500, or if the property stolen is a firearm, automobile, airplane, motorcycle, motor boat, or other motor-propelled vehicle, or in the case of theft by receiving stolen property, if the receiver is in the business of buying or selling stolen property.

(b) Theft not within the preceding paragraph constitutes a misdemeanor, except that if the property was not taken from the person or by threat, or in breach of a fiduciary obligation, and the actor proves by a preponderance of the evidence that the amount involved was less than $50, the offense constitutes a petty misdemeanor.

(c) The amount involved in a theft shall be deemed to be the highest value, by any reasonable standard, of the property or services which the actor stole or attempted to steal. Amounts involved in thefts committed pursuant to one scheme or course of conduct, whether from the same person or several persons, may be aggregated in determining the grade of the offense.

(3) *Claim of Right.* It is an affirmative defense to prosecution for theft that the actor:

(a) was unaware that the property or service was that of another; or

(b) acted under an honest claim of right to the property or service involved or that he had a right to acquire or dispose of it as he did; or

(c) took property exposed for sale, intending to purchase and pay for it promptly, or reasonably believing that the owner, if present, would have consented.

(4) *Theft from Spouse.* It is no defense that theft was from the actor's spouse, except that misappropriation of household and personal effects, or other property normally accessible to both spouses, is theft only if it occurs after the parties have ceased living together.

Section 223.2. Theft by Unlawful Taking or Disposition.

(1) *Movable Property.* A person is guilty of theft if he unlawfully takes, or exercises unlawful control over, movable property of another with purpose to deprive him thereof.

(2) *Immovable Property.* A person is guilty of theft if he unlawfully transfers immovable property of another or any interest therein with purpose to benefit himself or another not entitled thereto.

Section 223.3. Theft by Deception.

A person is guilty of theft if he purposely obtains property of another by deception. A person deceives if he purposely:

(1) creates or reinforces a false impression, including false impressions as to law, value, intention or other state of mind; but deception as to a person's intention to perform a promise shall not be inferred from the fact alone that he did not subsequently perform the promise; or

(2) prevents another from acquiring information which would affect his judgment of a transaction; or

(3) fails to correct a false impression which the deceiver previously created or reinforced, or which the deceiver knows to be influencing another to whom he stands in a fiduciary or confidential relationship; or

(4) fails to disclose a known lien, adverse claim or other legal impediment to the enjoyment of property which he transfers or encumbers in consideration for the property obtained, whether such impediment is or is not valid, or is or is not a matter of official record.

The term "deceive" does not, however, include falsity as to matters having no pecuniary significance, or puffing by statements unlikely to deceive ordinary persons in the group addressed.

Section 223.4. Theft by Extortion.

A person is guilty of theft if he purposely obtains property of another by threatening to:

(1) inflict bodily injury on anyone or commit any other criminal offense; or

(2) accuse anyone of a criminal offense; or

(3) expose any secret tending to subject any person to hatred, contempt or ridicule, or to impair his credit or business repute; or

(4) take or withhold action as an official, or cause an official to take or withhold action; or

(5) bring about or continue a strike, boycott or other collective unofficial action, if the property is not demanded or received for the benefit of the group in whose interest the actor purports to act; or

(6) testify or provide information or withhold testimony or information with respect to another's legal claim or defense; or

(7) inflict any other harm which would not benefit the actor.

It is an affirmative defense to prosecution based on paragraphs (2), (3) or (4) that the property obtained by threat of accusation, exposure, lawsuit or other invocation of official action was honestly claimed as restitution or indemnification for harm done in the circumstances to which such accusation, exposure, lawsuit or other official action relates, or as compensation for property or lawful services.

Section 223.5. Theft of Property Lost, Mislaid, or Delivered by Mistake.

A person who comes into control of property of another that he knows to have been lost, mislaid, or delivered under a mistake as to the nature or amount of the property or the identity of the recipient is guilty of theft if, with purpose to deprive the owner thereof, he fails to take reasonable measures to restore the property to a person entitled to have it.

Section 223.6. Receiving Stolen Property.

(1) *Receiving.* A person is guilty of theft if he purposely receives, retains, or disposes of movable property of another knowing that it has been stolen, or believing that it has probably been stolen, unless the property is received, retained, or disposed with purpose to restore it to the owner. "Receiving" means acquiring possession, control or title, or lending on the security of the property.

(2) *Presumption of Knowledge.* The requisite knowledge or belief is presumed in the case of a dealer who:

(a) is found in possession or control of property stolen from two or more persons on separate occasions; or

(b) has received stolen property in another transaction within the year preceding the transaction charged; or

(c) being a dealer in property of the sort received, acquires it for a consideration which he knows is far below its reasonable value.

PART II. DEFINITION OF SPECIFIC CRIMES   401

"Dealer" means a person in the business of buying or selling goods including a pawnbroker.

Section 223.7. Theft of Services.

(1) A person is guilty of theft is he purposely obtains services which he knows are available only for compensation, by deception or threat, or by false token or other means to avoid payment for the service. "Services" includes labor, professional service, transportation, telephone or other public service, accommodation in hotels, restaurants or elsewhere, admission to exhibitions, use of vehicles or other movable property. Where compensation for service is ordinarily paid immediately upon the rendering of such service, as in the case of hotels and restaurants, refusal to pay or absconding without payment or offer to pay gives rise to a presumption that the service was obtained by deception as to intention to pay.

(2) A person commits theft if, having control over the disposition of services of others, to which he is not entitled, he knowingly diverts such services to his own benefit or to the benefit of another not entitled thereto.

Section 223.8. Theft by Failure to Make Required Disposition of Funds Received.

A person who purposely obtains property upon agreement, or subject to a known legal obligation, to make specified payment or other disposition, whether from such property or its proceeds or from his own property to be reserved in equivalent amount, is guilty of theft if he deals with the property obtained as his own and fails to make the required payment or disposition. The foregoing applies notwithstanding that it may be impossible to identify particular property as belonging to the victim at the time of the actor's failure to make the required payment or disposition. An officer or employee of the government or of a financial institution is presumed: (i) to know any legal obligation relevant to his criminal liability under this Section, and (ii) to have dealt with the property as his own if he fails to pay or account upon lawful demand, or if an audit reveals a shortage or falsification of accounts.

Section 223.9. Unauthorized Use of Automobiles and Other Vehicles.

A person commits a misdemeanor if he operates another's automobile, airplane, motorcycle, motorboat, or other motor-propelled vehicle without consent of the owner. It is an affirmative defense to prosecution under this Section that the actor reasonably believed that the owner would have consented to the operation had he known of it.

ARTICLE 224. FORGERY AND FRAUDULENT PRACTICES

Section 224.0. Definitions.

In this Article, the definitions given in Section 223.0 apply unless a different meaning plainly is required.

Section 224.1. Forgery.

(1) *Definition.* A person is guilty of forgery if, with purpose to defraud or injure anyone, or with knowledge that he is facilitating a fraud or injury to be perpetrated by anyone, the actor:

(a) alters any writing of another without his authority; or

(b) makes, completes, executes, authenticates, issues or transfers any writing so that it purports to be the act of another who did not authorize that act, or to have been executed at a time or place or in a numbered sequence other than was in fact the case, or to be a copy of an original when no such original existed; or

(c) utters any writing which he knows to be forged in a manner specified in paragraphs (a) or (b).

"Writing" includes printing or any other method of recording information, money, coins, tokens, stamps, seals, credit cards, badges, trade-marks, and other symbols of value, right, privilege, or identification.

(2) *Grading.* Forgery is a felony of the second degree if the writing is or purports to be part of an issue of money, securities, postage or revenue stamps, or other instruments issued by the government, or part of an issue of stock, bonds or other instruments representing interests in or claims against any property or enterprise. Forgery is a felony of the third degree if the writing is or purports to be a will, deed, contract, release, commercial instrument, or other document evidencing, creating, transferring, altering, terminating, or otherwise affecting legal relations. Otherwise forgery is a misdemeanor.

Section 224.2. Simulating Objects of Antiquity, Rarity, Etc.

A person commits a misdemeanor if, with purpose to defraud anyone or with knowledge that he is facilitating a fraud to be perpetrated by anyone, he makes, alters or utters any object so that it appears to have value because of antiquity, rarity, source, or authorship which it does not possess.

Section 224.3. Fraudulent Destruction, Removal or Concealment of Recordable Instruments.

A person commits a felony of the third degree if, with purpose to deceive or injure anyone, he destroys, removes or conceals any will, deed, mortgage, security instrument or other writing for which the law provides public recording.

Section 224.4. Tampering with Records.

A person commits a misdemeanor if, knowing that he has no privilege to do so, he falsifies, destroys, removes or conceals any writing or record, with purpose to deceive or injure anyone or to conceal any wrongdoing.

Section 224.5. Bad Checks.

A person who issues or passes a check or similar sight order for the payment of money, knowing that it will not be honored by the drawee, commits a misdemeanor. For the purposes of this Section as well as in any prosecution for theft committed by means of a bad check, an issuer is presumed to know that the check or order (other than a postdated check or order) would not be paid, if:

(1) the issuer had no account with the drawee at the time the check or order was issued; or

(2) payment was refused by the drawee for lack of funds, upon presentation within 30 days after issue, and the issuer failed to make good within 10 days after receiving notice of that refusal.

Section 224.6. Credit Cards.

A person commits an offense if he uses a credit card for the purpose of obtaining property or services with knowledge that:

(1) the card is stolen or forged; or

(2) the card has been revoked or cancelled; or

(3) for any other reason his use of the card is unauthorized by the issuer.

It is an affirmative defense to prosecution under paragraph (3) if the actor proves by a preponderance of the evidence that he had the purpose and ability to meet all obligations to the issuer arising out of his use of the card. "Credit card" means a writing or other evidence of an undertaking to pay for property or services delivered or rendered to or upon the order of a designated person or bearer. An offense under this Section is a felony of the third degree if the value of the property or services secured or sought to be secured by means of the credit card exceeds $500; otherwise it is a misdemeanor.

Section 224.7. Deceptive Business Practices.

A person commits a misdemeanor if in the course of business he:

(1) uses or possesses for use a false weight or measure, or any other device for falsely determining or recording any quality or quantity; or

(2) sells, offers or exposes for sale, or delivers less than the represented quantity of any commodity or service; or

(3) takes or attempts to take more than the represented quantity of any commodity or service when as buyer he furnishes the weight or measure; or

(4) sells, offers or exposes for sale adulterated or mislabeled commodities. "Adulterated" means varying from the standard of composition or quality prescribed by or pursuant to any statute providing criminal penalties for such variance, or set by established commercial usage. "Mislabeled" means varying from the standard of truth or disclosure in labeling prescribed by or pursuant to any statute providing criminal penalties for such variance, or set by established commercial usage; or

(5) makes a false or misleading statement in any advertisement addressed to the public or to a substantial segment thereof for the purpose of promoting the purchase or sale of property or services; or

(6) makes a false or misleading written statement for the purpose of obtaining property or credit; or

(7) makes a false or misleading written statement for the purpose of promoting the sale of securities, or omits information required by law to be disclosed in written documents relating to securities.

It is an affirmative defense to prosecution under this Section if the defendant proves by a preponderance of the evidence that his conduct was not knowingly or recklessly deceptive.

Section 224.8. Commercial Bribery and Breach of Duty to Act Disinterestedly.

(1) A person commits a misdemeanor if he solicits, accepts or agrees to accept any benefit as consideration for knowingly violating or agreeing to violate a duty of fidelity to which he is subject as:

(a) partner, agent or employee of another;

(b) trustee, guardian, or other fiduciary;

(c) lawyer, physician, accountant, appraiser, or other professional adviser or informant;

(d) officer, director, manager or other participant in the direction of the affairs of an incorporated or unincorporated association; or

(e) arbitrator or other purportedly disinterested adjudicator or referee.

(2) A person who holds himself out to the public as being engaged in the business of making disinterested selection, appraisal, or criticism of commodities or services commits a misdemeanor if he solicits, accepts or agrees to accept any benefit to influence his selection, appraisal or criticism.

(3) A person commits a misdemeanor if he confers, or offers or agrees to confer, any benefit the acceptance of which would be criminal under this Section.

Section 224.9. Rigging Publicly Exhibited Contest.

(1) A person commits a misdemeanor if, with purpose to prevent a publicly exhibited contest from being conducted in accordance with the rules and usages purporting to govern it, he:

(a) confers or offers or agrees to confer any benefit upon, or threatens any injury to a participant, official or other person associated with the contest or exhibition; or

(b) tampers with any person, animal or thing.

(2) *Soliciting or Accepting Benefit for Rigging.* A person commits a misdemeanor if he knowingly solicits, accepts or agrees to accept any benefit the giving of which would be criminal under Subsection (1).

(3) *Participation in Rigged Contest.* A person commits a misdemeanor if he knowingly engages in, sponsors, produces, judges, or otherwise participates in a publicly exhibited contest knowing that the contest is not being conducted in compliance with the rules and usages purporting to govern it, by reason of conduct which would be criminal under this Section.

Section 224.10. Defrauding Secured Creditors.

A person commits a misdemeanor if he destroys, removes, conceals, encumbers, transfers or otherwise deals with property subject to a security interest with purpose to hinder enforcement of that interest.

Section 224.11. Fraud in Insolvency.

A person commits a misdemeanor if, knowing that proceedings have been or are about to be instituted for the appointment of a receiver or other person entitled to administer property for the benefit of creditors, or that any other composition or liquidation for the benefit of creditors has been or is about to made, he:

(a) destroys, removes, conceals, encumbers, transfers, or otherwise deals with any property with purpose to defeat or obstruct the claim of any creditor, or otherwise to obstruct the operation of any law relating to administration of property for the benefit of creditors; or

(b) knowingly falsifies any writing or record relating to the property; or

(c) knowingly misrepresents or refuses to disclose to a receiver or other person entitled to administer property for the benefit of creditors, the existence, amount or location of the property, or any other information which the actor could be legally required to furnish in relation to such administration.

Section 224.12. Receiving Deposits in a Failing Financial Institution.

An officer, manager or other person directing or participating in the direction of a financial institution commits a misdemeanor if he receives or permits the receipt of a deposit, premium payment or other investment in the institution knowing that:

(1) due to financial difficulties the institution is about to suspend operations or go into receivership or reorganization; and

(2) the person making the deposit or other payment is unaware of the precarious situation of the institution.

Section 224.13. Misapplication of Entrusted Property and Property of Government or Financial Institution.

A person commits an offense if he applies or disposes of property that has been entrusted to him as a fiduciary, or property of the government or of a financial institution, in a manner which he knows is unlawful and involves substantial risk of loss or detriment to the owner of the property or to a person for whose benefit the property was entrusted. The offense is a misdemeanor if the amount involved exceeds $50; otherwise it is a petty misdemeanor. "Fiduciary" includes trustee, guardian, executor, administrator, receiver and any person carrying on fiduciary functions on behalf of a corporation or other organization which is a fiduciary.

Section 224.14. Securing Execution of Documents by Deception.

A person commits a misdemeanor if by deception he causes another to execute any instrument affecting or purporting to affect or likely to affect the pecuniary interest of any person.

OFFENSES AGAINST THE FAMILY

ARTICLE 230. OFFENSES AGAINST THE FAMILY

Section 230.1. Bigamy and Polygamy.

(1) *Bigamy*. A married person is guilty of bigamy, a misdemeanor, if he contracts or purports to contract another marriage, unless at the time of the subsequent marriage:

(a) the actor believes that the prior spouse is dead; or

(b) the actor and the prior spouse have been living apart for five consecutive years throughout which the prior spouse was not known by the actor to be alive; or

(c) a Court has entered a judgment purporting to terminate or annul any prior disqualifying marriage, and the actor does not know that judgment to be invalid; or

(d) the actor reasonably believes that he is legally eligible to remarry.

(2) *Polygamy*. A person is guilty of polygamy, a felony of the third degree, if he marries or cohabits with more than one spouse at a time in purported exercise of the right of plural marriage. The offense is a continuing one until all cohabitation and claim of marriage with more than one spouse terminates. This section does not apply to parties to a polygamous marriage, lawful in the country of which they are residents or nationals, while they are in transit through or temporarily visiting this State.

(3) *Other Party to Bigamous or Polygamous Marriage*. A person is guilty of bigamy or polygamy, as the case may be, if he contracts or purports to contract marriage with another knowing that the other is thereby committing bigamy or polygamy.

Section 230.2. Incest.

A person is guilty of incest, a felony of the third degree, if he knowingly marries or cohabits or has sexual intercourse with an ancestor or descendant, a brother or sister of the whole or half blood [or an uncle, aunt, nephew or niece of the whole blood]. "Cohabit" means to live together under the representation or appearance of being married. The relationships referred to herein include blood relationships without regard to legitimacy, and relationship of parent and child by adoption.

Section 230.3. Abortion.

(1) *Unjustified Abortion.* A person who purposely and unjustifiably terminates the pregnancy of another otherwise than by a live birth commits a felony of the third degree or, where the pregnancy has continued beyond the twenty-sixth week, a felony of the second degree.

(2) *Justifiable Abortion.* A licensed physician is justified in terminating a pregnancy if he believes there is substantial risk that continuance of the pregnancy would gravely impair the physical or mental health of the mother or that the child would be born with grave physical or mental defect, or that the pregnancy resulted from rape, incest, or other felonious intercourse. All illicit intercourse with a girl below the age of 16 shall be deemed felonious for purposes of this subsection. Justifiable abortions shall be performed only in a licensed hospital except in case of emergency when hospital facilities are unavailable. [Additional exceptions from the requirement of hospitalization may be incorporated here to take account of situations in sparsely settled areas where hospitals are not generally accessible.]

(3) *Physicians' Certificates; Presumption from Non-Compliance.* No abortion shall be performed unless two physicians, one of whom may be the person performing the abortion, shall have certified in writing the circumstances which they believe to justify the abortion. Such certificate shall be submitted before the abortion to the hospital where it is to be performed and, in the case of

abortion following felonious intercourse, to the prosecuting attorney or the police. Failure to comply with any of the requirements of this Subsection gives rise to a presumption that the abortion was unjustified.

(4) *Self-Abortion.* A woman whose pregnancy has continued beyond the twenty-sixth week commits a felony of the third degree if she purposely terminates her own pregnancy otherwise than by a live birth, or if she uses instruments, drugs or violence upon herself for that purpose. Except as justified under Subsection (2), a person who induces or knowingly aids a woman to use instruments, drugs or violence upon herself for the purpose of terminating her pregnancy otherwise than by a live birth commits a felony of the third degree whether or not the pregnancy has continued beyond the twenty-sixth week.

(5) *Pretended Abortion.* A person commits a felony of the third degree if, representing that it is his purpose to perform an abortion, he does an act adapted to cause abortion in a pregnant woman although the woman is in fact not pregnant, or the actor does not believe she is. A person charged with unjustified abortion under Subsection (1) or an attempt to commit that offense may be convicted thereof upon proof of conduct prohibited by this Subsection.

(6) *Distribution of Abortifacients.* A person who sells, offers to sell, possesses with intent to sell, advertises, or displays for sale anything specially designed to terminate a pregnancy, or held out by the actor as useful for that purpose, commits a misdemeanor, unless:

(a) the sale, offer or display is to a physician or druggist or to an intermediary in a chain of distribution to physicians or druggists; or

(b) the sale is made upon prescription or order of a physician; or

(c) the possession is with intent to sell as authorized in paragraphs (a) and (b); or

(d) the advertising is addressed to persons named in paragraph (a) and confined to trade or professional channels not likely to reach the general public.

(7) *Section Inapplicable to Prevention of Pregnancy.* Nothing in this Section shall be deemed applicable to the prescription, administration or distribution of drugs or other substances for avoiding pregnancy, whether by preventing implantation of a fertilized ovum or by any other method that operates before, at or immediately after fertilization.

Section 230.4. Endangering Welfare of Children.

A parent, guardian, or other person supervising the welfare of a child under 18 commits a misdemeanor if he knowingly endangers the child's welfare by violating a duty of care, protection or support.

Section 230.5. Persistent Non-Support.

A person commits a misdemeanor if he persistently fails to provide support which he can provide and which he knows he is legally obliged to provide to a spouse, child or other dependent.

OFFENSES AGAINST PUBLIC ADMINISTRATION

ARTICLE 240. BRIBERY AND CORRUPT INFLUENCE

Section 240.0. Definitions.

In Articles 240–243, unless a different meaning plainly is required:

(1) "benefit" means gain or advantage, or anything regarded by the beneficiary as gain or advantage, including benefit to any other person or entity in whose welfare he is interested, but not an advantage promised generally to a group or class of voters as a consequence of public measures which a candidate engages to support or oppose;

(2) "government" includes any branch, subdivision or agency of the government of the State or any locality within it;

(3) "harm" means loss, disadvantage or injury, or anything so regarded by the person affected, including loss, disadvantage or injury to any other person or entity in whose welfare he is interested;

(4) "official proceeding" means a proceeding heard or which may be heard before any legislative, judicial, administrative or other governmental agency or official authorized to take evidence under oath, including any referee, hearing examiner, commissioner, notary or other person taking testimony or deposition in connection with any such proceeding;

(5) "party official" means a person who holds an elective or appointive post in a political party in the United States by virtue of which he directs or conducts, or participates in directing or conducting party affairs at any level of responsibility;

(6) "pecuniary benefit" is benefit in the form of money, property, commercial interests or anything else the primary significance of which is economic gain;

(7) "public servant" means any officer or employee of government, including legislators and judges, and any person participating as juror, advisor, consultant or otherwise, in performing a governmental function; but the term does not include witnesses;

(8) "administrative proceeding" means any proceeding, other than a judicial proceeding, the outcome of which is required to be based on a record or documentation prescribed by law, or in which law or regulation is particularized in application to individuals.

Section 240.1. Bribery in Official and Political Matters.

A person is guilty of bribery, a felony of the third degree, if he offers, confers or agrees to confer upon another, or solicits, accepts or agrees to accept from another:

(1) any pecuniary benefit as consideration for the recipient's decision, opinion, recommendation, vote or other exercise of discretion as a public servant, party official or voter; or

(2) any benefit as consideration for the recipient's decision, vote, recommendation or other exercise of official discretion in a judicial or administrative proceeding; or

(3) any benefit as consideration for a violation of a known legal duty as public servant or party official.

It is no defense to prosecution under this section that a person whom the actor sought to influence was not qualified to act in the desired way whether because he had not yet assumed office, or lacked jurisdiction, or for any other reason.

Section 240.2. Threats and Other Improper Influence in Official and Political Matters.

(1) *Offenses Defined.* A person commits an offense if he:

(a) threatens unlawful harm to any person with purpose to influence his decision, opinion, recommendation, vote or other exercise of discretion as a public servant, party official or voter; or

(b) threatens harm to any public servant with purpose to influence his decision, opinion, recommendation, vote or other exercise of discretion in a judicial or administrative proceeding; or

(c) threatens harm to any public servant or party official with purpose to influence him to violate his known legal duty; or

PART II. DEFINITION OF SPECIFIC CRIMES

(d) privately addresses to any public servant who has or will have an official discretion in a judicial or administrative proceeding any representation, entreaty, argument or other communication with purpose to influence the outcome on the basis of considerations other than those authorized by law.

It is no defense to prosecution under this Section that a person whom the actor sought to influence was not qualified to act in the desired way, whether because he had not yet assumed office, or lacked jurisdiction, or for any other reason.

(2) *Grading.* An offense under this Section is a misdemeanor unless the actor threatened to commit a crime or made a threat with purpose to influence a judicial or administrative proceeding, in which cases the offense is a felony of the third degree.

Section 240.3. Compensation for Past Official Action.

A person commits a misdemeanor if he solicits, accepts or agrees to accept any pecuniary benefit as compensation for having, as public servant, given a decision, opinion, recommendation or vote favorable to another, or for having otherwise exercised a discretion in his favor, or for having violated his duty. A person commits a misdemeanor if he offers, confers or agrees to confer compensation acceptance of which is prohibited by this Section.

Section 240.4. Retaliation for Past Official Action.

A person commits a misdemeanor if he harms another by any unlawful act in retaliation for anything lawfully done by the latter in the capacity of public servant.

Section 240.5. Gifts to Public Servants by Persons Subject to Their Jurisdiction.

(1) *Regulatory and Law Enforcement Officials.* No public servant in any department or agency exercising regulatory functions, or conducting inspections or investiga-

tions, or carrying on civil or criminal litigation on behalf of the government, or having custody of prisoners, shall solicit, accept or agree to accept any pecuniary benefit from a person known to be subject to such regulation, inspection, investigation or custody, or against whom such litigation is known to be pending or contemplated.

(2) *Officials Concerned with Government Contracts and Pecuniary Transactions.* No public servant having any discretionary function to perform in connection with contracts, purchases, payments, claims or other pecuniary transactions of the government shall solicit, accept or agree to accept any pecuniary benefit from any person known to be interested in or likely to become interested in any such contract, purchase, payment, claim or transaction.

(3) *Judicial and Administrative Officials.* No public servant having judicial or administrative authority and no public servant employed by or in a court or other tribunal having such authority, or participating in the enforcement of its decisions, shall solicit, accept or agree to accept any pecuniary benefit from a person known to be interested in or likely to become interested in any matter before such public servant or a tribunal with which he is associated.

(4) *Legislative Officials.* No legislator or public servant employed by the legislature or by any committee or agency thereof shall solicit, accept or agree to accept any pecuniary benefit from any person known to be interested in a bill, transaction or proceeding, pending or contemplated, before the legislature or any committee or agency thereof.

(5) *Exceptions.* This Section shall not apply to:

(a) fees prescribed by law to be received by a public servant, or any other benefit for which the recipient gives legitimate consideration or to which he is otherwise legally entitled; or

PART II. DEFINITION OF SPECIFIC CRIMES

(b) gifts or other benefits conferred on account of kinship or other personal, professional or business relationship independent of the official status of the receiver; or

(c) trivial benefits incidental to personal, professional or business contacts and involving no substantial risk of undermining official impartiality.

(6) *Offering Benefits Prohibited.* No person shall knowingly confer, or offer or agree to confer, any benefit prohibited by the foregoing Subsections.

(7) *Grade of Offense.* An offense under this Section is a misdemeanor.

Section 240.6. Compensating Public Servant for Assisting Private Interests in Relation to Matters Before Him.

(1) *Receiving Compensation.* A public servant commits a misdemeanor if he solicits, accepts or agrees to accept compensation for advice or other assistance in preparing or promoting a bill, contract, claim, or other transaction or proposal as to which he knows that he has or is likely to have an official discretion to exercise.

(2) *Paying Compensation.* A person commits a misdemeanor if he pays or offers or agrees to pay compensation to a public servant with knowledge that acceptance by the public servant is unlawful.

Section 240.7. Selling Political Endorsement; Special Influence.

(1) *Selling Political Endorsement.* A person commits a misdemeanor if he solicits, receives, agrees to receive, or agrees that any political party or other person shall receive, any pecuniary benefit as consideration for approval or disapproval of an appointment or advancement in public service, or for approval or disapproval of any person or transaction for any benefit conferred by an official or agency of government. "Approval" includes

recommendation, failure to disapprove, or any other manifestation of favor or acquiescence. "Disapproval" includes failure to approve, or any other manifestation of disfavor or nonacquiescence.

(2) *Other Trading in Special Influence.* A person commits a misdemeanor if he solicits, receives or agrees to receive any pecuniary benefit as consideration for exerting special influence upon a public servant or procuring another to do so. "Special influence" means power to influence through kinship, friendship or other relationship, apart from the merits of the transaction.

(3) *Paying for Endorsement or Special Influence.* A person commits a misdemeanor if he offers, confers or agrees to confer any pecuniary benefit receipt of which is prohibited by this Section.

ARTICLE 241. PERJURY AND OTHER FALSIFICATION IN OFFICIAL MATTERS

Section 241.0. Definitions.

In this Article, unless a different meaning plainly is required:

(1) the definitions given in Section 240.0 apply; and

(2) "statement" means any representation, but includes a representation of opinion, belief or other state of mind only if the representation clearly relates to state of mind apart from or in addition to any facts which are the subject of the representation.

Section 241.1. Perjury.

(1) *Offense Defined.* A person is guilty of perjury, a felony of the third degree, if in any official proceeding he makes a false statement under oath or equivalent affirmation, or swears or affirms the truth of a statement previously made, when the statement is material and he does not believe it to be true.

(2) *Materiality.* Falsification is material, regardless of the admissibility of the statement under rules of evidence, if it could have affected the course or outcome of the proceeding. It is no defense that the declarant mistakenly believed the falsification to be immaterial. Whether a falsification is material in a given factual situation is a question of law.

(3) *Irregularities No Defense.* It is not a defense to prosecution under this Section that the oath or affirmation was administered or taken in an irregular manner or that the declarant was not competent to make the statement. A document purporting to be made upon oath or affirmation at any time when the actor presents it as being so verified shall be deemed to have been duly sworn or affirmed.

(4) *Retraction.* No person shall be guilty of an offense under this Section if he retracted the falsification in the course of the proceeding in which it was made before it became manifest that the falsification was or would be exposed and before the falsification substantially affected the proceeding.

(5) *Inconsistent Statements.* Where the defendant made inconsistent statements under oath or equivalent affirmation, both having been made within the period of the statute of limitations, the prosecution may proceed by setting forth the inconsistent statements in a single count alleging in the alternative that one or the other was false and not believed by the defendant. In such case it shall not be necessary for the prosecution to prove which statement was false but only that one or the other was false and not believed by the defendant to be true.

(6) *Corroboration.* No person shall be convicted of an offense under this Section where proof of falsity rests solely upon contradiction by testimony of a single person other than the defendant.

Section 241.2. False Swearing.

(1) *False Swearing in Official Matters.* A person who makes a false statement under oath or equivalent affirmation, or swears or affirms the truth of such a statement previously made, when he does not believe the statement to be true, is guilty of a misdemeanor if:

(a) the falsification occurs in an official proceeding; or

(b) the falsification is intended to mislead a public servant in performing his official function.

(2) *Other False Swearing.* A person who makes a false statement under oath or equivalent affirmation, or swears or affirms the truth of such a statement previously made, when he does not believe the statement to be true, is guilty of a petty misdemeanor, if the statement is one which is required by law to be sworn or affirmed before a notary or other person authorized to administer oaths.

(3) *Perjury Provisions Applicable.* Subsections (3) to (6) of Section 241.1 apply to the present Section.

Section 241.3. Unsworn Falsification to Authorities.

(1) *In General.* A person commits a misdemeanor if, with purpose to mislead a public servant in performing his official function, he:

(a) makes any written false statement which he does not believe to be true; or

(b) purposely creates a false impression in a written application for any pecuniary or other benefit, by omitting information necessary to prevent statements therein from being misleading; or

(c) submits or invites reliance on any writing which he knows to be forged, altered or otherwise lacking in authenticity; or

(d) submits or invites reliance on any sample, specimen, map, boundary-mark, or other object which he knows to be false.

(2) *Statements "Under Penalty."* A person commits a petty misdemeanor if he makes a written false statement which he does not believe to be true, on or pursuant to a form bearing notice, authorized by law, to the effect that false statements made therein are punishable.

(3) *Perjury Provisions Applicable.* Subsections (3) to (6) of Section 241.1 apply to the present section.

Section 241.4. False Alarms to Agencies of Public Safety.

A person who knowingly causes a false alarm of fire or other emergency to be transmitted to or within any organization, official or volunteer, for dealing with emergencies involving danger to life or property commits a misdemeanor.

Section 241.5. False Reports to Law Enforcement Authorities.

(1) *Falsely Incriminating Another.* A person who knowingly gives false information to any law enforcement officer with purpose to implicate another commits a misdemeanor.

(2) *Fictitious Reports.* A person commits a petty misdemeanor if he:

(a) reports to law enforcement authorities an offense or other incident within their concern knowing that it did not occur; or

(b) pretends to furnish such authorities with information relating to an offense or incident when he knows he has no information relating to such offense or incident.

Section 241.6. Tampering With Witnesses and Informants; Retaliation Against Them.

(1) *Tampering.* A person commits an offense if, believing that an official proceeding or investigation is pending

or about to be instituted, he attempts to induce or otherwise cause a witness or informant to:

(a) testify or inform falsely; or

(b) withhold any testimony, information, document or thing; or

(c) elude legal process summoning him to testify or supply evidence; or

(d) absent himself from any proceeding or investigation to which he has been legally summoned.

The offense is a felony of the third degree if the actor employs force, deception, threat or offer of pecuniary benefit. Otherwise it is a misdemeanor.

(2) *Retaliation Against Witness or Informant.* A person commits a misdemeanor if he harms another by any unlawful act in retaliation for anything lawfully done in the capacity of witness or informant.

(3) *Witness or Informant Taking Bribe.* A person commits a felony of the third degree if he solicits, accepts or agrees to accept any benefit in consideration of his doing any of the things specified in clauses (a) to (d) of Subsection (1).

Section 241.7. Tampering with or Fabricating Physical Evidence.

A person commits a misdemeanor if, believing that an official proceeding or investigation is pending or about to be instituted, he:

(1) alters, destroys, conceals or removes any record, document or thing with purpose to impair its verity or availability in such proceeding or investigation; or

(2) makes, presents or uses any record, document or thing knowing it to be false and with purpose to mislead a public servant who is or may be engaged in such proceeding or investigation.

Section 241.8. Tampering With Public Records or Information.

(1) *Offense Defined.* A person commits an offense if he:

(a) knowingly makes a false entry in, or false alteration of, any record, document or thing belonging to, or received or kept by, the government for information or record, or required by law to be kept by others for information of the government; or

(b) makes, presents or uses any record, document or thing knowing it to be false, and with purpose that it be taken as a genuine part of information or records referred to in paragraph (a); or

(c) purposely and unlawfully destroys, conceals, removes or otherwise impairs the verity or availability of any such record, document or thing.

(2) *Grading.* An offense under this Section is a misdemeanor unless the actor's purpose is to defraud or injure anyone, in which case the offense is a felony of the third degree.

Section 241.9. Impersonating a Public Servant.

A person commits a misdemeanor if he falsely pretends to hold a position in the public service with purpose to induce another to submit to such pretended official authority or otherwise to act in reliance upon that pretense to his prejudice.

ARTICLE 242. OBSTRUCTING GOVERNMENTAL OPERATIONS; ESCAPES

Section 242.0. Definitions.

In this Article, unless another meaning plainly is required, the definitions given in Section 240.0 apply.

Section 242.1. Obstructing Administration of Law or Other Governmental Function.

A person commits a misdemeanor if he purposely obstructs, impairs or perverts the administration of law or other governmental function by force, violence, physical interference or obstacle, breach of official duty, or any other unlawful act, except that this Section does not apply to flight by a person charged with crime, refusal to submit to arrest, failure to perform a legal duty other than an official duty, or any other means of avoiding compliance with law without affirmative interference with governmental functions.

Section 242.2. Resisting Arrest or Other Law Enforcement.

A person commits a misdemeanor if, for the purpose of preventing a public servant from effecting a lawful arrest or discharging any other duty, the person creates a substantial risk of bodily injury to the public servant or anyone else, or employs means justifying or requiring substantial force to overcome the resistance.

Section 242.3. Hindering Apprehension or Prosecution.

A person commits an offense if, with purpose to hinder the apprehension, prosecution, conviction or punishment of another for crime, he:

(1) harbors or conceals the other; or

(2) provides or aids in providing a weapon, transportation, disguise or other means of avoiding apprehension or effecting escape; or

(3) conceals or destroys evidence of the crime, or tampers with a witness, informant, document or other source of information, regardless of its admissibility in evidence; or

(4) warns the other of impending discovery or apprehension, except that this paragraph does not apply to a warning given in connection with an effort to bring another into compliance with law; or

(5) volunteers false information to a law enforcement officer.

The offense is a felony of the third degree if the conduct which the actor knows has been charged or is liable to be charged against the person aided would constitute a felony of the first or second degree. Otherwise it is a misdemeanor.

Section 242.4. Aiding Consummation of Crime.

A person commits an offense if he purposely aids another to accomplish an unlawful object of a crime, as by safeguarding the proceeds thereof or converting the proceeds into negotiable funds. The offense is a felony of the third degree if the principal offense was a felony of the first or second degree. Otherwise it is a misdemeanor.

Section 242.5. Compounding.

A person commits a misdemeanor if he accepts or agrees to accept any pecuniary benefit in consideration of refraining from reporting to law enforcement authorities the commission or suspected commission of any offense or information relating to an offense. It is an affirmative defense to prosecution under this Section that the pecuniary benefit did not exceed an amount which the actor believed to be due as restitution or indemnification for harm caused by the offense.

Section 242.6. Escape.

(1) *Escape.* A person commits an offense if he unlawfully removes himself from official detention or fails to return to official detention following temporary leave granted for a specific purpose or limited period. "Official detention" means arrest, detention in any facility for custody of persons under charge or conviction of crime or alleged or found to be delinquent, detention for extradition or deportation, or any other detention for law enforcement purposes; but "official detention" does not include supervision of probation or parole, or constraint incidental to release on bail.

(2) *Permitting or Facilitating Escape.* A public servant concerned in detention commits an offense if he knowingly or recklessly permits an escape. Any person who knowingly causes or facilitates an escape commits an offense.

(3) *Effect of Legal Irregularity in Detention.* Irregularity in bringing about or maintaining detention, or lack of jurisdiction of the committing or detaining authority, shall not be a defense to prosecution under this Section if the escape is from a prison or other custodial facility or from detention pursuant to commitment by official proceedings. In the case of other detentions, irregularity or lack of jurisdiction shall be a defense only if:

(a) the escape involved no substantial risk of harm to the person or property of anyone other than the detainee; or

(b) the detaining authority did not act in good faith under color of law.

(4) *Grading of Offenses.* An offense under this Section is a felony of the third degree where:

(a) the actor was under arrest for or detained on a charge of felony or following conviction of crime; or

(b) the actor employs force, threat, deadly weapon or other dangerous instrumentality to effect the escape; or

(c) a public servant concerned in detention of persons convicted of crime purposely facilitates or permits an escape from a detention facility.

Otherwise an offense under this section is a misdemeanor.

Section 242.7. Implements for Escape; Other Contraband.

(1) *Escape Implements.* A person commits a misdemeanor if he unlawfully introduces within a detention facility, or unlawfully provides an inmate with, any weapon, tool or other thing which may be useful for escape. An

inmate commits a misdemeanor if he unlawfully procures, makes, or otherwise provides himself with, or has in his possession, any such implement of escape. "Unlawfully" means surreptitiously or contrary to law, regulation or order of the detaining authority.

(2) *Other Contraband.* A person commits a petty misdemeanor if he provides an inmate with anything which the actor knows it is unlawful for the inmate to possess.

Section 242.8. Bail Jumping; Default in Required Appearance.

A person set at liberty by court order, with or without bail, upon condition that he will subsequently appear at a specified time and place, commits a misdemeanor if, without lawful excuse, he fails to appear at that time and place. The offense constitutes a felony of the third degree where the required appearance was to answer to a charge of felony, or for disposition of any such charge, and the actor took flight or went into hiding to avoid apprehension, trial or punishment. This Section does not apply to obligations to appear incident to release under suspended sentence or on probation or parole.

ARTICLE 243. ABUSE OF OFFICE

Section 243.0. Definitions.

In this Article, unless a different meaning plainly is required, the definitions given in Section 240.0 apply.

Section 243.1. Official Oppression.

A person acting or purporting to act in an official capacity or taking advantage of such actual or purported capacity commits a misdemeanor if, knowing that his conduct is illegal, he:

(a) subjects another to arrest, detention, search, seizure, mistreatment, dispossession, assessment, lien or other infringement of personal or property rights; or

(b) denies or impedes another in the exercise or enjoyment of any right, privilege, power or immunity.

Section 243.2. Speculating or Wagering on Official Action or Information.

A public servant commits a misdemeanor if, in contemplation of official action by himself or by a governmental unit with which he is associated, or in reliance on information to which he has access in his official capacity and which has not been made public, he:

(1) acquires a pecuniary interest in any property, transaction or enterprise which may be affected by such information or official action; or

(2) speculates or wagers on the basis of such information or official action; or

(3) aids another to do any of the foregoing.

OFFENSES AGAINST PUBLIC ORDER AND DECENCY

ARTICLE 250. RIOT, DISORDERLY CONDUCT, AND RELATED OFFENSES

Section 250.1. Riot; Failure to Disperse.

(1) *Riot.* A person is guilty of riot, a felony of the third degree, if he participates with [two] or more others in a course of disorderly conduct:

(a) with purpose to commit or facilitate the commission of a felony or misdemeanor;

(b) with purpose to prevent or coerce official action; or

(c) when the actor or any other participant to the knowledge of the actor uses or plans to use a firearm or other deadly weapon.

(2) *Failure of Disorderly Persons to Disperse Upon Official Order.* Where [three] or more persons are participating in a course of disorderly conduct likely to cause

substantial harm or serious inconvenience, annoyance or alarm, a peace officer or other public servant engaged in executing or enforcing the law may order the participants and others in the immediate vicinity to disperse. A person who refuses or knowingly fails to obey such an order commits a misdemeanor.

Section 250.2. Disorderly Conduct.

(1) *Offense Defined.* A person is guilty of disorderly conduct if, with purpose to cause public inconvenience, annoyance or alarm, or recklessly creating a risk thereof, he:

(a) engages in fighting or threatening, or in violent or tumultuous behavior; or

(b) makes unreasonable noise or offensively coarse utterance, gesture or display, or addresses abusive language to any person present; or

(c) creates a hazardous or physically offensive condition by any act which serves no legitimate purpose of the actor.

"Public" means affecting or likely to affect persons in a place to which the public or a substantial group has access; among the places included are highways, transport facilities, schools, prisons, apartment houses, places of business or amusement, or any neighborhood.

(2) *Grading.* An offense under this section is a petty misdemeanor if the actor's purpose is to cause substantial harm or serious inconvenience, or if he persists in disorderly conduct after reasonable warning or request to desist. Otherwise disorderly conduct is a violation.

Section 250.3. False Public Alarms.

A person is guilty of a misdemeanor if he initiates or circulates a report or warning of an impending bombing or other crime or catastrophe, knowing that the report or warning is false or baseless and that it is likely to cause evacuation of a building, place of assembly, or facility of public transport, or to cause public inconvenience or alarm.

Section 250.4. Harassment.

A person commits a petty misdemeanor if, with purpose to harass another, he:

(1) makes a telephone call without purpose of legitimate communication; or

(2) insults, taunts or challenges another in a manner likely to provoke violent or disorderly response; or

(3) makes repeated communications anonymously or at extremely inconvenient hours, or in offensively coarse language; or

(4) subjects another to an offensive touching; or

(5) engages in any other course of alarming conduct serving no legitimate purpose of the actor.

Section 250.5. Public Drunkenness; Drug Incapacitation.

A person is guilty of an offense if he appears in any public place manifestly under the influence of alcohol, narcotics or other drug, not therapeutically administered, to the degree that he may endanger himself or other persons or property, or annoy persons in his vicinity. An offense under this Section constitutes a petty misdemeanor if the actor has been convicted hereunder twice before within a period of one year. Otherwise the offense constitutes a violation.

Section 250.6. Loitering or Prowling.

A person commits a violation if he loiters or prowls in a place, at a time, or in a manner not usual for law-abiding individuals under circumstances that warrant alarm for the safety of persons or property in the vicinity. Among the circumstances which may be considered in determining whether such alarm is warranted is the fact that the actor takes flight upon appearance of a peace officer, refuses to identify himself, or manifestly endeavors to conceal himself or any object. Unless flight by the actor or other circumstance makes it impracticable, a peace officer shall prior to any arrest for an offense under this section afford the actor an opportunity to dispel any alarm which would otherwise be warranted, by requesting him to identify himself and explain his presence and conduct. No person shall be convicted of an offense under this Section if the peace officer did not comply with the preceding sentence, or if it appears at trial that the explanation given by the actor was true and, if believed by the peace officer at the time, would have dispelled the alarm.

Section 250.7. Obstructing Highways and Other Public Passages.

(1) A person, who, having no legal privilege to do so, purposely or recklessly obstructs any highway or other public passage, whether alone or with others, commits a violation, or, in case he persists after warning by a law officer, a petty misdemeanor. "Obstructs" means renders impassable without unreasonable inconvenience or hazard. No person shall be deemed guilty of recklessly obstructing in violation of this Subsection solely because of a gathering of persons to hear him speak or otherwise communicate, or solely because of being a member of such a gathering.

(2) A person in a gathering commits a violation if he refuses to obey a reasonable official request or order to move:

(a) to prevent obstruction of a highway or other public passage; or

(b) to maintain public safety by dispersing those gathered in dangerous proximity to a fire or other hazard.

An order to move, addressed to a person whose speech or other lawful behavior attracts an obstructing audience, shall not be deemed reasonable if the obstruction can be readily remedied by police control of the size or location of the gathering.

Section 250.8. Disrupting Meetings and Processions.

A person commits a misdemeanor if, with purpose to prevent or disrupt a lawful meeting, procession or gathering, he does any act tending to obstruct or interfere with it physically, or makes any utterance, gesture or display designed to outrage the sensibilities of the group.

Section 250.9. Desecration of Venerated Objects.

A person commits a misdemeanor if he purposely desecrates any public monument or structure, or place of worship or burial, or if he purposely desecrates the national flag or any other object of veneration by the public or a substantial segment thereof in any public place. "Desecrate" means defacing, damaging, polluting or otherwise physically mistreating in a way that the actor knows will outrage the sensibilities of persons likely to observe or discover his action.

Section 250.10. Abuse of Corpse.

Except as authorized by law, a person who treats a corpse in a way that he knows would outrage ordinary family sensibilities commits a misdemeanor.

Section 250.11. Cruelty to Animals.

A person commits a misdemeanor if he purposely or recklessly:

(1) subjects any animal to cruel mistreatment; or

(2) subjects any animal in his custody to cruel neglect; or

(3) kills or injures any animal belonging to another without legal privilege or consent of the owner.

Subsections (1) and (2) shall not be deemed applicable to accepted veterinary practices and activities carried on for scientific research.

Section 250.12. Violation of Privacy.

(1) *Unlawful Eavesdropping or Surveillance.* A person commits a misdemeanor if, except as authorized by law, he:

(a) trespasses on property with purpose to subject anyone to eavesdropping or other surveillance in a private place; or

(b) installs in any private place, without the consent of the person or persons entitled to privacy there, any device for observing, photographing, recording, amplifying or broadcasting sounds or events in such place, or uses any such unauthorized installation; or

(c) installs or uses outside a private place any device for hearing, recording, amplifying or broadcasting sounds originating in such place which would not ordinarily be audible or comprehensible outside, without the consent of the person or persons entitled to privacy there.

"Private place" means a place where one may reasonably expect to be safe from casual or hostile intrusion or surveillance, but does not include a place to which the public or a substantial group thereof has access.

(2) *Other Breach of Privacy of Messages.* A person commits a misdemeanor if, except as authorized by law, he:

(a) intercepts without the consent of the sender or receiver a message by telephone, telegraph, letter or other means of communicating privately; but this paragraph does not extend to (i) overhearing of messages through a regularly installed instrument on a telephone party line or on an extension, or (ii) interception by the telephone company or subscriber incident to enforcement of regulations limiting use of the facilities or incident to other normal operation and use; or

(b) divulges without the consent of the sender or receiver the existence or contents of any such message if the actor knows that the message was illegally intercepted, or if he learned of the message in the course of employment with an agency engaged in transmitting it.

ARTICLE 251. PUBLIC INDECENCY

Section 251.1. Open Lewdness.

A person commits a petty misdemeanor if he does any lewd act which he knows is likely to be observed by others who would be affronted or alarmed.

Section 251.2. Prostitution and Related Offenses.

(1) *Prostitution.* A person is guilty of prostitution, a petty misdemeanor, if he or she:

(a) is an inmate of a house of prostitution or otherwise engages in sexual activity as a business; or

(b) loiters in or within view of any public place for the purpose of being hired to engage in sexual activity.

"Sexual activity" includes homosexual and other deviate sexual relations. A "house of prostitution" is any place where prostitution or promotion of prostitution is regularly carried on by one person under the control, management or supervision of another. An "inmate" is a person who engages in prostitution in or through the agency of a house of prostitution. "Public place" means any place to which the public or any substantial group thereof has access.

(2) *Promoting Prostitution.* A person who knowingly promotes prostitution of another commits a misdemeanor or felony as provided in Subsection (3). The following acts shall, without limitation of the foregoing, constitute promoting prostitution:

(a) owning, controlling, managing, supervising or otherwise keeping, alone or in association with others, a house of prostitution or a prostitution business; or

(b) procuring an inmate for a house of prostitution or a place in a house of prostitution for one who would be an inmate; or

(c) encouraging, inducing, or otherwise purposely causing another to become or remain a prostitute; or

(d) soliciting a person to patronize a prostitute; or

(e) procuring a prostitute for a patron; or

(f) transporting a person into or within this state with purpose to promote that person's engaging in prostitution, or procuring or paying for transportation with that purpose; or

(g) leasing or otherwise permitting a place controlled by the actor, alone or in association with others, to be regularly used for prostitution or the promotion of prostitution, or failure to make reasonable effort to abate such use by ejecting the tenant, notifying law enforcement authorities, or other legally available means; or

(h) soliciting, receiving, or agreeing to receive any benefit for doing or agreeing to do anything forbidden by this Subsection.

(3) *Grading of Offenses Under Subsection (2).* An offense under Subsection (2) constitutes a felony of the third degree if:

(a) the offense falls within paragraph (a), (b) or (c) of Subsection (2); or

(b) the actor compels another to engage in or promote prostitution; or

(c) the actor promotes prostitution of a child under 16, whether or not he is aware of the child's age; or

(d) the actor promotes prostitution of his wife, child, ward or any person for whose care, protection or support he is responsible.

Otherwise the offense is a misdemeanor.

(4) *Presumption from Living off Prostitutes.* A person, other than the prostitute or the prostitute's minor child or other legal dependent incapable of self-support, who is supported in whole or substantial part by the proceeds of prostitution is presumed to be knowingly promoting prostitution in violation of Subsection (2).

(5) *Patronizing Prostitutes.* A person commits a violation if he hires a prostitute to engage in sexual activity with him, or if he enters or remains in a house of prostitution for the purpose of engaging in sexual activity.

(6) *Evidence.* On the issue whether a place is a house of prostitution the following shall be admissible evidence: its general repute; the repute of the persons who reside in or frequent the place; the frequency, timing and duration of visits by non-residents. Testimony of a person against his spouse shall be admissible to prove offenses under this Section.

Section 251.3. Loitering to Solicit Deviate Sexual Relations.

A person is guilty of a petty misdemeanor if he loiters in or near any public place for the purpose of soliciting or being solicited to engage in deviate sexual relations.

Section 251.4. Obscenity.

(1) *Obscene Defined.* Material is obscene if, considered as a whole, its predominant appeal is to prurient interest, that is, a shameful or morbid interest, in nudity, sex or excretion, and if in addition it goes substantially beyond customary limits of candor in describing or representing such matters. Predominant appeal shall be judged with reference to ordinary adults unless it appears from the character of the material or the circumstances of its dissemination to be designed for children or other specially susceptible audience. Undeveloped photographs, molds, printing plates, and the like, shall be deemed obscene notwithstanding that processing or other acts may be

required to make the obscenity patent or to disseminate it.

(2) *Offenses*. Subject to the affirmative defense provided in Subsection (3), a person commits a misdemeanor if he knowingly or recklessly:

(a) sells, delivers or provides, or offers or agrees to sell, deliver or provide, any obscene writing, picture, record or other representation or embodiment of the obscene; or

(b) presents or directs an obscene play, dance or performance, or participates in that portion thereof which makes it obscene; or

(c) publishes, exhibits or otherwise makes available any obscene material; or

(d) possesses any obscene material for purposes of sale or other commercial dissemination; or

(e) sells, advertises or otherwise commercially disseminates material, whether or not obscene, by representing or suggesting that it is obscene.

A person who disseminates or possesses obscene material in the course of his business is presumed to do so knowingly or recklessly.

(3) *Justifiable and Non–Commercial Private Dissemination*. It is an affirmative defense to prosecution under this Section that dissemination was restricted to:

(a) institutions or persons having scientific, educational, governmental or other similar justification for possessing obscene material; or

(b) non-commercial dissemination to personal associates of the actor.

(4) *Evidence; Adjudication of Obscenity*. In any prosecution under this Section evidence shall be admissible to show:

(a) the character of the audience for which the material was designed or to which it was directed;

(b) what the predominant appeal of the material would be for ordinary adults or any special audience to which it was directed, and what effect, if any, it would probably have on conduct of such people;

(c) artistic, literary, scientific, educational or other merits of the material;

(d) the degree of public acceptance of the material in the United States;

(e) appeal to prurient interest, or absence thereof, in advertising or other promotion of the material; and

(f) the good repute of the author, creator, publisher or other person from whom the material originated.

Expert testimony and testimony of the author, creator, publisher or other person from whom the material originated, relating to factors entering into the determination of the issue of obscenity, shall be admissible. The Court shall dismiss a prosecution for obscenity if it is satisfied that the material is not obscene.

ADDITIONAL ARTICLES[2]

[At this point, a State enacting a new Penal Code may insert additional Articles dealing with special topics such as narcotics, alcoholic beverages, gambling and offenses against tax and trade laws. The Model Penal Code project did not extend to these, partly because a higher priority on limited time and resources was accorded to branches of the penal law which have not received close legislative scrutiny. Also, in legislation dealing with narcotics, liquor, tax evasion, and the like, penal provisions have been so intermingled with regulatory and procedural provisions that the task of segregating one group from the other presents special difficulty for model legislation.]

2. Model Penal Code 241 (Proposed Official Draft 1962).

PART III. TREATMENT AND CORRECTION—TABLE OF CONTENTS AND SELECTED PROVISIONS

ARTICLE 301. SUSPENSION OF SENTENCE; PROBATION

Section 301.1. Conditions of Suspension or Probation.

Section 301.2. Period of Suspension or Probation; Modification of Conditions; Discharge of Defendant.

Section 301.3. Summons or Arrest of Defendant Under Suspended Sentence or on Probation; Commitment Without Bail; Revocation and Re-sentence.

Section 301.4. Notice and Hearing on Revocation or Modification of Conditions of Suspension or Probation.

Section 301.5. Order Removing Disqualification or Disability Based on Conviction.

Section 301.6. Suspension or Probation is Final Judgment for Other Purposes.

ARTICLE 302. FINES

Section 302.1. Time and Method of Payment; Disposition of Funds.

Section 302.2. Consequences of Non–Payment; Imprisonment for Contumacious Non-Payment; Summary Collection.

Section 302.3. Revocation of Fine.

ARTICLE 303. SHORT–TERM IMPRISONMENT

Section 303.1. State and Local Institutions for Short–Term Imprisonment; Review of Adequacy; Joint Use of Institutions; Approval of Plan of New Institutions.

(1) Within the appropriation allotted therefor, the several counties, cities and [other appropriate political subdivisions of the State] and the Department of Correction may construct, equip and maintain suitable buildings, structures and facilities for the operation and for the necessary expansion and diversification of local short-term institutions, including lockups, jails, houses of correction, work farms and such other institutions as may be required for the following purposes:

(a) the custody, control, correctional treatment and rehabilitation of persons sentenced or committed to imprisonment for a fixed term of one year or less;

(b) the custody, control and temporary detention of persons committed to the Department of Correction, until they are removed to the reception center or to another institution in the Department;

(c) the detention of persons charged with crime and committed for hearing or for trial;

(d) the detention of persons committed to secure their attendance as witnesses, and for other detentions authorized by law.

(2) The Director of Correction shall annually review, on the basis of visitation, inspection and reports pursuant to Section 401.11, the adequacy of the institutions for short-term imprisonment in the several counties, cities and [other appropriate political subdivisions of the State] in the light of the number of persons committed thereto, the physical facilities thereof and programs conducted therein. No later than his next annual report, the Director shall report on any inadequacies of such facilities, including his recommendations for the alteration or ex-

pansion of existing institutions, for the construction of new institutions, for the combination of two or more local institutions of the same or of different political subdivisions of the State, or for such other measures to meet the situation as may be appropriate. In making his recommendations, the Director may indicate whether, in his opinion, the alteration, expansion or new construction can best be undertaken by the political subdivisions concerned, or by the Department of Correction.

(3) In reviewing the adequacy of the institutions for short-term imprisonment, the Director of Correction shall consider whether the facilities available in the several political subdivisions of the State afford adequate opportunity for the segregation and classification of prisoners, for the isolation and treatment of ill prisoners, for the treatment of alcoholic and drug-addicted prisoners, for diversified security and custody, and for opportunities for vocational and rehabilitative training.

(4) Upon the recommendation or with the approval of the Director of Correction, counties, cities, and [other appropriate political subdivisions of the State] having institutions for short-term imprisonment may establish joint institutions, or combine two or more existing facilities for short-term imprisonment, and may make such agreements for the sharing of the costs of construction and maintenance as may be authorized by law.

(5) No county, city, or [other appropriate political subdivision of the State] shall construct or establish an institution for short-term imprisonment, unless the plans for the establishment and construction of such institution are approved by the Director of Correction.

Section 303.2. Records of Prisoners; Classification; Transfer.

(1) The Warden, or other administrative head of an institution for short-term imprisonment, shall establish and maintain, in accordance with the regulations of the

Department of Correction, a central file in the institution containing an individual file for each prisoner. Each prisoner's file shall as far as practicable include: (a) his admission summary; (b) his pre-sentence investigation report, if any; (c) the official records of his conviction and commitment, as well as earlier criminal records, if any; (d) progress reports from treatment and custodial staff; (e) reports of his disciplinary infractions and of their disposition; and (f) other pertinent data concerning his background, conduct, associations and family relationships. The content of the prisoners' files shall be confidential and shall not be subject to public inspection except by court order for good cause shown and shall not be accessible to prisoners in the institution.

(2) The [governing body of each] county, city [or other appropriate political subdivision of the State] having one or more institutions for short-term imprisonment shall appoint a Classification Committee consisting of [ ] members of the institutional staffs and of qualified citizens of the county, city or [other appropriate political subdivision]. If a physician has been appointed to serve the institutions, he shall be an ex officio member of the Committee. All Committee members shall serve without compensation but shall be paid their necessary expenses.

(3) As soon as practicable after a prisoner who has been sentenced to a definite term of thirty days or more is received in the institution, and no later than the expiration of the first third of his term, the Classification Committee shall study his file and interview him, and shall [determine] [aid the Warden or other administrative head of the institution in determining] the prisoner's program of treatment, training, employment, care and custody. The Classification Committee may also recommend the transfer of the prisoner to another institution which in its opinion is more suitable for him.

(4) The Warden or other administrative head of the institution may, on his own motion or upon the recom-

mendation of the Classification Committee, apply to the Court for an order to transfer the prisoner to another institution for short-term imprisonment, within or outside of the county, city [or other appropriate political subdivision of the State].

Section 303.3. Segregation of Prisoners; Segregation and Transfer of Prisoners With Physical or Mental Diseases or Defects.

(1) In institutions for short-term imprisonment the following groups shall be segregated from each other:

(a) female prisoners from male prisoners; and

(b) prisoners under the age of twenty-two from older prisoners; and

(c) persons detained for hearing or trial from prisoners under sentence of imprisonment or committed for contumacious default in the payment of fines; and

(d) persons detained for hearing or trial or under sentence from material witnesses and other persons detained under civil commitment.

(2) When an institutional physician finds that a prisoner suffers from a physical disease or defect, or when an institutional physician or psychologist finds that a prisoner suffers from a mental disease or defect, the Warden or other administrative head may order such prisoner to be segregated from other prisoners, and if the physician or psychologist, as the case may be, is of the opinion that he cannot be given proper treatment at that institution, the Warden or other administrative head may transfer him to another institution in the county, city or [other appropriate political subdivision of the State] where proper treatment is available, or to a hospital, if any, operated by the county, city or [other appropriate political subdivision of the State] if such hospital has adequate facilities, including detention facilities when necessary, to receive and treat the prisoner. If proper treatment or facilities are not available in an institution or a hospital operated by the

county, city, or [other appropriate political subdivision of the State] the Warden or other administrative head may transfer him to an institution or hospital operated by another county, city or [other appropriate political subdivision of the State], where such treatment and facilities are available, if such hospital or institution is ready to receive him, under such arrangements for reimbursement of costs as may be authorized by law. The Warden or other administrative head may request the Director of Correction to permit such prisoner to be transferred for examination, study and treatment to the medical-correctional facility, if any, or to another institution in the Department where proper treatment is available. The Director of Correction shall permit such transfer whenever such institutions in the Department have available room to receive the prisoner.

(3) When an institutional physician finds upon examination that a prisoner suffers from a physical disease or defect that cannot, in his opinion, be properly treated in any institution or hospital of the county, city or [other appropriate political subdivision of the State] or of another county, city or [other appropriate subdivision of the State], or in the Department of Correction, such prisoner, upon the direction of the Warden or other administrative head [and with the approval of the Director of Correction], may receive treatment in, or may be transferred to, for the purpose of receiving treatment in, any other available hospital. The Warden or other administrative head, in accordance with regulations of the Department of Correction, shall make appropriate arrangements with other public or private agencies for the transportation to, and for the care, custody and security of the prisoner in such hospital. While receiving treatment in such hospital, the prisoner shall remain subject to the jurisdiction and custody of the institution to which he was committed, and shall be returned thereto when, prior to the expiration of his sentence, such hospital treatment is no longer necessary.

(4) When two psychiatrists approved by the Department of Mental Hygiene [or other appropriate department] find upon examination that a prisoner suffers from a mental disease or defect that cannot, in their opinion, be properly treated in any institution in the Department of Correction, such prisoner, upon the direction of the Warden or other administrative head [and with the approval of the Director of Correction], may be transferred for treatment, with the approval of the Department of Mental Hygiene [or other appropriate department], to a psychiatric facility in such department. The Warden or other administrative head, in accordance with the regulations of the Department of Correction, shall make appropriate arrangements with the Department of Mental Hygiene [or other appropriate department] for the transportation to, and for the custody and security of the prisoner in such psychiatric facility. A prisoner receiving treatment in such a psychiatric facility shall remain subject to the jurisdiction and custody of the institution to which he was committed, and shall be returned thereto when, prior to the expiration of his sentence, treatment in such facility is no longer necessary. A prisoner receiving treatment in a psychiatric facility in the Department of Mental Hygiene [or other appropriate department] who continues in need of treatment at the time of his release or discharge shall be dealt with in accordance with Subsection (5) of this Section.

(5) When two psychiatrists approved by the Department of Mental Hygiene [or other appropriate department] find upon examination that a prisoner about to be discharged from an institution suffers from a mental disease or defect of such a nature that his release or discharge will endanger the public safety or the safety of the prisoner, the Warden or other administrative head, with the approval of the Director of Correction, shall transfer him to, or if he has already been transferred, permit him to remain in, the Department of Mental

Hygiene [or other appropriate department] to be dealt with in accordance with law applicable to the civil commitment and detention of persons suffering from such disease or defect.

Section 303.4. Medical Care; Food and Clothing.

(1) Upon admission to a facility for short-term imprisonment, each prisoner shall [whenever practicable] be given a physical examination, and if he is suspected of having a communicable disease, he shall be quarantined until he is known to be free from such disease. Each prisoner shall receive such medical and dental care as may be necessary during his period of commitment [, but at his request, he may be permitted to provide such care for himself at his own expense].

(2) Each prisoner shall be adequately fed and clothed in accordance with regulations of the Department of Correction. No prisoner shall be required to wear stripes or other degrading apparel.

Section 303.5. Program of Rehabilitation.

The Warden or other administrative head of an institution for short-term imprisonment shall establish, subject to regulation of the Department of Correction, an appropriate program for his institution, designed as far as practicable to prepare and assist each prisoner to assume his responsibilities and to conform to the requirements of law. In developing such a program, the Warden or other administrative head shall seek to make available to each prisoner capable of benefiting therefrom academic or vocational training, participation in productive work, religious and recreational activities and such therapeutic measures as are practicable. No prisoner shall be ordered or compelled, however, to participate in religious activities.

Section 303.6. Discipline and Control.

(1) The Warden or other administrative head of each correctional institution shall be responsible for the disci-

pline, control and safe custody of the prisoners therein. No prisoner shall be punished except upon the order of the Warden or other administrative head of the institution or of a deputy designated by him for the purpose; nor shall any punishment be imposed otherwise than in accordance with the provisions of this Section. The right to punish or to inflict punishment shall not be delegated to any prisoner or group of prisoners and no Warden or other administrative head shall permit any such prisoner or group of prisoners to assume authority over any other prisoner or group of prisoners.

(2) Except in flagrant or serious cases, punishment for a breach of discipline shall consist of deprivation of privileges. In case of assault, escape, or attempt to escape, or other serious or flagrant breach of discipline, the Warden or other administrative head may order that a prisoner's reduction of term for good behavior in accordance with Section 303.8 be forfeited. For serious or flagrant breach of discipline, the Warden or other administrative head may confine the prisoner, in accordance with the regulations of the Department of Correction, to a disciplinary cell for a period not to exceed [ten] days, and may order that the prisoner, during all or part of the period of such solitary confinement, be put on a monotonous but adequate and healthful diet. A prisoner in solitary confinement shall be visited by a physician at least once every twenty-four hours.

(3) No cruel, inhuman, or corporal punishment shall be used on any prisoner, nor is the use of force on any prisoner justifiable except as provided by Article 3 of the Code and the rules and regulations of the Department of Correction consistent therewith.

(4) The Warden or other administrative head of an institution shall maintain a record of breaches of rules, of the disposition of each case, and of the punishment, if any, for each such breach. Each breach of the rules by a

prisoner shall be entered in his file, together with the disposition or punishment therefor.

Section 303.7. Employment and Labor of Prisoners.

(1) To establish good habits of work and responsibility, for the vocational training of prisoners, and to reduce the cost of institutional operation, prisoners shall be employed so far as possible in constructive and diversified activities in the production of goods, services and foodstuffs to maintain the institution and its inmates, for the use of the county, city or [other appropriate political subdivision of the State], State [and for other purposes expressly authorized by law]. To accomplish these purposes, the Warden or other administrative head, with the approval of the Director of Correction, shall establish and maintain work programs, including, to the extent practicable, prison industries and prison farms in his institution, and may enter into arrangements with the departments of the State, or of the county, city or [other appropriate political subdivision of the State], for the employment of prisoners in the improvement of public works and ways, and in the improvement and conservation of the natural resources owned by the State.

(2) No prisoner shall be required to engage in excessive labor, and no prisoner shall be required to perform any work for which he is declared unfit by the institutional physician.

(3) The Director of Correction shall make rules and regulations governing the hours and conditions of labor of prisoners in correctional institutions of the counties, cities or [other appropriate political subdivision of the State] and the rates of prisoners' compensation for employment. In determining the rates of compensation, such regulations may take into consideration the quantity and quality of the work performed by a prisoner, whether or not such work was performed during regular working hours, the skill required for its performance, as well as the

economic value of similar work outside of correctional institutions. Prisoners' wage payments shall be set aside by the Warden or other administrative head in a separate fund. The regulations may provide for the making of deductions from prisoners' wages to defray part or all of the cost of prisoner maintenance, but a sufficient amount shall remain after such deduction to enable the prisoner to contribute to the support of his dependents, if any, to make necessary purchases from the commissary, and to set aside sums to be paid to him at the time of his release from the institution.

(4) The labor or time of a prisoner shall not be sold, contracted or hired out, but prisoners may work for other departments of the State or of the county, city or [other appropriate political subdivision of the State] in accordance with arrangements made pursuant to Subsection (1) of this Section.

(5) All departments and agencies of the county, city or [other appropriate political subdivision of the State] and institutions and agencies which are supported in whole or in part by such political subdivision, shall purchase [or draw] from the correctional institution all articles and products required by them which are produced or manufactured by prison labor in such correctional institutions, unless excepted from this requirement by the [appropriate authority] of the county, city or [other appropriate political subdivision of the State] in accordance with rules and regulations of such [appropriate authority] to carry out the purposes of this Subsection. Any surplus articles and products not so purchased shall be disposed of to the departments and agencies of the State and of other counties, cities or [other appropriate political subdivisions of the State]. The Governor [or other appropriate authority] may, by rule or regulation, provide for the manner in which standards and qualifications for such articles and products shall be set, for the manner in which the needs of departments, agencies and institutions of the State and

its political subdivisions shall be estimated in advance, for the manner in which the price for such articles and products shall be determined, and for the manner in which purchases shall be made and payment credited.

(6) Within the appropriation allotted therefor, the Warden or other administrative head shall make appropriate arrangements for the compensation of prisoners for damages from injuries arising out of their employment.

Section 303.8. Reduction of Term for Good Behavior.

For good behavior and faithful performance of duties, the term of imprisonment of a prisoner sentenced or committed for a definite term of more than thirty days shall be reduced by [five] days for each month of such term. Such reductions of terms may be forfeited, withheld or restored by the Warden or other administrative head of the institution, in accordance with the regulations of the Department of Correction.

Section 303.9. Privilege of Leaving Institution for Work and Other Purposes; Conditions; Application of Earnings.

(1) When a defendant is sentenced or committed for a fixed term of one year or less, the Court may in its order grant him the privilege of leaving the institution during necessary and reasonable hours for any of the following purposes:

(a) to work at his employment;

(b) to seek employment;

(c) to conduct his own business or to engage in other self-employment, including, in the case of a woman, housekeeping and attending to the needs of her family;

(d) to attend an educational institution;

(e) to obtain medical treatment;

(f) to devote time to any other purpose approved by the Court.

(2) Whenever a prisoner who has been granted the privilege of leaving the institution under this Section is not engaged in the activity for which such leave is granted, he shall be confined in the institution.

(3) A prisoner sentenced to ordinary confinement may petition the Court at any time after sentence for the privilege of leaving the institution under this Section and may renew his petition in the discretion of the Court. The Court may withdraw the privilege at any time by order entered with or without notice.

(4) If the prisoner has been granted permission to leave the institution to seek or take employment, the Court's probation department shall assist him in obtaining suitable employment. Employment shall not be deemed suitable if the wages or working conditions or other circumstances present a danger of exploitation or of interference in a labor dispute in the establishment in which the prisoner would be employed.

(5) If a prisoner is employed for wages or salary, the [probation service] [Warden or other administrative head] shall collect the same, or shall require the prisoner to turn over his wages or salary in full when received, and shall deposit the same in a trust account and shall keep a ledger showing the status of the account of each prisoner. Earnings levied upon pursuant to writ of attachment or execution or in other lawful manner shall not be collected hereunder, but when the [probation service] [Warden or other administrative head] has requested transmittal of earnings prior to levy, such request shall have priority. When an employer transmits such earnings to the [probation service] [Warden or other administrative head] pursuant to this Subdivision he shall have no liability to the prisoner for such earnings. From such earnings the probation service shall pay the prisoner's board and personal expenses both inside and outside the institution, shall

deduct so much of the costs of administration of this Section as is allocable to such prisoner, and shall deduct installments on fines, if any, and, to the extent directed by the Court, shall pay the support of the prisoner's dependents. If sufficient funds are available after making the foregoing payments, the [probation service] [Warden or other administrative head] may, with the consent of the prisoner, pay, in whole or in part, any unpaid debts of the prisoner. Any balance shall be retained, and shall be paid to the prisoner at the time of his discharge.

(6) A prisoner who is serving his sentence pursuant to this Section shall be eligible for a reduction of his term for good behavior and faithful performance of duties in accordance with Section 303.8 in the same manner as if he had served his term in ordinary confinement.

(7) The Warden or other administrative head may deny the prisoner the exercise of his privilege to leave the institution for a period not to exceed five days for any breach of discipline or other violation of regulations.

(8) The Court shall not make an order granting the privilege of leaving the institution under this Section unless it is satisfied [the Warden or other administrative head has certified] that there are adequate facilities for the administration of such privilege in the institution in which the defendant will be confined.

Section 303.10. Release from Institutions.

When a prisoner sentenced or committed for a definite term of one year or less is discharged from an institution, he shall be returned any personal possessions taken from him upon his commitment, and the Warden or other administrative head shall furnish him with a transportation ticket, or with the cost of transportation, to the place where he was sentenced, or to any other place not more distant.

ARTICLE 304. LONG–TERM IMPRISONMENT

Section 304.1. Reception Center; Reception Classification Boards; Reception Classification and Reclassification; Transfer of Prisoners.

Section 304.2. Institutions; Review of Adequacy; Use of Institutions of Another Jurisdiction.

Section 304.3. Central Prisoner File; Treatment, Classification and Reclassification in Institutions.

Section 304.4. Segregation and Transfer of Prisoners with Physical or Mental Diseases or Defects.

Section 304.5. Medical Care, Food and Clothing.

Section 304.6. Program of Rehabilitation.

Section 304.7. Discipline and Control.

Section 304.8. Employment and Labor of Prisoners.

Section 304.9. Compassionate Leave; Pre–Parole Furlough.

Section 304.10. Release from Institutions.

ARTICLE 305. RELEASE ON PAROLE

Section 305.1. Reduction of Prison Term for Good Behavior.

Section 305.2. Reduction of Parole Term for Good Behavior.

Section 305.3. Award of Reduction of Term for Good Behavior.

Section 305.4. Forfeiture, Withholding, and Restoration of Reduction of Term for Good Behavior.

Section 305.5. Report of Reductions Granted, Forfeited and Restored.

Section 305.6. Parole Eligibility and Hearing.

Section 305.7. Preparation for Hearing; Assistance to Prisoner.

Section 305.8. Decision of Board of Parole; Reconsideration.

Section 305.9. Criteria for Determining Date of First Release on Parole.

Section 305.10. Data to Be Considered in Determining Parole Release.

Section 305.11. Eligibility for Discharge from Parole.

Section 305.12. Termination of Supervision; Discharge from Parole.

Section 305.13. Conditions of Parole.

Section 305.14. Parole Residence Facilities.

Section 305.15. Revocation of Parole for Violation of Condition; Hearing.

Section 305.16. Sanctions Short of Revocation for Violation of Condition of Parole.

Section 305.17. Duration of Re-imprisonment and Re-parole after Revocation.

Section 305.18. Parole to Detainers.

Section 305.19. Finality of Determinations with Respect to Reduction of Terms for Good Behavior and Parole.

ARTICLE 306. LOSS AND RESTORATION OF RIGHTS INCIDENT TO CONVICTION OR IMPRISONMENT

Section 306.1. Basis of Disqualification or Disability.

Section 306.2. Forfeiture of Public Office.

Section 306.3. Voting and Jury Service.

Section 306.4. Testimonial Capacity; Testimony of Prisoners.

Section 306.5. Appointment of Agent, Attorney-in-Fact or Trustee for Prisoner.

Section 306.6. Order Removing Disqualifications or Disabilities; Vacation of Conviction; Effect of Order of Removal or Vacation.

PART IV. ORGANIZATION OF CORRECTION—
TABLE OF CONTENTS

ARTICLE 401. DEPARTMENT OF CORRECTION

Section 401.1. Department of Correction; Creation; Responsibilities.

Section 401.2. Director of Correction; Appointment; Powers and Duties.

Section 401.3. Organization of Department of Correction.

Section 401.4. Division of Treatment Services; Deputy Director for Treatment Services.

Section 401.5. Division of Custodial Services; Deputy Director for Custodial Services.

Section 401.6. Division of Young Adult Correction; Deputy Director for Young Adult Correction.

Section 401.7. Division of Prison Industries; Deputy Director for Prison Industries.

Section 401.8. Division of Fiscal Control; Deputy Director for Fiscal Control.

Section 401.9. Division of Research and Training; Deputy Director for Research and Training.

Section 401.10. Commission of Correction and Community Services; Organization; Functions.

Section 401.11. Visitation and Inspection of Institutions.

Section 401.12. Appointment and Promotion of Employees; Department Under Civil Service Law [Merit System].

ARTICLE 402. BOARD OF PAROLE

Section 402.1. Board of Parole; Composition and Tenure.

Section 402.2. Powers and Duties of the Board of Parole.

Section 402.3. Young Adult Division of Board of Parole.

ARTICLE 403. ADMINISTRATION OF INSTITUTIONS

Section 403.1. Appointment of Personnel.

Section 403.2. Powers and Duties of Wardens and Other Administrative Heads of State and Local Institutions.

Section 403.3. Separation of Female Prisoners.

ARTICLE 404. DIVISION OF PAROLE

Section 404.1. Division of Parole; Parole Administrator.

Section 404.2. Powers and Duties of the Parole Administrator.

Section 404.3. Field Parole Service; Organization and Duties.

ALTERNATIVE ARTICLE 404. DIVISION OF PROBATION AND PAROLE

Section 404.1. Division of Probation and Parole; Probation and Parole Administrator.

Section 404.2. Powers and Duties of the Probation and Parole Administrator.

Section 404.3. Field Probation and Parole Service; Organization and Duties.

ARTICLE 405. DIVISION OF PROBATION

Section 405.1. Division of Probation; Probation Administrator.

Section 405.2. Powers and Duties of the Probation Administrator.

Section 405.3. Extension of Probation Field Services by Division of Probation.

Section 405.4. Field Probation Service; Organization and Duties.

TABLE OF CASES

References are to Pages.

Ayers v. State, 222

Backun v. United States, 116
Berkowitz, People v., 164
Booth v. State, 153, 154
Bowens, State v., 194
Boyd, United States v., 261
Brawner, United States v., 278
Breakiron, State v., 270
Brim, People v., 243
Bryan v. United States, 105

Callanan v. United States, 144, 162
Calley, United States v., 250
Calvano, People v., 259
Cameron, State v., 70, 87
Campbell, People v., 161
Carr, People v., 7
Ceballos, People v., 222
Chicago, City of v. Morales, 44
Chisler v. State, 141
City of (see name of city)
Coe, People v., 105
Commonwealth v. _____ (see opposing party)
Cornell, United States v., 86
Craig, People v., 200
Cunningham, Regina v., 105

Dlugash, People v., 146, 154
Donahue, Commonwealth v., 205

TABLE OF CASES

Donton, Commonwealth v., 149
Dotterweich, United States v., 127, 180
Dudley & Stephens, Regina v., 199, 207
Dugdale, Regina v., 40
Duffy, People v., 110
Durham v. United States, 277

Faulkner, Regina v., 63
Flayhart, People v., 120

George, State v., 243
Godwin, State v., 262
Goetz, People v., 193
Griffin, People v., 139

Haines, Commonwealth v., 176
Hamilton, United States v., 137
Harmelin v. Michigan, 58
Haupt v. United States, 67
Henley, Commonwealth v., 153, 154

In re (see name of party)

Jacobson v. United States, 250, 261
Jaffe, People v., 153
Johnson v. State, 109

Kaczynski, United States v., 191
Kelly, State v., 205
Kemp, State v., 168
Kibbe, People v., 139
Koczwara, Commonwealth v., 127
Krulewitch v. United States, 171

Lambert v. California, 263
Lauria, People v., 117
Lennard, Rex v., 94
Leidholm, State v., 205, 213, 230
Leland v. Oregon, 188, 275
Liberta, People v., 240
Liparota v. United States, 104
Lovercamp, People v., 252
Lubow, People v., 175
Lyerla, State v., 159

TABLE OF CASES

Maiorino v. Scully, 121
Malone, Commonwealth v., 65
Manini, People v., 121
Marrero, People v., 237, 263
Martin v. Ohio, 96, 188
McGee, People v., 114, 168
McMillan v. Pennsylvania, 189
M'Naghten's Case, 277
Montana v. Egelhoff, 86
Morissette v. United States, 54
Mosley, United States v., 261
Mullaney v. Wilbur, 188
M.W., United States v., 7

Papachristou v. City of Jacksonville, 44
Parker, State v., 168
Patterson v. New York, 96, 188, 267
Peacock, People v., 215
Pena, People v., 237
Penn Valley Resorts, Commonwealth v., 126
Peoni, United States v., 116
People v. _____ (see opposing party)
Pestinikas, Commonwealth v., 36
Peterson, United States v., 231
Petrie v. Cartwright, 235
Pinkerton v. United States, 113, 144, 171
Powell v. Texas, 34, 86
Prince, Regina v., 91, 93, 98

R. v. _____ (see opposing party)
Ratzlaf v. United States, 105
Regina v. _____ (see opposing party)
Register, People v., 75, 115
Rementer, Commonwealth v., 139
Rex v. _____ (see opposing party)
Robinson v. California, 33
Rogers v. Tennessee, 138
Rowe v. United States, 227, 228
Ryan, People v., 150

Sandstrom v. Montana, 189
Schmidt, People v., 279
Schwimmer, People v., 164
Scofield, Rex v., 143

Sette, State v., 90
Sherman v. United States, 261
Stamp, People v., 140
Standefer v. United States, 111, 121, 124
Staples, People v., 158
State v. _____ (see opposing party)
Steinberg, People v., 36, 38, 73
Steven S., In re, 7
Stewart v. State, 178
Stoffer v. State, 228
Strong, People v., 77
Studifin, People v., 263

Tally, State v., 113, 131
Tavares, Commonwealth v., 110
Taylor, People v., 124
Tennessee v. Garner, 235
The Cotton Planter, 263
Thompson, Commonwealth v., 93 Mass. 23 (1865), 56
Thompson, Commonwealth v., 88 Mass. 591 (1863), 55
Tolson, R. v., 49
Toscano, State v., 256

United States v. _____ (see opposing party)
United States Gypsum Co., United States v., 7, 73

Warner–Lambert Co., People v., 126, 139
Weston v. State, 194, 216
Winship, In re, 95, 188
Wood v. State, 217
Wyant, State v., 65

TABLE OF MODEL PENAL CODE SECTIONS AND STATUTES

MODEL PENAL CODE

Sec.	This Work Page
1.01	14
1.02	10, 13, 23–28, 43, 105, 127, 184–85
1.03	20
1.04	20, 57
1.05	9, 20, 37
1.06	20
1.07	20
1.09	199
1.10	199
1.12	20, 96, 177, 187, 189
1.13	20, 30, 33, 44, 93, 189–90, 193, 199, 214
2.01	20, 33–42, 67, 255
2.02	2, 20, 42–82, 92, 105, 120, 135, 192, 199, 264
2.02(2)	60–80
2.02(2)(a)	63–65
2.02(2)(b)	65–67
2.02(2)(c)	67–76
2.02(2)(d)	76–78
2.02(3)	53–54
2.02(4)	54–55
2.03	20, 128–41
2.04	20, 83–84, 90–105, 112, 116, 189, 206, 232, 260, 262–64
2.05	20, 55–56, 95
2.06	20, 105–27, 164, 170–71, 176, 178, 254, 260
2.07	96, 125, 189
2.08	20, 83–90, 199
2.09	21, 109, 198, 248, 251–59, 270, 279
2.10	21, 198, 250, 279
2.11	21, 199, 209, 238–46
2.12	21, 180–82, 199, 201, 262

MODEL PENAL CODE

Sec.	This Work Page
2.13	96, 189, 260, 261
3.02	6, 21, 192, 194–202, 204, 206, 240, 249
3.03	21, 192, 231, 233
3.04	21, 192, 198–99, 203–18, 221, 223–31, 233, 258
3.05	21, 217–18, 221
3.06	6, 21, 192, 198–99, 205, 215, 218–23
3.07	21, 192, 198, 199, 215, 225, 231–38
3.08	21, 232, 241
3.09	202, 205, 215, 232–33
3.10	198, 204
3.11	92, 208–11, 222, 224, 230, 239
4.01	21, 133, 199, 210, 271–81
4.02	270, 275, 280
4.03	275–77
4.08	276
4.10	21, 210, 274–75
5.01	21, 46, 65, 125, 141–62, 176–79, 198
5.02	21, 112, 144, 173–76, 177, 179
5.03	21, 119, 162–73, 177, 179
5.04	144
5.05	100, 144, 155, 172, 175
5.06	21, 41, 150–51, 173
5.07	21, 96, 151, 177, 189
7.08	15
210.1	36, 62, 66, 128
210.2	75, 115
210.3	6, 265–71
210.4	76
210.5	62, 106, 110, 143, 246
210.6	15, 65, 133
211.1	75, 76, 136, 143, 182, 224, 232
211.2	155, 160
212.1	92, 231, 246
212.3	231
212.5	256
213.1	94
213.6	94, 189
220.1	12, 146
220.3	76, 204, 246
221.1	62, 143
221.2	92, 255
223.1	242
223.2	92

TABLE OF STATUTES

MODEL PENAL CODE

Sec.	This Work Page
223.3	36, 246
223.9	239
224.3	92
224.7	143
224.8	143
224.9	143
230.3	23
240.1	143, 146
240.3	143
240.5	143
240.6	143
240.7	143
241.6	143, 246
242.2	215
250.11	239
250.12	239, 245
251.2	143
251.3	143
251.4	143
303.1	16
303.10	16
303.2	16
303.3	16
303.4	16
303.5	16
303.6	16
303.7	16
303.8	16
303.9	16

FEDERAL

18 U.S.C. § 81	7
18 U.S.C. § 844	191
18 U.S.C. § 1716	191
Prop. New Fed. Crim. Code § 608	213
Prop. New Fed. Crim. Code ch. 10	142

LOUISIANA

Crim. Code §§ 10–12	70

NEW JERSEY

Code Crim. Just. § 2C:2–9 256

NEW YORK

Penal Law § 15.00 41
Penal Law § 15.05 .... 61, 62, 77
Penal Law § 15.20 102
Penal Law § 25.00 188
Penal Law § 35.05 .... 195, 200, 202
Penal Law § 35.20 221
Penal Law § 35.25 221
Penal Law § 35.30 237
Penal Law § 70.15 57
Penal Law § 115.00 .... 117, 141
Penal Law § 120.00 76
Penal Law § 120.03 76
Penal Law § 125.05 23
Penal Law § 125.10 76
Penal Law § 125.12 76
Penal Law §§ 125.40–.60 23
Penal Law § 145.00 204
Penal Law § 255.17 52
Penal Law tit. G 141
Family Court Act § 1012(f)(i)(A) 38
Veh. & Traf. Law § 1192(3) 44

NORTH DAKOTA

Crim. Code § 12.1–05–07 230
Crim. Code § 12.1–05–08 213

TEXAS

Penal Code ch. 15 141

RESTATEMENT (SECOND) OF TORTS

§ 2 .... 33, 35
§ 9 129
§ 11 214
§ 22 147
§ 65 215
§ 67 215
§ 76 218
§ 261 204

RESTATEMENT (SECOND) OF TORTS

§ 431(a)	131
§ 435	132
§ 890	213

GERMANY

StGB § 20	88
StGB § 21	88
StGB § 23	143
StGB § 32	252
StGB § 323a	88
StGB § 34	197, 252
StGB § 35	252
StPO §§ 153 et seq.	181

*

INDEX

References are to pages

ACT
Defined, 33–34
Voluntary, 34–35

ACTUS REUS
Criminal Conduct, this index
Model Penal Code, 19

AGE
Mistake as to, generally, 91–99

AGREEMENT
Criminal conduct, agreement as core of conspiracy, 163

AIDING ANOTHER'S CONDUCT
Complicity, 110–125

AMBIGUOUS MENTAL STATE REQUIREMENTS
Rules of interpretation, 52–59

AMERICAN LAW INSTITUTE (ALI)
Model Penal Code, 6–12

ANALYSIS OF CRIMINAL LIABILITY
Model Penal Code, 28–31, 285–287

ANTICIPATORY OFFENSES
Inchoate Offenses, this index

ARREST
Justification, this index

ATTEMPT
Impossibility, 152–153
Inchoate offenses, 144–162

INDEX

References are to pages

ATTENDANT CIRCUMSTANCE ELEMENT
Criminal Conduct, this index

ATTITUDINAL AXIS OF MENS REA
Criminal conduct, 73

AWARENESS
Knowledge, this index

BLUEPRINT FOR MODEL PENAL CODE
Wechsler, 8–9

CAUSATION
Criminal Conduct, this index

CHARTS
Criminal Conduct, this index
Analysis of criminal liability, 285–287

CHILDREN
Excuse, this index

COMMON LAW
Criminal Conduct, this index
Model Penal Code, 31

COMPLICITY
Criminal Conduct, this index

CONDUCT
Criminal Conduct, this index

CONSENT
De minimis, 181–182
Justification, 239–246
Level one defense, 238–239
Unlawful force, 208–209, 214

CONSPIRACY
Inchoate offenses, 162–173

CONTRIBUTING CAUSE
Criminal conduct, 131

CORPORATIONS
Liability for another's conduct, 125–127

CORRECTIONAL CODE
Generally, 14–17

CRIMINAL CONDUCT
Generally, 32–185
Abetting another's conduct, liability for, 112–113
Act defined, 33, 34
Actus reus
    Generally, 33–42
  Act defined, 33, 34
  Common law duties, 37
  Complicity, 110–116
  Conspiracy, 165
  Duties, generally, 37, 38
  Indirect omission, 36
  Nonacts, 39
  Omission, 34, 34–40
  Possession, 40–42
  Voluntariness, 34, 35
Age, mistake as to, generally, 91–99
Agreement as core of conspiracy, 163
Aiding another's conduct, liability for, 112–113
Ambiguous mental state requirements, 59
Another's conduct, liability for
    Generally, 105–127
  Actus reus of complicity, 110–116
  Aiding and abetting, 112–113
  Complicity, generally, 110–125
  Conspiracy as implying complicity, 113, 114
  Corporations, 125–127
  Entrapment, 109
  Ignorance of law, 109
  Imputation, 107, 108
  Instruments, 107–110
  Jury verdicts, inconsistency of, 124, 125
  Knowledge, 116–120
  Means to an end, 107
  Mens rea of complicity, 116–120
  Purpose, 116–120
  Result element, 118, 119
  Termination of complicity, 122–124
Attempt, generally, 144–162
Attendant circumstance element, 32, 43–46
Attitudinal axis of mens rea, 73
Burden of proof. Presumptions and burden of proof, below

References are to pages

CRIMINAL CONDUCT—Cont'd
CAR elements, generally, 43–46
Causation
    Generally, 128–141
  Attempt causation distinguished from, 145, 146
  But-for test, 128–129
  Contributing cause, 131
  Factual cause, generally, 128, 129
  Intervening cause, 132, 138, 145
  Knowledge test for causation, 134
  Legal cause, generally, 129
  Modes of culpability, 134
  Negligence test for causation, 134
  Proximate cause, 129
  Purpose test for causation, 134
  Recklessness test for causation, 134
  Result offenses, 128
  Strict liability test for causation, 134, 139, 140
  Tests for causation, 134
Charts. Mens rea and offense elements, below
Common law
  Actus reus, 37
  Liability scheme, 29–30
Complicity
  Another's conduct, liability for, above
  Conspiracy distinguished from, 169, 170
  Pinkerton rule, 113–116, 169–171
Conduct element, generally, 43–46
Conspiracy. Inchoate offenses, below
Contributing cause, 131
Corporations, 125–127
Culpability, modes of. Mens rea and offense elements, below
Dangerousness, generally, 147, 167, 178
De minimis infractions, 182
Default rule of mens rea, 53
Element types, 43–52
Entrapment, 109
Facial liability, generally, 42
Fact and law mistakes, distinction between, 102–105
Factual cause, generally, 128, 129
Ignorance of law, 109
Imputation, 107, 108
Inchoate offenses
    Generally, 141–179
  Actus reus of conspiracy, 165

CRIMINAL CONDUCT—Cont'd
Inchoate offenses—Cont'd
    Agreement as core of conspiracy, 163
    Attempt, generally, 144–162
    Causation distinguished from attempt, 145, 146
    Complicity distinguished from conspiracy, 169, 170
    Conspiracy
        Generally, 162–173
        Pinkerton rule, 113–116, 169–171
    Dangerousness, generally, 147, 167, 178
    Facilitation, 111–112, 116–117
    Mens rea of conspiracy, 166
    Overt act required for conspiracy, 165
    Preparation distinguished from attempt, 149, 150
    Renunciation, 177–179
    Solicitation, 173–176
    Treatmentism, generally, 143, 144, 162, 173, 174
Indirect omission liability, 36
Individual or public interests, generally, 183–185
Instruments, liability for another's conduct, 107–110
Intent v Modes of Culpability, 70–78
Intent, general and specific, 68–71, 85–86
Interpretation, rules of, 52–59
Intoxication
      Generally, 82–90
    Excuse, intoxication as, 84
    Intent, general and specific, 69, 85–87
    Involuntary intoxication, 88–90
    Knowledge or purpose, 87
    Negligence, 85
    Pathological intoxication, 89, 90
    Recklessness, 85, 87
    Self-induced intoxication, 87, 88
Involuntary intoxication, 88–90
Knowledge
    Another's conduct, liability for, 116, 117
    Causation, knowledge test for, 134
    Intoxication, 87
    Mens rea, 65–67
Law and fact mistakes, distinction between, 102–105
Legal or proximate cause, generally, 129
Matching conduct to offense definition, 80–82
Mens rea and offense elements
      Generally, 42–82

CRIMINAL CONDUCT—Cont'd
Mens rea and offense elements—Cont'd
    Absence means absence (strict liability), Rule 3 of interpretation, 55–59
    Absence means presence I (default), Rule 1 of interpretation, 53
    Absence means presence II (one-for-all), Rule 2 of interpretation, 54, 55
    Ambiguous mental state requirements, 52–59
    Another's conduct, liability for, 119, 120
    Attendant circumstance element, generally, 43–46
    Attitudinal axis, 73
    CAR elements, generally, 43–46
    Charts
        Modes of culpability by offense element, 61
        Modes of culpability (including strict liability), 79, 80
        Modes of culpability (Mental States), 78
        Modes of culpability (MPC) v Intent (common law), 70
        Modes of culpability (N.Y. Penal Law), 63
        Rules of Interpretation (ambiguous mental state requirements), 59
    Conduct element, generally, 43–46
    Conspiracy, mens rea of, 166
    Culpability, modes of
        Generally, 60–80
        Attitudinal axis, 73
        Causation, 134
        Charts, above
        Intent v Modes of Culpability, 70–78
        Knowledge, 65–67
        Model Penal Code, generally, 61, 62
        Negligence, 76–78
        New York Penal Law, 62–70
        Probabilistic axis, 71–73
        Purpose, 63–65, 72, 73
        Recklessness, 67–70
        Strict liability, 79, 80
        Varieties, generally, 46
    Default rule, 53
    Element types, 43–52
    Facial liability, generally, 42
    Intent v Modes of Culpability, 70–78
    Interpretation, rules of, 52–59
    Knowledge, 65–67
    Matching conduct to offense, 80–82

CRIMINAL CONDUCT—Cont'd
Mens rea and offense elements—Cont'd
- Mistake, 93–96
- Model Penal Code modes, 61, 62
- Modes of culpability. Culpability, modes of, above
- Negligence, 76–78
- N.Y. Penal Law, 63
- One-for-all rule, 54, 55
- Prima facie liability, generally, 42
- Reckless default rule, 53
- Result element, generally, 43–46
- Rules of interpretation, 52–59
- Strict liability, 55–59, 79, 80
- Types of elements, 43–52

Mistake
- Generally, 82-84, 90–105
- Age, mistake as to, generally, 91–99
- Aggravating factor, mistake as, 101
- Burden of proof, 95–97
- Excuse, mistake as, generally, 84
- Fact and law mistakes, distinction between, 102–105
- Level one defense, generally, 90
- Mens rea requirement, 93–96
- Mitigating factor, mistake as, 101
- Reasonableness, 93–95
- Recklessness, 90, 91
- Scienter requirement, 92
- Strict liability, 91–94

Model Penal Code modes of culpability, generally, 61, 62
Modes of culpability. Mens rea and offense elements, above
Negligence
- Causation, test for, 134
- Intoxication, 85
- Mens rea, 76–78

Nonacts, generally, 39
N.Y. Penal Law, mens rea and offense elements, 63
Omission, 34–40
One-for-all rule of mens rea, 54, 55
Overt act required for conspiracy, 165
Pathological intoxication, 89, 90
Possession, actus reus, 40–42
Preparation distinguished from attempt, 149, 150
Presumptions and burden of proof
- Possession, 150–151
- Mistake, burden of proof of, 95–97

CRIMINAL CONDUCT—Cont'd
Presumptions and burden of proof—Cont'd
    Varieties, generally, 187–188
Prima facie liability, generally, 42
Purpose
    Causation, test for, 134
    Mens rea, 63–65
Reasonableness of mistake, 93–95
Recklessness
    Causation, test for, 134
    Default rule of mens rea and offense elements, 53
    Intoxication, 85, 87
    Mens rea, 67–76
    Mistake, 90, 91
Renunciation, inchoate offenses, 177–179
Result element
    Complicity, 118, 119
    Causation, 128
    Mens rea and offense elements, 43–46
Rules of interpretation, mens rea, 52–59
Scienter. Knowledge, above
Self-induced intoxication, 87, 88
Solicitation, inchoate offenses, 173–176
Strict liability
    Causation, test for, 134, 139, 140
    Mens rea, 55–59, 79, 80
    Mistake, 91–94
Substantial harm
    De minimis infractions, 182
    Individual or public interests, generally, 183–185
    Substantial harm, generally, 179–182
Termination of complicity, 122–124
Third persons. Another's conduct, liability for, above
Treatmentism, generally, 143, 144, 162, 173, 174
Voluntariness, 34, 35

CULPABILITY
Criminal Conduct, this index

DANGEROUSNESS
Attempt, 147–149, 151–162
Complicity, 113
Conspiracy, 162–173
Intoxication, 87
Possession, 149–151
Renunciation, 177–179

INDEX
References are to pages

DANGEROUSNESS—Cont'd
Solicitation, 173–176
Treatmentism, 12–13

DE MINIMIS INFRACTIONS
Criminal conduct, 182

DEADLY FORCE
Duress, 256
Justification, this index

DEFAULT RULE OF MENS REA
Rules of interpretation, 53

DEFENSES
Affirmative, 186–190
Excuse and justification, 186–194
Level one, 83–84, 88, 90–91, 104, 239, 270–271
Level three (excuse), 84, 88–89, 103–104, 238, 247–281
Level two (justification), 186–246

DEFINITIONS
Crimes and criminals, 24–28
Unlawful force, 208

DIMINISHED CAPACITY
Extreme mental disturbance, 270, 271
Insanity, 264
Intoxication, 88

DURESS
Excuse, 248, 251–259

ELEMENTS
Criminal Conduct, this index

EMERGENCY
Necessity, 195

EMOTIONAL DISTURBANCE
Provocation, 265–270

ENTRAPMENT
By estoppel, 262
Excuse, 259–262

ESTOPPEL
Entrapment by, 262

INDEX

EXCUSE
Generally, 186–194, 247–281
Children. Insanity and infancy, below
Diminished capacity, 270, 271
Duress, generally, 251–259
Emotional disturbance, 265–270
Entrapment, 259–262
Estoppel, entrapment by, 262
Executive estoppel, 262
Extreme mental or emotional disturbance, 265–270
Ignorance of law, 262–264
Infancy, 273–275
Insanity
    Generally, 271–281
    Cognitive incapacity, 277
    Common law, 273, 274
    Durham test, 277
    Irresistible impulse, 281
    M'Naghten rule, 277–280
    Presumption of sanity, 275
    Treatmentism, 273
Mistake of law, entrapment as attempt to induce, 260
Model Penal Code, generally, 247–251
Provocation, 265-270

EXECUTIVE ESTOPPEL
Ignorance of law, 262

FACIAL LIABILITY
Criminal conduct, 42

FACILITATION
Complicity, 111–112, 116–117

FAILURE–OF–PROOF DEFENSE
Level One Defense, this index

FEDERAL CRIMINAL LAW
Efforts to recodify, 18

FRAUD
In the factum and in the inducement, 245, 246

GENERAL PART
Criminal law, 20, 23, 179, 223
Model Penal Code, 15, 19–20, 81–82, 180, 190, 250, 265

HOMICIDE
Attempt, 158–159
Causation, 128
Complicity, 119
Duress, 256
Felony murder, 115, 140
Manslaughter, 68, 265–270
Murder, 66, 68, 72, 85–86, 134, 145
Necessity defense, 207
Negligent homicide, 76
Omission liability, 36
Self-defense, 223–224
Voluntary manslaughter, 265–270

HOUSE OR WORK EXCEPTION
Self-defense, 230

IGNORANCE OF LAW
Excuse, 262–264

IMMEDIACY OF THREAT
Duress, 256
Self-defense, 215, 216

INCHOATE OFFENSES
Criminal Conduct, this index
Model Penal Code, 21, 22

INDIRECT OMISSION
Actus reus, 36

INDIVIDUAL OR PUBLIC INTERESTS
Criminal conduct, 183–185

INFANCY
Excuse, this index

INITIAL AGGRESSOR
Self-defense, 226–228

INSANITY
Excuse, this index

INTENT
Criminal Conduct, this index

INTERPRETATION, RULES OF
Mens rea, 52–59

INDEX

INTOXICATION
Criminal Conduct, this index

INVOLUNTARY INTOXICATION
Criminal conduct, 88–90

JUSTIFICATION
    Generally, 186–246
Arrest
    Justification for, 231–238
    Self-defense, unlawfulness of arrest, 215
Belief, self-defense and defense of others, generally, 205, 206
Consent, generally, 238–246
Deadly force
        Generally, 223–231
    Arrest, 231, 234–238
    Escalation of force by initial victim, 226–228
    Forfeiture rule, 226–228
    House or work exception, 230
    Initial aggressor rule, 226–228
    Property, defense of, 220–222
    Proportionality requirement, 224–226
    Provocation, 226
    Resistance to arrest, 231
    Retreat requirement, 228–230
    Self-defense and defense of others, 202, 203
Defenses in general, 186–194
Definition of unlawful force, 208
Emergency situations, 195
Escalation of force by initial victim, 226–228
Fear of future harm, 216
Force
    Deadly force, above
    Self-defense and defense of others, 204, 205, 207
Forfeiture rule, 226–228
Fraud, consent obtained by, 245, 246
House or work exception to deadly force, 230
Immediacy, self-defense and defense of others, 215, 216
Law enforcement, generally, 231–238
Mens rea, attacker's, 210
Mistake, 192, 200, 201, 205
Necessity
        Generally, 194–202
    Self-defense and defense of others, 202, 204, 206, 207
Negligence, 202
Privilege to use force, 213

INDEX

JUSTIFICATION—Cont'd
Property, defense of, generally, 218–223
Proportionality requirement, 224–226
Protection, self-defense and defense of others, 215–217
Provocation, use of deadly force after, 226
Reasonable belief, 193
Recklessness, 202
Resistance to arrest, 231
Retaliation for past harm, 216
Retreat requirement, 228–230
Self-defense and defense of others
      Generally, 202–218
  Arrest, unlawfulness of, 215
  Belief, 205, 206
  Deadly force, 202, 203
  Definition of unlawful force, 208
  Fear of future harm, 216
  Force, use of, generally, 204, 205, 207
  Immediacy, 215, 216
  Imperfect, 194
  Mens rea, attacker's, 210
  Mistake, 205
  Necessity, generally, 202, 204, 206, 207
  Privilege to use force, 213
  Protection, 215–217
  Retaliation for past harm, 216
  Retreat requirement, 228–230
  Tortious force, self-defense against, 211
  Unlawfulness, generally, 208–215
Tortious force, self-defense against, 211
Treatmentism, 198
Unlawfulness, generally, 208–215

KNOWLEDGE
Criminal Conduct, this index

LAW AND FACT MISTAKES
Ignorance of law, 262–264
Model Penal Code, 102–105

LAW ENFORCEMENT
Justification, 231–238

LEGAL PROCESS SCHOOL
Model Penal Code, 7–12

LEVEL ONE DEFENSE
Failure-of-proof, 83–84, 88, 90–91, 104, 239, 270–271

LEVEL THREE DEFENSE
Excuse, 84, 88–89, 103–104, 238, 247–281

LEVEL TWO DEFENSE
Justification, 186–246

MANSLAUGHTER
Homicide, this index

MATCHING CONDUCT TO OFFENSE DEFINITION
Criminal conduct, 80–82

MENS REA
Attacker's in self-defense cases, 210
Criminal Conduct, this index

MILITARY ORDERS
Excuse, 238, 250
Justification, 250

MISTAKE
Criminal Conduct, this index
Entrapment as attempt to induce mistake of law, 260
Justification, 192, 201, 205

MODEL CORRECTIONAL CODE
Generally, 14–17

MODEL PENAL CODE
    Generally, 1–31
Actus reus, 19–20
American Law Institute (ALI), generally, 6–12
Analysis of criminal liability, 28–31, 285–287
Blueprint for code, 9
Casebooks, 5
Chart showing analysis of criminal liability, 285–287
Coherence of code, 4
Common law and the code, 28–31
Comprehensiveness of code, 10
Conduct. Criminal conduct, this index
Correctional Code, 14–17
Criminal conduct, this index
Criminal propensities, 12–14
Defenses, generally, 20, 21, 186–194
Definitions of crimes and criminals, 24–28

MODEL PENAL CODE—Cont'd
Excuse, this index
Federal criminal law, efforts to recodify, 18
General part, 15, 19–20, 81–82, 180, 190, 250, 265
Inchoate crimes, 21, 22, 141–179
Introduction, 1–31
Justification, this index
Legal Process School, 7–12
Mens rea, 19–20
Model Correctional Code, 14–17
New York Penal Law, importance of, 6
Origins, 7–12
Pragmatic nature of code, 10
Prerequisites of criminal liability, 26–28
Prevention of crime, generally, 13
Roadmap for analysis of criminal liability, code as, 19
Section 1.02 as key to Code, 23–26
Sentencing, general purposes of provisions governing, 25, 26
Special part, 15, 17, 22–23, 43, 46, 60, 80–82, 179, 183–184, 250, 265
Structure of code, 5, 17–23
Treatmentism, generally, 7–17

MURDER
Homicide, this index

NECESSITY
Justification, this index

NEGLIGENCE
Criminal Conduct, this index
Justification, mistake as to, 202

NEW YORK PENAL LAW
Affirmative Defenses, 187
Attempt, 146
Causation, 139
Model Penal Code and, 6
Modes of culpability, 63, 74, 77, 105
Necessity defense, 199–200
Omission liability, 32

NONACTS
Actus reus, 39

OMISSION
Actus reus, 34, 34–40

ONE-FOR-ALL RULE OF MENS REA
Rules of interpretation, 54, 55

OVERT ACT
Conspiracy, 165

PATHOLOGICAL INTOXICATION
Criminal conduct, 89, 90

PINKERTON RULE
Complicity, 113–116
Conspiracy, 169–171

POSSESSION OFFENSES
Actus reus, 40–42
Inchoate offenses, 150
Strict liability, 57–58

PREPARATION
Distinguished from attempt, 149, 150

PRESUMPTIONS AND BURDEN OF PROOF
Criminal Conduct, this index

PRIMA FACIE CRIMINALITY
Criminal conduct, 42

PRIVILEGE TO USE FORCE
Unlawful force, 213

PROPERTY
Defense of, 218–223

PROPORTIONALITY REQUIREMENT
Justification, 224–226

PROTECTION
Self-defense and defense of others, 215–217

PROVOCATION
Excuse, 265–270
Self-defense, 226

PURPOSE
Criminal Conduct, this index

REASONABLENESS
Duress, 257–258
Ignorance of law, 262–264
Mistake, 93–95, 205, 213–214, 217
Provocation, 269, 270

INDEX
References are to pages

RECKLESSNESS
Criminal Conduct, this index
Justification, mistake as to, 202

RENUNCIATION
Attempt, 122–123, 177–179
Complicity, 122–124
Conspiracy, 177–179
Solicitation, 177–179

RESISTANCE TO ARREST
Justification, 230–231

RESULT ELEMENT
Criminal Conduct, this index

RETALIATION FOR PAST HARM
Self-defense, 216

RETREAT REQUIREMENT
Self-defense, 228–230

SELF–DEFENSE
Justification, this index

SELF-INDUCED INTOXICATION
Criminal conduct, 87, 88

SENTENCING
Model Penal Code, 25, 26

SEVERITY OF THREAT
Duress as affected by, 256

SOLICITATION
Inchoate offenses, 173–176

SPECIAL PART
Criminal law, 17, 80–81, 179, 222
Model Penal Code, 15, 17, 22–23, 43, 46, 60, 80–82, 179, 183–184, 250, 265

STRICT LIABILITY
Criminal Conduct, this index

TERMINATION
Complicity, 122–124

TORTIOUS FORCE
Self-defense against, 211

TREATMENTISM
Criminal conduct, 143, 144, 162, 173, 174
Insanity, 273
Justification, 198
Model Penal Code, 7–17

UNLAWFULNESS
Justification, 208–215

VICARIOUS LIABILITY
Conspiracy, 168–169
Corporations, 126–127

VOLUNTARINESS OF ACT
Actus reus, 34, 35

WILFULNESS
Mens rea, 104–105

†